Super B -   onys
108.

MW00934537

Made up By Howard!

page
113
Killer
B.S.

The Phoenix Suns:
The View From Section 101

Horizon Books
P. O. Box 4342
Scottsdale, AZ. 85261-4342

E Mail: Howard217@aol.com

First Published 2012

ISBN: 1-4819-5939-5
ISBN-13: 9781481959391
Library of Congress Control Number: 2013900852
CreateSpace Independent Publishing Platform, North Charleston, SC

The Phoenix Suns:
The View From Section 101

Howard A. DeWitt

TABLE OF CONTENTS

ROCK N ROLL BOOKS BY HOWARD A. DEWITT

Van Morrison: Them and the Bang Era, 1945-1968 (2005)

Stranger In Town: The Musical Life of Del Shannon (with D. DeWitt (2001)

Sun Elvis: Presley In The 1950s (1993)

Paul McCartney: From Liverpool To Let It Be (1992)

Beatle Poems (1987)

The Beatles: Untold Tales (1985, 2nd edition 2001)

Chuck Berry: Rock 'N' Roll Music (1981, 2nd edition1985)

Van Morrison: The Mystic's Music (1983)

Jailhouse Rock: The Bootleg Records of Elvis Presley (with Lee Cotton) (1983)

HISTORY AND POLITICS

Obama's Detractors: In The Right Wing Nut House (2012)

The Road to Baghdad (2003)

A Blow To America's Heart: September 11, 2001, The View From England (2002)

Jose Rizal: Philippine Nationalist As Political Scientist (1997)

The Fragmented Dream: Multicultural California (1996)

The California Dream (1996)

Readings In California Civilization (1981, 4th edition revised 2004)

Violence In The Fields: California Filipino Farm Labor Unionization (1980)

California Civilization: An Interpretation (1979)

Anti Filipino Movements in California: A History, Bibliography and Study Guide (1976)

Images of Ethnic and Radical Violence in California Politics, 1917-1930: A Survey (1975)

NOVELS

Stone Dead: A Rock 'N' Roll Mystery (2012)

PREFACE

The inner workings of a professional basketball and the fan enjoyment are intertwined. As a former full and part time season ticket holder in a previous life with the Seattle Super Sonics and the Golden State Warriors, I enjoy NBA basketball. That is to a point. Both teams were sold twice in the middle of my season ticket experience, and the changes were never pleasant ones. When the Seattle Super Sonics were winning I was ignored, as they started to lose I was called on the phone weekly. This was fun as I was the only Super Sonic mini season plan holder who lived in Fremont, California.

From 1971 to 2005, I was a Golden State Warrior ticket holder of one type or another, and I flew to Seattle to watch my mini season ticket games until 1995. Fortunately, I had no trouble with my wife, Carolyn; she is even more of a fan.

When Franklin Mieuli owned the Golden State Warriors, you could call the front office and the general manager might answer the phone. I was sent books, memorabilia and autographs. I took my wife on our first serious date to San Francisco's Cow Palace to see her first Warrior game. She loved it, and Carolyn became an instant fan. The next year the Warriors moved to the Oakland Coliseum, and we moved nearby to Fremont, where I was a professor of history. Carolyn taught in the public school system. We had fifteen great years with the Warriors. Then the roof fell in as they were sold to an ownership group that was more interested in the money than the fans.

When Mieuli sold the Warrior's in 1986, I looked to purchase a home in Scottsdale. I didn't have enough money for a home, so I bought tickets to assorted Suns' games, and Carolyn and I flew in to watch our new team. Then in 1989 we purchased a home in the Phoenix area. I was going to retire in 1995 but that was delayed for ten years. Finally, in 2005 we moved to Scottsdale, and I purchased season tickets in section 101. As the eighth year begins we are still rabid fans.

As I sat in my seat during the first few years, I realized that the Suns were a different organization. They loved the fans. They were everywhere in the community. Despite a few scandals in the past, there were no wife beatings, no incidents in gentleman's clubs and the worst thing that you say about the Suns players is that they were seen having ice cream with their families. I see the Suns' players all over Scottsdale. Steve Nash' dad is regularly seen beating his son in a tennis match.

Scottsdale is full of breast enhanced Barbie's, people who view golf as a religion, Happy Hour devotees, maladjusted fans from Chicago, right wing political nuts as well as most of the Phoenix Suns who live in and around Scottsdale and Paradise Valley. The players love the U. S. Airways Arena, the training staff and good living in the Valley of the Sun. This prompts some players to sign for a little less money. Grant Hill and Shannon Brown are examples of players who love the Phoenix area. The owner, Robert Sarver, contrary to popular opinion, spends some of that money on the players as well as the fans. More on that subject later.

This book is a reflection of seven plus years as a season ticket holder and more than twenty-five years of attending Suns' games. The private life of the players, the Internet gossip, the less than credible reporting (don't worry Dan Bickley and Paul Coro you passed the test you are great reporters), and the constant barrage of criticism from some quarters about ownership is not a part of this book. I am not a shill for the Suns, but I value the experience of going to the games.

Peter: "I think you are a shill."

The gossip mongering folks will not like this book. Most of the stories in this book are true but the real people have been disguised. There are quotes from Peter and Claude but they are fictional characters. Peter is modeled on Clarence Buttonwillow, a British expatriate, who owns 21 Circle K's in Phoenix and 29-7-11s in Southern California. He is married to a former Miss India and his financial adviser in Mumbai is working on a deal to bring Hertz Rent A Car franchises to his 7-11s. Claude is modeled after Solly "The Intimidator" Lukowitz. After a professional wrestling career, christened the El Sereno California brawler early in his WWF fame, he became a well-known yachtsman. After his retirement, and after he almost qualified for the America's Cup, he invented the world's most expensive toilet. Solly's Soilers sell for more than $200,000, and his product is in the homes of Donald Trump, Bill Gates, Vladimir Putin, Warren Buffett, Queen Elizabeth, the Italian Count Pietero Serenostein and Warren Johansen. Solly lives in Bisbee Arizona where he continues to work on new products from his home in Brewery Gulch. There will be comments from Claude and Peter throughout the book.

My close Scottsdale friends wonder if I have lost my mind. They can't imagine anyone that would be interested in my ramblings. Claude and Peter's comments reflect this feeling.

When I began this book, I intended to reflect on the strife torn, lock out season that took place in 2011-2012. The strike dominated period led to a great deal of grumbling, criticism of the owner, Robert Sarver, and there were rumors that the franchise face, Steve Nash, was moving on to another team. Not surprisingly, there was a fan backlash when Nash signed with the enemy, the Los Angeles Lakers. Then Grant Hill went to the Los Angeles Clippers. Then the Suns moved half their roster. A series of new faces after free agent signings, trades and releases created a new group of Phoenix Suns.

In 2006-2007, the Suns were 61-21 and five years later they were 33-33 in a strike-shortened season. This is an indication that change is needed. Hence, it was the hiring of Lon Babby to run the franchise as the President of Basketball Operations that began the turnaround. This next year is one of rebuilding the franchise. It will be an interesting time.

HOW THE SUNS TREAT THEIR FORMER PLAYERS

Most NBA franchises treat two or three of their past stars with reverence. The Suns are a family that treats the majority of its former players well. The Phoenix Suns employ so many retired players, and honor many others, that if there were an old timers league the Suns would win the title every year. The franchise is loyal to its history.

There is a Suns history that is important to the franchise. This book, as well as one I will write next year, suggests the importance of the Suns historical legacy.

Why write a book about Phoenix Suns? The answer is a simple one. I have spent more than twelve thousand plus dollars a year to enjoy forty-one home games, a few pre-season games and until the last few years the NBA playoffs. In our eight seasons as ticket holders, we have loved every minute of it. There is no dollar better spent than on an NBA season ticket.

Why does someone spend that much money on basketball? This is a good question. In my case, it is not only to keep my wife happy, but the anticipation of standing outside the arena and taking in the colorful spectacle. When one enters the arena, the smell of food, the excitement of cheering Steve Nash, and the friends that we have made is important to our enjoyment. Maybe it's a good game. Maybe it's a stiff. Either way it is a good time.

One of the problems with being a Phoenix Suns fan is reading the newspaper. At this point there is more criticism than praise for the owner Robert Sarver, the teams progress and the amenities offered the fans. This is what happens when you purchase a sports franchise, but the Suns are trying reenter the elite NBA team status.

The press is only one of many distractions that the owner faces. Sarver runs the team as a business. Unlike Dallas Maverick owner, Mark Cuban, who spends what he feels like regardless of the salary cap, or Los Angeles Clipper owner, Donald Sterling, who spends as little as possible, Sarver is a hands on owner with a budget. Alvin Gentry is a great coach, and, as the NBA goes, the players have high character, good community relations and they like living in the Valley of the Sun.

Perhaps the most important plus of the Phoenix Suns is accessibility. You can actually meet with and talk to the owner. You can give him your opinions and he listens. By putting himself so close to the fans, Sarver sometimes gets in uncomfortable situations. I talked to him in May 2012 and he was genial and good humored. Then a fan showed up and spent half an hour complaining about the loud music during the games. The jury is still out on DJ Dizzie, but he looks like a keeper.

At one of the periodic meetings with fans that Sarver holds, I pointed out that Donald Sterling is an incredible inept owner, a personal disaster and a jackass. Sarver looked uncomfortable. "I like Donald Sterling, he is a good guy," Sarver remarked. He didn't look happy or comfortable, but he was nice to me. I do that to people at times. Sarver also ran away from me as quickly as possible. Why am I telling this lame story? The answer is a simple one. Robert Sarver is a good listener, and he is not prone to tooting his own horn. Sorry for that last cliché. He listens to people. Even to irate and somewhat misinformed fans. I couldn't imagine standing next to Los Angeles Lakers owner, Jerry Buss, talking basketball. That is unless I was a nineteen-year-old beauty queen with cosmetic enhancements. Sarver is not an average guy, but he does his best to act like one. That is he is an owner who cares about the team, and he will not disparage anyone. But he is realistic. He realizes that he will be more popular when the Suns win.

The Suns from top to bottom treat the fans well. When Sol welcomes me at the ticket gate at U. S. Airways arena, he always has a positive spin on the night's game. This is reason enough to purchase season tickets. One of the purposes behind this book is to suggest what you are missing if you don't have season tickets. Stay tuned.

X   Basketball is a metaphor for life. The one year I played high school basketball I learned more from the coaches and playing than I did from my ten years in college. I went ten years to get a BA, MA and PHD. I never wanted to real day job, so I became a college professor. So who better to write a fan's look at the Phoenix Suns? Hence, the sub-title: "The View From Section 101." Harold Schifman is responsible for the title.

The main reason for this book is to show how fan friendly the Phoenix Suns are in a business where huge television revenues, mammoth stadium naming deals, shoe deals, other advertising and foreign rights to the product make owning an NBA team a lucrative business. The Suns' owner, Robert Sarver, does everything he can to make the fan experience a positive one. Some fans show their appreciation at games by hollering: "Sarver you suck." Others blame everything that goes wrong on Sarver. The extreme fans think that Sarver caused the war in Iraq. I pointed out that he didn't own the team then.

This intense and at times unfair criticism is the price for owning a franchise. He ignores these personal insults and fan diatribes, and he goes about his business. There is no bodyguard with Mr. Sarver. He has his wife and two children with him. Maybe his wife is the bodyguard.

There is another reason for this book. That is that the Phoenix Suns are an extension of the community. When I had Golden State Warrior tickets under owner Franklin Mieuli, I could call the office and talk to the general manager. That ended when the corporate guys bought the team. The new owner made his money in advertising and he had little, if any, interest in the fans. The Golden State owner was a cable television magnate who was a pain in the ass for the fans, the players and the NBA. He bought the team to maximize his money. The team declined in attendance, the roster no longer had players like All Star and Hall of Famer Rick Barry and Coach Alvin Attles moved to the front office before running away from the franchise. But he did sell the Golden State Warriors for a nice profit.

I had sporadic communication with the Warriors. Rick Barry lost his hair, and I dropped my season tickets. Barry ran off to the Houston Rockets to finish his career. I continued as a mini season ticket holder until 2005. Then I fled the San Francisco Bay Area in retirement to the Valley of the Sun. We didn't know a soul. We live in Gainey Ranch in the Greens with Glenn Campbell, Steve Nash, Alvin Gentry, Scott Williams, Charles Barkley and Marc Iavaroni. Living nearby for some folks is in Paradise Valley. The Valley of the Sun is a great place to live, and the players have a certain amount of privacy. Fortunately, for them, they don't know me. I talk to Iavaroni once in a while, but he thinks I am just some crazed fan. He is probably right. He is also a nice guy. He tries to have some quiet time with his wife at the Paradise Bakery, but he is not able to escape the fans. That's me I am talking about. I told him he is a better coach as the lead assistant to Vinny Del Negro for the Los Angeles Clippers because he now has a point guard, Chris Paul. It was funny. He didn't laugh.

In 2005, when I purchased my first set of Suns season tickets, I was astonished at the fan friendly atmosphere. I wondered what was wrong with the Suns. They actually cared about the fans. Robert Sarver was at the games; the Los Angeles Lakers' Jerry Buss was seldom at their home games. I guess he was embarrassed to be seen with his two or three of his eighteen-year-old girl friends. The Los Angeles Clippers owner, Donald Sterling, was seen clipping coupons and figuring out ways to save money. My favorite Sterling story is when he asked a hooker what to do about his team. They made the playoffs that year.

Peter" "Howard I think you are jealous of Jerry Buss. I know I am."

What do my lame stories suggest? It is another way of saying that the Suns' owner, Robert Sarver, is not clipping coupons or riding around in a limo with young ladies who look like his daughters. He is paying attention to business and keeping the Suns fan friendly. Or at least a few of the Suns' fans are happy. There is progress for the Suns. He no longer runs along the sidelines with a finger, and he has only been on the trampoline once. Is this a sign Mrs. Sarver is running a part of the Suns' organization?

No one from the Phoenix Suns' organization was involved in this book. I have sniffed around the U. S. Airways Arena for almost eight years as a season ticket holder and almost twenty years as a casual fan. So everything I write about is from my own experiences. I hope that you are not bored. If you are buy a ticket to a Clippers' game and say hi to my kids in Los Angeles. Not only is the Phoenix Suns experience a fun one; there is a great deal to learn about life from watching the games.

The main reason for writing a fans perspective on the Suns is to show how people who do not have season tickets are missing a great experience. Enjoy the ride and e-mail me at Howard217@aol.com., with praise or condemnation Preferably praise. The last time I gave out my e-mail for one of my twenty-one books, it was for an Elvis book. I said something that the fans didn't approve of and I received over 5,000 e-mails. I hope I get more than ten on this book. But, then again, the Suns aren't Elvis. Well maybe Steve Nash is a bit of Elvis. While I also take criticism, I prefer praise. A portion of the profits from this book will be donated to a Suns charity. Enjoy the ride and send me your inner thoughts.

Professional sports at times gets a bad rap. The fans are often obnoxious. (I think of my Oakland Raider days.) The fans are often too pompous. (I think of my San Francisco 49er days) The fans are often rude and a bit provincial. (I think of my Seattle Super Sonics days) The fans are often trendy and a bit too latte oriented. (I think of my Los Angeles Lakers days) The fans looks like hookers trying to look like movie stars. Or like gang bangers trying to look like Ice T. (I think of my Los Angeles Clipper days). The fans are too cool and casual. (I think of my Portland Trail Blazers games I attended. I stood out because I didn't wear any L. L. Bean clothing.). I don't' have any of these problems with the Phoenix Suns. It is a fun experience.

There is a culture to the Phoenix Suns. It is a positive one that celebrates the community. This culture is not just fan friendly; it embraces the skill of watching the best basketball players on the planet while being comfortable and well fed. It doesn't get any better than that.

The best part of the experience is going to the games. Almost as good is the experience with my 6th man. This is the person assigned to season ticket holders. My 6th man, Khalif Fortune, is typical of the Phoenix Suns organization. He is helpful, intelligent and personable. Khalif makes the Suns experience a memorable one. He has helped me select new seats, he has invited me to special events at the Montelucia and Donovan's Steakhouse, and he does everything to make the experience a positive one. Thanks Khalif Fortune for helping me enjoy the ultimate Suns' experience. Melissa Fender is a previous 6h Man who was great. All my 6th Men get promoted. Is this a trend? My first 6th Man now heads the Oklahoma City Thunder 6th Man program.

This book is a love letter to the Phoenix Suns. I didn't ask for any interviews, I didn't talk to anyone in the organization, but the Suns are open with their fans. So I have been in the locker room, the weight room, the pressroom, the practice court, but I have not been in Coach Alvin Gentry's office. Like most fans, the Suns extend these privileges to me as a season ticket holder. I also grabbed an energy bar, a peanut butter one, from the Suns training table. I ate it and felt like going on the court and dunking. Fortunately, I regained my sanity.

The purpose of this book is to weave the 2012 season with a personal mini history of the Phoenix Suns. There is a great deal of Suns lore that needs to be examined. Enjoy the ride.

My apologies to Eddie Johnson, Walter Davis, Shawn Marion, Amare Stoudemire and everyone else who scored a lot of points. You will be in next years book: **The Phoenix Suns: My Year Without Steve Nash and Grant Hill**. Stay tuned.

PROLOGUE

"I'M SUPER EXCITED...THAT"S WHY I THINK I'M BANGED UP, GOING A LITTLE TOO HARD IN PRACTICE. BUT I'M SUPER AMPED." SEBASTIAN TELFAIR, SUNS POINT GUARD

The quote from Sebastian Telfair suggests the joy and commitment of Suns' players. He is typical in that playing in the Valley of the Sun is a sheer joy.

As I was putting the finishing touches on this book, I didn't have a title. I was sitting in the Paradise Bakery at Gainey Ranch on a beautiful May morning. Coach Alvin Gentry walked in with a smile, at lunch Steve Nash was in the corner having a salad with his kids and I still needed a title.

I went to my financial guru and spiritual advisor, Harold Schifman. He showed up talking about his latest girl friend and his investments. He is a great guy. Harold is also a poet, a short story writer, a working artist, a financial genius and an inveterate party planner. He had the title in minutes. **The Phoenix Suns: The View From Section 101** was the working title. I loved it.

I meet with a group of people at three different coffee shops, and we are all interested in the Phoenix Suns' gossip. One of the crew at my favorite Hayden Avenue bagel shop said to me: "Why don't you write a book? That way you can get a life." I pointed out to my coffee group that we needed to dissect the Suns. We needed to help them get back to being a deep playoff team.

At that point Coach Alvin Gentry came in. Claude hollered: "Coach you are the man." Ernie wanted a free ticket or an upgrade because they weren't winning. Gentry walked over and talked to us. This is the beauty of the Suns. No one acts like a star. Well maybe Peter. I said: "Coach I'm working on my outside shot." He smiled.

Claude took Gentry aside and said: "Coach when you get into the playoffs, you will get a Solly's Soiler in every bathroom in your house."

New York Ernie: "Claude are you nuts, Gentry has four toilets, that's $800,000 dollars. I need just one of your toilets."

Claude: "No problem New York Ernie, I can get you one that Bill Gates returned, it doesn't always flush."

The table looked at me like I was nuts. Gentry asked us what we like about the Suns. It's the experience the table called out in unison. It is about having dinner at Kincaid's before the game. It is about hanging out with your friends. It is about the bar at Legends or Cooperstown, where rock star Alice Cooper might wait on you. I agreed. The Phoenix Suns were like no other team. They actually cared about their season ticket holders. They also made it fun.

Claude: "Howard you sound like a shill."

Peter: "No, he sounds like an obsessed fan." Remind me to fire Claude and Peter.

The next morning Coach Alvin Gentry, broadcaster Scott Williams and former Suns' coach Marc Iavaroni and his lovely wife came into the Paradise Bakery for coffee. None of these people know me. They do recognize me as a crazy fan that asks too many questions. They are all nice to me.

The owner's right hand man, Ed Zito, comes in for coffee. He is a great guy and probably knows as much about the Suns as anyone. Don't worry he doesn't talk basketball to me.

None of my friends are responsible for anything that follows in written form, and all mistakes, insights, etc. are mine The purpose of this book is to present a fans view of the Phoenix Suns. In this book mini-biographies of Suns past players, a look inside the organization from the fans perspective, and a recap of the strike shortened season make a case for a great fan experience. The Phoenix Suns organization, the players and everyone involved had no input into this book. It is strictly my ranting and raving. If you are looking for gossip about the ownership, the players or the league, this is not the book for you. Go to the Internet and read what those morons have put up on their blogs. Sorry, Peter, I know you have the word moron copyrighted.

Jack McCallum, a reporter for **Sports Illustrated**, was granted season long access to the Phoenix Suns for a book that came out in 2006. My first Sun's season ticket was in 2005-2006 and I was around to watch McCallum. I felt like Zelig in the Woody Allen movie, as I watched McCallum ask all the wrong questions. He had an annoying habit of asking what Steve Nash thought in the book. It was a device I adopted when I invented a character known as Peter to criticize my book. Remember Peter is a fictional character.

McCallum's book, **:07 Seconds Or Less: My Season On The Bench With The Runnin' And Gunnin' Phoenix Suns** is not only a thoughtful and intelligent book, but it is one that is honest beyond a fault. That said there is one heavy bias. For some reason, McCallum did not like Robert Sarver. He is not only consistently unfair to Sarver, but he blames the new owner for all the things that have gone wrong with the Suns. This mars an otherwise excellent book. It is also a book that made some Suns' players angry. I won't be sitting on the bench or going on a team flight. Neither will McCallum. He also worshipped the first Suns general manager and future owner, Jerry Colangelo. He was really nasty toward Amare Stoudemire. There is also a tendency to want to manage the Suns business. He should remember that is Dan Bickley's job. The tone of **:07 Seconds or Less: My Season On The Bench With The Runnin' and Gunnin' Phoenix Suns** is so anti-management that Robert Sarver comes off as the grinch who stole Christmas. The beat reporter, Paul Coro, and the columnist, Dan Bickley, for the **Arizona Republic**, Phoenix's excellent daily newspaper, have at times the same affliction. Everyone wants to spend Robert Sarver's money. Fortunately, Sarver does a good job spending his own money. There is no word from Mrs. Sarver.

The Suns franchise began in 1968 as an expansion team. In translation, that means you are at the bottom of the league with marginal players. It didn't work out that way for the Suns. They had a commitment to winning, and by 1976 they were in the NBA finals. They were the little team that could, and Jerry Colangelo's vision was rewarded with loyal fans.

The last two seasons were ones that a lot of fans were unhappy with but there were some positives. In the 2010-2011 season, the Suns had the fourth best historical record in the NBA. This is a major accomplishment for a team in a small market, with a low paying television contract compared to the New York Knicks or the Los Angeles Lakers.

In 2012, the Suns are celebrating forty-four years in the Valley of the Sun. It is a great franchise, but it is now in transition. Jerry Colangelo is leaving the franchise, Steve Nash is leaving the franchise, Grant Hill is also leaving the franchise, and the team hasn't made the playoffs in two years. It is time to look back and to look forward.

chapter

ONE

THE SECRET HISTORY OF THE SUNS: ESTABLISHING THE BRAND TO 1976

"YOU MUST BE CRAZY. PHOENIX WILL NEVER SUPPORT PRO BASKETBALL." NBA COMMISSIONER J. WALTER KENNEDY IN CONVERSATION WITH RICHARD BLOCH AT NEW YORK'S TOOTS SHOR'S RESTAURANT SUMMER 1968

The chances of Phoenix getting an NBA franchise appeared to be zero and none in the mid-1960s. Then Seattle Super Sonics owner, Sam Schulman, told his tennis-playing partner, Richard Bloch, that he needed a new toy. Bloch was president and chairman of the board of Filmways Inc. This was a $100 million entertainment and publishing business. Bloch needed a tax write off. He loved to come to the Valley of the Sun. The Biltmore Hotel was his favorite haunt. He would be seen playing tennis there and in the evening he drove down Lincoln Avenue for cocktails and dinner at El Chorro. It was Bloch's buddy, Schulman, who praised the lifestyle in the Valley of the Sun. Bloch was soon a convert.

The conversations with Schulman piqued Bloch's interest. He began researching professional basketball. Bloch was not only athletic, but he had a knack for business. Bloch also realized that celebrities loved to invest in professional sports. He worried that he knew little about basketball. Then Bloch recalled that his buddy Schulman knew nothing about sports.

Schulman was an egomaniac that suddenly had a new toy. Bloch was an athlete who had little interest in basketball, but, unlike Schulman, he had a sense of basketball's economic potential. He saw a strong return on his investment. Bloch liked the 12,500 seat Phoenix Memorial Coliseum. He was a Tucson native with Arizona business interests. His partners were also University of Arizona graduates. They included Karl Eller, who owned an outdoor advertising company in Phoenix, Donald Pitt, a Tucson attorney and Don Diamond, a Tucson real estate investor.

Of all the Suns' investors, Diamond was the most financially sophisticated. He was savvy when it came to business and leverage. He was a commodities trader from New York, who may have been the person behind leveraging the Suns. He probably told the management group that the celebrities would provide most of the funds for establishing the franchise.

The Suns management group persuaded their celebrity clients Andy Williams, Henry Mancini, Ed Ames and Bobby Gentry to bankroll their attempt to bring NBA basketball to Phoenix. They needed to raise $100,000 to make the application for a franchise. The check was presented to NBA Commissioner J. Walter Kennedy. He informed them that a two million dollar entry fee was required. They had one million and Bloch began lobbying for a million dollar league loan. To everyone's amazement the NBA Board of Governors agreed. Only New York Knick owner, Ned Irish, complained that it was money "the cactus people could never pay back."

THE DOUBTS ABOUT THE PHOENIX FRANCHISE

Sam Schulman made fun of Bloch for attempting the coup. After depositing the check with the NBA, the Phoenix Suns were awarded a franchise in 1968. There was excitement in the Valley of the Sun. Richard Bloch felt important. He was in New York for the NBA All Star game. "Where do I get my tickets to the All Star game?" Bloch asked. Kennedy responded: "Go to the ticket booth and purchase them." When Bloch walked over to Madison Square Garden, he wondered about the commissioner. He wasn't a friendly person.

After Commissioner Kennedy didn't bother to give him tickets to the game, he told a friend that the wondered what he got for the $100,000 application fee. Bloch still needed to come up with the two million dollars to be formally granted a franchise. He was furious with Commissioner Kennedy and those who ran the league. His business partner, Donald Pitt, laughed at the NBA Commissioner, and he told Bloch there was money to be made in professional basketball. They were still a million dollars short of funding the franchise as they raised the first million from celebrity investors.

The New York Knicks Ned Irish said: "This is the Phoenix coup, we have some desert folks thinking that they can play big city basketball." The doubts about the Suns future angered Bloch. He had more important problems. He had to raise the rest of the money to bring the franchise to fruition.

Not only did the Suns intrigue the other owners, but also there was enough money in the NBA to provide a loan to the demanding but very convincing Richard Bloch. He was a man with a mission. He wanted to use someone else's money to found the Suns.

LET'S USE SOMEONE ELSES MONEY TO FOUND THE SUNS

On January 22, 1968 the twelve existing NBA owners met in New York's St. Regis Hotel, and they listened to Bloch's proposal for a Phoenix franchise. The New York Knicks Ned Irish called Phoenix "a backwater burg," and he opposed the franchise. In Phoenix there was little booster support. There was only casual mention in the press of the new basketball franchise. What no one realized was that the NBA owners agreed to front one million of the two million dollar franchise fee. The Suns would pay the money back to the league over the next five years. Singer Andy Williams put up $300,000, and the other celebrities kicked the remainder of the $700,000. Bloch and his partners spent very little of their own money to be awarded an NBA franchise. It was a sweetheart deal. But Bloch did have some problems. He had no idea how to run an NBA franchise. He also had a downtown Coliseum that was not a first class basketball venue.

It was Bloch who joked that they had used somebody else's money to establish the Phoenix Suns. The large number of unsophisticated investors turned into a nightmare. He had so many people who wanted jobs that he had to give Jerry Colangelo unprecedented power.

Bloch and his partners had other problems. They had brought in economic hillbillies to support the franchise. Almost every investor had a relative that they wanted the Suns to employ. Singer Bobbie Gentry wanted one of her boyfriends hired for public relations. Andy Williams had friends that he thought could help the franchise. When Bloch and his partners hired Jerry Colangelo the economic hillbillies receded into the woodwork. There was still the problem of a business plan.

Sam Schulman was on the phone to Bloch every day giving him advice. Finally, Schulman said to talk to Commissioner Kennedy. The Suns ownership group was now split into two factions, and there was concern about how to get the franchise off the ground.

It was the positive change in the NBA front office that got the Suns franchise down the road to completion. Commissioner Kennedy said: "I talked to half a dozen shoeshine boys, a couple of barbers and some taxi drivers, and I was surprised and gratified how aware they were of the NBA. I came away with strong feelings that Phoenix was ready." This was little more than a public relations gesture as Kennedy realized that the owners would approve the franchise. Privately, he was not happy about the prospect of professional basketball in the Valley of the Sun.

Bloch needed help finding out how to run a professional basketball team. In an act of insidious juvenile behavior, Kennedy wouldn't answer his phone. He didn't want to talk to the Phoenix Suns ownership group. So Bloch went to Commissioner Kennedy's office to obtain instructions on how to operate the Phoenix Suns. He found that there was no owner's manual. What Bloch knew was business. So he set up a corporation to make the Suns a for profit enterprise. He wouldn't be a dilettante like Sam Schulman. He structured DRD Sports, as the general partner to run the Suns business operation. With more than a dozen owners, the early days were often confusing ones. Bloch had a sense of the future, and he was a consummate and optimistic businessman. Everyone was impressed with the organizational structure. From top to bottom they were highly professional.

The main problem was that the ownership didn't know very much about basketball. Some critics called the Suns ownership a combination of tax right offs and ego. There was some truth to this criticism. To counter this criticism, Bloch remained in the background and reporters found it difficult to obtain an interview.

The reason was a simple one. Bloch wasn't sure that Phoenix had a suitable arena. Bloch needed help. So he called his friend Sam Schulman who would tutor the Suns' owner. Schulman told Bloch to get in touch with the Seattle Super Sonics General Manager Don Richman. Bloch called. He asked for a basketball mind that the organization could hire. Richman responded: "I know a kid who's working for the Chicago Bulls and while this may sound crazy, I got a hunch he just could be a general manager." Bloch wasn't sure. The kid was twenty-seven years old. He didn't want to waste the resources of a two million dollar franchise on a young and unproven kid. He thought about it for a week. Finally, Bloch called the kid and invited him out to Beverly Hills to talk about the general manager's job. The Phoenix Suns needed someone with basketball knowledge to bring order out of chaos. This answer to the Suns problems came in the form of Jerry Colangelo.

JERRY COLANGELO: THE EARLY YEARS

When the Suns ownership contacted young Jerry Colangelo everyone asked: "Who is this kid?" The answer was a complicated one. He was a young man committed to a life in the athletic arena. He was a good basketball player, but he was not talented enough to play in the NBA. So he entered the NBA as a scout, a coach and eventually he became a general manager. It is his Chicago background that is important in his rise to prominence in the NBA.

While growing up, Colangelo was a competitive athlete in Chicago Heights playing guard on the Bloom Township basketball team that was 49-8 his junior and senior years. In baseball, Colangelo was a pitcher on a high school team that included future New York Yankee star Jim Bouton.

Then Colangelo was off to the University of Kansas to play with Wilt Chamberlain. "I wanted to play on a national college championship team," Colangelo remarked. When Wilt left to play for the Harlem Globetrotters during Colangelo's sophomore year, he transferred to the University of Illinois. His leadership skills led him to captain the Illinois basketball team during his senior year.

Things got more confusing when the second new NBA franchise, the Milwaukee Bucks, called to talk about a management position. He turned down that offer and he flew to Los Angeles. After meeting with the new Suns' owners, Colangelo told them that he needed to talk to the Chicago Bulls. He had to get permission to fully explore the job. Then the Bulls owner, Dick Klein, refused to give Colangelo permission to talk to the Phoenix Suns about a job offer. This infuriated Colangelo. He told Klein that he was going to meet the Suns' managing partner.

After Bloch made his spiel, Colangelo looked at Bloch and remarked: "Phoenix!" He was flummoxed by the offer. Then Colangelo told Bloch that he had turned down an offer to go to work for both the Seattle Super Sonics and the Milwaukee Bucks. The reason, Colangelo stated, was that he felt a strong loyalty to the Chicago Bulls. He was working as a scout for the Bulls, and he soon became an assistant coach. When the Bulls' owner attempted to block Colangelo from the general manager interviews, his loyalty to the Bulls dissipated.

The meeting with Bloch was not a positive one. Colangelo had strong differences with Bloch on how to run an NBA franchise. Then there was a meeting in Phoenix with the primary partners, Bloch, Diamond and Pitt. They asked Colangelo: "What makes you think that a young kid like you can run an NBA franchise?" He replied: "You wouldn't have me here if you didn't think I could run the show." He also asked for increased decision-making powers. They agreed. He got the job. Jerry called his wife in Chicago, and told her to pack her bags they were heading to the Valley of the Sun. Colangelo's wife asked: "Where is the Valley of the Sun?" He replied: "Phoenix." She asked: "Why?" Jerry didn't answer.

As he returned to Chicago, Colangelo had two hundred dollars in his wallet. He had come a long way since his first job after graduating from college. He started out working at the House of Charles, a tuxedo rental shop, and more than five years later he was the Phoenix Suns general manager. But he still had to give notice to the Chicago Bulls.

The Chicago Bulls tried to change Colangelo's mind. Klein offered him a substantial raise. He offered him more authority. None of this prevailed. Then Klein threatened Colangelo: "Remember if you leave you can't come back, this is a jungle." This threat only heightened Colangelo's resolve to be successful.

JERRY COLANGELO FLIES INTO SKY HARBOR

On March 1, 1968 Jerry Colangelo flew into Sky Harbor Airport and took over the Phoenix Suns. To his surprise, the locals didn't greet him warmly. There was no hostility, just general indifference to the new franchise. Colangelo and Bloch put their heads together and came up with a sure means of winning over local fans. He had to hire a recognizable coach.

On April 24, 1968 John "Red" Kerr signed a three year contract as the Suns' first head coach. He was a former Illinois star who had played in 917 consecutive NBA games with the Syracuse Nationals. He also coached the Chicago Bulls for two years. Colangelo raided the Bulls front office and brought the secretary, Ruth Dryjanski, and the trainer, Joe Proski, to Phoenix.

For thirty-two seasons, Proski was known as "Magic Fingers" for his healing powers. He was inducted into the Suns ring of honor after his retirement. He was given the name magic fingers when Connie Hawkins fell in a game. Proski rushed out. "What's wrong Hawk," he said. Hawkins smiled. "Wave to all your buddies in Green Bay. You are on national TV." Hawkins got up quickly. Hot Rod Hundley, the Suns' TV announcer, remarked: "Proski must have magic fingers." When Proski looked back on the Suns he remarked that Connie Hawkins, Charles Barkley and Jason Kidd were the greatest Suns' players.

COACH JOHN RED KERR: THE WORST CHOICE FOR THE SUNS AND OTHER DIFFICULTIES

When John "Red" Kerr was hired as the Suns first coach there was euphoria. He was a great player who was not ready to coach in the NBA. Kerr was from another basketball era. He was hard-nosed, authoritarian, and he wasn't a top-notch basketball mind. As a result, he never translated into an effective NBA coach. His recognition would come later as the broadcasting voice of the Chicago Bulls. For the Suns he was a good public relations choice, as a coach he was a disaster.

The first year was difficult as the Suns went 16-66 and finished twenty games out of the playoffs. Out of this early misery, Dick Van Arsdale came into the fold. Colangelo said Arsdale was: "The ideal player to start an expansion team with." Van Arsdale became known as the "Original Sun." The Suns didn't do so well in the early drafts. They lost a coin flip to draft Lew Alcindor, before he changed his name to Kareem Abdul Jabbar, and the American Basketball Association was raiding the NBA.

Then Colangelo began advertising season tickets. When someone called and asked: "How much are season tickets?" The answer was "$185."

Coach Red Kerr looked to be a wonderful fit for the Suns. While with the Chicago Bulls, Kerr was named NBA Coach of the Year for achieving a winning season and a playoff spot in the Bulls inaugural season. It was all-downhill after that for Kerr, and when he went into broadcasting for the Suns in the 1969-1970 season, after he was fired as the coach, he found his niche. He teamed with Hot Rod Hundley, and they were a popular local duo. He left to work for the Chicago Bulls and

Kerr remained as their color commentator until the end of the 2007-2008 season.

THE STATISTICAL SUNS: THE FIRST YEAR AND SOME OBSCURE SUNS

In 1968-1969, former UCLA star Gail Goodrich was the Suns' scoring leader with 1931 points as he averaged 23.8 points a game. The Suns picked up Goodrich in the expansion draft from the Los Angeles Lakers. As one of the team's first stars, Goodrich teamed with Van Arsdale to provide a potent scoring duo. He also got a chance to start for the first time in his NBA career. Throughout his career, Goodrich was labeled a gunner, but with the Suns he ranked seventh in the league in assists with 6.4 a game. After Goodrich played in the 1969 NBA All Star game, the Suns traded him to the Lakers for center Mel Counts. That was a mistake, as Goodrich led the Lakers to a 69-13 record. He did have some help from Jerry West and Wilt Chamberlain. Goodrich was the scoring leader for four seasons with the Lakers.

There are a number of obscure Suns' players who were important to the franchise. During the 1968-1969 season, Dick Snyder was the Suns' field goal scoring leader at .472 percent. Who was Dick Snyder? Snyder played his college ball at Davidson, and he was with the Suns for two years. Snyder was a shooting guard who was a diamond in the rough. He was traded to the Seattle Super Sonics, and he became one of their early stars averaging in double figures for four years. He was a 6-5 shooting guard or small forward who was among the NBA's best percentage shooters.

The best foul shooter in 1968-1969, a former New York University star, Stan McKenzie, played for the first two years of the franchise, and he was a .763 three-throw shooter. South Carolina's Jim Fox was the top rebounder the first year with 3.5 a game. Dick Van Arsdale played the most minutes and Fox was the person who fouled out the most.

The Arizona Veterans' Memorial Coliseum had a 12,096 capacity and there were plenty of seats and a great deal of money was lost. But it was fun and Colangelo had a plan for the future.

THE RED INK OF THE FIRST SEASON

The Suns first season was brutal. They won sixteen games and lost $185,000. They averaged 4,300 fans a game. Basketball wasn't exactly a hot commodity in the Valley of the Sun. Things got so bad that at a New York press conference Coach John "Red" Kerr started talking about the beauty of the Grand Canyon when he was questioned on the Suns' woes during press conferences. In New York, he was asked:

"How do you get to the Grand Canyon?" Kerr responded: "I'm not sure but if we keep losing I am going to find it and jump into the canyon."

Jerry Colangelo knew that the Suns had to be a state brand. So on September 26, 1968 the Suns first exhibition game was played in a high school gym in front of local fans in Miami, Arizona. This small town is located in a mining area and the Suns coming to town was an event that everyone anticipated. Local restaurants had dinner specials named for a Suns player. The Neal Walk meatloaf was a big seller. The Suns beat the Seattle Super Sonics 104-99. The Suns were led by David "Big Daddy" Lattin, Dick Snyder and McCoy McLemore who each scored twenty points in the Suns inaugural exhibition game; it was fun for the local fans. The result was a small, but energetic, fan base in Miami.

The Suns went on to play other exhibition games in Fort Huachuca, Flagstaff, and Mesa Arizona before opening the regular season. When the season opened Dick Van Arsdale scored the first basket. But it was a difficult time, as the Suns' roster couldn't compete with the established teams.

When the 1968-1969 season opened the Suns beat the Seattle Super Sonics in their first game 116-107 and they were 4 and 3 after seven games. Then the roof fell in, and they won only twelve more games during the inaugural season.

During the first season Colangelo traded players to improve the team but nothing worked. It would take some time to clear the red ink. The Suns desperately needed help. It came from an unexpected source. In a secret coin flip with Seattle, the Suns won the right to sign Connie Hawkins.

Connie Hawkins was a hot commodity. The Pittsburgh Condors of the American Basketball Association made a number of offers to Hawkins. He turned them down. Hawkins wanted to play in the NBA. He also wanted to get away from New York and the distractions that almost ruined his career. He loved the Valley of the Sun, and after playing for one season, he remarked: "I am extremely happy in Phoenix." The Hawk was above all else loyal. He was also smarter than people realized, and the Hawk knew that if he played hard he would be the new face of the franchise. That happened.

THE HAWK SAVES THE FRANCHISE AND THEN MOVES ON

His impact on the Suns was immediate. They went from a 16-66 team selling eight hundred season tickets to a fan base that loved Hawkins floating dunks, his ball wizardry and his fun loving personality. In 1973, Hawkins was traded to the Los Angeles Lakers but his four years in Phoenix boosted the franchise. "No other athlete ever captured this town's fancy like Connie Hawkins," remarked Verne Boatner, the **Arizona Republic** sports editor.

The tragedy is that NBA officials never apologized to Hawkins for banning him from the league without evidence. When he began playing the head factotum, Commissioner J. Walter Kennedy, announced that Hawkins contract was approved paying him $85,000 a year for five years. The league paid him $25,000 a year beginning in 1987 for twenty-four years for banning him without cause. There was still no formal apology.

It was not all roses with Hawkins. He missed wake up calls, he missed practices, he missed transportation connections and Colangelo and Hawkins had heated arguments. In 1973, Colangelo traded him to the Los Angeles Lakers. The trade caused a local furor but in time people got over it.

Hawkins was a legend in the community. The December 1970 issue of **Phoenix** magazine had the Hawk on the cover giving gifts to young kids sitting under a Christmas tree. Not only was Hawkins well liked; he was active in charities and promoting the team. But somewhere along the line, he became angry that he wasn't appreciated, and that the Suns played him too many minutes. He got into arguments with Jerry Colangelo and things did not go well in his last year in the Valley of the Sun.

The controversy over the Hawk is an interesting one. He was pure and simple a great player. The Suns recognized that and retired his jersey. End of argument; he remains a legend.

THE STATISTICAL SUNS: THE SECOND YEAR

Connie Hawkins was the leading scorer in 1969-1970 averaging 24.6 points a game. This was a club record, and Hawkins also played 40.9 minutes a game. With that much time on the floor, Hawkins had the highest number of fouls. Jim Fox continued with the most games fouled out, but he also had a .524 shooting percentage. The addition of Paul Silas led to his 11.7 rebounds a game, which was a club record. Most of Fox's shoots were close to the basket. He was a center with limited offensive skills, but he had a physical presence. It is difficult to miss two feet from the basket. Hence, the over .500 shooting percentage.

Gail Goodrich continued to star as he had a .808 free throw shooting percentage, and he also was the top playmaker. When he was taken in the 1968 supplemental draft, Goodrich played for two years in the Valley of the Sun. He led the club in scoring during the first season with a 23.8 points a game average, and he was one of the Suns' All-Stars.

In the second year, the Suns were not only getting better but the crowds were increasing. They finished third in the NBA's Western Division and Jerry Colangelo took over for Coach Red Kerr and he went 24-20. The team went to the playoffs and lost in seven games to the Los Angeles Lakers. Colangelo had brought the Suns back. He was about the fire the coach. He was the coach. So he fired himself. He brought in Cotton Fitzsimmons, which was a smart move. Fitzsimmons went 48-34, and the Suns attendance of 332,945 ranked them seventh in the league. The little team that could was on the move.

THINGS GET BETTER, SORT OF: 1970-1976

In the early 1970s, Colangelo had to twice take over the coaching reins, and he was pretty good at it. But it was a stopgap measure, as running the Suns business side was a full time job. What is striking about Colangelo's coaching is that he knew the game and how to motivate his players. He was responsible for Connie Hawkins performing at a mythical level. That is he could take over a game and win it single handedly. The Lakers had so much trouble with Hawkins in the playoff that a few years later they traded for him.

Throughout the early 1970s, the Suns improved dramatically. In 1976, they advanced to the NBA finals. The 1975-1976 season brought the Suns to the forefront of NBA teams. They brought in deadly shooting Paul Westphal, increased center Alvan Adams scoring role, and they had point guard Ricky Sobers take a more active role in the offense. It worked. But the team took some time to find its mojo. The Suns didn't jell in the regular season as they finished 42-40. In the playoffs it was a different story. They beat the Seattle Super Sonics and the Golden State Warriors to advance to the NBA championship series. They lost in six games to the Boston Celtics. By 1975, the arena on McDowell was filled. The fans were jubilant as the 12,500 seats sold out regularly.

When Colangelo fired himself as coach in 1970, he brought in Cotton Fitzsimmons who won 97 games in two seasons. It looked like Fitzsimmons was the long-term coach of the future. Then, surprisingly, he accepted a higher paying job coaching the Atlanta Hawks. In 1972-1973, Colangelo had to return to coaching after Butch Van Breda Kolff was fired after just seven games. Van Breda Kolff was a nasty personality with a dictatorial style, and he clashed with everyone. He got along with his players because he went out drinking with them. One former Suns' player said of Van Breda Kolff: "He coached more than 1300 games at the college and pro levels and he had 2600 drinks. I loved him."

DRINKING AND HAVING FUN WITH COACH VAN BREDA KOLFF

Butch Van Breda Kolff was a great basketball mind in a body that never left the Playboy Mansion or the nearest cocktail lounge When Colangelo discovered that Van Breda Kolff was out drinking with his players during pre-season training camp, he went ballistic. In 1972, the Suns training camp at Lake Havasu City High was in a gym where the NBA Suns shared lockers with high school football players After practice, Van Breda Kolff would meet his players at a local lounge, the Watering Hole, and they would drink until closing time.

For some reason he was hired at the Suns head coach. The reason is that Van Breda Kolff was a great coach. He didn't care about his public image and his drinking bouts with Suns announcer Hot Rod Hundley created an urban legend. Hundley had an interest in a Phoenix bar, and they spent their nights downing scotch and waters. Colangelo made so many great decisions he can be forgiven for hiring Van Breda Kolff. The problems at the training camp at Lake Havasu escalated when players didn't show up for practice. In an atmosphere that Allan Iverson would approve of, Van Breda Kolff was more interested in drinking, playing cards and chasing women than he was in creating a structured Suns offense. When he coached the Los Angeles Lakers, his team was losing in San Antonio, and he left the bench during a game to get a scotch and water from a bar behind the team bench. He was colorful. He was also fired everywhere for not paying attention to his team.

When Colangelo called Van Breda Kolff on his laziness, the coach responded: "Quit being a little Old Italian in tennis shoes." Van Breda Kolff thought he was funny. Colangelo was furious. Then the season began and things got worse. Colangelo found vodka in the locker room. One day after practice there were fifteen good-looking women in the Lake Havasu High School locker room. One player said: "There aren't fifteen good looking women in Lake Havasu." One of the women remarked: "We are Mr. Van Breda Kolff's Las Vegas friends." That night the Watering Hole was particularly raucous. Things were out of control.

The managing partner, Robert Bloch, back from a European vacation, criticized the coach in an early loss to the Los Angeles Lakers. He told Colangelo: "I could substitute players better than that guy." Van Breda Kolff was called to Colangelo's office and fired.

The problem was that the players liked Van Breda Kolff because they didn't have to practice or perform. It was like a vacation as the Suns went 3-4 in their first seven games. Colangelo took over and began the process of righting the ship. It wasn't an easy task.

JOE PROSKI AND JOHN MACLEOD: STABILITY IN THE FRANCHISE

Joe Proski, the Suns trainer, recalled that while at training camp, Eddie Biedenbach, whom the Suns had acquired from the Los Angeles Lakers, was in charge of the cooler and it vanished. Proski said he found the cooler in a rental house in Phoenix with Biedenbach sampling the wares. Biedenbach for his training camp escapades only played seven games with the Suns.

The franchise coaching merry go around ended when John MacLeod was hired in 1973, and he remained until 1987 winning 579 games while losing 543. Stability and good coaching became MacLeod's reputation. Integrity, brilliant coaching, a calm personality and an indepth knowledge of the game made MacLeod a winner.

By the mid-1970s, the Suns were established as a premier team. Now the problem was to keep them competitive. In 1975, the Phoenix Suns were an enviable franchise. Most of the good things were due to Jerry Colangelo.

COACH JOHN MACLEOD AND RIGHTING THE SHIP

The Phoenix Suns began their turnaround when John MacLeod was named the head coach. It was 1973 and the Suns were struggling to establish their brand. He spent two years weeding out players, with Jerry Colangelo's help, and the 1975-1976 Suns went to the NBA finals. It was the coaching style, the integrity and the control over the players that allowed MacLeod keep his job until 1987.

During his thirteen and a half years with the Suns, MacLeod coached seventy-two players and four went on to become NBA head coaches. He was a professor who taught his players the subtle nuances of the NBA game.

He reached the NBA playoffs nine times, and this included a run of eight straight years from 1978 to 1985. The knock against MacLeod was that he couldn't win the big ones. He was a great coach with integ-

14

rity and the will to win within the competitive system. The best thing
that can be said about MacLeod was that to a man his players remarked
that he taught them how to play the game.

THE PHOENIX SUNS BRAND IS ESTABLISHED: 1976

In 1976, the Phoenix Suns established the brand in the Valley of
the Sun by losing to the Boston Celtics in the NBA finals. In September 1975 Coach John MacLeod blew the whistle for the first practice
at Yavapai College. The players were not happy to be practicing in the
middle of nowhere. Prescott Arizona has a beautiful downtown; a wonderful set of local bars and it is great for tourists. If you are a twenty
something basketball player it is boring. The upside is that there were
virtually no distractions. Coach MacLeod refined his system, and, as the
season progressed, there was no doubt that the Suns had done something special in training camp. The Suns had gone through two of the
worst seasons in the franchise history but Jerry Colangelo struck with
Coach MacLeod. He could see progress.

In training camp the team had fun kidding Alvan Adams. In a
Prescott restaurant Adams came in and asked Jerry Colangelo what he
was eating. Colangelo said: "Bavarian cream pie, order a piece kid I am
paying."

Adams said: "I don't like chocolate. Then order a vanilla Bavarian
cream pie." Most of the team was eating with Colangelo, and they were
all laughing. There was no such thing as vanilla Bavarian cream pie.
Adams ordered the pie and the waitress tried to tell him that there was
no such thing. She took Dick Van Arsdale aside and asked him what
was wrong with the kid. Van Arsdale said: "He's from Oklahoma." The
waitress smiled and went back into the kitchen. She came out with three
scoops of ice cream and two cookies. She put it down in front of Adams
and said: "Vanilla Bavarian Cream Pie Oklahoma style."

The story doesn't end there. During the early part of the season,
Coach MacLeod's wife, Joannie, heard a horse clopping down the street.
She looked out and Alvan Adams rode up on a horse that he had brought
to Phoenix. He knocked on the door. He smiled and handed Joannie a
dozen roses with a French cookbook recipe for Vanilla Bavarian pie. It
was at this point that Coach MacLeod knew that he had an intelligent
center.

What MacLeod recognized was that the 1975-1976 Suns had immediate team chemistry. The roster was filled with future coaches like
Pat Riley, rugged and intelligent front line players like Curtis Perry,

Keith Erickson, Garfield Heard, Alvan Adams and Dennis Awtrey. At the guards and the wings Ricky Sobers, Paul Westphal, John Wetzel, Phil Lumpkin, Nate Hawthorne and the face of the franchise Dick Van Arsdale made for a formidable roster.

There was one player in the mix that no one thought about as the season started. He was a rookie John Shumate. Although he was drafted in 1974 out of Notre Dame, Shumate sat out his rookie season with a blood clot. In 1975, he was under the radar, as he joined the Suns roster. Not only was Shumate selected to the All NBA Rookie First Team in 1975-1976, he averaged 12.4 points a game with 7.5 rebounds. He was the final piece in a team that surprised everyone in the NBA.

It took almost six months for the Suns to be recognized as the NBA's newest super team and Coach MacLeod was hailed as a genius. What happened in the 1975-1976 season? The answer is a simple one. Good coaching. There was also a great front office. The appreciative fans made the players energetic, and during the season there was a great deal of luck.

There were glimpses of the Sun's future greatness in the 1975 Summer Pro League when Alvan Adams and Paul Westphal shot the lights out. The summer games in Los Angeles saw Westphal average 27 points a game and Adams 24 points. It was a portent of things to come. In the twelve summer league games the chemistry amongst Suns players was outstanding.

Jerry Colangelo: "I got the feeling for the first time that Alvan was really something special."

OPENING THE 1975-1976 SEASON

The Suns opened the 1975-1976 season with six road games. They returned home with two wins and four losses. MacLeod was amazed at the optimism and the eagerness in the opening game at the Arizona Veterans Memorial Coliseum. The home opener against the New York Knicks was an indication of things to come. The Suns destroyed the Knicks 112 to 81. The new player in the mix, John Shumate, was a monster.

When the Suns showed up in Chicago to play the Bulls early in the season, center Dennis Awtrey had coffee with his old buddy Jerry Sloan. "We really got a much better team this year, and it won't take long to prove it," Awtrey said. Sloan laughed at him. Awtrey was furious. He scored eleven points against the Bulls in the second quarter and the Suns defeated the Bulls 96-80. After the game, Sloan remarked: "I thought the coach told you not to shoot." Awtrey agreed that was the case. "When I'm mad I shoot."

What happened was that the Suns dominated the boards. Alvan Adams also played a high post and caught the cutting Suns with pin-point passes. Then on November 26, John Shumate had the first of many career nights when he scored 25 points and pulled down seven rebounds in only twenty-three minutes on the floor.

On December 26, 1975, 11,482 fans turned out at the Phoenix Coliseum to welcome back former Sun Charlie Scott. He had played with the Suns from 1971 to 1975, and he was a three time All Star who was popular in the Valley of the Sun. When he was traded to the Celtics, it was an unpopular move. The fans cheered his return. The Celtics won the game; Scott remarked that he still loved the Suns' fans.

In late January 1976, Alvan Adams became the fist rookie since 1972 to be named to the All Star game. The press and fans began to use the term "The Rising Suns," as the Suns played like one of the best teams in the Western Conference. The Suns found their missing piece in forward Garfield Heard. He was a tenacious rebounder and a scorer. He was also a late season addition arriving in the middle of the season. There were some other strange occurrences. Alvan Adams wife, Sara, said she would only kiss him if he scored in double figures. He did for most of the rest of the season.

As the 1975-1976 season progressed, the Golden State Warriors riding super star Rick Barry's hot shooting were on their way to a 59-23 season and a .720 winning percentage. The Suns were only the third best team in the Western Conference, but they had a chemistry that was better than their record. On March 3, Paul Westphal scored 33 points, as the Suns won their tenth game in the last fifteen. That night his wife gave birth to a 7 pound 6 ounce baby girl. Westphal said: "I'm taken you to the NBA finals." It turned out the statement was no idle boast.

It wasn't until March 25 that the Suns reached .500 with a 36-36 record. They won six of their last ten games, but no one realized that they were jelling on offense, as well as on defense. An overflow crowd of 13,306 squeezed into the Coliseum on April 8 to watch the Suns dismantle the Los Angeles Lakers 113-98, as they clinched their first playoff berth since 1970. The standing ovations from the fans energized the Suns players. Then arena announcer, Stan Richards, remarked that play-off tickets were about to go on sale. The Suns sold out the playoffs. They were officially the team in the Valley of the Sun.

The media began calling Alvan Adams "The Find," and he became the **Sporting News** rookie of the year. For a team just above .500 the Suns caught the media's eye. As the Suns closed the season they prepared to play the Super Sonics in the playoffs. The fans selected Paul Westphal as the most popular player, and the MVP award was given to all twelve players. The Suns were psychologically and physically ready for the 1976 playoffs. As the team ended the 1975-1976 regular season, the Suns final twelve home games were victories.

THE SUNS MAGIC IN THE 1976 PLAYOFFS

When the 1976 NBA playoffs began the defending NBA champs, the Golden State Warriors, looked like a sure lock to come out the West. In the East, the Boston Celtics were loaded, and their coach, Tommy Heinsohn, had an All Star roster that included a frontcourt of John Havlicek, Dave Cowens and Paul Silas. All three players were named to the NBA's All Defensive First Team. Don Nelson, another strong front line player, came off the bench, but the Celtics were grey beards and their window of opportunity for another NBA title was closing rapidly. Everyone was looking forward to a Golden State-Boston final. It didn't happen. The upstart Phoenix Suns, riding the hot shooting of Paul Westphal, and the coaching of John MacLeod beat the Seattle Super Sonics in the first round four games to two. No one gave the Suns a chance in the Western Conference finals against the Golden State Warriors. The national media ignored the Suns and Coach MacLeod used this to motivate his team. The 6-4 Westphal also had a breakout season, as he was unstoppable on the offensive end. The Arizona newspapers printed stories that headlined: "The Suns Versus The East." The Coliseum was sold out every night for the playoffs, and there was an air of euphoria in the Valley of the Sun. The rest of the league laughed when Suns players talked openly of reaching the NBA finals. When they did everyone was stunned.

By the time that the Suns reached the NBA finals, after beating defending champions the Golden State Warriors four games to three there was a renewed respect for the Suns. There was also one key addition that helped the Suns. They picked up Garfield Heard in a trade with the Buffalo Braves. At 6-6 and 219 pounds Heard was one of the toughest players in the NBA.

THE GREATEST NBA GAME: CELTICS-SUNS GAME SIX, 1976

As the Suns advanced to the 1976 NBA finals, there was euphoria in the Valley of the Sun. For the first time in NBA history, there was extensive television coverage of the finals. As television dictated starting times and staggered the days between the games, this helped the aging Boston Celtics.

As they faced the Celtics, the Suns were aware of their legacy. The Celtics had twelve NBA championships and a team staffed with future Hall of Famers. The Celtics had not lost a home game in the 1976 playoffs going 6-0. CBS sports helped the Celtics by delaying the championship series for six days so it could start with a Sunday television broadcast. John Havlicek was thirty-six years old with bad knees and not much left in the gas tank. He soaked his knees and Dave Cowens and Paul Silas rested. The **Boston Globe** called the Suns "a Minnie Pearl basketball team." The rest helped as the Celtics won the first two games, and John Havlicek excelled as he poured on 23 points in the Celtics 105-90 victory in game two. Then the Suns returned home to win 109-107 in overtime in Phoenix. From the beginning game four was a war. The Celtics tried to intimidate the Suns. It didn't work. When game four started referees Don Murphy and Manny Sokol whistled twenty-one fouls in the first ten minutes. Tom Heinsohn, the Celtics coach, became angry and screamed at the officials that they were calling "stupid fouls." The game was close to the end. The Suns were up by four points with ninety seconds left. The Celtics cut it to a basket but the Suns prevailed.

The series was tired as 2-2 when game five opened to a sell out crowd in the Boston Garden. This game turned into a triple overtime affair, and it was filled with controversy. The first problem occurred with the score tied 95 all when Boston's Paul Silas attempted to call a timeout near the end of regulation. The problem was that the Celtics didn't have any timeouts left and referee Richie Powers didn't grant a timeout. As 15,320 screaming Celtic fans looked on, the game was tied as regulation time ended. Then it was 101 at the end of the first overtime.

In the second overtime, the Celtics went ahead on a Havlicek shot 111-110 as the horn sounded. The Celtics went to the locker room and the Suns coach pointed out that there were still two seconds on the game clock. The Celtics had to come back out of the locker room. Havlicek had taken the tape off his legs. A fan assaulted referee Richie Powers and CBS Analyst Rick Barry got into a fight with a fan. Things were out of control.

The teams came back onto the floor. Then Paul Westphal called a time out. The Suns didn't have a time out. So referee Richie Powers awarded a free throw to Boston. The technical shot by Jo Jo White was converted and Boston led 112-110. Although two seconds remained on the game clock, Boston fans streamed onto the floor. Jerry Colangelo screamed at the referees and the game resumed. The Suns players had to push fans off the court. Colangelo threatened never to bring his team back if security wasn't increased. The Suns players were not only verbally harassed but drinks and objects were thrown at them. When play resumed the Suns' Garfield Heard hit a shot to tie it up.

The Suns-Celtics were ready for a third overtime. Boston took a 128-122 lead in the third overtime but Westphal scored four quick points to make it 128-126 but the Celtics won. The sixth game was anti-climatic as the Celtics won the NBA championship.

Game five is considered the greatest in Suns' history, and it is one of the premier championship games in NBA history. John MacLeod continued to coach the Suns for another eleven years, and it wasn't until 1993 that the Suns reached the NBA finals under then head coach Paul Westphal.

Looking back at game five, Coach John MacLeod remarked: "Some people didn't want us to be there. We were not considered a team with much appeal at the time. They wanted Golden State and Boston in the finals." There was no doubt that everyone underestimated the Suns.

From the Celtic-Suns series there were nine players who went on to become NBA head coaches. It was a historic television series. It was one that established the NBA as a major sports television attraction, and put the Valley of the Sun on the professional sports map. It was also an indication that the little town in the Valley of the Sun had arrived in major league sports.

The publicity from the triple overtime thriller in game five of the 1976 NBA finals remains a legendary game. Rick Barry, the Golden State Warrior, hot shooting star was a guest broadcaster and he remarked of the June 4, 1976 game: "It was the most exciting basketball game I've ever seen." It was the Suns Garfield Heard who remains the star as he sank a shot with no time remaining to send the game into the third overtime. The Celtics won that game and the next to wrap up their 13th NBA championship. The Suns, however, became the Valley of the Sun team with their gritty performance.

chapter

TWO

FAMOUS AND NOT SO WELL KNOWN BUT FAMOUS SUNS FROM THE PAST

**"I'M NOT A ROLE MODEL...JUST BECAUSE I DUNK A BAS-KETBALL DOESN'T MEAN I SHOULD RAISE YOUR KIDS."
CHARLES BARKLEY**

The Phoenix Suns culture is one emphasizing family, respect, community service, excellent player relations and strong character. The following people are not only a big part of the present day Suns legacy, but they are also important to the history of the NBA. The following list of ten has no scientific basis. They are people I respect, admire, and enjoy listening to, occasionally talking to while placing them in the context of the Phoenix Suns. The next book will have ten new icons, and the vote from readers will determine the next ten. That is if enough books are sold to warrant the book that is tentatively titled: **The Phoenix Suns: My Year Without Steve Nash and Grant Hill**. So stay tuned.

In order to understand the Phoenix Suns culture it is important to look into some of the past historical windows. They are a small market franchise that attracts some fine players. As Grant Hill said to me at the Montelucia: "You come to Scottsdale, play for a few years with the Phoenix Suns and never leave the Valley of the Sun." Hill's Duke education makes him the second smartest person in the Suns organization. He said that his agent, Lon Babby, is the smartest man he ever met. Robert Sarver is tied for first or second because he signs the paychecks.

The Suns players, as well as their coaches, and the varying levels of management define the organization. The management is first rate. Unlike teams like, the Golden State Warriors, there are clear lines of authority. To appreciate and understand the Suns, it is necessary to examine the careers of ten people who have impacted the franchise. The ten people listed below are among the most important in Suns history. My apologies to those I left out. You will be in next year's book. Remember the list is arbitrary and everyone on it has made an important contribution to the Suns. The people who typify the Suns commitment to character, excellence and community service, are included, and there is no ranking system. The only criteria is my good judgment

The ten famous Suns included in this section represent a cross section of the type of person who finds a home in the Valley of the Sun.

1. THE SECOND SUN
SIR CHARLES BARKLEY: THE WARRIOR WHO WAS AN INSIDE FORCE

In 1984, Charles Barkley entered the NBA, after being cut from the U. S. Olympic team by Coach Bob Knight. The cut was something that Barkley never forgot. He worked hard on his game. He also committed himself to a rigid personal training regime. There were still some good nights in the bars, but not just as many of them. With the ubiquitous nickname, the Round Mound of Rebound, the three hundred plus pound Barkley proved that talent also came with brains and wit. He honed his talents and dropped his weight. He couldn't get away with the same things in the NBA as he did at Auburn University.

BARKLEY'S YEARS AT AUBURN
Barkley's college career at Auburn University is the stuff of legend. Although he had constant problems with his weight, Barkley led the SEC in rebounding for four years. He played center, and, while he was

closer to 6-4 than the 6-6 he was listed at in the program, Barkley was a prolific scorer. He still holds the Auburn University field goal percentage title at 62.6%. At Auburn, Barkley averaged 14.8 points a game and 9.6 rebounds. He was the consummate team player with the most assists amongst big man in SEC history. He also developed an all around game with passing skills that were unparalleled. That is when he passed the ball, which was a rarity. The ubiquitous nickname, "The Round Mound of Rebound," was not only cruel, but it brought Charles regularly into the training room. He did have one bad influence-Dan Majerle, but that is another story.

The 1984 draft was one that produced a number of Hall of Fame legends. In addition to Barkley, Michael Jordan, John Stockton and Hakeem Olajuwon were brought into the NBA fold.

In the NBA, Barkley quickly developed into playing shape. For ten straight seasons, he was either a first or second team All Star. He was a power forward. In his day, power forwards were 6-9 and weighted two hundred fifty pounds. Despite his lack of size, he led the NBA in rebounding in one season. He was among the top ten rebounding leaders for the remainder of his career.

What did everyone underestimate about Barkley's talent? The answer is a simple one. He has the heart of a Lion. When he was drafted by the Philadelphia 76ers, Matt Goukas commented: "When I coached him in Philly in 1985, he was very, very young and his game had not formed yet. He was not big for forwards, and defensively, he was bad. But at the end of the game he wanted to guard Larry Bird." Barkley was a fierce competitor. This is something Bobby Knight missed. A teammate, Kevin Loughery, called Barkley "pound for pound the greatest rebounder in the history of the game." Not bad for a guy who wasn't even 6-5.

In Philadelphia, Barkley played with some stars. In his rookie season the 76ers reached the Eastern Conference finals on a team that included Moses Malone, Julius Erving, Andrew Toney and Bobby Jones.

In 1990, Barkley finished second to Magic Johnson in MVP voting. Barkley claimed that he was robbed. He scored three more points a game than Johnson, he had as many rebounds, and he shot sixty per cent from the field. The difference was that Barkley played for the 76ers and Johnson was with the Los Angeles Lakers.

The Los Angeles Times had a weekly column or a story about why and how Magic deserved the MVP. Magic Johnson was playing his first season without Kareem Abdul Jabbar, and the sportswriters were impressed with his leadership, playmaking and scoring. Magic also had a supporting case that included James Worthy, A. C. Green, Byron Scott and a young rookie Vlade Divac. Johnson caught the attention of sportswriters and beat Barkley by only 22 votes.

WHY IS SIR CHARLES A FAMOUS SUN?

Charles Barkley is the most famous former Sun. Why is he the most famous? There are many reasons. He is articulate and bright. He is also an over the top as a television analyst. Just turn on his NBA basketball shows with Ernie, Kenny the Jet and Shaq. He is the verbal star. His commentary on NBA games reminds fans that his finest days were with the Suns.

While in Philadelphia, the outspoken Barkley accused the 76ers of racism by keeping a white player, Dave Hoppen, as the twelfth man. He is independent minded and honest. The 76ers sent him packing.

In the 1992-1993 season, Barkley was traded from the 76ers to the Suns. It worked out well for both teams. Barkley averaged almost 26 points his first year and had a career high 5.1 assists per game. During the regular season, Barkley was a monster. He led the Suns in scoring in 46 games and in rebounding in 58 games. He also led the team in assists in 22 games. He was fifth in the league in scoring, he was sixth in rebounds and for a big man he averaged 5.1 assists a game. Not surprisingly, the Suns were an elite team.

He also led Phoenix to the NBA Finals. The Suns were 62 and 20 that year, but it was with the fans that Barkley made his biggest impact. He established the run and gun Phoenix Suns long before Mike D'Antoni introduced the system. He was a perennial All Star during his four years with the Suns.

Many of the critics believe that the Suns should have won the 1993 NBA title. They had Kevin Johnson, Dan Majerle, and Cedric Ceballos as starters to compliment Charles Barkley's talent. When they lost to the Chicago Bulls, the local press blamed Barkley. The worst comments about Barkley came from Michael Jordan who said: "Barkley didn't want to put in the time to win an NBA title. He didn't want it enough." This is of course nonsense. Charles answered the criticism. He pointed out that the Bulls had all the tools to win the NBA title. He also weighed in on the MVP race by criticizing Magic Johnson's 1989-1990 selection. "Magic Johnson got to raise the level of James Worthy's game, Michael Jordan got to raise the level of Scottie Pippin's game. I got to raise the level of Shelton Jones's game," Barkley said. He made it clear he needed a stronger supporting cast. This didn't always sit well with his teammates, but this is Barkley's charm. He spoke his mind.

When he won the NBA MVP award in 1993, it was Charles' ultimate triumph. Barkley not only revitalized the Suns' franchise, he brought a swagger to the NBA. There is no doubt that Michael Jordan was still the best NBA player, but no one turned a franchise around better than Sir Charles. No one was more entertaining.

When Jack McCallum's book **:07 Seconds or Less: My Season On The Bench With he Runnin' And Gunnin' Phoenix Suns**, pictured Barkley as a person "whose shadow looms over the franchise." (p. 30) He described how Barkley dominated key games. Many players were jealous of Sir Charles' theatrics and constant demand for the ball. This is great writing, but it is not close to the truth. Barkley's assists, his offensive rebounding, his fast break points, his shooting percentage, and his newly acquired defensive made him the best all around player in Suns history. They expected too much of Barkley. He responded in typical Barkley fashion by suggesting that it is a team game.

Never one to shy away from controversy, he stated that sports figures did not need to be role models. It was almost like Charles had committed a grievous error. No one believed what he said. A translation might be to leave me alone, let me play the game and be myself.

In 1996, Barkley was traded to the Houston Rockets. After a few years of recrimination, the Suns were once again back in his good graces. As one of the more outspoken and controversial players, Barkley sold tickets. He was also a dominant player. In 2004, the Phoenix Suns retired his jersey. The Barkley years are among the best for the Suns. His legacy is to point out how great the Suns teams of the 1990s performed in an age of super stars. The Suns generally do not have a bevy of super stars; their success is achieved with teamwork and precision. This model provides an incentive for the present day Suns. For me, Charles Barkley is the number one Sun.

In politics, Barkley startled everyone by being a Republican. When he mother told him that President George H. W. Bush only worked for rich people. Barkley responded: "But Mom I am rich."

THE OTHER CHARLES BARKLEY

Charles Barkley is an independent thinker and he is a man of conviction. So it is not surprising that from time to time he is a bit over the top. When he left the Philadelphia 76ers and joined the Suns, Barkley made it clear that he wasn't a hot head or a troublemaker. He had had enough of the Philadelphia mentality, and he accused the city of brotherly love of overt racism. He was so angry at his treatment by the Philadelphia fans that he pushed the Sun to the NBA finals. A little anger was good for Barkley's game. He also had a strong supporting cast in the Valley of the Sun.

When Barkley won the NBA MVP award in 1993, his statistics were outstanding. Barkley is still mad that he didn't win the 1990 MVP. "I had the most first place votes and didn't win the award!" Barkley continued. "I think you should vote for only one guy-I don't get why you have to rank the votes." There is no doubt that the NBA needed a charisma injection. This is what Barkley gave the 76ers, the Suns and finally the Houston Rockets. He spoke his mind and played at an MVP level. That is all you could ask.

Charles Barkley is one of the shrewdest and more honest observers of the NBA. He remarked: "The Suns are built for the regular season." This was a shrewd observation, as Coach Mike D'Antoni's system used fewer players down the stretch, and this made it difficult for the players to remain fresh. They played too many minutes. So D'Antoni's teams did not do well in the playoffs. After he left Phoenix, Barkley observed: "It is going to be tough for them because when you live by your offensive three point shooting, then any off night you could lose a game."

CHARLES BARKLEY'S LAST GREAT GAME

As one of the NBA's greatest players, Barkley worried that his skills would decline. When he was traded from Phoenix to the Houston Rockets, before the 1997 season, he took time to assess his game. He had great talent in Houston with Clyde Drexler and Hakeem Olajuwon. In 1999, Scotty Pippin joined the mix. But with Pippin as a slashed to the basket and Barkley posting up his defender, the team didn't mesh.

But there was still some gas in Barkley's tank. On May 13, 1999, Charles watched as the media christened the Los Angeles Lakers the new NBA superpower. With Shaquille O'Neal and an emerging star, Kobe Bryant, the Lakers were beginning a dynasty. In interviews with the local media, Shaq talked about the new Kings of the NBA. He laughed and said that there should be a coronation. As the Rockets left the locker room, Barkley told his teammates to watch him.

They did in awe, that night Barkley scored thirty points, brought down twenty-three rebounds and had five assists. The Rockets beat the Lakers 102-88. As he left the floor Barkley told Shaq: "Save the coronation for later in your career."

BARKELEY ON THE DREAM TEAM AND LEGACY

In 1992 and 1996, Barkley was a member of the U. S. Olympic basketball teams, and he won two gold medals. In the 1996 Atlanta Summer Olympics, Barkley led the team in scoring, rebounding and field goal percentage. He remembered Coach Bobby Knight cutting him from the 1984 team. These two Olympic appearances redeemed him.

Barkley's NBA career was one of constant controversy. This has obscured his game. He is a player who excelled at all parts of the game. He wasn't just a scoring machine and rebounder, Barkley played solid defense, and he had a strong sense of strategy.

When Barkley stated that athletes didn't need to be role models, he weathered a storm of criticism. His larger than life personality didn't help, as he wouldn't back down. "I don't create controversies," Barkley continued, "I just bring them to your attention." It is his playoff statistics that set Barkley apart from his contemporaries. He has the eleventh best rating among players to 2010 in playoff scoring, assists and rebounds.

In summing up Charles Barkley's career, one can make a case for greatness. He appeared on five NBA first teams and as many second teams. He won one NBA MVP award, and he finished in the top six in four other years. When Barkley lost out to Magic Johnson for the 1990 NBA MVP award he polled 48 first place votes to 27 for Magic. It was the second through fifth votes that prevented him from being the MVP. In career rebounds, Barkley ranks sixth on the all time NBA list. When he won the MVP award in 1993, he was fifth in scoring, sixth in rebounding and he averaged a career high 5.1 assists per game.

2. THE FIRST SUN
JERRY COLANGELO: HE IS THE FRANCHISE

Jerry Colangelo is tied with Charles Barkley as the number one Sun. As I write this article a friend reminded me that Colangelo is worth 25 million dollars, he is the Suns founder, and he developed the culture that defined professional sports in the Valley of the Sun. He is the most understated millionaire in the Valley of the Sun. An entire book is necessary to describe Colangelo's commitment to excellence.

While growing up in the working class Italian section know as Hungry Hill in Chicago Heights south of the city, Colangelo learned about hard work. He still has a photo of his family's two story flat in his office. He learned from his mother to make quick decisions. Colangelo watched as his mother threw his father out of the house. His commitment to school and sports was the result of his father's lack of discipline. Colangelo was determined to be a strong man, a leader and a savvy decision maker. He made his decisions with knowledge and research. He was perfect to run an NBA franchise. Jerry's combination of integrity, hard work and knowledge led him to unprecedented success.

COLANGELO ARRIVED IN THE VALLEY OF THE SUN

When he arrived in Phoenix, the twenty-eight year old Colangelo was a perfect choice to establish NBA basketball in the Valley of the Sun. In 1968, Colangelo, an assistant coach with the Chicago Bulls, pulled up stakes and left with his family for Arizona. He had $200 to his name and a great deal of ambition. He was the Phoenix Suns general manager, and his first job was to oversee the supplemental draft. This allowed the Suns to pick players from other NBA teams who were unprotected. There were some great players in the mix and Colangelo demonstrated his basketball knowledge by making the right choice on the first Sun taken in the draft.

In the supplemental draft, the Suns selected, Dick Van Arsdale. He quickly became known as "the Original Sun." It sounds strange to say that this was a great draft choice. It was because it defined the integrity, the character and the quality of play of the Phoenix Suns. He was the Suns first choice taken from the New York Knicks in the dispersal draft. The next choice was not a good one. The Suns selected in the 1968 draft Gary Gregor from the University of South Carolina. In his six year NBA career, Gregor played for six teams and he was a role player. He averaged about ten points a game.

Things did not go well in the 1969 draft as the Suns lost the coin flip to the Milwaukee Bucks, and they took UCLA's Lew Alcindor, soon to be Kareem Abdul Jabbar. The Suns took Neal Walk.

Jerry Colangelo did push some of the right buttons early on with the Suns. The managing partners were so happy with him that he was awarded an ownership share. The owners gave Colangelo a six-year contract, as well as partial ownership.

COLANGELO PURCHASES THE TEAM

From 1968, Jerry Colangelo was the face of the Suns. But he had opposition within his kingdom. Richard Bloch, Donald Pitt and Don Diamond increased their ownership from twenty to eighty percent. This took place in October 1983, and they demanded decisions by committee. This not only took the power out of Colangelo's hands, but it made for a clumsy and often confusing business model. This began the negotiations for Colangelo to purchase the team for twenty times the original franchise tag.

The early Suns' owners were impressive and none more so than Donald Diamond, who not only developed an expensive gated community, Pima Canyon Estates, but he also had a second career as the commodities businessman. His importance is that he knew the demographics of the Valley of the Sun. He also had business interests in Tucson. What Donald Diamond provided was the influence to make the Suns' a formidable Arizona brand. He eventually became a prime mover in bringing major league baseball to Phoenix.

Donald Pitt was equally impressive with Tucson based businesses. A lawyer turned jeweler, businessman and land developer, Pitt saw the future of NBA basketball. He helped Richard Bloch put together the sophisticated financial package that brought the NBA to the Valley of the Sun. They all worked well together and by hiring the young Jerry Colangelo, as the general manager, the Suns brand was assured of success. They also were responsible for educating Colangelo to the point where he could purchase the Suns with his investment group.

In 1987, Colangelo was part of an investment team that bought the Suns for $44.5 million dollars. When Colangelo represented the new owner's group it had been nineteen years since he began the Suns as an expansion team. He knew much more about basketball than the original franchise group led by Los Angeles businessman Richard Bloch. There was a storied history behind the Suns when Colangelo made his bid to purchase the franchise.

It was the Phoenician, Karl Eller, with his partners Bloch, Diamond and Pitt, along with local investment celebrities Andy Williams, Bobby Gentry and Ed Ames that helped bring the team to the Valley of the Sun. Eller dropped out to pursue other sports interests, but his integrity and name helped to establish the Suns. There was a lot of skepticism and minimal interest when Colangelo arrived, and he single handedly changed the local culture. He established a loyal and at time frenetic fan base.

The **Arizona Republic** held a contest to name the team the Suns. Some early popular choices were the Scorpions, the Rattlers, the Wranglers and the Mavericks. Fortunately, the name Suns prevailed.

What Colangelo had that no other owner possessed was that he was a scout, a player, a general manager and he probably cleaned up the stadium in the early days. "The game itself," Colangelo remarked, "is everything to me."

On July 1, 2012 the Phoenix Suns, for the first time in their history, were without Jerry Colangelo. Since selling the team to Robert Sarver, Colangelo spent eight years as a consultant. He was a visible presence in the arena. Until the end of the 2011-2012 season, Colangelo sat in Section 101 Row 8 on the aisle. When he sold the franchise in 2004 for $401 million, he negotiated an agreement to remain as chief executive for three years and chairman for five years. That contract is at an end. After forty-four years with the Phoenix Suns, the longest tenure of anyone in the NBA, Colangelo is enjoying retirement.

What are some of Colangelo's accomplishments: 1.) He pushed to get a first day commitment from Steve Nash to sign a multi-year contract in 2004. Mark Cuban was telling everyone who would listen that Nash was too old and his body too frail. It is a good thing that no one listened to Cuban. 2.) He brought in the legendary Connie Hawkins. 3.) He revived the fortunes of the U. S. Olympic basketball team. 4.) He organized and promoted the Ring of Honor, which honors past Suns and he maintains a solid interest in Suns' history. 5.) He was a prime mover in the construction of the downtown arena. 6.) He organized the earliest Suns' charities and outreach programs. 7.) He hired and maintained a broadcast crew that was independent, thoughtful and not cheerleaders for the Suns. 8.) He defined character. 9.) He initiated the earliest season ticket fan celebrations. 10.) He created a strong state wide market for the Suns.

Jerry Colangelo is known for much more than Suns basketball. He personally took charge of the U.S. Olympic Basketball team and brought it back to glory. Since the 2004 Summer Olympics, when Tim Duncan made it clear that NBA players had little concern about the Olympics, Colangelo has changed the culture. The player's stay in 5 Star hotels, they are encouraged to bring their families and practices are kept to a minimum. When you see Kobe Bryant or Lebrun James attending a swimming event and waving an American flag, you realize that they are enjoying the Olympics. In 2008, Jason Kidd was everywhere taking in as many events as possible. When Carmelo Anthony scored 37 points in fourteen minutes the television ratings were the highest of any Olympic event. One of the ironies of the 2012 games is that spectators from other nations were screaming "USA, USA." That is the magic of the NBA. That is the magic of Jerry Colangelo.

COLANGELO IN EUROPE

During his career, Colangelo was always a visionary. In the 1980s, he began looking into Europe for players. The Cleveland Cavaliers took the first player that Colangelo scouted, Stefano Ruston, in the 1990 draft. The 6-10 center had great shooting skill, but he was soft on defense. When Paul Westphal weighed in on Ruston, the Suns didn't draft him.

What Colangelo did was to remind the Suns scouting staff that players outside the U.S. were worth a look. In 1985, Colangelo traveled to Bulgaria to take a look at Georgi Glouchkov a 6-8 forward who was one of Europe's top players. He averaged 28 points and 10 rebounds when his team won the European championship. Colangelo was impressed. The Suns selected him in the 1985 draft in the seventh round as the 148th overall pick.

When the Suns signed Glouchkov, there was a great deal of publicity. But when he showed up in Phoenix he proved that he could not compete in the NBA. John MacLeod attempted to help Glouchkov's game, but he had little success. The Suns' general manager, Bryan Colangelo, bought out Glouchkov's contract and he returned to star in Europe.

In 2003, the Suns drafted Zarko Cabarkapa, a Serbian power forward, as their first round draft choice, and he was the seventeenth overall draft pick. He played for two years with the Suns, and then he was traded to the Golden State Warriors. He left the NBA in 2006, and he retired from professional basketball at twenty-five.

The European players were a mixed bag, but this doesn't diminish Colangelo's foresight in scouting that market.

COLANGELO LISTS HIS TEN GREATEST INFLUENCES
1. COTTON FITZSIMMONS: "COTTON EPITOMIZES WHAT A COACH IS ALL ABOUT. I DON'T BELIEVE HE EVER HAD A BAD DAY BECAUSE HE WAS ONE OF THE MOST POSITIVE PEOPLE YOU WOULD EVER MEET...." (DID CHARLES BARKLEY STRAIN THE POSITIVE SIDE?)
2. DAVID STERN: "DAVID IS CONSIDERED ONE OF THE GREAT COMMISSIONERS IN THE HISTORY OF MAJOR LEAGUE SPORTS."
3. PETE NEWELL: "A HALL OF FAME COACH IN HIS OWN RIGHT, PETE SERVED AS A MENTOR TO ME ON A PERSONAL

BASIS REGARDING PHILOSOPHY OF THE GAME AND THE
HISTORY OF THE GAME."
4. COACH MIKE KRZYZEWSKI: "WE HAVE BEEN JOINED AT
THE HIP SINCE 2005 AS HE HELPED ME RESTORE DIGNITY
TO THE USA BASKETBALL PROGRAM."
5. BOBBY KNIGHT: "ANOTHER ONE OF THE GREAT ALL TIME
COACHES AND STUDENTS OF THE GAME. HE IS A FIERCE
COMPETITOR WHO SHARED MUCH OF HIS JOURNEY WITH
ME BECAUSE OF OUR PERSONAL RELATIONSHIP."
6. WAYNE EMBRY: "ONE OF THE REAL PIONEERS REPRE-
SENITNG THE AFRICAN AMERICAN COMMUNITY IN BASKET-
BALL, AS A HALL OF FAMER, OUTSTANDING GENERAL MAN-
AGER AND A TERRIFIC FRIEND."
7. RUSS GRANIK: "RUSS SPENT THREE DECADES IN THE NBA
AND MANY YEARS AS DEPUTY COMMISSIONER. HE MADE
GREAT CONTRIBUTIONS TO THE NBA...RUSS WAS A SOOTH-
ING INFLUENCE ON RELATIONSHIPS INSIDE AND OUTSIDE
THE GAME."
8. RED HOLZMAN: "RED HELPED BREAK ME INTO THE NBA
BACK IN 1966 WITH THE CHICAGO BULLS. I LEARNED A
GREAT DEAL ABOUT THE NUANCES OF THE GAME, THE
GAME'S HISTORY AND THE CHARACTERS WHO PLAYED IT."
9. ARNOLD "RED" AUERBACH: "HIS MERE PRESENCE DE-
MANDED RESPECT AND HIS TRACK RECORD AS A COACH
AND GENERAL MANAGER ARE UNPARALLELLED."
10. EDDIE GOTTLIEB: "EDDIE IS TRULY ONE OF THE FOUND-
ERS OF OUR GREAT GAME. HE DEVLEOPED MUCH OF MY
PHILOSOPHY TOWARDS THE GAME AND THE RULES OF THE
GAME...."
SOURCE: WILLIAMS AND CONNELLY, NBA LIST JAM, PP. 184-
185

JERRY COLANGELO: CONCLUDING THOUGHTS

When Jerry Colangelo arrived in the Valley of the Sun, he was just shy of thirty, and he was virtually unknown outside of basketball. He was a young kid with extraordinary talent who turned down many job offers. Colangelo spent twenty six years shaping the franchise prior to putting together an investment group to purchase the Suns.

When he helped a group of investors purchase the team after the drug scandal, they paid forty plus million dollars to purchase the team. Colangelo had a one per cent share. By April 2004, when he sold the Suns, Colangelo owned 38%. From 1968 to 2004, Colangelo made the decisions on players and the franchise direction. When Dennis Johnson and Jason Kidd had personal problems that made the newspapers, they were traded. Kidd was innocent of spousal abuse, and it is alleged that Colangelo apologized.

The hiring of the no nonsense Coach, Cotton Fitzsimmons, identified the franchise's direction. That was a good thing, and Colangelo's decisive leadership marked the franchise with one word-integrity.

It is Colangelo's commitment to the community that is outstanding. He was never afraid to make an unpopular decision. When Colangelo supported a full state holiday honoring Dr. Martin Luther King, he was heavily criticized. This suggests his commitment to civil rights. He also quietly helped the Phoenix Symphony Orchestra solve its financial problems. He supported the integration of the white only country clubs. There has never been a question of fairness with Colangelo. He is not only civic minded, he is personally beyond reproach.

3. THE COACHING SUN WITH A RUN AND SHOOT SYSTEM MIKE D'ANTONI: 0:7 SECONDS TO SHOOT OR GO TO THE BENCH

Mike D'Antoni is a basketball legend in Italy. He is the purest shooter in Italian professional basketball history. He is also one of the NBA's most creative, fiery and respected head coaches. He also speaks fluent Italian. How did a farm boy from West Virginia acquire these credentials? It is a long story. Here is the short version.

When he was a kid growing up in Mullens, West Virginia, D'Antoni became a basketball junkie. He developed one of the best jump shots in the game. When he attended Marshall University, he was a star, and then the Kansas City-Omaha Kings in the second round of the 1973 NBA draft selected him. He was named to the All NBA rookie second team in 1974. After three seasons in the NBA, D'Antoni, who was a role player, jumped to the Spirits of St. Louis in the American Basketball Association. The next year he signed with the San Antonio Spurs and after two games he was released. He quickly signed a contract to play in Italy.

D'ANTONI: AN ITALIAN BASKETBALL LEGEND

In Milano, the Olimpia team signed D'Antoni, and he became the Italian clubs all-time leading scorer. He was also voted the top point guard in Italian history. He led his teams to five Italian league titles, one Korac Cup and one intercontinental cup. D'Antoni played for the Italian national team in the 1989 European championship.

What did D'Antoni learn from playing in Italy? He learned how to manage players, impart his basketball philosophy, and he developed a playing style based on his Italian experiences. There are three things NBA players hate. They can't stand long and highly structured practices. No problem. D'Antoni has a system of half hour practices. The players dislike a structured defense. There was a free flowing Suns defense, if there even was a defensive philosophy, and the players loved the lack of a formal defense. Finally, NBA players dislike the Los Angeles Lakers' triangle that scientifically separates players on the court so that they can more easily find a good shot. Constant motion, the double screens, the back door cuts and the precise discipline of placing players on the floor define the Princeton offense and this is what got Coach Mike Brown fired by the Los Angeles Lakers. D'Antoni wouldn't think of employing this antiquated system. NBA players love the pick and roll, they love the freedom to take a three point shot and they love pushing the ball. They don't like structure or a defined system. When D'Antoni told his players to shot within seven seconds, he sold them on his system. It was also a fan favorite with fast paced games that had high scores, ferocious dunks and dramatic endings. It was also a system that many believed could get the Suns into the NBA finals. D'Antoni won 61 games with the Suns in 2006-2007, and it was only because of Tim Donaghy's referee calls that they didn't go to the finals. Donaghy subsequently pleaded guilty to making erroneous calls to help gamblers. He went to prison and the Suns went home.

It was D'Antoni's playing days in Italy that framed his basketball philosophy. He learned to shoot quickly and often. He liked playing two games a week. He loved drinking red wine, and he became used to limited practices. He loved the rabid fans. D'Antoni used these experiences to mold his unique system.

COACHING IN ITALY IN D'ANTONI'S FOUNDATION

When he was through playing in Italy, D'Antoni evolved into a legendary coach. He spent four seasons as Olimpia's coach. From 1990 to 1994, he coached Olimpia and the club won the European Championship in 1992 and the Korac Club the following year. He moved to the Benetton Treviso club from 1994 to 1997, and this team won the Cup of Europe and the Coppa Italia in 1995.

The Olimpia experience was an important one. The team, located in Milan, was so rabid about identifying with the NBA that the ownership imported Scarepette Rosse shoes (Little Red Shoes) from the United States and the list of import players from America included Bill Bradley, Antoine Carr, Earl Cureton, Joe Barry Carroll, Bob McAdoo, Albert King, Marc Iavaroni and Darryl Dawkins. It was an NBA type team in one of Italy's best towns for food and drink. In the 1980s, Olimpia won five Italian championships. Not surprisingly, D'Antoni was a big part of that run.

The following season they won the national title. He was twice voted Italy's coach of the year. D'Antoni's star attracted NBA interest. He went to the NBA but continued to coach in Italy in the offseason. The road back to the NBA was a long and strange one. It was his scouting and jobs as an assistant coach that defined his system.

ON TO THE NBA

While he played and coached in Italy, D'Antoni found that NBA teams were interested in his knowledge and passion for the game. In 1997-1998, the Denver Nuggets hired D'Antoni as their director of player personnel. He was also a part time broadcaster for TNT. When the Nuggets hired D'Antoni as their head coach for the 1998-1999 season, he got off to a poor start and he was fired in the strike-shortened season.

D'Antoni left to became a scout for the San Antonio Spurs in the 1999-2000 season, and he was an assistant coach for the Portland Trailer Blazers in 2000-2001. By this time D'Antoni was well regarded in the NBA in all aspects of the game.

In 2002, D'Antoni was hired as a Suns assistant coach. The hiring was an interesting one. D'Antoni's wife is Italian, the general manager, Bryan Colangelo, is also married to a beautiful and vivacious Italian woman. They knew each other and were good friends. This isn't why D'Antoni was hired. He was brought in for his running and gunning style.

D'ANTONI AND THE SUNS: A GREAT RUN

When Mike D'Antoni became the Suns head coach, he had a lot in common with his All Star point guard, Steve Nash. They were both gym rats. They were students of the subtle points of the NBA game. They didn't worry about defense. When they were brought together for the first time in 2004-2005 the Suns averaged 110.4 points a game. The previous year they had averaged 94.2. The Suns were off on one of the most prolific scoring and victory runs in NBA history. It was due as much to D'Antoni's system, as it was to the players.

In his five seasons as the Suns' head coach, D'Antoni won the Pacific Division three times, and he was second the year that he left for the New York Knicks. In two of those years, D'Antoni lost in the conference finals. When the Suns lost in 2006-2007, in the conference semifinals, it was due to referee Tim Donaghy's phantom calls. He eventually went to jail. The other part of that season was when San Antonio's Robert Horry almost decapitated Steve Nash and the Suns players who came to his rescue from the bench were suspended. Good old David Stern. He never met a rule he didn't like. He never met an exception in his life."

Peter: "Howard, how do you really feel about David Stern?"

WHAT IMPACT DID STEVE NASH HAVE ON D'ANTONI?

When Steve Nash won back-to-back NBA Most Valuable Player Awards there was the usual grumbling from the sports writers, the fans and the owners. The question that no one asked is: "What impact did Steve Nash have upon Coach Mike D'Antoni's system? The answer is a simple one. Nash legitimized a playing structure that was suspect among coaches.

When D'Antoni signed a lucrative contract with the New York Knicks, he had little, if any, success. The Knicks failed to crack the 100 plus point mark. They made the playoffs in the 2012 season after finishing 18-6 under interim Coach Mike Woodson. This was the time when D'Antoni quit. Jeremy Lin had a run that helped the Knicks, but when he went down with a knee injury, D'Antoni's system fell apart.

Not only did D'Antoni quit, he cast doubts on the team's ability to blend Carmelo Anthony and Amare Stoudemire into a winning tandem. D'Antoni made an important point, that is super stars need to complement each other. He also pointed out that an All Star point guard is needed.

What is obvious is that the D'Antoni methods worked only with an All-Star point guard and a power forward that can work the pick and roll. Consistency and efficiency are the trademarks of Nash's style, and this helped D'Antoni sell his system to his players. In New York, D'Antoni's point guards Stephon Marbury, Raymond Felton, Toney Douglas and Chris Duhon were underachievers. He resigned as the Knicks' coach due to Carmelo Anthony's rebellion, as well as the point guard fiasco.

Steve Nash believed that D'Antoni leaving the Knicks was a mistake. "It was a shame," Nash told Marc Berman of the **New York Post**. "He never got a great opportunity. The team was constantly in flux. Amare and Carmelo didn't play much together." The point is that Nash was the engine that ran the D'Antoni system and without his MVP point guard he was doomed in New York.

For a time, Jeremy Lin ran the D'Antoni system but Carmelo Anthony constantly disrupted it. Amare Stoudemire's knees made him ineffective and everyone else stood around waiting for Anthony or Stoudemire to shoot the ball. Lin was the only person on board with the D'Antoni system. Then D'Antoni quit. He wasn't fired. He has integrity.

Mike D'Antoni is a great coach. He coaches at times by the seat of his pants, but his teams are invariably exciting. D'Antoni is a player's coach. The Suns had two sets of game tapes. One for the coaches showing player mistakes and a gentle one for the players that didn't intrude upon their egos. When D'Antoni played video games in the Suns locker room an hour before tip off the players were relaxed. He is the consummate player's coach.

PAUL SHIRLEY SUMS UP MIKE D'ANTONI

In the later days of the 2005 season Paul Shirley received some notoriety as a blogger. He was twenty-seven, 6-11 and played center or power-forward. He was also slow, white and couldn't shoot. He could write up a storm. His book **Can I Keep My Jersey? 11 Teams, 5 Countries and 4 Years in My Life As A Basketball Vagabond**, tells us the cruel fate of professional basketball. When he played for the Suns or more appropriately watched from the bench, Shirley has some interesting observations.

He saw fire and brimstone in Coach D'Antoni's character. "I know my role with the Phoenix Suns. I'm the white guy at the end of the bench," Shirley wrote. (p. 319) The journal that Shirley kept while playing with the Suns in 2004-2005 has very nice things to say about management and the players. He played for thirteen different professional teams, not eleven as his book suggests. He is the most literate basketball player. Sorry Charles Barkley you are number two.

Shirley's time with the Suns provided an interesting book. He stated that the transition to Robert Sarver's ownership altered the Suns culture. He was negative or critical of Sarver, Shirley simply points out that everything changes.

4. THE COACHING-PLAYER BRAINY SUN
MARC IAVARONI: THE BRAIN WHO IS THE SCHOLAR AS
PLAYER AND COACH

Marc Iavaroni appears to be the most unlikely player-coach to impact the Suns. But he has had an enormous influence on how they play the game. You may wonder what Iavaroni is doing as one of the early top ten Suns. The reasons are many for his inclusion. The primary one is his knowledge of basketball, as well as game planning. He is a private person and it is difficult to penetrate his basketball mind. Since his greatest asset is as a basketball brain that is where he impacted the Suns.

In Iavaroni's career there were twists and turns that he navigated to play in the NBA. He had to reinvent his game in Italian pro basketball, and he had to learn the ropes of the fiercely competitive and often unfair NBA. He learned along the way the road to coaching. His career represents all aspects of drive, determination and talent that is required to play professional basketball. It wasn't easy, and his road to the Phoenix Suns was a long and torturous one.

He was born in Jamaica New York in 1956, and he was a star at Plainview New York's John F. Kennedy High School. He played with Seth Greenberg, a head coach at Virginia Tech. Then it was off to college in Virginia.

THE LONG ROAD TO THE SUNS

He attended the University of Virginia from 1974 to 1978. At Virginia, he averaged in double figures all four years with a ten to twelve point scoring spread, and his rebounds were just over six a game. He ranks in the top ten in scoring and rebounding among all players at the University of Virginia. At 6-8 and two hundred ten pounds, he was a consistent performer. Iavaroni was the fifty-fifth pick in the 1978 draft by the New York Knicks.

But he didn't survive the cut in his rookie year, and it was off to Italy to work on his game. The hard work and determination paid dividends, as he became an all around player. Iavaroni also displayed an innate knowledge of the game.

It took Iavaroni four years to make it back to the NBA. He went on to a fourteen-year professional playing career, and it was one where he moved around constantly. He learned a number of different systems. When he didn't start his pro career in the NBA, it was a plus as his basketball IQ increased. For whatever reason, NBA teams believed that

Iavaroni was not ready for prime time NBA basketball. He thought otherwise, and he proved it.

What is impressive about Iavaroni is his work ethic. He went overseas, and he developed his game so well that he became an NBA starter. Former coaches and players often describe Iavaroni as "the brain," and this explains a great deal about his approach to the game. He plans meticulously.

When he left the U. S. to play for Basket Brescia in Italia from 1978 to 1980, he was in the midst of an offensive explosion. He also learned a great deal about the European offensive while his defensive skills continued to develop. He played for Fulgor Libertas Forli also an Italian team. It was in Italy that, as Iavaroni refined his game, he attracted NBA scouts. He developed into a strong front line player with a smooth shot. NBA scouts were impressed with his improvement, and he was offered a contract.

Iavaroni also played for Fulgor Libertas Forli from 1979 to 1982 and later in his career for Olimpia Milano in 1988-1989 and Unicaja Malaga in Spain. But before he came back to Italy and Spain, Iavaroni had a solid NBA career. He was getting ready for coaching but he didn't know it. It was on to the NBA in 1982, and he made the most of his opportunity. The irony of Iavaroni's career is that he had some common traits with Mike D'Antoni.

ON TO THE NBA

In 1982, Iavaroni was twenty-six when he began a two-year stint with the Philadelphia 76ers. Mike D'Antoni, who was a scoring legend in Italy, had little concern with defense. When Iavaroni played in Italy, he was a defensive legend. D'Antoni used offensive coaching schemes to return to the NBA. Iavaroni used defense and a high basketball IQ to return to the NBA. They coached together in Phoenix. Go figure!

In 1983, when Iavaroni was a starter for the Philadelphia 76ers NBA championship team, he was a perfect fit in a roster that included Julius Erving, Moses Malone, Andrew Toney and Maurice Cheeks. Iavaroni is often described as a role player with the 76ers, but he was a tough, blue-collar guy who gave one hundred percent each night.

The 1983 Philadelphia 76ers were a team ready for a championship, as they acquired Moses Malone to go along with Julius Erving to create Showtime before the Los Angeles Lakers. When Malone came to the 76ers he remarked: "It Doc's show and I'm here to make it better." Malone was the key offensive piece, and Iavaroni was the defensive stopper. It was a special team with a great deal of camaraderie. Iavaroni remembered: "To be around these type of guys was special for me. They didn't make me feel like an outsider." When the 76ers reached the playoffs they only lost one game on their way to the NBA title. It was magic the first year in the league for Iavaroni.

As the eleventh best scorer on the 76ers, Iavaroni was in the starting lineup for defense, and he did the little things for a championship team. He was one of the best passing big men in the game, and he had a sixth sense on the court when it came to rebounds.

He moved on to the San Antonio Spurs from 1984 to 1986 and then he finished his NBA career with the Utah Jazz from 1986-1989. His teams qualified for the playoffs every year that he played in the NBA.

During his NBA career Iavaroni scored 2328 points and he brought down 1725 rebounds. He averaged five points and more than three rebounds a game.

He returned to Italy for part of 1989 and played with Olimpia Milano and then in 1991-1992 he signed with Caja de Rona Malaga in Spain. He returned to America and from 1991 to 1992, he played with the Sioux Falls Skyforce in the CBA.

THE ROAD TO A COACHING CAREER

Now it was time to get a real day job. He returned to his alma mater, the University of Virginia, as a graduate assistant. Then he moved on as an assistant coach at Bowling Green State University from 1992 to 1994.

In 1997, Iavaroni landed a job in the NBA with the Cleveland Cavaliers. He worked with the forwards, and in 1999 he moved into the Miami Heats front office, as the director of player development. With this experience, Mike D'Antoni brought Iavaroni to Phoenix in 2002. After five years of drawing up x's and o's for the Suns' big men, he was named the Memphis Grizzlies head coach on May 30, 2007.

The journey to an NBA head-coaching job was a tough one. It got worse when Iavaroni joined the Grizzlies. He not only inherited a team with no stars, but Memphis was twenty-ninth in the league in attendance. Barbecue and music still ruled Memphis.

After an 11-30 start during the 2008-2009 Iavaroni was fired. What went wrong? Memphis was a coach's nightmare. Rudy Gay, only twenty-one, shot all the time and averaged twenty points a game. Pau Gasol was soft on defense but great on the offensive end. He hit for eighteen points a game, while a creaky Mike Miller scored sixteen a game and a skinny, but ferocious, Hakim Warrick was the fourth leading scorer at eleven a game. Pau Gasol was traded to the Los Angeles Lakers and in the 2008-2009 season, a young gunner, who wasn't a team player, O. J. Mayo, didn't help in the offensive mix. On defense the Grizzles were among the three worst teams in the NBA. In his first season Iavaroni was 22 and 60 and not surprisingly, he was on the coaching hot seat.

When he left Memphis after one and a half tough seasons, he joined the Toronto Raptor's coaching staff. Then it was on to the Los Angeles Clippers working under Vinny Del Negro.

Did Iavaroni have any success with the Grizzlies? The answer is yes. He helped to develop Rudy Gay as a premier scorer, and his first year record of 25 and 57 was good enough considering the talent. The Grizzlies were 29th in the NBA in attendance and it was tough for the team in a city where music and barbecue were more popular than basketball.

WHAT DID IAVARONI TEACH?

As a coach Iavaroni had a mission. It was to educate the big men how to play the game. While with the Suns, he used his experiences from his playing days to bring toughness to the team. It is how he approaches the game that makes Iavaroni a great coach. The knuckleheads who play in the NBA are not easy to coach.

During the 2005-2006 Suns season, a **Sports Illustrated** writer, Jack McCallum, following the team around for a season, and he wrote an analytical and highly readable book about the Suns' season. His comments on Iavaroni were positive ones. The attention to detail, the sophisticated game plans, the ability to work with the big men and in-depth knowledge of the game made Iavaroni a candidate for the Portland Trail Blazers head-coaching job. He didn't get it; that was in 2005-2006 and Iavaroni continued to prepare sophisticated game plans for the Suns.

Iavaroni worked well with head coach D'Antoni. As the lead assistant, Iavaroni had more input than other coaches. Yet, he was very careful in his dealings with D'Antoni. Iavaroni would spend hours, sometimes days, watching film. D'Antoni spent minutes in the film room.

The main contribution from Iavaroni was when he held the "bigs" meeting before each game. In the meetings, he suggests to the centers and the power forwards what they need to do to help the team. He uses the locker room with its big board, and then he moves to a smaller area in the locker room where paper slogans are taped to the wall. The precision in Iavaroni's preparation is legendary. Amare Stoudemire had his best season working with Iavaroni. Others like Shawn Marion and Boris Diaw refined their inside game due to his coaching.

Then Iavaroni gives the players some questions to answer. This didn't go over well with everyone. Since grade school big men have been coddled, handled with kid gloves and seldom criticized. They don't like pop quizzes. They are all near seven feet, and there is no need to force them to answer questions. Many of the bigs don't like to play the game. Iavaroni's system is one predicated upon knowledge as well as ability. This didn't sit well with some players.

The problem that Iavaroni faced with the Suns was that the starting five was only on the floor for a few minutes. D'Antoni is much like the mad scientist former Dallas coach Don Nelson. It was Nelson who revolutionized the game by having 7-7- center Manute Bol shoot three point shots. Nelson, at times, would have four guards on the floor. He loved to create strange matchups. D'Antoni was a different version of Nelson. The problem for Iavaroni, as an assistant coach, is that D'Antoni didn't watch film. As Iavaroni held in-depth strategy sessions, he had a firm mind set on what he wanted. Still Iavaroni worked well with D'Antoni and they remain good friends. Those close to the Suns told me that Iavaroni could have helped the Suns defensive woes if D'Antoni had listened in more depth.

As the Suns defensive guru, Iavaroni made a number of contributions. He was one of the few people to get Amare' Stoudemire and Boris Diaw to play defense. He also came up with defensive plans to stop the Lakers' Kobe Bryant. Iavaroni's biggest contribution was the chalkboard. He had a board filled with lines, slogans, reminders, strategy and statistics. One hour before tip off Iavaroni was still writing on the board. It is low post defense that Iavaroni is superb at diagramming, and this was shown in Amare Stoudemire's increasingly dominant low post presence.

The big men coaching sessions that brought in the centers and power forwards, were so well organized that the players had a distinct advantage. Shawn Marion often came to the bigs meetings to learn what he could, and when he was tired of Iavaroni's in depth blackboard and pristine analysis, he met with the wing players. Marion remarked that the wing players dealt with minor chaos. The bigs, said Marion, knew where to position themselves in the game. The rest of the team did as they pleased.

Marc Iavaroni as a player and coach epitomizes a Phoenix Sun. He is a strong competitor. He is bright and a student of the game. He is a typical family man. He also loves NBA basketball. As an assistant coach with Vinny Del Negro for the Los Angeles Clippers, Iavaroni continues to work his coaching magic. In 2012-2013, former Sun Grant Hill joined the Clippers and along with Iavaroni and Del Negro they will mentor a team that is on the rise.

Perhaps the best testimony of Iavaroni's teaching ability is the emergence of Los Angeles Clipper DeAndre Jordan. The twenty four year old center in his fifth season with the Clippers worked hard in the off-season with Iavaroni, and his post game and free throws make him a starter. In working with Jordan, Iavaroni displayed the same attention to detail that made him an NBA starter. He is even better as a coach.

Mark Iavaroni is one of the best examples of sacrifice, intelligence and love for the game of basketball. It has served him well, and he has a lot left in the coaching gas tank. He has also worked for some of the best coaches in the game, and he has integrated their philosophical bent and game planning into his coaching. It was in 2006, when Iavaroni assisted with the U. S. Men's Senior National Team, that he worked with legendary Hall of Fame Coach Pete Newell. For years Newell and Iavaroni were in touch about the NBA game. Iavaroni credits much of his knowledge to Newell's influence, and he also learned a great deal from Mike Fratello. Iavaroni remains the consummate student of the game. In time, he will once again become an NBA head coach.

5. THE FIRST LEGEND
THE HAWK: CONNIE HAWKINS GRACE IN THE AIR

Connie Hawkins is one of the greatest players in the NBA. He was Dr. J before Julius Irving was a household name. You are wondering have I lost my mind? Hawkins averaged just over sixteen points a game in a brief seven year NBA career. How is it possible that he is one of the best players in the NBA? My argument is how he played the game, and how he was unjustly denied a fifteen-year career. The story is an intriguing one.

As he grew up, Hawkins was a star on New York's Rucker Park outdoor courts. It was on this legendary court in Brooklyn's Bedford-Stuyvesant section where he learned to handle the ball, float and dunk. He always played against the older kids and his game was one of the

44

best ever seen. When NBA stars showed up to showcase their talents, Hawkins invariably upstaged them. Yet, he would not play high school ball very much until his junior year, he would not star in college, and he would be twenty-seven before he entered the NBA.

The eight years that Connie Hawkins spent attempting to enter the NBA and escape the erroneous charge of gambling influences were spent honing his showmanship in the minor basketball leagues and with the Harlem Globetrotters. By the time that he entered the NBA, a number of knee operations made the Hawk a shadow of his former self. The irony is that even as a shadow of his former self, he was an All Star, and a Hall of Famer.

HAWKINS' EARLY YEARS AND THE ERRONEOUS CHARGES

While attending Boys High School in the Bedford-Stuyvesant section of Brooklyn, Hawkins walked down to Rucker Park, and at this legendary outdoor court he played with some of the best basketball wizards. In high school, Hawkins led his team to the PSAL title scoring sixty points in one game, and he accepted a scholarship to the University of Iowa.

In high school, Hawkins averaged 25.5 points a game, and he passed up many shots to let his teammates score. He was the ultimate team player, and he seldom showboated. He was a solid player on both ends of the court.

In 1961, while a freshman at the University of Iowa, Hawkins was rumored to be involved in a gambling scandal. The rumors were not true. There wasn't an ounce of evidence linking Hawkins to wrongdoing. The point shaving allegations were in New York and Hawkins wasn't charged. His name came up in the investigation. He was a good kid who cooperated with authorities. The NCAA ruined his college career because no one would give him a scholarship. NBA Commissioner J. Walter Kennedy ruled that he would not approve a contract for Hawkins. His persecution for a crime that he didn't commit is one of the greatest injustices in sports history.

J. Walter Kennedy didn't treat Hawkins equitably. He represented the owners; he also made it clear that Hawkins was guilty of misdeeds. It didn't matter that he was cleared in the courts. It was Kennedy's unsavory attitude that prompted sports writers and attorneys to take a closer look at Hawkins case. When they did, there was universal agreement that he had been railroaded. His crime was being a good, but naïve, young kid. The wheels were in motion for a court case.

HAWKINS' ROAD TO THE NBA

The road to the NBA began when David Wolf, a noted sports writer, had an investigative article published in the May 1969 issue of **Life**. The article pointed out that New York Police Detectives pressured Hawkins into making statements that were not true. He was told that he was a patriotic citizen helping to convict gamblers. Then came the coaches and college boosters. Hawkins was so good that Red Auerbach, the Boston Celtics coach, allegedly offered to pay him some money under the table if he attended nearby Providence College. Other colleges said that they would send his family $150 a month, as well as all college expenses. Hawkins knew all this was wrong, and he ignored the boosters who offered him money.

Hawkins is a man of integrity. He knew he was innocent, but he had to make a living. He signed with the Pittsburgh Rens of the American Basketball Association, and he was the league's Most Valuable Player. The Rens were owned by a Pittsburgh businessman, Lenny Littman, who was a nightclub mogul and a well known entertainment impresario When Littman's nightclub, the Copa, closed in 1959, he looked for a professional basketball franchise. He started the Pittsburgh Rens of the American Basketball League, and it was Connie Hawkins signing that kept the team financially solvent. The league folded and then Hawkins traveled for three years with the Harlem Globetrotters.

While touring with the Harlem Globetrotters, Hawkins took exception to their "Uncle Tom" style of basketball. He read and educated himself on history and politics, and by the time that he left the Globetrotters he had a sense of America's racial strife. There has been a great deal written about Hawkins that is inaccurate and the tales of his lack of education are hurtful and erroneous. He remains an intelligent and thoughtful person.

While playing with the Pittsburgh Rens, there were some hilarious moments. One night in the huddle as the coach was planning strategy; Art Heyman asked the Rens coach "Do you think this game will impact the Vietnam War?" Tom Washington, the Rens' power forward, did W. C. Fields imitations while guarding his man. One night only five players showed up. The rest went to a drunken party and thought they had missed the team bus. They rented a car and went to the site of the Rens next game. They found out that they were two days early and partied into the next two nights. Hawkins had fun with his fellow players, and when the Rens came to town the arena was filled. Everyone wanted to see the floating, dunking, ball wizardry of the Hawk. Long before Julius Irving thrilled Philadelphia fans with his antics, Connie Hawkins soared in the minor leagues.

While in Pittsburgh local attorneys, David and Roslyn Littman, became big fans. It didn't take them long to realize the injustice perpetrated upon Hawkins. They lined up a powerhouse group of attorneys who filed a six million dollar lawsuit against the NBA.

The NBA's attorneys, George Gallantz and David Stern, the later who became the NBA Commissioner, treated Hawkins with disdain and a lack of respect. Much to his credit, Hawkins was polite and deferential. He knew he was innocent. He knew that he had a winning case.

When Gallantz couldn't shake Hawkins' story, he became personally insulting. Then the Judge and Hawkins's attorney, David Littman, criticized him for his overbearing and gratuitous manner. Gallantz treated Hawkins like a criminal. Much to his credit, David Stern sat silently. It looked as though he believed Hawkins' story. With Stern barely uttering a word, the verdict was a clear one. Hawkins had been unfairly treated and convicted without evidence by the NBA.

When the lawsuit concluded it included a $1.295 million dollar settlement. The settlement also provided for a $600,000 annuity beginning at age 45 and $250,000 in cash. When the Seattle Super Sonics and the Phoenix Suns flipped a coin, the Suns won and the Hawk came to the Valley of the Sun. He became the second face of the franchise when the team needed a box office draw.

HAWKINS IN THE NBA

When Hawkins entered the NBA there was no question of his talent. He also had a lot to prove and on the nights he was on no one could touch him on the court. Some of the books written on Hawkins suggest that sometimes he took a night off or he was not up to par. This is a low blow, as he played more than forty minutes a game in his early years with the Suns, and there were games against the Los Angeles Lakers that he won single handedly. From day one, Connie Hawkins was a warrior who played his heart out. One can only imagine how bitter and hateful he could have been. He wasn't. He entered the NBA to prove that he was a legend. The Hawk left the NBA as a Hall of Famer.

When the Phoenix Suns quickly stepped in and signed Hawkins, Jerry Colangelo realized that he had a special player. Colangelo also deduced that Hawkins was a person of integrity and strong character. To his credit, as Hawkins persevered, he became an All Star and an

NBA legend. He seldom complained about his brutal treatment, but he had his personal moments. Jerry Colangelo was unhappy with him at times for missing practice. But Hawkins played more than forty minutes a game in the early years, and he needed a few days off.

His road to the Suns had been a long and circuitous one. The Hawk had his day in the NBA beginning at age 27, and there were those who said he was beyond his prime. They must have never seen him play. For his entire NBA career, Hawkins soared and scored, and he delighted the fans. I have never seen a more graceful and superb talent.

The Connie Hawkins story is about more than basketball. It highlights problems with race, unfair treatment of the players prior to the NBA players association, it also suggests the pervasive harm that sports can do in our society with owners, coaches and agents looking for a piece of the financial pie.

CONNIE HAWKINS SAVES THE EARLY FRANCHISE

What did Connie Hawkins mean to the Phoenix Suns? In 1970, the Suns created havoc for the Los Angeles Lakers led by Wilt Chamberlain, Jerry West and Elgin Baylor in the playoffs. In game two of the series Hawkins scored 34 points, pulled down 20 rebounds and had seven assists. The March 29, 1970 game was an important milestone as the Suns beat the Lakers 114-101. The next home game was the first sellout in Phoenix Suns history. Paul Silas had 25 points, and he dominated the boards. The Suns defense led by Gail Goodrich and Dick Van Arsdale held future Hall of Famers Elgin Baylor and Wilt Chamberlain to 14 and 19 points respectively. "That was the greatest individual performance I've ever seen," Jerry Colangelo remarked of Hawkins night. The Suns took a 3-1 lead in that series before losing to the Lakers in seven games. With more than 6300 points in his time with the Suns, Colangelo remarked that Hawkins 34 points and 20 rebounds against the Lakers displayed his whole package as a player. He wasn't one to toot his own horn, but that night Hawkins ruled the Lakers.

Connie Hawkins gave his all for more than forty minutes a game. In the 2011-2012 season, when the Suns honored one of its former coaches, John MacLeod, Hawkins sat with a litany of famous Suns on the floor. This was Robert Sarver's way of saying thanks for all the things that the Hawk did for the franchise.

As one long time fan suggested: "Connie Hawkins saved the franchise at a time that it needed a fresh face and a new level of excitement." The Hawk certainly brought that to the floor every night, and the number of sellouts suggests his box office luster. As the Hawk soared and swooped the cash box for the Suns franchise jingled.

The Suns retired Hawkins' number 42 jersey in 1976, and he was the first Suns player elected in 1992 to the Basketball Hall of Fame. In 1994, a Harlem Globetrotters "Legends' ring was presented to Hawkins during a game time ceremony.

CONNIE HAWKINS SUNS STATISTICS

1969-1970: MINUTES PG: 40.0-POINTS PG: 24.6-REBOUNDS PG: 10.4-AST: 4.8

1970-1971: MINUTES PG: 37.5-POINTS PG: 20.9-REBOUNDS PG: 9.1-AST: 4.5

1971-1972: MINUTES PG: 36.8-POINTS PG: 21-REBOUNDS PG: 8.3-AST: 3.9

1972-1973: MINUTES PH: 36.9-POINTS PG: 16.1-REBOUNDS PG: 8.5-AST: 4.1

There are so many highlights in Hawkins career it is difficult to pick one. My favorite came when as a freshman at the University of Iowa, when he outplayed and embarrassed Don Nelson who went on to play in the NBA and become one of its legendary coaches. Connie Hawkins has a huge billboard of his soaring shot outside the Suns' U. S. Airways Arena. It is a constant reminder of his greatness.

Connie Hawkins sported marvelous sideburns, and he was a whirling dervish as he attacked the basket. When his number 42 was retired, Hawkins had a sense of his greatness. Anyone who saw him play marveled at his hang time, his spectacular shots and his ability to make the game fun.

6. THE FIRST FACES OF THE FRANCHISE
THE VAN ARSDALE BROTHERS: THE ORIGINAL SUN DICK AND HIS BROTHER TOM

If there are two players who are Founding Fathers of the Phoenix Suns, it is the Van Arsdale brothers. Ironically, one of the brothers, Tom, only played for one year in the Valley of the Sun. Dick played in the early years of the franchise. They are linked to the franchise not because they are identical twins but due to their play, the strong character traits and their personal and playing charisma that they brought to the court and the community every night. The number of young ladies attending Suns' fames increased, and the Van Arsdale's good looks and their love for the Phoenix area made them ambassadors for the lifestyle in the Valley of the Sun. They were also married and great family men. There was another great thing about the Van Arsdale's. They could also play basketball with a creative flair, and their personalities were calm and understated. They were humble and unassuming. They became the marquee personalities and the Hollywood style twins of the NBA. They were the perfect players to sell the league.

In Indiana, Dick and Tom Van Arsdale are basketball Gods. They define the Hoosier state and its frenetic basketball culture.

THE VAN ARSDALE'S INDIANA HALL OF FAME YEARS

At Indianapolis' Emmerich Manuel High School, Dick and Tom led the school to the Indian Final Four, and Dick scored twenty-six points in a loss to Kokomo. Dick was All State and his grades were high enough to gain academic recognition. He shared the Indiana Mr. Basketball and Trester Award with his brother Tom who had equal recognition. They were among the most legendary high school basketball players.

The twins moved on to Indiana University, where they started for three years. The only reason that they didn't start during their four years at Indiana University is that freshmen had to play for the freshman team. Dick was the Hoosier's MVP, an All Big Ten selection, an All American and most importantly an Academic All American. Dick and Tom were also members of the U. S. Team that won a gold medal in the 1965 World University Games. That team included future NBA stars Bill Bradley, Billy Cunningham and Joe Ellis. Dick averaged just over six points a game in the eight tournament wins for the U. S. and Tom averaged just over five points a game. They were ready for the NBA.

In 1966, when the Van Arsdale's graduated from Indiana University, they were All Americans with a solid game. They were perfect for the NBA. At 6-5, Dick Van Arsdale was a great shooter who played for twelve years in the NBA. He was also among the best free throw shooters in the league, and he played solid defense. There was no part of his game that wasn't polished.

The New York Knicks drafted Dick in the second round in 1965. His play during his rookie year set the tone for the remainder of his career. He was a fierce competitor with a strong work ethic. Dick said: "I will do anything to beat you within the rules." He respected the game. It led to Van Arsdale being selected for the All Rookie team in 1966. After playing for three seasons with the Knicks, the Suns selected Van Arsdale in the expansion or supplemental draft. Each team had to put up three players as unprotected, and the Suns had the choice of any three from each NBA roster. Dick Van Arsdale is sometimes called the original Sun, because of his play and popularity, as well as the fact that he was the first player selected in the supplemental draft.

In Phoenix, Dick Van Arsdale was a three time All Star, and he was the first Steve Nash. That is he was the most reliable free throw shooter in the NBA as well as a scoring machine. After his playing days, Van Arsdale was for a time the Suns' general manager, and he served as the Senior Vice President of Player Personnel. In 1987, he was briefly the head coach when John MacLeod left for another position. The Suns retired his number 5. He continues to live in the Phoenix suburb of Paradise Valley.

There are a number of things that made Dick Van Arsdale a great player. He was versatile. He could play small forward or shooting guard. He had more than 2400 points with the Suns, but he also pulled down more than 2300 rebounds. He was the consummate team player. He loved to pass the ball and for a time when he played small forward, he had almost as many assists as the point guard.

TOM VAN ARSDALE

Tom Van Arsdale joined the Suns for one year, after he played for eleven years with five other teams. Like his brother, he was a three time All Star, and he was named to the NBA All Rookie team in 1966. He averaged 15.3 points a game with 4.2 rebounds and 2.2 assists. He was a fine all around player. Although they played together in the NBA for only one year, 1976-1977, the Van Arsdale's were the brand name in the Valley of the Sun.

When he graduated from Indiana University, the Detroit Pistons in the second round of the NBA draft selected Tom. He played for twelve seasons with the Pistons, the Cincinnati Royals, the Kansas City-Omaha Kings, the Philadelphia 76ers and the Atlanta Hawks. He was one of the NBA's most consistent free throw shooters. He also holds the NBA record for the most games played without a playoff appearance.

By playing for six teams over twelve seasons, it was difficult for Tom to develop an identity. He was also a top defensive player and this is why he was traded so often. He still was a scorer.

THE VAN ARSDALE'S IN RETIREMENT

Both Van Arsdale brothers are busy in retirement. They have Phoenix business interests, and they are strong Suns supporters. They only have good things to say about the Suns.

After suffering a stroke, Dick began painting and drawing, and he has turned into a much sought after artist. Dick's specialty is pen and ink drawings. There is a strong market for his product. He donates the money to local charities.

Tom Van Arsdale is a real estate investor and Phoenix businessman. He leads a quiet life with a commitment to the community. His brother's emergence as an artist is an important part of his recovery from the stroke. They remain respected icons of the Phoenix Suns. They are the original Suns. There is no better description.

In the Valley of the Sun, the Van Arsdale's stand as a monument to the work ethic, as well as the integrity, of the early franchise. It was just as Jerry Colangelo planned it. Find someone who exhibits the virtues of the Suns. He found two look a likes, and the Suns were in business. They defined the early success of the Suns, and they paved the way for Connie Hawkins, Paul Westphal and Charles Barkley.

7. PAUL WESTPHAL: NO ONE SHOT BETTER AND HE ALSO COACHED WELL

Paul Westphal is the most intriguing Phoenix Sun. He came to the franchise from Boston in May 1975, and he was an instant scorer. In his initial Sun's season, he averaged 20.5 points, and he had 5.4 assists. He was one of the key cogs in the Sun's reaching the 1976 NBA finals. In his six seasons with the Suns, he was a four time All Star from 1977 to 1980. He was one of the more popular players due to his deadly three point shot.

Where did Westphal come from? The answer is Torrance, California. He grew up amidst the Beach Boys legend, and he ate a few burgers and drank a few milk shakes at the Foster's Freeze where the Beach Boys hung out a decade earlier. He starred at USC. Westphal had overtures to play for the legendary Coach John Wooden at UCLA. But he didn't like the political activism on the Westwood campus, so he took his game down Highway 110 to USC. Hippies, beatniks and liberals were at the UCLA campus and Westphal wanted no part of it. He was a traditionalist, and the elitist USC atmosphere appealed to his sense of calm. As he listened to the music of the Kingston Trio, Bob Dylan and his friend John Stewart, Westphal was a solitary figure on the USC campus. He was a normal kid whose idea of fun was to buy and eat five hot dogs at Der Weinerschnitzel.

At USC, Westphal was one of five players who made it to the NBA. The 1970-1971 Trojans ended the season 24-2 and they were ranked number one in the nation for a portion of the year. The problem for USC is that they played UCLA twice and lost both times. The Trojans finished the season ranked fifth in the nation. They weren't selected for the NCAA tournament, because the Trojans didn't win the Pac 10. UCLA was the Los Angeles team that went to the NCAA tournament.

While he waited for the 1971 draft, he was unassuming, and this personality trait continued for the remainder of his playing and coaching career. Westphal's transition to the NBA was an interesting one. He would become an even bigger star than he was in college.

WESTPHAL MAKES HIS MARK IN THE NBA

In the 1972 draft, he was the tenth pick. His selection by the Boston Celtics led to a championship ring in 1974. He became known as a big time playmaker and shooter. While he was a role player on the Celtics 1974 championship team, his shot was one that caught NBA scout's attention.

The Suns traded for Westphal, and he came into the 1975-1976 season as the final piece in the drive for the NBA finals. The Suns shocked defending NBA champs, the Golden State Warriors, and employing Westphal's jump shot they went all the way to the NBA finals losing to the Boston Celtics.

In 1977-1978, Westphal averaged 25.6. points a game and the following season 24.0 points a game. In that year, he was seventh in league scoring. In four of Westphal's five seasons with the Suns, they had a winning record.

There was another side to Westphal. He had firm opinions about the game. When the Suns training staff wanted him to lift more weights to make him stronger for the three point shot, he called the trainer "a moron." Westphal had frequent clashes with Coach John MacLeod who Westphal believed had too many lengthy practices. Westphal wanted to save his energy for the game. He openly criticized MacLeod for his authoritarian attitudes.

Coach John MacLeod remarked: "It was Paul Westphal's philosophy that he could take his man out of the game by his scoring ability. But how many times do you have to give Paul Westphal the ball while the other four guys stood there watching him?" After MacLeod's comment, Westphal's days with the Suns were numbered.

Paul Westphal: "I didn't think I was disruptive. The only thing I bucked him on was weight training. John felt that was poor leadership on my part."

In 1979-1980, Westphal was traded to the Seattle Super Sonics for Dennis Johnson. It was one of Colangelo's toughest decisions, and he agonized about it for years. After one season, he went to the New York Knicks, and in 1983 he returned to the Phoenix Suns. His last season was one filled with injuries, and he played in only fifty-nine of the eighty-two games.

With an average of fifteen points a game for his NBA career and 4.4 assists a game, he was an all around player. He was also more complicated and driven than his public image.

PAUL WESTPHAL'S MISUNDERSTOOD PERSONALITY

There is no Suns player who is more misunderstood than Paul Westphal. As a player, Coach John MacLeod called him "anti-establishment." The reality is that Westphal is a traditionalist with his own thoughts and opinions. The sports culture is often a non-thinking one. The coach is right no matter what he decides. Westphal was the player who bucked the system.

When he coached at Grand Canyon College, his team had two free throws to win the NAIA, Division Two title. As Rodney Johns hit the shots to make Grand Canyon the champs, Westphal sat on the bench laughing. He told reporters he did so because he believed that he had no control over the outcome of the game. Jerry Colangelo sat in the stands, and he realized that Westphal was a successful coach. It is Westphal's misunderstood personality, which has caused people to misjudge him.

In many respects, Paul Westphal is a contradiction. He is a registered independent, as he doesn't support either Republican or Democratic politics. Yet, Rush Limbaugh, the conservative talk show host, is one of his closest friends. Westphal says that he doesn't agree with much of what Limbaugh represents, but he admires the commentator for speaking his mind. It is not uncommon where Westphal is coaching for his friends to have little or nothing to do with professional sports. He was frequently seen with folk singer John Stewart.

WESTPHAL'S COACHNG CAREER: A LITTLE COLLEGE AND A LOT OF THE PROS

His coaching career began in 1985 with Southwest Baptist Bible College in Phoenix. He moved over the Grand Canyon College, also in the Valley of the Sun. He won the NAIA championship with Grand Canyon in 1988, and he joined Cotton Fitzsimmons' Phoenix Suns staff. In 1992, Westphal was hired as the Suns head coach. He inherited a team that included the newly acquired Charles Barkley, deadly shooting guard Danny Ainge, rookie sensation Richard Dumas, long shot master Dan Majerle and point guard extraordinary Kevin Johnson. They went to the 1993 NBA Finals losing to the Chicago Bulls in six games. Although the Suns continued to make the playoffs Westphal was fired in the 1995-1996 season.

There was never an explanation for Westphal's firing. The pundits analyzed the firing with no firm conclusions, but NBA coaches do have a short shelf life. In his time in Phoenix, Westphal was an extraordinary player and coach. The NBA jobs are made to fire coaches. Westphal was fired. Now he needed to look for new opportunities.

After taking off two seasons and keeping busy by assisting a local high school team, Westphal was back in the mix as a Seattle Super Sonics assistant. He worked in Seattle until the 2000-2001 campaign concluded.

Westphal joined the college ranks once again taking Pepperdine University to a 22-9 record, and the NCAA tournament, where they lost to Wake Forest 83-74 in the first round. The dye was cast Westphal was back in the coaching ranks. After three years at Pepperdine, he left to work for Fox Sports Net West Prime Ticket. He spent some time broadcasting Los Angeles Clipper games.

In 2007, Westphal joined Avery Johnson's Dallas Maverick staff, and he moved into the front office assisting General Manager Donnie Nelson. In 2009, Westphal was hired to coach the Sacramento Kings. This was not a pleasant job. The Kings had a depleted roster, poor fan support and erratic owners. The Kings' owners, the Maloof brothers, make Mark Cuban look humble. They are casino owners who are more comfortable in a gentleman's club. They may be having difficulty in the casino business, and maybe this is why they wouldn't spend money for quality players. The fans were restive. The arena was not up to NBA standards, and the roster was filled with prima donna players who lacked maturity. There was no one more immature than Kings' center DeMarcus Cousins. When Cousins and Westphal argued in the teams locker room, owners Joe and Gavin Maloof took the young centers side. Why not! Cousins makes ten times more money than Westphal. There were also differences of opinions between Westphal and the Maloof brothers.

They owned the team so Westphal was fired. Geoff Petrie, the Kings President of basketball operations, remarked: "You start to keep seeing the same things over and over again, you can't sit around and meditate forever..." That statement by a former NBA player must have been a painful one. The Kings were the worst team in their division. Westphal was 51-120 in Sacramento and despite coaching this disastrous team with its temperamental casino owners, Westphal's NBA coaching percentage was .571. Just think what it would have been without the 120 Sacramento King losses.

DEMARCUS FIRES THE COACH

Who is DeMarcus Cousins? In two seasons with the Sacramento Kings, he is described as a player with character issues. His character issues began at the University of Kentucky where he put on weight and played with little flair. He is described by teammates as "immature and difficult to coach." While playing under Westphal, Cousins was fined, suspended, got into fights with teammates, and he demanded to be traded. Cousins argues that these issues are just a misunderstanding. One former player said: "He is temperamental and disliked." After one year at the University of Kentucky, Cousins declared for the NBA draft. Before he joined John Calipari at Kentucky, Cousins committed to three other colleges. He was a for hire basketball gun. One wonders did he complete any college units? He is an immature young person playing a man's game with the attitude of someone in kindergarten. No wonder Westphal suspended him. When Paul Westphal left him in Sacramento for a game against the New Orleans Hornets, the coach remarked that Cousins was "unwilling or unable to embrace traveling in the same direction as his team." There was only one thing left for the Maloof brothers to do, fire the coach. Don't look for a winning record anytime soon in Sacramento. Look for the team to head to Seattle or Anaheim. Look for the Maloof brothers to cut the odds at one of their casinos. Look for Cousins to continue to be a problem. Look for the present coach, Keith Smart, to be fired.

On December 23, 2012 the Sacramento Kings suspended DeMarcus Cousins indefinitely and the cause was "unprofessional behavior" and "conduct detrimental to the team." Coach Keith Smart had words with Cousins in the locker room. Maybe the Maloff brothers are not so bad after all. They supported the suspension. One wonders did they have a choice?

Peter: "Howard, quit asking the tough questions."

56

As a coach, Westphal was noted for his integrity and following the rules. He wasn't a strict disciplinarian, but, as the DeMarcus Cousin' incident suggested, the coach sometimes didn't have the last word. His coaching record is a good one. In the NBA he had 318 wins and 279 losses and at Pepperdine he was 75-71 with a college that put little emphasis upon basketball.

How does one summarize Paul Westphal? He was a great shooter, a firm coach, he was without scandal, he didn't beat up any of his teammates and he was a class act. Can the Maloof brothers say the same thing? How about DeMarcus Cousins?" Being a class act in Sacramento is not tolerated.

As the 2012-2013 season opened, the NBA suspended Cousins for two games for threatening the San Antonio Spurs announcer, Sean Elliott, as Cousins threatened to beat up Elliott for his opinions as a Spurs' analyst. Elliott was critical of Cousins selfish play, arrogance and personal behavior. When Cousins was asked to define defense. He responded: "Isn't it a country in Eastern Europe?" This is what Westphal had to deal with attempting to coach this pea-brained prima donna.

In 2012, Cousins hit Dallas Maverick O. J. May in the groin. It was a vicious and unnecessary blow. DeMarcus said it was accidental. O. J. Mayo had the last word: "That guy has some mental issues....Big maturity problems. Hopefully, he will grow out of it." Don't count on it O. J.

Peter: "Be nice Howard. Tell us how you really feel about DeMarcus Cousins.

PAUL WESTPHAL: THE SUNS COACH IS A SUCCESS

When Jerry Colangelo decided to hire Paul Westphal, as an assistant coach, it was due to the personality of Coach Cotton Fitzsimmons, who was often too strict. By nature, Fitzsimmons was a taciturn individual. There are some players who said: "it's a job working for Cotton." But it is a well paying job.

Fitzsimmons concurred that the Suns needed another personality; he saw a team that lacked the passion that he believed led to success. The Suns were a calm team that he believed needed fire. There was too much fire under Fitzsimmons, and this made Westphal the obvious coaching choice. He was calm, relaxed and nothing seemed to bother him. He wasn't demonstrative. The egos of NBA players are often fragile, and they don't accept criticism.

The players disliked Fitzsimmons, because he hollered at them on the floor. "Wake up, Tim Perry," Fitzsimmons said. Perry was furious.

He was the seventh player selected in the 1988 draft, and he believed that Fitzsimmons disrespected him. Unlike Westphal, Fitzsimmons had never played the game at a high level.

The Suns did have two winning seasons under Fitzsimmons, but he lost the team. Jerry Colangelo realized that Westphal had a defined coaching philosophy. While with the Boston Celtics, Westphal watched Red Auerbach work his psychological games with the lighted cigar at the end of the games the Celtics won. He also saw how Red used his bench. He also learned from Auerbach that the players would respect honest mistakes. Paul learned these techniques from Auerbach. Westphal knew how to manage players. Fitzsimmons was often too demanding for the modern player. Yet, he is one of the NBA's most successful coaches.

There were other parts of the Westphal's coaching background that helped him when he turned the Suns into an NBA finalist in the 1992-1993 season. He believed that playing for the NBA champions, against the Boston Celtics, was no more important than winning the small college basketball championship with Grand Canyon College. The players loved his demeanor.

The problem that Westphal had with the Suns was the inability to teach defense. He also attempted to control the hard partying Charles Barkley, while mollifying players who came to Westphal to complain that Barkley was a ball hog. A number of players simply did not like being in the same line up with Sir Charles. But he let Barkley know that he wasn't dictatorial, and the result was that Sir Charles had the best three years of his career under Westphal's careful eye.

When Barkley missed the team bus for a game with the Utah Jazz, Sir Charles caught a taxi to the game. Westphal laughed. The whole team thought it was hilarious. This translated into great team chemistry, and the Suns won 61 games the first year under Westphal's evenhanded tutelage.

While coaching the Suns, Westphal hung out with a mix of different personalities. During the 1993 NBA finals, Westphal was talking politics with a guy with a wrinkled shirt with stains on it. His name was Rush Limbaugh. What is interesting about the Westphal-Limbaugh friendship is that it is not based on politics but on the world of basketball.

When Barkley got into one of his usual bar difficulties, Westphal would tell Sir Charles to talk to A.C. Green. Not only is Green a Christian, but also he gave his all every night. "When my career gets to the end, I will give more," Barkley told Westphal, "till then I have got enough game to beat anyone." Charles is a humble soul.

Later that first season, Westphal coached the West NBA All Stars. Barkley was told that there would be a curfew and he would define and enforce it. In the long run, Westphal was viewed as too laid back. There were rumors he was losing the team.

Westphal had his hands full answering Barkley's press diatribes. When Sir Charles remarked, "training camp doesn't mean anything." Westphal said: "Charles said training camp doesn't mean nothing. But it does. That's how you build up your conditioning. We're so far from being in mid-season form, it's a joke."

Westphal brought some intangibles to the Suns. In practice, Westphal lectured the players on the need for complimentary players. This meant that he would use the bench effectively, and he let his team know that he had confidence in his bench.

In the 1995-1996 season, Paul Westphal was at a crossroads. During the past three seasons, the Suns had won more games than any other NBA team. He was on the hot seat to win an NBA title. Since he had taken over for Cotton Fitzsimmons in their 1992-1993 season, Coach Westphal had success, but he hadn't won an NBA title.

After three seasons, the critics complained that his teams couldn't play defense. There was also the problem of injury. Because of their fast paced style, the Suns players were prone to injury. As the 1995 season opened, the Suns had three players who were injury prone. The superstar Charles Barkley had bad knees, Danny Manning had blown out his knee and the talented and versatile center wasn't due back until January. Kevin Johnson, the point guard, was in rehab with leg muscle problems.

Then the press attacked Westphal for being too laid back and too much of a player's coach. Westphal didn't fit the image of a coach who was a strict disciplinarian and a drill sergeant. After the Suns started the 1995-1996 season at 14-19, Westphal was fired.

It was his inability to control Charles Barkley's quotes and game that cost Westphal his job. His team looked undisciplined and dispirited. This was the wrong perception. They played hard for Westphal and liked him. After three seasons he had won 177 games.

The firing brought out the critics. Many of them said that Westphal had lost a championship caliber team. The reasons were never clear and the gossip mongers had a field day.

After Colangelo and Fitzsimmons talked at length about Westphal, they came to the conclusion that he had lost control of the team. They didn't provide the press with a good reason for firing Westphal. The Suns were a mess. Barkley was in poor playing shape. Kevin Johnson was injured. They also appeared disorganized on offense as the Suns depended too heavily upon Barkley's offensive outbursts. But Charles was no longer the All Pro Barkley. His game was going south. But a Westphal quote told what was wrong. Westphal said: "We're strangers out there, the only time we are together is in front of 19,000 people." Colangelo fired Westphal shortly after this quote.

The truth is that Colangelo went to Westphal and told him that players needed more guidance. Westphal remarked that they were men and they should act like it. There was a quiet tension between the coach and the front office.

This led to unsubstantiated rumors that something was wrong. It was simple. Westphal started the season at 12-19, and this was unacceptable. He was fired. If there is someone to blame, it is Fitzsimmons. He was not a Westphal supporter, and he stabbed his former assistant in the back. It led to hard feelings.

PAUL WESTPHAL'S IMMEDIATE LIFE AFTER THE SUNS

Once Westphal was fired, he had time on his hands. He spent time with his family but he loved to drive Highway 66 and look at the historical sights. He picked up his friend folk singing legend, John Stewart, and along with the former Kingston Trio musician, they drove to Amarillo, Texas. Along the way Stewart wrote songs and Westphal told him the perils of professional basketball. "It was a lot of fun," Westphal said. "The funny thing was, we should have been driving a '59 Cadillac with tail fins and the top down. Instead. We are driving my Infiniti, and the romantic poet of the neon highway (John Stewart) was on his cellular phone half the time. It was the 50s meeting the 90s."

What irritated Westphal was the public perception that he was too laid back. "It's hard for me to sell myself as something other than what I am," Westphal said. The time at Grand Canyon College was the best coaching experience in Westphal's life. He could have cared less about the pros. John Stewart's "July You're A Woman" was constantly on his car stereo. He felt his time with his family was most important. The time coaching Charles Barkley was not among his favorite moments, but he persisted and the Suns had a good run.

It was Westphal's combination of self-deprecating humor, complete honesty and charisma that made him a popular NBA coach. He also knew his x's and o's. He didn't know how to keep Sir Charles out of the bars, and this was his downfall. He is one of the Suns great coaches, and this is the second best thing that Westphal does. The first is being a quality human being and a good family man.

When he left the Suns there were hard feelings. Give Robert Sarver some credit. He has brought Westphal and others back for a number of retirement ceremonies. The old antagonism is gone and Westphal remains a legend in the Valley of the Sun. Sarver has a strong understanding of the Suns' past history, and he is doing what he can to celebrate and preserve it.

8. WHAT IT TAKES TO MAKE A DIFFERENCE
COTTON FITZSIMMONS: THE WORLD'S GREATEST COACH
YOU NEVER HEARD OF

Cotton Fitzsimmons is the quietest legend in sports. He was always\ under the radar. As a coach, he has few peers. In the day before coaches were accorded mythical status (think Phil Jackson) and honored (think Red Auerbach), he went about his business with efficiency and marvelous results. It was always about the players with Fitzsimmons. It was never about the coach.

WHO WAS COTTON FITZSIMMONS?

Some people describe Cotton Fitzsimmons as born to coach. While growing up in the Mississippi river town of Hannibal, Missouri, Fitzsimmons was influenced by the good humor of local writer, Mark Twain. He moved to a small Missouri town, Bowling Green, in the fourth grade, and there because of his fluffy white hair, he was nicknamed Cotton. His father died when he was in the fifth grade, and his mother raised his brother and two sisters.

Cotton turned to basketball and town's basketball coach, James A. Wilson, made him into a player. From the seventh grade through high school; Fitzsimmons was taught the fine points of the game. At 5-7, he was not made for basketball, but the Bowling Green team went 65-7. As a small sized forward, Fitzsimmons was the team's second leading scorer.

But Cotton didn't go to college. He worked in a brick factory to help his mother. In time, he enrolled at a junior college in Hannibal. Then he was off to Wichita Falls, Texas to attend Midwestern State. He was called "the brash towheaded kid from Bowling Green," and this moniker was due to Cotton's prolific scoring. He was such a crowd favorite that Moberly Junior College hired him as a coach, and from the late 1950s into the early 1960s, he led this junior college team to national prominence.

What is unique about Fitzsimmons is that he coached the Suns on three different occasions. He may also be the only NBA coach to graduate from a junior college, LaGrange JC where he was a 5-9 shooting guard, and he played at a small four year school Midwestern State University in Wichita Falls, Texas.

When he returned to begin his coaching career at Moberly Junior College in Missouri in 1956, the NBA was the farthest thing from Fitzsimmons mind. After eleven years at Moberly he had won two national championships, and he was hired to coach at Kansas State University. He was there for only two seasons before leaving for the NBA.

THE FIRST TIME AROUND WITH THE SUNS

What did Fitzsimmons contribute to the Phoenix Suns? He had two separate coaching stints. The first one was brief but productive. From 1970 to 1972, Fitzsimmons helped the Suns find a winning identify. In 1970-1971, he brought the Suns their first winning season at 48-34. He was so successful that the Atlanta Hawks paid him substantially more money. When he moved on to the Hawks, Fitzsimmons walked into a coaching nightmare. The team depended upon a gunner, who had no time for team play, his name was Pete Maravich. He is one of the games great shooters. He was also a pain in the ass as a selfish, aloof and often erratic player. Fitzsimmons told close friends that he regretted taking the Hawks' coaching position.

The irony is that Fitzsimmons continued to live in the Valley of the Sun. His friends stated that his heart was always with the Suns. He loved Scottsdale, and his neighbors were Sandra Day O'Connor, Alice Cooper, Dan Quayle and Hugh Downs.

When he arrived in Atlanta, Fitzsimmons tried to bring discipline to the Hawks. Fitzsimmons believed that he had a championship team. This was due to one player that he wanted to coach because of his brilliant playmaking. In Atlanta, as Fitzsimmons coached Pete Maravich, he stated that this was the sole reason for taking the job. That was an ill-advised comment. The Atlanta Hawks move was a disaster from day one. The Hawks had trouble integrating Maravich's maverick playing style. He was also a selfish gunner with little thought of team play. A heavy drinker and a moody personality, Maravich was uncontrollable. Finally, Fitzsimmons benched him. After Pete got drunk on the team plane, played a subpar game and hollered incessantly at the referees, Fitzsimons had enough. He suspended Maravich. They hardly talked and a short time later the coach was sent packing.

On coaching Maravich, Fitzsimmons remarked: "I went against my own game those two years trying to make it work with Pete. It won't work. I'm going back to my old game." Before he was fired, Fitzsimmons said of Maravich: "Without a doubt, Pete is the most exciting player I've ever coached." What Fitzsimmons didn't say is that he couldn't coach a spoiled brat who wasn't a team player. When he left Atlanta, Fitzsimmons soured on coaching

He looked for a job in an NBA front office. In 1975, he moved to the Golden State Warriors, as the director of player personnel, and then in 1977 he took the head-coaching job for one year for the Buffalo Braves. Then the Kansas City Kings hired him, and he was the NBA coach of the year in 1979. By 1984 Fitzsimmons' run at Kansas City was over and after a 38-44 season in 1983-1984, he moved on to coach the San Antonio Spurs. In his two seasons with the Spurs, Fitzsimmons was 76-88, and he had a year left on his contract when he was fired.

When Colangelo brought Fitzsimmons back to the Suns, it was a bad time for the franchise. He helped to overcome the negative perception of the organization and the drug scandal faded into obscurity. Colangelo remarked: "I've got the right guy to right the ship."

THE DRUG SCANDAL AND JERRY COLANGELO TURNS THE FRANCISE AROUND: COTTON IS THERE

One of the craziest stories in the Suns history took place when the team returned from a road game against the Los Angeles Lakers in the 1988-1989 season. As they left the plane, three players jumped a fence as a short cut to get their cars. They literally fell into the hands of law enforcement, and they were arrested for entering a restricted area. Coach Cotton Fitzsimmons wrote on the team blackboard: "Don't jump any fences." It was a mirthful moment but the publicity for avoiding the law exceeded the crime. Then came the drug scandal. There is no incident in Phoenix Suns history that drew more press than the drug scandal.

When the drug scandal took place, Colangelo realized that he had not established close ties to his players. He was busy with business matters and personnel issues. Cotton Fitzsimmons watched the scandal unfold when he was sitting out a year with the San Antonio Spurs paying his salary. There is no doubt that Fitzsimmons wanted to return to the Suns.

The scandal took place at the end of the 1986-1987 season, when a Maricopa County Grand Jury indicted five Suns, as well as some former players on drug charges. The indicted players included center James Edwards, guard Jay Humphries and guard Grant Gondrezick on charges of possessing or trafficking in cocaine or marijuana. Former Suns' players Garfield Heard and Mike Bratz were also indicted. Walter Davis, the Phoenix guard, who had entered a drug rehab program in 1985, agreed to testify against his former teammates. It is unclear if the players were guilty or innocent. The damage was done in the community. The charges were dropped or reduced. This did little to undo the damage. Jerry Colangelo stepped in and took over. Colangelo remarked: "For a number of years we didn't have the personal contact with our players that we needed." Colangelo continued: "I think the fans were hurt by the drug charges...." What is the point of bringing up the drug scandal? The point is that over the years the Suns inquire about the character of their players better than anyone in the league. There was a strong reaction in the Phoenix area to the drug problem, but to his credit Colangelo worked on it. He also solved the problem.

COLANGELO ENDS THE DRUG SCANDAL

This didn't end the drug problem. The only Sun player to have serious drug issues, since the 1980s, is Richard Dumas who had to move to Israel to clean up his game and life. The point of the drug scandal is that the Suns are historically a team with great character. Jerry Colangelo traded one third of his team to other places. He made a statement. Character is first. Team play is important. Humphries, Edwards, Larry Nance and Mike Sanders were traded. This was not a popular move. People in Phoenix knew little about the new players, Mark West, Kevin Johnson and Tyrone Corbin, but they soon found out character and talent is one and the same. The Suns investigated their roster and much to Colangelo's credit, the Suns' culture came out clean. If there is one player who helped the Suns it was Eddie Johnson who arrived in the Valley of the Sun after playing for six years for the Kansas City/Sacramento Kings. He was considered an "old man" at twenty-nine, but he became one of the Suns most effective players. Johnson had played on only one winning team until he came to the Suns. After six seasons in Kansas City and with the Sacramento Kings, he wound up with his first winning team. On the court Johnson constantly displayed his deadly jump shot, as well as his stellar defense. T. R. Dunn was another defensive specialist, who at age thirty-four could still play.

Johnson and Dunn were family oriented individuals who had strong character, deep religious convictions, and they were topflight team players. They were the foundation stones that built the franchise. It didn't hurt to have a baby-faced kid from Utah by the name of Tom Chambers join the franchise. Chambers was 6-10 but had the skills of a shooting guard. Marc Iavaroni said Chambers was the toughest player to defend in the NBA. There was a quick turn around, and the Suns were ready for their best decade. The six seasons under Fitzsimmons were winning ones with the Suns posting 244 wins in his first five seasons.

Eddie Johnson epitomized the Suns player who was team oriented and unselfish. When he retired, Johnson had scored 19,202 points in over 1199 NBA games. Yet, he was never selected for the All Star game, but he did win the NBA Sixth Man of the Year in 1989. He is now the Suns TV color commentator.

To reshape the roster, the Suns dealt, Larry Nance, a popular player. The fans were upset. There was a plan. The Suns realized that the draft was a source for the shooter they needed to once again dominate the Western Conference The addition of Dan Majerle was another move that helped to turn the franchise from a team that won 28 games to one that won 54. Majerle's emergence as a star player was due as much to Cotton Fitzsimons coaching as it was to Jerry Colangelo's firm but fair hand. The late 1980s saw the Suns roaring back from the internal difficulties. Cotton Fitzsimmons was directing the resurgence.

The drug scandal is an important part of Suns' history because of the manner in which the franchise turned itself around. The press made matters worse by dubbing the scandal Waltergate. This was a reference to Walter Davis who testified against his teammates. Davis was granted immunity from prosecution and then no one was prosecuted. The press ignored this salient fact. Davis claimed: "The last thing I wanted to do was get my teammates and friends indicted. If I'd known I was going to do that, I'd have probably gone to jail instead." Come on, Walter, no one believes this self-serving quote.

COTTON FITZSIMMONS BRINGS TO SUNS TO THEIR PEAK

When Fitzsimmons returned to the Suns, as the head coach in 1988, he was the driving force behind the trade that brought Kevin Johnson and Mark West to the Suns. The trade was unpopular with the fans. Fitzsimmons was changing the team's culture. After the drug scandal, there was a new direction. No one personified this more than the Suns 1988 first round NBA, Dan Majerle. He came in with the other new players and turned the team around. In the 1988-1989 season, the Suns were back. Fitzsimmons won the NBA Coach of the Year award in 1989. By 1992, Fitzsimmons retired to work in the Suns front office. He was only the sixth NBA coach by 1992 to win 800 games. Before he left the Suns bench, Fitzsimmons worked with Colangelo to trade Jeff Hornacek, Andrew Lang and Tim Perry to the Philadelphia 76ers for Charles Barkley. Then Fitzsimmons joined Al McCoy for a time as a broadcaster.

It was a brief retirement as Fitzsimmons returned as the Suns head coach for the third time in 1996. After the Suns lost their first eight games in the 1996-1997 season, Fitzsimmons resigned. On July 25, 2003 the **Arizona Republic** informed the Valley of the Sun that he had died. After being diagnosed with lung cancer, Fitzsimmons had a series of brain strokes. His death brought an outpouring of grief. He was not only a great coach, but he had a level of integrity that defined the Suns' organization.

9. THE POINT GUARD MAYOR
KEVIN JOHNSON: A POINT GUARD WHO DID EVERYTHING AND THEN BECAME THE MAYOR

Kevin Johnson is the Mayor of Sacramento, California. A lady came up to him recently and said: "I know you are not interested in basketball, but see if you can keep our Kings in town." Johnson said: "We are working on an arena, so the team can stay." She smiled: "Thank you, I know the Mayor's job is more important than basketball." That is the kind of person Kevin Johnson is with people. He is shy, warm, and direct and he seldom talks about himself.

The shy nature that defines his personality is one that often hides his basketball greatness. Like Jason Kidd and Steve Nash, he was the point guard face of the Suns franchise. He is a much more diverse personality than the average NBA player. Johnson is a dedicated Christian, he has a high-level college education, he has multiple interests outside basketball, and he was one of the great point guards in the NBA.

WHERE DID JOHNSON COME FROM?

When Johnson arrived in the Valley of the Sun, he came off a sterling career at the University of California, Berkeley. He was also a star in the classroom. He studied political science but didn't graduate until after his NBA career ended. He also was a two time All Pac 10 conference player and an honorable mention All American. He made the honor role at UC regularly. He was different than other athletes. He was a Christian athlete before it was fashionable. Tim Tebow could learn a great deal from Johnson.

At the University of California, Johnson ranks second on the all time scoring list with 1,655 points, and he was a four-year starter. He led the California Bears to the NIT in his junior and senior years, and this was the first post-season appearance of California basketball in the last twenty-six years. Johnson also scored 27.2 points a game. When he left the University of California, Berkeley, Johnson was the school's assist and steals leader. He was a natural athlete, and he also played shortstop for the California baseball team. The Oakland Athletes drafted him in 1986 and between his junior and senior years, he played for Oakland's minor league team in the California League, Modesto. A year riding a bus to Bakersfield, Rancho Cucamonga and Visalia was enough for Johnson to concentrate on basketball.

ON TO THE NBA AND STARDOM

As a premier point guard, Johnson worked out for most NBA teams. There was no doubt that Johnson was going to be a lottery pick. This prompted teams to negotiate for his rights. When the Cleveland Cavaliers selected Johnson seventh in the 1987 draft many people were surprised The Cavaliers had an All Star point guard Mark Price. Johnson quickly became a back up to Price. On February 28, 1988, Johnson was traded along with Mark West and Tyrone Corbin to the Phoenix Suns. Phoenix also received a draft pick and used this pick to select swingman Dan Majerle. The pieces were in order for a championship Suns run.

The trade to the Valley of the Sun was a tonic for Johnson's game. He sat on the bench for the Cavaliers, and he didn't have a chance to showcase his skills. Johnson quickly took over the Phoenix offense. In April 1988, Johnson was rookie of the month in the NBA, as he averaged 15.1 points a game, he shot an 86.4% field goal percentage with 10.6 assists and 5.6 rebounds. The Suns couldn't wait for a full season of Kevin Johnson's backcourt magic. They weren't disappointed.

In 1988-1989, Johnson emerged as one of the NBA's newest stars. He won the NBA's most improved player award. As Johnson came West the Suns improved from 28 wins to 55. He was a three time All Star, and he was the starting point guard in the 1991 NBA All Star game. He started alongside Los Angeles Lakers legend Magic Johnson.

In the 1991 NBA All Star game in Charlotte, Johnson wore number 41 as a tribute to his teammate Mark West. Johnson told the press that his teammate did "the dirty work, the little things that made the Suns so successful."

From 1987 through the spring of 1992, Johnson was the glue that held the Suns potent offense together. After averaging 12.6 points a game in 1987-1988, Johnson averaged more than twenty points a game in the next three seasons. In 1991-1992 his average was 19.7 points, and he was the undisputed team leader. The Suns needed another ingredient to become NBA champions. The person turned out to be Philadelphia 76er star Charles Barkley. He was traded to the Suns, and his four years in the Valley of the Sun were ones that made Phoenix an elite team. The Suns were on national television more times in those four years than in the previous decade. Sir Charles brought stardom for himself and the team to Phoenix.

KEVIN JOHNSON'S SUPERSTAR SUNS' YEARS

During the 1992-1993 campaign, the Suns, with Charles Barkley leading the way, went to the NBA finals losing to the Chicago Bulls. Johnson was injured for much of that season, thanks to his belated attempt to lift Oliver Miller off the floor. The 300 plus pound Miller caused havoc with Johnson's body and he missed 33 games. By lifting a three hundred pound plus teammate, Johnson showed his team spirit. He also unwittingly shortened his NBA career.

When Charles Barkley arrived so did Kevin Johnson's injuries. During his four seasons playing with Barkley, Johnson missed 109 games. He was injured early in the year but Kevin was fine by the playoffs. It was a weird but consistent pattern as Johnson averaged 24.8 points a game in the 1995 postseason.

THE BANE OF KEVIN JOHNSON: CHARLES BARKLEY

The biggest problem for Kevin Johnson as a point guard was establishing where the ball went for shot selection. One of Johnson's problems was to control superstar Charles Barkley. In one game against the Houston Rockets, Chuck Brown told writer Mike Tulumello that he heard the following exchange between Johnson and Barkley.

Barkley: "Give me the fucking ball."

Johnson: "The play is called."

Barkley: "Forget the play. Give me the ball."

Johnson passed the ball to Barkley and he missed the shot. Then Barkley called for the ball.

Johnson "Are you going to score Charles?" The ball went to Charles and he missed another shot.

As they left the court, Barkley hit the last shot to help the Suns beat the Rockets 92 to 90. Johnson asked him: "Charles do you need the ball all the time?" Barkley smiled; "Yes, I win you games." Kevin Johnson was frustrated with Barkley's selfish demeanor and most of the team felt the same way.

JOHNSON'S INTERNATIONAL BASKETBALL FAME

In the summer of 1994, Johnson shared point guard duties with Utah's John Stockton as the member of the U. S. National Team, known as Dream Team II. In the FIBA World Championship, Johnson helped the team to a gold medal. U. S. Coach Don Nelson said: "I really like having KJ on the court. The thing that stood out is how he sacrificed his scoring to be a distributor of the ball and make this team win."

The twelve man Dream Team II included Larry Johnson, Shawn Kemp, Dan Majerle, Reggie Miller, Alonzo Mourning, Joe Dumars, Shaquille O'Neal and Dominique Wilkins among others.

This team was younger and more immature than Dream Team I, but they also had more fun. There were some hilarious moments. With Cuba down by thirty points one of their players attempted to start a fight. Shaq walked over and glared at him. That ended the so-called fight. The game resumed, Shaq got the ball and dunked it with thunder. The Cuban center was already running to the other end of the court.

Because there were so many scorers, Johnson and John Stockton were facilitators, and the players all enjoyed scoring. Shaq led Dream Team II in scoring with 18 a game, followed by Reggie Miller with 17.1 and Dominque Wilkins and Joe Dumars averaged just over twelve points a game. Kevin Johnson averaged five points a game, as he directed the offense.

KEVIN JOHNSON'S SUNS LEGACY

Johnson retired after the 1997-1998 season, but returned in the 1999-2000 campaign to replace the injured Jason Kidd. After the Suns lost in the second round to the Los Angeles Lakers, Johnson retired for good.

After he retired the second time, Johnson looked back upon an incredible NBA career. He was also single handedly responsible for much of the mystique and success of the Phoenix Suns. He was a master of consistency. In his first seven Suns seasons, he was on a team that won more games than any team in NBA history. In addition to being selected five times for the NBA All Star team, Johnson was a prolific scorer and a team leader. The Suns averaged 56 wins a year, and he is one of only three players in NBA history to average 20 points and 12 assists in a season. The other two are Isaiah Thomas and Magic Johnson.

Consistency was a hallmark of Johnson's career. He is only one of three players to average at least 20 points and 10 assists three seasons in a row. The others are Oscar Robertson and Magic Johnson. The playing honors continue as he was the first NBA player to average twenty points, ten assists, a .500 field goal percentage along with two steals a game. He did this in the 1990-1991 season.

KEVIN JOHNSON OFF THE BASKETBALL COURT

Off the basketball court, he enrolled in divinity school and finished his B.A. at the University of California. There is much more to Johnson than basketball. He used his B. A. in political science to secure election as Sacramento's Mayor.

His charities support education and community growth. Johnson organized a program, READS, to help students improve their reading. He also founded St. Hope to work toward educational reform. St. Hope means Helping Others Pursue Excellence. Since the St. Hope Development Corporation was founded in 1994, it has enabled Sacramento to renovate its downtown area for small business. This has also led to low cost housing and affordable condominiums. In the schools, St. Hope supports charter schools and provides an education for 2,000 students in seven small schools. The honors go on and on. Kevin Johnson is the best representative of the Suns in government. That is until Charles Barkley becomes Alabama's governor.

The Kevin Johnson Corporation is an active member of the Sacramento business community. This business conglomerate specializes in real estate development, sports management and developing new businesses in and around Sacramento.

Not only is Kevin Johnson one of the most heralded Suns, he remains a community advocate who has gone beyond his basketball roots to make a difference as Sacramento's mayor.

10. TOM CHAMBERS: HE PLAYED LIKE A 6-FOOT GUARD AT 6-10 AND BOY CAN HE TALK ON THE AIR

Tom Chambers frightened players who guarded him. He played with the skills of a six-foot shooting guard. The problem is that he was almost seven feet tall. He starred at the University of Utah, and then he went on to a superlative sixteen year NBA career. He was not only a four time NBA All Star, but he emerged as one of the most prolific scorers in league history. Chambers possessed power forward skills unparalleled in the NBA. He was a thunderous dunker, a great ball handler, a deadly jump shooter, and he was quick to the basket. His dribble was more like that of a point guard than of a power forward He even played a little defense.

What is strange about Chambers is that at Fairview High School in Boulder, Colorado, he was a talented point guard. He was also a sophomore in high school, and he was only six feet tall. Then almost overnight he grew seven inches and he still played like a backcourt phenomenon. He broke his wrist in his last year in high school, and he had to play with his left hand. He had also grown to 6-10. The college recruiters came calling, and he selected the University of Utah.

At the University of Utah, Chambers led his team to two Western Athletic Conference titles. He was also the consummate team player. When **Sports Illustrated** came to the University of Utah campus to report on Chambers, the magazine noted that with Danny Vranes and Karl Bankowski the Utes had the best front line in college basketball. In his senior year, Chambers averaged nineteen points a game and nine rebounds. He concluded his four-year career at Utah with a fifteen points a game average and eight rebounds. His teammates called him "Mr. Consistency."

In 1981, the San Diego Clippers selected Chambers with the eighth pick in the NBA draft. What a way to start an NBA career playing for Donald Sterling. He went on to play for sixteen seasons in the NBA. He was the Clippers top score at 17.2 points a game in his rookie year. The next year the Clippers drafted Terry Cummings, and they decided to trade one of their players. Chambers was sent packing to Seattle in August 1983. He joined center Jack Sikma and guard Gus Williams to make the Super Sonics formidable. He scored 18.1 a game at Seattle and played great defense. The next year Seattle traded Williams and the new point guard Gerald Henderson couldn't set up Chambers to score. Henderson resented Chambers' star status. He did what he could to keep the ball from Tom. Chambers still had team high 21.5 points per game, but he wasn't getting the same amount of touches. There was a strained relationship between Chambers and Henderson. This tiff ended when rookie Nate McMillan came in to reinvigorate Chambers' scoring. He averaged 23.3 a game the next year for the Super Sonics, and he made the All Star team. He had his finest year.

The 1987 NBA All Star game played in Seattle was Chambers show. He scored 34 points and made 13 of 25 shots. He was selected as the game's MVP. But Chambers had problems in Seattle. He didn't get the ball. He was the leading scorer, but he was third in shots taken. There was no doubt that his time in Seattle was close to an end. The high scoring career made him a hot trade item. The Super Sonics didn't trade Chambers, and he became a restricted free agent. The Super Sonics refused to match the Phoenix Suns contract offer.

The Phoenix Suns made Chambers what was then a very high-end contract. It came close to ten million dollars during his five years in the Valley of the Sun. The ability to sign Chambers was due to his outdoor interests. The New York Knicks and the Chicago Bulls wanted Chambers, but he preferred to remain in the Far West. He is a hunter and outdoorsman.

Cotton Fitzsimmons, the Phoenix coach, made it clear that Chambers was his go to scorer. Tom didn't disappoint as he averaged 25.7 points a game in 1988-1989, and for five seasons in Phoenix, he was the dominant scorer. By 1990-1991, Chambers game was more team oriented, and his old Seattle teammate Xavier McDaniel joined him.

Everything changed in 1992-1993 when Charles Barkley joined the Suns. Chambers, now 33 years old, became a sixth man. Along with Dan Majerle, he was one of the Suns' top scorers. The Suns went 62-20 and they played the Chicago Bulls in the NBA Finals. They lost. Barkley's arrival prompted change. Chambers was traded to the Utah Jazz. He backed up Karl Malone at the power forward position. But Chambers made history as the first unrestricted NBA free agent.

CHAMBERS LOOKS BACK ON HIS SUNS CAREER; 1993 WAS THE BEST

When the Phoenix Suns signed Tom Chambers on July 8, 1988 as the first unrestricted NBA free agent, this began a journey that was amongst the best in his career. In his five years with the Suns, he reached the NBA Finals in 1993, and he was an All Star.

As he looked back upon 1993, Chambers saw it as a magic season. He was the key ingredient off the bench that saw the Suns beat Chambers old team, the Seattle Super Sonics in game seven of the NBA Western Conference finals. The Suns were on their way to the NBA finals.

When he arrived in the Valley of the Sun no one picked the Phoenix team to do much. As Chambers looked back fondly on 1988-1989, he saw a strong potential for the future. What Chambers didn't count on was the return of Cotton Fitzsimmons, who molded the Suns into a surprise team that finished second with a 55-27 record in the NBA's Pacific Division. When Phoenix went to the Western Conference finals losing 4-0 to the Los Angeles Lakers, the Suns were a team of the future.

Tom Chambers: "We weren't even picked to do anything. Cellar dwellers, if you will. By the end of the season the stands were full."

The 1989-1990 season saw the Suns advance to the Western Conference finals, and the team continued to sell out, as they posted a 54-28 record. They lost to the Portland Trail Blazers in the Western Conference Finals.

CHAMBERS FINEST MOMENTS AS A SUN

Then the changes came for Chambers. A new coach, Paul Westphal, arrived and a super star, Sir Charles Barkley, as the Suns became a national TV favorite. By 1993 Chambers was not the main option, as Barkley took most of the shoots. It didn't matter Chambers was the ultimate team player.

Chambers finest moment as a Sun came in game 7 of the Western Conference NBA finals when he lobbied Coach Paul Westphal to start.

Tom Chambers: "I just said that I had always guarded Derrick and I always had success. I was taller, being 6-10." Chambers referred to the fact that Richard Dumas had trouble guarding Derrick McKey, who was part of the Seattle Super Sonics mammoth front line that included Xavier McDaniel and Nate McMillan. Chambers not only shut down McKey, but also he was so embarrassed him that the Super Sonics traded him to the Indiana Pacers.

CHAMBERS ON SIR CHARLES BARKLEY

One of the knocks on Barkley is that some players didn't like sharing the floor with him. This wasn't the case with Tom Chambers. He had a good on and off the court relationship with Barkley. "Charles and I did a lot of things off the court. We went out, we ate, we hung out. We had a lot of things we enjoyed doing together, playing cards. I really enjoyed my time with him," Chambers concluded.

On the court, Chambers gave up a part of his game to facilitate Barkley's prodigious scoring. When the Suns signed power forward A. C. Green, Chambers realized that his career in the Valley of the Sun was nearing an end. "Right after the playoffs I was released so they could use my money, because of the way that the collective bargaining agreement was at the time," Chambers continued, "I went and signed with the Jazz...."

Charles Barkley complained publicly about losing Chambers. He was a friend to Tom until the end.

THE END OF HIS SUNS CAREER AND OFF TO UTAH AND RETIREMENT

In 1994, Chambers was a key player off the bench as the Jazz reached the Western Conference Finals. He was a back up to power forward Karl Malone, and he finished his first season with eleven points a game, and during the second year he played fifteen minutes or less and his NBA career in Utah ended. Chambers attempted to play with other teams in the NBA, but he had to go overseas to restart his game. He left to play for Maccabi Tel Aviv for a season in Israel. Upon returning to the U. S., Chambers had a brief stint with the Charlotte where he played in twelve games. Then he re-signed with the Suns. He never played a game for the Suns, they traded him to the Philadelphia 76ers. He played one game for the 76er and he retired.

Chambers retired with a 20,000 plus point scoring total in 1107 NBA games. He averaged 18 points a game, four rebounds and two assists. He was a four time NBA All-Star.

When he left basketball, Chambers began working as a broadcaster for the Suns. In 1999, he was the first inductee into the Suns' Ring of Honor. He is now the color commentator for the Suns on local television. He spends his off-season at the Tom Chambers Shooting Star Ranch in North Ogden, Utah.

He spends much of his time doing charity work and he remains an avid outdoorsman.

CHAMBERS NBA AWARDS

The awards that Tom Chambers received in the NBA attests to his high level of skill and the smart way that he played the game. He was a four time All Star. He was a leader in field goal attempts, and he was among the top free throw shooters. In three of his seasons, Chambers was in the top ten in NBA scoring. His humility was demonstrated at the 1986-1987 All Star game when he was selected the MVP. Chambers gave credit to his All Star teammates passing and game planning that set him up for the award.

There was another part of Chambers game that was important and that was his relationship with point guard Kevin Johnson. They performed at a high level together and Johnson liked to joke that his high assist totals were due to Chambers ability to take a pass and quickly sink a basket.

As the pre, half time and post game television analyst for the Suns, Chambers continues to work for the organization that helped define his Hall of Fame credentials. He remains one of the faces of the franchise.

chapter

THREE

THE END OF THE 2010-2011 AND 2011-2012 SEASONS: LESSONS LEARNED

PAUL CORO, ARIZONA REPUBLIC BEAT WRITER: "WHAT'S YOUR FAVORITE PLACE IN PHOENIX? MARKIEFF MORRIS: "THAT GYM DOWNSTAIRS IN THE US AIRWAYS PRACTICE COURT."

When the Phoenix Suns ended their 2010-2011 season on April 13, I sat in my Section 101 Row 17, seat 7 looking and acting like Vince Carter. That is I felt like I had one leg and didn't hustle well. The season was not a good one. We went 40-42 and missed the playoffs. I didn't mind. The experience was the best I have had in years. The next year in the strike shortened 2011-2012 season, the Suns rebounded to a 33-33 record. Both years were tough on me. I am used to the playoffs. As I reflected, however, things were still fine. The team was fun. The food was good before the games. The drinks still flowed, and the arena was filled with happy people. That is how I felt. Others grumbled about not getting to the playoffs.

So I began writing this book. I looked at the Suns' legacy. It is a franchise that has achieved greatness for decades. When Robert Sarver purchased the team in 2004, the good times and the winning continued. Then like all franchises, the changes in the NBA's collective bargaining agreement, the difficulty of maintaining a core of players, due to salary negotiations, and the desire of players to find other teams led to a decline in wins in 2010-2011. Then in the summer of 2012 the Suns blew up their roster and brought in a host of new players.

THE ROBERT SARVER: OWNERSHIP QUESTION AND MANAGEMENT

The question is whether or not Sarver is a good owner. In my opinion, he is an excellent owner. He is also a businessman. When he didn't sign Amare Stoudemire and the New York Knicks moved in and offered Amare a maximum contract, Sarver gave his side of the story. The Suns medical staff pointed out that Amare had three good years and then injury would catch up with him. Sarver looks pretty good in December 2012, as Stoudemire is out with injuries. Although he is constantly criticized, Sarver is open to fans suggestions, he has no bodyguards and he does want to win. So the best is yet to come.

Lon Babby, Lance Blanks and Mark West provide a front office expertise that is slowly turning the Suns from a run and gun team to one with a big front line and good wing and point guards. It is a time of transition. Sarver is a patient owner, and the front office knows what it is doing. So the Suns are on the rise. It will take some time and a great deal of patience.

HIGH HOPES FOR THE 2011-2012 SEASON

For the 2011-2012 season, I had high hopes. Then came the strike. The Suns had changed their roster slightly, and there were rumors of players being traded, there were Internet stories of strife on the team, the owner, Robert Sarver, had the usual nut cases complaining about his management style and the fans were unhappy without basketball. I reflected that this would change. It did. The strike concluded and thirty-three home games in one hundred twenty three days made me cranky.

Peter: "You are a cranky bastard day and night."

The Suns are still a great franchise. They have good guys on the roster, excellent management and the season ticket holders are provided with some many extras it is hard to describe. Not to mention that the tickets are a good value. For my seats, $11,600 is a bargain, it is less expensive than a divorce lawyer. You see my wife, Carolyn, is the real fan. On our first date we went to see Rick Barry, when he still had hair and his first wife, and the Golden State Warriors beat up on the Philadelphia 76ers. She let me know basketball was her passion. I immediately got Golden State Warrior season tickets, and she reluctantly agreed to marry me. I think it was the season tickets that did it. Now forty plus years later we are still married. We are retired in Scottsdale. A good part of our life is the Phoenix Suns. For seven years our season tickets provided five playoff seasons and two others with drama and excitement.

AS THE 2012-2012 SEASON BEGAN

The 2012-2013 season will be a fun one. The Suns are practicing Moneyball. It will be great to watch. Although the early part of the season was a tough one, Elston Turner's defense and head coach Alvin Gentry's x's and o's brought the Suns back from the early problems. By January 7, 2013 the Suns had twelve wins and twenty three losses. The Suns play hard and the changes in their lineup suggested that they would continue to be fun. The Suns were working on their future lineups as the roster shakeup changed the culture.

CHAPTER

FOUR

ARE ROBERT SARVER OR LON BABBY BRAD PITT?: THE MONEYBALL FACTOR

"WHAT ARE THE DIFFERENCES WHEN DWYANE WADE DRIVES LEFT INSTEAD OF RIGHT? WHAT IS THE IMPACT OF RUSSELL WESTBROOK'S DRIVING ABILITY ON THE OKLAHOMA CITY THUNDER? HOW MUCH OF THE COURT CAN LEBRON JAMES DEFEND EFFECTIVELY?" PROFESSORS RAJIV MAHESWARAN AND YU-HAN CHANG, USC ON THE NEED FOR MONEYBALL STATISTICS.

The University of Southern California has assembled the largest database of basketball statistics ever collected. The goal is to take the more than one million pieces of data from the championship series between the Miami Heat and the Oklahoma City Thunder and quantify the strengths and weaknesses of the players. The bottom line is that the statistics may provide scouts, coaches and general mangers new evidence on what to pay the players. Or for that matter what players to sign.

The concept is christened moneyball. In simplest terms, moneyball is a means of building a franchise without spending millions on free agents, who may or may not perform to their financial worth. If they don't play up to their ability, the franchise has to continue the contract. The New York Knicks are an example of a team with large contracts and diminishing talent. They should have embraced the moneyball concept.

Another problem with basketball is that individual statistics create the market for a larger contract. This is contrary to the interests of the team. On the Phoenix Suns roster, Jared Dudley is a good example of a moneyball player. He is described as not particularly athletic. Yet, on the court his teammates get better due to his passing, his ability to play defense, his shooting and his knack for getting the ball to teammates who can score. Dudley also commits very few turnovers and for his size he has a large number of rebounds. On defense, Dudley routinely guards some of the NBA's most prolific scorers, and he generally keeps them below their average.

WHAT IS MONEYBALL?

Moneyball is a system of analyzing basketball talent using sabermetric's. This is a scientific means of evaluating players. Billy Beane, the Oakland A's General Manager, created the system and Michael Lewis' 2003 book **Moneyball: The Art of Winning An Unfair Game** highlighted the process.

A movie in 2011, featuring Brad Pitt, was released with considerable success. "Moneyball," was nominated for six Academy Awards including Best Actor and Best Picture. The major theme to moneyball is that analytical evidence based on statistics can help a team assemble a roster that is value laden. In other words, expensive free agents are not always the best way to win.

One of the key elements in moneyball is that the manger, the general manager, the scouts and the owner are often biased and generally flawed in their analysis. Much of the success of moneyball results from taking college educated talent rather than high school players. The notion is that the extra years of physical maturity, combined with an education, makes for a better player. This is the baseball model. The basketball model is more difficult, as the trend is for players to leave college early. They have less training, fewer developed skills and they lack the maturity of baseball players. So for basketball the money ball model is recast.

The scientific approach to analyzing statistics has attracted a great deal of attention from NBA teams. They all use one form of moneyball or another. When Robert Sarver hired Lon Babby to resurrect the Suns, moneyball was a factor. In his previous positions with the Washington Redskins from 1977 to 1980 and the Baltimore Orioles from 1979 to 1994, Babby practiced an early form of moneyball. As a former player agent, he is first and foremost a financial analyst, but he also has an unusually strong knowledge of how players perform and what they are capable of in the future. So Babby used an early moneyball approach to recommend changes in the Suns roster. Those changes took place as the 2012-2013 season opened.

LON BABBY SHEDS LIGHT ON THE MONEYBALL PHILOSOPHY

In the summer of 2012, Lon Babby shed some light on the Suns' money ball philosophy. It is Babby's contention that the Suns are assessing where they stand in the Western Conference. In other words, what does the franchise need to do to compete at a high level in the NBA?

"We have moved through a wonderful era," Babby continued, "hopefully into a bright new era and we've done it with grace." The translation is that they granted Steve Nash's wishes for a trade and they are rebuilding the roster. In a press conference, Babby suggested that it takes two years to put a new team into place. Babby explained: "You only have a certain amount of money you're allowed to spend under the rules...Our job-my job in particular is to allocate how you're going to spend that." To sign Nash to a thirty million dollar contract, Babby said, made it difficult to bring in young talent. So the painful decision to let Nash and Grant Hill leave was necessary to rebuilding the franchise.

STEVE ILARDI MAKES MONEYBALL WORK FOR THE SUNS

To make moneyball work the Suns hired a consultant, Steve Ilardi, a professor of clinical psychology at the University of Kansas. He also works as a consultant to the KU men's basketball team. It is Ilardi who developed a system known as the adjusted plus-minus model of player evaluation. This system is one that makes its way into the statistics that teams keep. The player is awarded a net offensive plus minus by a statistical system that combines offensive and defensive plays.

In simplest terms moneyball is a system that allows management to decide which players give the most for their salary. It also identifies those who are of great value. When Jared Dudley received his long-term contract, he was a moneyball player. Sebastian Telfair is another bargain for the money. Whether or not he is a moneyball player is too soon to analyze, but he is heading in that direction.

To build an NBA team with the right balance of skills and personality is a difficult task. The Dallas Mavericks provided some moneyball statistics for the Phoenix Suns' 2011-2012 season. Mark Cuban spent a great deal of money analyzing the strengths and weaknesses of the Suns. Why? Who knows! Maybe Cuban has too much money and needs to spend it.

The conclusions of the Dallas Mavericks attempt to identify the Suns strengths and weaknesses is interesting. The league scoring average was 91.42 and the Suns scored at 92.41 to rank seventh. In terms of offensive efficiency, the Suns ranked eighteenth in the NBA. This statistic is flawed as the Suns use an offense that relies on more passing than other teams. This sets the efficiency bar lower for the Suns, but the scoring results are higher. The Mavericks' moneyball statistics ranked lineups that worked the best for the Suns. These combinations included Marcin Gortat, Steve Nash, Grant Hill, Markieff Morris and Ronnie Price. This statistic appears incongruous, as Price played very little. The moneyball statisticians considered a lineup of Steve Nash, Shannon Brown, Jared Dudley, Channing Frye and Marcin Gortat equally strong.

Maybe Mark Cuban needs to get a life. Why he would spend this amount of money to identify the Suns weaknesses and strengths is beyond comprehension. Cuban needs to get back on Dancing With the Stars so that he has a life.

MONEYBALL AND THE SUNS' ROSTER

Moneyball is one means of analyzing the Suns roster, but it is nothing more than another means of ranking the talent and the team. The auto-generated statistics provided by the Dallas Mavericks don't tell the whole story. There is no simple way to approach the problem of how to win in the NBA.

During the offseason, Lon Babby provided some clues to the Suns approach to moneyball. When Babby was asked what the Suns would do to return to the playoffs, he remarked: "Steps to achieve this goal began last season when basketball operations upgraded the scouting department and implemented an analytics-based player evaluation...." Sounds like moneyball. Markieff Morris was drafted and signed due to his moneyball evaluation.

There is no clear means of identifying basketball talent. When New York Knicks point guard, Jeremy Lin, scored thirty-eight points against the Los Angeles Lakers in February 2012, he exemplified the moneyball concept. The irony is that when Lin's talent was analyzed in 2010, he was not rated a candidate with a strong game. So much for moneyball, as Lin signed a twenty-five million dollar plus contract with the Houston Rockets. Jeremy Lin suggests the tentative nature of moneyball. It is a concept. Sometimes it works. Sometimes it doesn't.

As a moneyball player, Jeremy Lin's skills were touted my Mike Qaissaunee, a Professor of Engineering and Technology at Brookdale Community College in Lincroft, New York. "The best candidate to pull off a surprise is Harvard's Jeremy Lin," Professor Qaissaunee wrote in May 2010. No one noticed the professor, but he was right on. As the 2012-2013 season progresses, Lin's numbers have increased and he is a solid addition to the Houston Rockets. Not only does moneyball work, but it is an important tool in the salary cap conscious NBA.

MONEYBALL FREE AGENTS

In the moneyball marketplace free agents are important. In August 2012, the Suns signed Jermaine O'Neal as a backup to center Marcin Gortat. At thirty-four years of age with bad knees and sixteen years in the league, O'Neal is a gamble. During the first nineteen games of the season, O'Neal averaged 8.2 points a game, 4.9 rebounds, 1.8 blocked shots and almost a steal a game. These statistics are for a player who played only eighteen minutes a game. From a salary and performance standpoint the deal is a slam-dunk. He costs the Suns only the veteran's minimum, and he brings inside scoring, defense, a great basketball mind and a team player into the fold. Not bad for a guy with supposedly bad knees. Lon Babby, Lance Blanks and Mark West made a smart choice. The Jermaine O'Neal signing brought strong inside play and, more significantly, leadership.

There are some other positives about O'Neal. He is a Christian athlete with a strong work ethic. He is a team player. He has skills that can be exploited in a few minutes of the game, thereby negating his tender knees. He is also mentoring Marcin Gortat.

Moneyball is a strategy for small market teams. It is important in creating a roster this is financially equipped to handle the NBA's high level of play. In basketball, moneyball is a less predictable science. As a team game, basketball requires players to mesh on a first or second unit.

Of all the moneyball free agents, the signing of Michael Beasley is considered money well spent. Only time will tell. The reason for Beasley's moneyball value is that he comes with an average salary a strong offensive game that is improving, while he has a weak defensive side that Coach Elston Turner can turn into a plus. After nineteen games in the 2012-2013 season, Coach Alvin Gentry said that the Suns were working on making Beasley the go to guy. They weren't giving up on him. Then after thirty-five games, Beasley temporarily was relegated to less playing time. Coach Alvin Gentry told Paul Coro not to read too much into the move. It was about match ups and experimentation.

Peter: "Howard, why don't you say that the Beasley experiment isn't working?" Remind me to have Ba Ba visit Peter.

Claude: "Do it soon, Peter will get us in trouble with Mr. Donaghy." Remind me to fire Claude and Peter.

When the Suns claimed Luis Scola from the Houston Rockets, who was released under the amnesty clause, they believed the veteran big man was a moneyball selection. To acquire Scola the Suns had to bid at least 3.3 million dollars. The player also can't be traded for a year. It was a smart move as Scola began the season strongly. He started for a time and then he came off the bench. In both instances, he demonstrated his veteran leadership, and he played well in either situation. Scola is the ultimate team player.

What makes Scola an important moneyball pick is that he has a hidden game. What this means is that his rebounding skill, his defensive smarts and his shooting skill make him a strong player who gives the team a hundred per cent every night.

WHAT DOES THE MONEYBALL CONCEPT MEAN TO THE SUNS?

Moneyball is a concept created by Billy Beane to make the Oakland A's baseball team competitive. Basketball is a different game. It has more individual components and there is not a farm system. While many view college, the minor basketball leagues and Europe as a farm system, the reality is that most teams develop the tenth through twelfth man on the roster in hopes of bringing them in as rotation players. It is in this system that moneyball works. The major impact of moneyball is to control the payroll while creating a competitive team.

The use of moneyball is also designed to store cash for future signings. The problem is that teams often talk about cap money without using it. That is what drives the fans crazy.

Moneyball challenges the status quo, and is a new way of thinking about constructing a basketball team. For the Suns, it provides a means of bringing in under valued players and with the training staff, the coaching and the quality of life in the Valley of the Sun there is success. Moneyball also shows that Sarver and Babby know what they are doing. They have a defined strategy for future growth, but this does not stop the pundits from excessive criticism. The salary cap, the free agent market and the vagaries of NBA business are elements that moneyball handles well. Rather than cost cutting measures, moneyball allows a team to spend wisely. It also takes time to invoke the moneyball strategy. Stay tuned. The Suns are on the road to becoming a perennial playoff team once again.

chapter

FIVE

A BRIEF LOOK AT THE SUNS DRAFT HISTORY: 1968-2011

"I'M GOING TO BE VERY LEARY IF ANTHONY DAVIS ENDS UP IN BROOKLYN. YOU KNOW, I'M GOING TO BE VERY LEARY BECAUSE I KNOW THE NBA HAS A LOT RIDING ON THAT NEW ARENA...." CHARLES BARKLEY

At 12:01 Eastern time on July 1, 2012 Midnight Madness took off with a bang. It was the opening of free agency. There was no free agency in 2011 due to the strike. The rumors around free agency were many, but the first few days brought no surprises. The Suns twenty three million dollars in cap space remained intact.

The publicity from the Suns camp was that Minnesota small forward Michael Beasley, the second pick in the 2008 draft, and Eric Gordon, the twenty three year old New Orleans Hornets shooting guard, were on the Suns radar. The New Orleans Hornets matched the Suns offer for Gordon. The Suns offered fifty-eight million dollars over four years. This should end the speculation that Robert Sarver doesn't want to sign players to long term, expensive contracts. Michael Beasley signed a three year eighteen million dollar contract. Beasley is an example of moneyball. He is a strong player, who is on the verge of developing his full game. While he was with the Miami Heat and the Minnesota Timberwolves, he was often inconsistent. Both teams got rid of him quickly and this has cast unfair aspersions about his talent. He can play. Everyone agrees that he has an enormous upside. Lebron James remarked: "Michael Beasley has the tools to be one of the premier players in the NBA."

As soon as free agency began, the Suns made qualifying offers to center Robin Lopez and guard Aaron Brooks. The reason for these offers was to make them restricted free agents. Brooks played in China during the strike-shortened season. Brooks won't be back. The Suns released him. He signed with the Sacramento Kings. Lopez was sent, via the trade route, to the New Orleans Hornets.

THE MYSTERY OF THE NBA DRAFT

The NBA draft is full of conspiracy-oriented analysts. If the worst team doesn't get the top choice there invariably is a conspiracy. The truth is that the draft is much like gambling in Las Vegas. That is unless you are selecting Wilt Chamberlain, Bill Russell, Tim Duncan, Elgin Baylor, Lebron James or Dwyane Wade.

Paul Coro, writing in the **Arizona Republic**, remarked: "It has been a decade since the Suns selected and kept a player from the NBA drafts top ten." What this quotation fails to mention is that you have to finish low enough to select a top ten pick. There are also trades, and the shifting of draft selection positions.

The draft is an inexact science. When the Golden State Warriors drafted Todd Fuller rather than Kobe Bryant in 1996 with the eleventh pick they passed up a potential Hall of Fame player. With the twelfth pick in the 1996 NBA draft the Cleveland Cavaliers selected Vitaly Potapenko from the Ukraine. The Los Angeles Lakers were jubilant as they worked out a deal to have the Charlotte Hornets select Kobe with the thirteenth overall selection. The Lakers traded their starting center, Vlade Divac, for Kobe, and it was one of the biggest steals in NBA history.

A brief history of the Phoenix Suns draft suggests the strengths and weaknesses of the process.

THE ORIGINAL SUNS

The Suns selected the New York Knicks, Dick Van Arsdale, who became known as "the Original Sun," in the NBA supplemental draft. It sounds strange to say that this was a great draft choice. As a player, he defined the integrity, the character and the Suns high-level quality of play. The next choice was an average one. In the 1968 draft the Suns selected Gary Gregor from the University of South Carolina. In his six year NBA career, Gregor played for six teams, and he was no more than a role player.

Things did not go well in the 1969 draft as the Suns lost the coin flip to the Milwaukee Bucks who selected UCLA's Lew Alcindor, soon to be Kareem Abdul Jabbar. After Abdul Jabbar was no longer available in the 1968 NBA draft.

Alvan Adams is one of the Suns greatest players. He was selected in 1975 with the number four pick, and he played thirteen NBA seasons. As the NBA Rookie of the Year, Adams began a career that was not only high scoring but he had a complete game. He remains the Suns all time rebounds and steals leader. If you can imagine a big man who could score at will and take the ball away from you it is Alvan Adams. He continues to work with the Suns as the US Airways Vice President of Facility Management.

Alvin Scott is one of the Suns more interesting performers, and he was a steal in the draft. He was nicknamed "The Space Needle" or "T-Bone." The nickname "T-Bone" was due to the way that he changed the game. He came in to give the Suns backbone. He had a tremendous work ethic, and he was a Christian athlete who attended Oral Roberts University. He was a consistent role player in eight seasons. He was a seventh round draft choice in 1977, and Scott epitomized what it was to be a Sun.

In eight seasons with the Suns, Scott averaged five points a game with three rebounds, but his leadership, court sense and his work ethic defined what is was to be a Sun.

SUNS WINNERS IN THE DRAFT

The Suns did have some draft winners. There were two draft picks that were rookies of the year, Alvan Adams, taken in 1975, as the fourth pick who played for thirteen seasons, Walter Davis selected in 1977, as the fifth pick, was a six time All Star who played at a high level for eleven seasons. Davis leads the Suns in all time shooting percentage with 51%. Adams and Davis remain legendary Suns.

The best recent Suns pick, Amare Stoudemire, was taken with the ninth pick in the 2002 NBA draft. He is a five time Phoenix All Star prior to signing a lucrative, long term deal with the New York Knicks.

One of the problems that management had with Stoudemire was his inability to maintain a rehab schedule when his knee was injured. The training staff winced when he showed up with a bag of burgers from McDonald's, and he was frequently late for practices, rehab and team meetings. He preferred to work in rehab at his own pace, and he was inconsistent. He was by all accounts a good citizen, but, with his enormous talent, he could do as he pleased. The Suns training staff said he had three good years before his knee reduced his effectiveness. This report looks like gold.

There are also some draft value picks. A value pick is a player who performs for a long time at a consistent level. When Larry Nance was selected as a first rounder in 1981, he played for six and a half seasons with the Suns and had an All Star year. In his NBA career, he scored 15,687 points, and he was the first winner of the NBA Slam Dunk contest.

The most surprising value pick is Jeff Hornacek. He was selected with the 46th pick in 1986. His six years with the Suns led to a 20.1 scoring average, and he was also a major piece in the trade for Charles Barkley. Hornacek ended every game looking like he had had been beaten up in a street fight. He was tired, bruised and needed rest. This is a testimony to how hard he played the game. In his last season with the Suns, he averaged 20.1 points a game, then he was dealt to the Philadelphia 76ers.

Don't forget Steve Kerr. He was a low draft choice, number 50 in the 1988 draft, but he turned into one of the NBA's best pure shooters. He is also a Suns investor, and for a time he was the general manager. As a player, he had a remarkably long career. He is best known for getting a pass from Michael Jordan and sinking a jump shot to win the Chicago Bull's fifth NBA title in 1997. He won three straight titles with the Bulls, and he had a .454 percentage point rating from three-point range. He worked for the Suns from 2004 to 2010, and then he went back into broadcasting. Despite rumors of bad feelings, he parted company without regrets from the Suns. Every indication is that Kerr and managing partner, Robert Sarver, are still good friends. Kerr is one of the most respected and highest integrity guys in the league. The irony is that Kerr is a well-known Sun's general manager and an esteemed player. What people often forget is that Kerr only played in Phoenix for one year, 1988-1989, averaging 2.1 points a game.

What made Steve Kerr popular was his decision to have the Phoenix Suns wear the Los Suns jerseys in game two of the 2010 playoffs against the San Antonio Spurs. Kerr was critical of the Arizona immigration law and his boss, Robert Sarver, supported him. This took a great deal of courage as most Arizonians supported immigration restrictions. What Kerr is, as is Robert Sarver, is a person who wants justice for everyone. When they wore the Los Suns jerseys, the strong statement from the franchise suggested where the organization stood on the controversial immigration bill. This tells one a great deal about the franchises liberal integrity.

There were three other players that fit into this category. Mark Eaton was drafted with the107th pick in 1979, but he opted to continue his college career. The rules of the draft were different, and he continued to refine his game. Eaton was the 72nd pick in the 1982 draft, and he played eleven seasons for the Utah Jazz. Had the Suns persuaded him to sign, he would have been a serviceable center and backup. He is the only player in NBA history to be drafted twice.

Stephen Jackson, always a talented head case, was drafted 42nd in 1997 but a lack of maturity, a raw talent that was not yet developed forced him to leave the NBA before his career started. He played in the CBA, Australia, Venezuela and the Dominican Republic before beginning an NBA career that has him presently with the San Antonio Spurs. He turned into an All Star, but he is still a head case. Gregg Popovich is presently administering Jackson's head with good results. Next year, who knows?

Jayson Williams was selected with the 21st pick in 1990, and he was adamant about not playing in Phoenix. He was traded to the Philadelphia 76ers where he starred, and he was a 1998 All Star before he was charged with murder. He has written two books that explain his life. The Suns must breathe a sigh of relief, as they look at his potential for trouble in a storied but tragic career. His books suggest that he hasn't learned a thing about life. The books apologize for his mistakes without understanding how his poor decisions and excessive ego ruined his life. He should be featured on a reality TV s program like Basketball Wives. The shows title could be "I'm Almost Seven Foot, So I Don't Have To Follow The Rules."

In many respects, Williams is the poster child for what is wrong with professional sports. In 2010, he pleaded guilty to assault in the shooting death of a limousine driver. He served eight months in prison.

When he was released, he took the Tim Donaghy approach. Donaghy is the NBA referee who threw games. Williams wrote a book **Loose Ball**, which is a humorous recollection of his life. In this book, he talks about loving guns and playing with them. In 2012, when he was released from jail, he authored an autobiography **Humbled**. He blamed his erratic behavior on being abused as a kid. Somewhere Jerry Colangelo is breathing easier. Williams didn't want to come to Phoenix. When he married Kellie Batistste in 1999, she divorced him a year later. He married Tanya in 2000 and they are divorcing. Tanya is a member of the VH 1 TV reality shows Basketball Wives. When you hang out with Barbie barracudas you get eaten alive. Williams would have never made it as a Sun. His gun would have gotten him in trouble.

Peter: "Howard is there a hidden meaning in the above paragraph? Just a thought."

Howard: "Remind me to fire Peter."

The worst Suns draft choice was the infamous, talented, seven footer, William Bedford, who was a sixth round selection in 1986. He turned into a complete bust. He did last for six seasons in the NBA, but it was not a distinguished career. In his defense, Bedford did average 6.7 points a game and 4.9 rebounds, but the Suns could have selected Ron Harper with the same pick. In 1972, Corky Calhoun was selected as the fourth pick in the NBA draft. He was a star at the University of Pennsylvania, and at 6-7 with a deft shooting touch, he looked like a long-term NBA star. He was nothing more than a role player. He spent three years with the Suns before being traded to the Los Angeles Lakers. He signed with the Portland Trail Blazers as a free agent, and he spent his last year with the Indiana Pacers. He managed to spend seven years in the NBA. Calhoun was released in 1980, and he entered the corporate world where he works for Exxon Mobil. He graduated with a marketing degree, and he knows how to sell a product. He is smart, educated and a role player. He was not the fourth best player in the 1972 draft.

The irony is that Calhoun won on an NBA championship team in 1977 with the Bill Walton led Portland Trail Blazers. He also won the Robert V. Geasey Trophy in 1972. This is awarded to the most outstanding basketball player in the Philadelphia Big 5. This is an organization of five colleges and it is a prestigious award. This is amazing as Calhoun averaged 5.3 points a game, 3.6 rebounds and 1.1 assists a game. It was a good career for Calhoun. It was just an awful draft pick. Not for Calhoun, but for the Suns.

THE HOWARD A. DEWITT BEST SUNS DRAFT PICKS, 1968-1980

The Suns did a lot of things right in the draft. Here are the Top DeWitt draft picks from 1968 to 1980. In 1969, Neal Walk was an excellent draft choice. He was 6-10 quick and lean at 220 pounds. He was the second overall pick in the draft, some guy who changed his name was number one, and Walk played until 1977. In five seasons with the Suns, he was in double figures during four of the campaigns. In 1970, UCLA Center Steve Patterson arrived and in his five season the 6-9 center was serviceable. He would have been a star had it not been for knee problems. Patterson is best known as the starting UCLA center between Lew Alcindor and Bill Walton.

Don Buse, who played for the Suns for three seasons, is my next pick because he was one of the few Suns to play defense. He also dated Betsy V. and his active social life didn't decrease his playing time. In 1979, Buse's defense helped the Suns go deep into the playoffs while star players Paul Westphal, Walter Davis, Alvan Adams and Truck Robinson got the publicity. He was a starting guard with the Suns for much of his career. Don Buse was also a mover and shaker with the ladies. He had a disco haircut and with an average of eight to nine points a game, he was a crowd favorite. Betsy V. could be seen smiling in the stands.

Then in 1977, he was selected to the NBA All-Star game. One person called it a fluke. That person was Don Buse. Bill Walton was injured and Buse took his place. In a Cinderella ending, Buse led the West to victory in the All Star game with his passing and defense.

Tim Perry was the number seventh pick in the 1988 draft. He was an average pick for his play, but a great selection as he was included in the trade for Charles Barkley. As a Sun, Perry averaged four points a game in three seasons. With the Philadelphia 76ers, Perry had a break out season averaging 12.3 points a game. The next year he was back to an average performance. The Charles Barkley trade would have been impossible without Perry. The 76ers believed that he was ready for a long career. He was in a mediocre way.

Ron Lee, from the University of Oregon, is my next favorite unknown draft choice. I have a Master's degree in history from the University of Oregon. That clinched his selection. My wife and I lived in the San Francisco Bay Area, and we came down to see our first Suns' game in Lee's rookie year. One of my high-end friends gave us courtside tickets. We met Ron Lee. He landed in my lap during a game. With his bad Afro and my bad mustache, long hair and blue leisure suit I knew we had something in common. Bad hair. Bad clothes. Bad taste. At least Lee could play basketball. In 1976-1977, with Paul Westphal taking all the shots, Ron Lee was a prodigious defender and in 1977-1978 he led the NBA in steals. He was also a community guy, and he had no issues at a time when the NBA was filled with disco guys. He was arguable, after the Van Arsdale's, the Suns most popular player. Oh, he could also play. He did the unthinkable. He played defense. He was also selected tenth in the 1978 NBA draft. He went on to have an eleven-year NBA career followed by three years in Italy, As he nears fifty he is still playing in Sweden.

When he played with the Suns, Lee's nickname "The Tasmanian Devil" came from his constant motion on the court. He remains the University of Oregon's top basketball scorer. He lives in Solna, a beautiful suburb of Stockholm, with his Swedish fiancée and their two children. He loves Swedish meatballs and the local delicacy the shoemaker's box. This is steak with root vegetable and potato's. He is a player/coach for a second division in Skru. Alvan Adams remarked of Lee: "I remember him eating powdered sugar donuts and a Coca Cola for breakfast twenty minutes before practice…." A Phoenix sportswriter observed: "Lee attacks the fame of basketball like Howard Cossell attacks silence."

Stanford University is an elite educational institution. Lately, it has had wonderful football and basketball teams. In 1977, the Suns took Mike Bratz from Stanford in the second round as the sixty-sixth selection. He only spent three years with the Suns, but he was a strong defensive player. He was a great bench guy. Unfortunately, Bratz is remembered as the last person to wear number 23 for the Chicago Bulls. After Bratz, Michael Jordan took the 23 jersey. Bratz has gone on to a career as an NBA executive.

The DeWitt list of great unknowns ends in the late 1970s. Stay tuned. In next years book look for the 1980s and a part of the 1990s. There are so many good draft picks it will take a number of books to laud their accomplishments.

IS KENDALL MARSHALL THE ANSWER?

In 2012, the Suns drafted Kendall Marshall from the University of North Carolina. He is a great passer, he has excellent court vision and he will be a solid back up as a rookie. Is it the right draft choice? Who knows! With a 9.7 assist a game college career, Marshall looks like a sure bet to remain in the NBA. At present he is honing his skills with the Bakersfield Jam. He is averaging ten points and seven assists after four games. When he completed his assignment, Marshall led the D League in assists, he improved his defensive game and he took more shots. The bad news is that he shot just over thirty per cent from the floor, but he played like a first round draft choice. He did come back with a new beard, but that is another story.

The draft gurus gave the Suns a C grade alleging that Marshall is not athletic enough to star at the next level. The claims that he has little lateral quickness put him in the same league with Steve Nash or Jeff Hornacek. About sixteen years ago they said the same thing about Steve Nash. There is one guru who disagreed. In the **USA Today**, Adi Joseph gave the Suns an A plus, and he stated that Marshall has all the tools to be a floor general much like Nash. Time will tell.

Here is what the guru's missed.1.) Marshall is a deadly passer. 2.) He makes excellent decisions. 3.) He has demonstrated repeatedly in his college shot selection, that he knows when, where and how to shoot the ball. He was a 47 per cent shooter his last year at North Carolina. In the NCAA tournament with the pressure on he converted 12 of 15 from the field in two games. 4.) He led the nation in assist to turnover ratio. For the Phoenix Suns, Marshall is the perfect fit. It will take some time.

The problem with Kendall Marshall is that the starting point guard, Goran Dragic, players about thirty minutes a game and Sebastian Telfair is the best back up point guard in the NBA. It will take a season to find room in the rotation for Marshall. The Suns need to sign Telfair to a contract extension, and they also need to find a place for Marshall.

In the early weeks of the 2012-2013 campaign, Marshall was relegated to the bench. As Goran Dragic and Sebastian Telfair logged the major of the minutes, Marshall sat and he learned and listened. It was a tough time for the number thirteen pick in the 2012 NBA draft. The Portland Trail Blazers' point guard, Damian Lilliard, was the sixth pick in the draft, and he is lighting up the NBA. The difference may be as much in opportunity as talent. There is no doubt that Marshall was the second best point guard in the draft.

Coach Alvin Gentry pointed out that it was not fair to compare Marshall with Lilliard. "Kendall is a pure point guard a distributor," Gentry continued. "He's more of an old school point guard....Kendall will be a very good NBA player." It is obvious that Marshall is still the right choice. His time will come.

SOME RANDOM THOUGHTS ON THE DRAFT

The draft is unknown territory. The science of drafting a player is well developed, but it is still an inexact process. What does into the process? At the moment teams send out scouts to colleges, Europe, the minor leagues and to high schools. They return and talk to the scouting director. In the Suns case, they have a University of Kansas psychology professor who devises tests to separate candidates. The results are sometimes great as with Amare Stoudemire, the results are sometimes excellent as with Markieff Morris and sometimes the scouts miss the mark as with D.J. Strawberry or Earl Clark.

The draft process cannot predict drive, intensity or the will to achieve. With moneyball now a concept in the NBA, there is continually striving for the best player for the money. In the Suns case, the majority of these performers come from free agency and not the draft.

Because the draft is an inexact science, it takes time to build a team through free agency.

chapter

SIX

THE NBA STRIKE, THE LOCK OUT AND MY LIFE

DURING AN EARLY OCTOBER MEETING IN MANHATTAN, MICHAEL JORDAN OF THE CHARLOTTE BOBCATS SPARRED WITH WASHINGTON WIZARDS' OWNER ABE POLLIN IN FRONT OF NBA COMMISSIONER DAVID STERN, OTHER OWNERS AND MORE THAN 100 PLAYERS. AFTER AN IMPASSIONED POLLIN, THE LEAGUE'S SENIOR OWNER, TALKED OF HIS STRUGGLE TO KEEP HIS TEAM, JORDAN INTERRUPTED. "IF YOU CAN'T MAKE IT WORK ECONOMICALLY, YOU SHOULD SELL THE TEAM."

The 2011-2012 NBA strike and lockout was responsible for preventing teams from working out their drafted rookies and selected free agents. The Suns drafted Markieff Morris out of Kansas. They loved his game. The Suns had to wait to sign him. This delayed his transformation into a rotation player. This was one of many obstacles that the Suns faced during the NBA lockout.

THE 2011 LOCKOUT

When the NBA lockout took place for 181 days in 2011, it was the fourth time in league history that there was a failure to reach an accord on the NBA's collective bargaining agreement. The season was delayed from November 1 to December 25 until an agreement was reached.

The primary issues separating the owners and the players evolved around the salary cap, the division of revenue and the luxury tax. In other words, it was about money, not working conditions. The National Basketball Players Association, led by Billy Hunter, faced some serious obstacles. The owners claimed that long-term contracts didn't work out. The irony was that the owners didn't recognize that they willingly negotiated and signed these agreements.

The strike impacted the league in a number of ways. The players couldn't workout in their home facilities, the trainers and staffs were not allowed to help the players and the teams could not trade, sign or contact players. It was a total shutdown.

When a tentative agreement was reached on November 28, the owners allowed players to engage in voluntary workouts. The deal was ratified on December 8, and the next day the NBA was back in business with free agency signings, the beginning of a brief two-week training camp, and a strong public relations effort to win back the fans.

THE 2011 NBA LOCKOUT AND STRIKE

July 1, 2011: The lockout begins

September 23, 2011: The NBA canceled training camp, which was to begin October 3, and the first week of preseason games, which were to run October 9 through 15.

October 4, 2011: The NBA canceled the remainder of the preseason.

October 10, 2011: The first two weeks of the regular season canceled.

October 28, 2011: All games through November 30 canceled.

November 14, 2011: The NBPA dissolves labor union and resurrects it into a trade association.

November 15, 2011: The NBA canceled all games through December 15. Players file antitrust lawsuits against the NBA in California and Minnesota federal courts.

November 26, 2011: The NBA owners and players reached a tentative agreement to end the lockout.

December 1, 2011: The NBPA re-formed as a union.

December 8, 2011: The new CBA is ratified, officially ending the lockout.

WHAT WAS THERE TO TALK ABOUT DURING THE LOCKOUT?

There wasn't much to talk about during the lockout so the media gurus and those in the press had to search long and hard for topics. The fans learned things that were both unimportant and trivial. The Phoenix press scrutinized the Suns first round draft choice Markieff Morris.

The NBA gurus and talking heads on ESPN wondered why the Suns didn't take Morris' brother in the draft. The answer was obvious. Markieff is a power forward and his brother is a small forward. After visiting Phoenix prior to the lockout, Morris left for Los Angeles to work out with former NBA player Pooh Richardson. Why Pooh Richardson? The reason is a simple one. Richardson was one of the great defenders during his decade long pro career. Pooh also had some ideas about taking the three point shot. No one even considered that Morris would have some brilliant three-point moments.

No one realized that Morris was doing something special in Los Angeles. He was learning to shoot three pointers. He was developing his already formidable defensive skills, and he was learning the Sun's system.

THE SUNS OPTIONS DURING THE NBA LOCKOUT

The main concern with the NBA lockout was that free agency was delayed. Normally the free agent process begins on July 1. However, the strike put an end to the traditional wooing of free agents.

As the strike and lockout continued the Suns had to figure out how not to go over the $70 million luxury tax. It didn't seem to be a problem, as they had a payroll well under the cap. As the 2011-2012 season approached, the Suns had nine players under guaranteed contracts? Those without guaranteed agreements Garret Siler, Gani Lawal and Zabian Dowdell were soon gone. The total payroll appeared to be about $57 million. Then the Suns decided to bring Grant Hill back and this brought their payroll to $60 million. Over his years with the Suns, Hill was underpaid, but he was appreciated and honored by the franchise.

After the 2011-2012 season concluded, Suns management realized, before the season began, that they had two high priced players they needed to move. After the season concluded Hakim Warrick was traded to New Orleans and Josh Childress was let go using the amnesty clause in the Collective Bargaining Agreement.

The 2011-2012 campaign was not a good one for signing new Suns' free agents. At least not high profile ones. When the Suns failed to pursue some of the available free agents there was concern. Michael Redd was signed during the season, but he was a much-injured player who was once an All Star. He turned out fine.

The Suns were a team in transition as the 2011-2012 season opened. They did get rid of some dead wood sending Vince Carter packing and avoiding his mammoth contract. The Hedo Turkoglu mistake was recognized, and he was traded to the Orlando Magic. Mickael Pietrus was another player who couldn't fit into the Suns system, and he was off to greener pastures. No pun intended. He eventually helped the Boston Celtics in their failed drive to the NBA finals.

What is obvious is that the Suns were planning for the 2012-2013 season. In retrospect, they were looking to change the roster. It worked. After a 33-33 record in the strike shortened 2011-2012 season, they were ready to blow up the roster. They did. This is the reason that free agency was a relative quiet period. The Suns were looking to the future.

When the strike ended Robert Sarver and Lon Babby looked at an aging and often stagnant roster. They vowed to remake the team. They failed to tell Dan Bickley and Paul Coro and the **Arizona Republic** reporters roasted them for much of the summer and fall of 2012. Time will tell if the new roster works out.

BEFORE THE LOCK OUT: WHAT THE LEAGUE CLAIMED

In early 2011, the league argued that it was losing $300 million a year and they claimed that twenty-two were losing money. They proposed a 40% reduction in player's salaries. The NBA moneymen knew that the players wouldn't agree to this ridiculous demand. They were paving the way for a lockout and prolonged negotiations.

The players union, led by Billy Hunter, challenged the statistics. In May 2011, the National Basketball Players' Association filed a complaint with the National Labor Relations Board. The war began. NBA owners wanted a forty five million dollar hard salary cap per team, as opposed to the soft cap of fifty eight million.

The May and June negotiations produced no results. Then the owners proposed a flexible salary cap. The players responded by offering a five hundred million dollar salary reduction over five years and they offered to have their take of the revenue reduced to 54.3%. None of this worked and a lockout took place.

THE LOCKOUT AND THE RESULTS

The main problem with the NBA lockout was the perception that the players were taking too much of the pie. Maybe this was true. Maybe not! The media word was that the players were greedy. The owners developed some sympathy from the fans. This was a unique trend. Most of the time, no one cared about the owners. What followed was a one hundred forty nine day lockout. When it ended the strike produced some interesting results.

The NBA owners clearly were the winners in the new labor agreement. There is now a 50-50-revenue split, while under the old deal the players received 57% of the revenue. The concessions granted the owners were more than $300 million a year under the new contract. This is the sum of money that the owners claimed that they lost each year. There were also shorter guaranteed contracts, a lower salary cap and restrictions on the wealthier teams overspending for players. The rookie contracts were worth less.

The prolonged contract negotiations forced unsigned and drafted rookies to take out loans during the lockout. Reggie Jackson drafted from Boston College by the Oklahoma City Thunder explained: "While most veteran players have had their paychecks suspended, they at least have, or should have, some kind of coin in reserve."

There were also concessions to the fans. The labor agreement is for ten years. This makes it easier for owners to competitively price seats. The labor agreement provides for no strikes, no labor lockouts and no interruptions in the schedule. In this ten-year contract, there are specific guarantees for the players that will avoid future labor disagreements. At least this is the theory. This is not bad for the hardcore fan. The average salary for an NBA player is $5.15 million dollars a season. Major league baseballs average is $3.31 million, the National Hockey League average is $2.4 million and the National Football League average is $1.9 million. So the NBA players will not have to apply for food stamps anytime soon.

The 2011 NBA lockout is the fourth in league history. The division of revenue and the salary cap modifications were the key issues, and they were solved apparently without rancor. Or so it appears. The fans were worn out and ready for the season.

But not all was well with the strike. The NBA players association was divided about the deal. As late as mid-November, it appeared that there would not be a season. On November 15, 2011 NBA Commissioner David Stern and NBA Player Executive Director, Billy Hunter, met and agreed to disagree. That is they could only agree on one thing, and that was that the season was in jeopardy. Commissioner Stern is not popular among Phoenix Suns fans for suspending Amare Stoudemire and Boris Diaw during the 2007 playoffs. It took Stern almost five years to sneak back into the U.S. Airways Center. He came unnoticed with bodyguards, and he wasn't announced as a visitor. He wasn't bothered. The Suns' fans are forgiving.

In 2012, when Stern met with Suns Managing Partner, Robert Sarver, they spent two hours discussing the season. Stern told Sarver that the increase in TV ratings was a critical factor in the popularity of the NBA game aboard. One wonders what Sarver thought. He is an intelligent businessman and a caring owner. Stern is a self-serving bureaucrat with a smooth personality. He is not a disingenuous man. He simply enforces the rules. They are his rules, his game and the league enforcement officer is a former player, Stu Jackson. He makes sure that players follow league guidelines in dress and deportment. There is no deviation from league policy. These rules cost the Suns a trip to the NBA finals a few years ago, but that is another story.

WHAT PHOENIX SUNS PLAYERS DID DURING THE LOCKOUT

Steve Nash spent the lockout going to the gym and working out. He also spent a lot of time in the Paradise Bakery eating a salad for lunch with his twin girls. His parents live in Gainey Ranch, and he was able to indulge his creative passion. That is to watch and help with the progress of his major league soccer team, the Vancouver Whitecaps. Not only did Nash practice with this soccer team, but also he was able to give advice on the future. As a part owner, Nash is looking to make the Canadian franchise a major league soccer power.

Grant Hill stayed in shape, increased his African American art collection, listened to his wife's CDs, played with his children and appeared in community charity events. Perhaps Hill's toughest job was to provide Jalen Rose with the ability to explain his actions without sounding gratuitous. Now that Hill is gone to the Los Angeles Clippers, he will be missed. Working for Donald Sterling will not be easy. Grant Hill is the player who can pull it off while making Sterling look good.

Sebastian Telfair was back in New York working on his three point shot and his defense. He is a tough street kid whose career appeared to be on the down side until he joined the Suns. He learned the D work.

Defense. He became an excellent backup point guard. He worked hard on his game and took it to a new level. He also spent time raising money for New York's Lincoln High School, where he is a legend. He talked a lot about playing poker with his brother. My thought is that Robert Sarver needs to up his pay; I suspect his brother won most of those games. Don't tell David Stern, he might want to get into the game. Or he might want to suspend Telfair for winning or maybe losing.

Not only is Telfair one of the more underrated players in the NBA, he has shown in Phoenix that he has a high basketball IQ. The best is yet to come from Telfair's game.

The NBA strike and lockout compressed the schedule to sixty-six games in one hundred and twenty three days. The compressed schedule with more back-to-back games and heavy travel led to more player injuries. The schedule demonstrated that while the fans were loyal, they did have a breaking point. The NBA constantly trotted out doctors who claimed that the rash of injuries had little, if anything, to do with the compact schedule. The truth is that there were too many games in too few days. Don't tell NBA Commissioner David Stern. He is a constant cheerleader for the game. He should be with his salary.

WEIRD TALES FROM THE NBA LOCKOUT

The NBA lockout had many strange twists and turns. On September 29, 2011 it was reported that Kobe Bryant signed a ten game $3 million deal to play in Italy with Virtus Bologna. It was a story that had little merit, but the upside was that the next day serious discussions began among the players and owners.

The July 1 lockout led to bad feelings on both sides and months of charges and counter charges of greed and unfairness. Finally, on October 1, there was some consensus as both sides agreed after a seven-hour meeting that compromise was essential. It was a nice thought, but it didn't materialize. By the end of October, lengthy meetings brought little progress to end the lockout. Then Commissioner David Stern canceled all games through November 30.

The star players became increasingly involved. On November 8, Carmelo Anthony and Blake Griffin were part of a forty-three-player group that met to discuss the owner's proposal. They rejected it. The players were asked to accept 47% of the revenue whereas in the past they had as much as 57%. There were threatened lawsuits and hard feelings persisted.

Finally, on November 25-26, NBA owners and the players reached a tentative agreement to end the one hundred and forty nine day lockout. By December 8, the owners and players ratified a ten-year collective bargaining agreement, and the season was scheduled to begin. The agreement provided a 50-50 split of basketball related income, a higher luxury tax and a soft salary cap. The maximum length of player contracts was five years, where it previously had been six. David Stern remarked: "This collective bargaining agreement will help us move toward a better business model, a more competitive league and better alignment between compensation and performance."

Peter: "How did you spell bullshit." Remind me to fire Peter.

LOSERS AND WINNERS UNDER THE NBA AGREEMENT

What impact did the lockout and strike have upon the league? One of the changes is that free agents may not have the same market value or flexibility in signing contracts. When Channing Frye signed a $30 million dollar deal for five years, it was good for both sides. Under the new agreement, Frye would sign a three-year contract. He might or might not make more money in the remaining years. In other words players may not get the same long-term contracts.

A victory for the players in the new agreement is that teams must pay a minimum salary that is ten percent higher than in the previous year. There is more money available for lower tier players. The impact is to equalize salaries, or at least increase them, for the ninth to twelfth men on the active roster.

The NBA hopes to make it easier for the less competitive teams to add bench strength. If the top free agents sign with the best teams that means that the Miami Heat, the Los Angeles Lakers, the New York Knicks and the Dallas Mavericks have a competitive edge. The notion is that the new collective bargaining agreement helps to balance the talent. This is, in many ways, a specious argument.

Many of the players approve the new collective bargaining agreement because it allows them to live and work where they desire. There are also some other provisions. The amnesty clause allows teams to waive players. They must still be paid, and they can sign somewhere else. The notion is that their skills will develop playing and not on the bench. When the Suns exercised their amnesty rights on Josh Childress, he signed with the Brooklyn Nets.

When the Suns released Childress two years into a five year $33.5 million contact the money no longer counted against the salary cap.

While Childress was paid the Suns saved over $21 million dollars over the next three years. Childress commented: "I'm not upset at all…It's part of the business and now I'm just looking forward to my next opportunity…." Always the consummate professional, Childress left with good wishes, and he will help another team.

The new rules in the NBA agreement allow a team to dump a salary under the amnesty clause. The player is still owed the money but it doesn't count against the cap. When a player is released, under the amnesty clause, teams can bid on him. When the Suns acquired Luis Scola, released by the Houston Rockets, they put in a 3.3 million dollar bid, and they were awarded Scola. Both sides were winners. The Rockets dumped a contract, and the Suns signed a big man. Win! Win!

chapter

SEVEN

HILARIOUS SUNS FAN TALES: SOME NOT SO HILARIOUS

"THE PHOENIX SUNS ARE MORE IMPORTANT TO ME THAN MY WIFE AND MY DOG, WELL AT LEAST MY WIFE," A SUNS FAN IN DIVORCE COURT

The level of strange and hilarious tales in professional sports knows no bounds. The fans loyalty makes them a special breed. They react strongly to any attack on the Suns. The support for their team is unequivocal. They often worship their team. In a sports bar another team's shirt will at times lead to derisive hoots. Or perhaps even to a fistfight.

There is no better description of this behavior than when the Phoenix Suns mascot, the Gorilla, went to Dave and Buster's a local Phoenix video game-eating emporium. While mingling with the crowd, the Gorilla began to give the fans high fives. When the Gorilla approached Timothy Austin, this Miami Heat fan refused the high five. When the Gorilla playfully and lightly kicked Austin, the young man punched the

Gorilla in the face. The good news is that the Gorilla, Robert Woolf, is not the same Gorilla who performs at games. I breathed a deep sigh of relief, my Gorilla was safe and I couldn't believe Austin's stupidity. The police arrived and they determined that both men could be charged with assault. The police were trying not to laugh and the incident ended.

THE REALLY STRANGE FAN TALES

Stupid fan reactions are not confined to the games. In Gilbert, Arizona, a Phoenix suburb, the police were called when a domestic incident took place when a man pulled a gun on his girl friend, because she had misplaced his season ticket renewal form. This fool probably didn't have a phone, and he didn't know he could get a replacement form. He is no longer with his girl friend. Rumor has it; he is purchasing Los Angeles Clipper tickets.

Perhaps the strangest Phoenix Suns fans are those who shout obscenities and wear a t-shirt that reads: F**K KOBE. But Phoenix Suns' fans also go after Tim Duncan. Can't figure out why. Tim is a solid citizen, he is a great player, and he beats the Suns. Even if Duncan walks on half his offensive possessions, while complaining to the referee constantly; he is still a marquee player. He is a great player. He needs to smile once in a while.

One of the best stories is a divorce case. The husband of fifty years left the wife for a younger partner. The wife didn't care. Then came the question of the tickets. The wife wanted them and the husband desired them. The wife asked: "How does you new girl friend feel?" The husband answered: "What girl friend? I have a partner." The wife screamed at him. "We are going to Court." The husband was so irate that he told the judge his wife had breast enhancements. "Do I also get one of the breasts in the divorce decree? She has no right to half my tickets." The Judge awarded each party half a season. The smile on the Judge's face told all one needed to know about obsessive fans.

One of the strangest season ticket stories took place when a couple from Albuquerque, New Mexico bought season tickets two years before they moved to Phoenix. They sold separate tickets when they could, and when they finally moved to Scottsdale, the husband died. The wife spent one season sitting with an empty seat. This was in the days of Charles Barkley.

The tales of fan stupidity are legendary. Here are some of my favorites. The guy who talks on his cell phone the whole game. The guy who asks for free tickets because the Suns aren't winning. The guy who eats half a hot dog, that is the dollar hot dog, then he takes it back and asks for the ten dollar hot dog. "My time is worth something," the fan bellows. They give it to him. The guy who spills his drink at the inside bar after downing two thirds of his drink; he also gets a free refill. Why do women never do these stupid things? It is only men. I have a friend who is a master of the freebee, he could learn from these folks.

In the restaurants around the arena, there is a fan that goes into each eatery to have a meal. He tells the waiter it is his birthday, when he takes his wife, it is his wedding anniversary, when he has a buddy they are celebrating their survival in the Vietnam War. Who wouldn't be nice to Vietnam vets? They get a ticket to park to eat in Kincaid's restaurant, and then they park with the Suns season ticket holders. These two guys, Harvey and Lou, are adept at the freebee. They go to Whole Foods and purchase one sandwich. They divide the sandwich and take it back. They complain that it is not properly seasoned. Whole Foods gives them two sandwiches and they sneak them into the arena. They order two drinks and spill the last quarter and they get a free drink. Does this explain why Robert Sarver is occasionally testy?

Big Boy Roberts, this is a fictional character, but his story is real. It began in the 2010-2011 season as a first time season ticket holder at age sixty. Big Boy Roberts was retired and he lives in Patagonia Arizona. When he arrived in Phoenix, he purchased a home in Gainey Ranch in the Estates. These are fancy multi-million dollar homes. Then Big Boy started attending the games. He got the flu one night and he decided to sell his ticket. It was for a Los Angeles Lakers game. For his $125 tickets he received $225. Suddenly Big Boy became an entrepreneur. He sold 20 of 41 home games for a grand total of $4000. He paid six thousand for the season tickets. Then in the 2012 season, Big Boy Roberts stood outside the arena, near Legend's, and he became a ticket broker. This is a nice phrase for a scalper. So you want tickets go to the corner near Legends and ask for Big Boy. Remind him that he lives in a million dollar home in Scottsdale's plush Gainey Ranch. He will tell you to mind your own business.

Boris "Rob" Krueger, known as B. R., is a dedicated Suns fan. He is not a season ticket holder, but he purchases ten to twelve game tickets from the scalpers. He runs one of the higher end Scottsdale bakeries and coffee shops. I should call it a gourmet bagel place, but that would ignore the rest of a great menu. It is an independent bakery that Alvin Gentry and other Suns frequent. B. R. is a quiet fan. He has a buddy who gives him upgrades, and he attends only the Los Angeles Lakers, the Los Angeles Clippers, the Chicago Bulls, Houston Rockets, the New Orleans Hornets, the Miami Heat, the Golden State Warriors and the New York Knicks games. He is a strange fan. I asked him "B. R. that doesn't add up to ten games." B. R. responded: "What are you stupid?" "How am I stupid?" B. R. was perplexed: "The Western Conference teams come in twice and I sit next to owner Robert Sarver, a $200 scalper ticket." Sarver is a nice guy and he actually talked to B. R. " What did Sarver say to you?" I asked B. R. He responded: "He thinks that he is practicing moneyball, I hollered at him and told Sarver to look up Billy Beane. He knows about moneyball" What does Sarver say to you? "Have a nice day."

THE SUBURBS OF PHOENIX TALES

Paradise Valley is the richest suburb in the Phoenix area. It makes Scottsdale look like Los Angeles' Central District. In Paradise Valley, a couple that has been married fifty years filed for divorce. Irreconcilable differences. It happens. The divorce headed for the courts, and then the issue of Suns' season tickets came up. The couple had first row seats in the same section as owner Robert Sarver. To make a long story short, they stayed married. They solved their problems a simple way. The couple bought the home next door. The wife lives there and the husband, a former music executive in Los Angeles, lives in their primary home. The music mogul bought a third house. The three homes sit side by side. The middle one is filled with Suns' memorabilia. Rumor is that they are adding a Steve Nash room with a throne to go with the Charles Barkley room. One wonders if the trade ended the Nash memorabilia throne. They still go to the games together. They claim the Suns solved all their marital problems. So now Robert Sarver is a marriage counselor!

Queen's Creek is to the East of the Phoenix area. It is a lovely, if somewhat strange, area for a wide variety of reasons. It is also the home to a lot of old folks. That is the snowbirds that troop in about November and leave in April. There are some hilarious Phoenix Sun tales from Queens Creek. This is a beautiful location in the San Tan Foothills, and it is the perfect residence for those afflicted with the mobile home disease. The first tale involves a $225,000 mobile home. We used to call them trailers. There are also no more trailer parks they are now called mobile home retirement communities. Jim and Alice purchased a mobile home and bought some land on North Thompson Road in Queen's Creek. They spent ten years watching Suns games, and they retired to their 2003 luxury mobile home. Then disaster struck. Jim went off to

Scottsdale, met one of the local Barbie's, got divorced and moved in with a woman ten years his junior. As his divorce wove its way through the court, it was held up by the question of who would get the Suns' season tickets? They couldn't decide. Finally the decision was made to have joint custody of the tickets. Am I missing something? Joint custody of the tickets!

Roger is an advertising executive. He spends days thinking up slogans for milk. He is also an inveterate bar fly. That is he loves Happy Hour in and around Phoenix. Scottsdale is his favorite Happy Hour destination, and he is seen at the Camelback Inn trolling for young ladies. Roger is thirty-five, handsome, well dressed, and he has five sports cars. He is also a Suns' season ticket holder. He met Connie at Downside Risk, a sports bar in Scottsdale, as he stood at the crowded bar. Connie played basketball for the University of Arizona women Wildcats. She is five years older than Roger and twenty years more intelligent. They began dating. She is a cougar. That is she likes younger men. She also loves the Phoenix Suns, and she has tickets in Section 224. Roger has seats in section 100. His seats are more desirable. Roger fell in love with Connie. They dated for five months and the 2012-2013 season was about to begin when Connie presented Roger with a contract. He would sit in her seats in section 224, and she would sit in his seats in section 100. I could only guess what the contract stipulated. Roger happily agreed to it. They have a happy, healthy (no this is not about sex) and full social life. In 2012, Roger proposed to Connie. She is thinking it over. She said yes if he purchased seats in the third or fourth row. He is currently thinking over her proposal. There is a pre-nuptial agreement. Then he told her that he couldn't spend $24,000 for the seats that she wanted. He continues sitting in section 224, while she is in section 100. She said that they had to postpone the wedding. He agreed. It is not easy to get a Cougar to get married and Roger tells anyone who will listen, it is due to the Phoenix Suns season tickets. The good thing is that Connie sits near me. She is a babe.

Amanda is an eighty-year-old grandmother. She sits in the upper deck. She and her husband, Bill, have been season ticket holders since day one. He died five years ago. She continues to go to the games. At times she takes friends. When no one is available, she puts a picture of Bill on the seat next to her. She vows to keep both seats until the day that she dies. Her doctor told her that was going to be for a long time. She was recently seen at Costco getting a large life size picture of her husband. The extra seat makes her happy. "I think Bob is still with me," she remarked. I reminded her husband's name was Bill. She said: "Whatever."

Suns season tickets often pass from one family member to another, and there is seldom any disagreement. Not always. A few years ago as the will was read, the youngest son contested it. After the will was read and each family member understood it, the will was still contested. The house in Paradise Valley would be sold and the proceeds distributed to the four kids. The wife died a few years before the husband and her jewelry was divided amongst the wives. The Suns' season tickets went through an arbitrator who awarded the son 25% of the tickets, and the rest sold last year on the Suns website.

TALES OF FANS FROM OUT OF TOWN

Jim and Alice live in Prescott. He is a retired lawyer, and she is a retired high school history teacher. They love to come to Phoenix. They can't make all forty-one home games. They plan for twenty and gift the tickets for the remainder to their kids, their friends and sometimes to a charity. They are robust Suns fans. They are fans that on their seventieth birthdays made a change in their will. It has been a decade, and the couple is now entering their eighties. They left their Suns season tickets to their two dogs. The lawyer has a provision to allow the dogs to keep the seats for one year after their death. Does this mean the dogs go to the games? There is no more to this story, but stay tuned.

The fans that come to Phoenix Suns games from out of town are many and they have legendary tales. From Bisbee Arizona, Joe comes up for one game a year. He gets into his rental car on Bisbee's Mountain View Avenue, this is the street where he has lived for forty-seven years, and he says a short prayer. He was once a Buddhist Monk, and now he is a retired philosophy professor. Before he drives to Phoenix for the game, there is a search for tickets. He goes on the Internet and he purchases two of the best seats. In 2012, he spent $500 on the tickets; he stayed where the visiting players luxuriously reside in the Biltmore area of Phoenix. The hotel, the Ritz Carlton, cost Joe another $295. That is with his AARP discount. Then it was off to dinner at Kincaid's. He always orders steak and lobster and during the game he has two beers and a snack. He goes down to the bar for two double Scotch and waters. The food and bar bill comes to over two hundred dollars. Then the next morning it is back to Bisbee in the rental car. The rental car and gas is another $75. I asked Joe: "Is this a bargain?" He responds: "This is an experience you can only get in one place." I forgot to mention that he purchases about $250 worth of Suns shirts and memorabilia each year. For just under a thousand dollars, Joe considers the Phoenix Suns a bargain. That's just for one game.

TALES OF SUNS FANS FROM OUT OF STATE

Basketball fans are a strange lot. Those who are truly fanatics will follow their team anywhere. In Albuquerque, New Mexico there is a Suns' fan that is not a season ticket holder. Yet, he attends at least half of the home games. He wears all the Suns t-shirts; he is a visible presence in the arena with specially made t-shirts showing pictures of the Suns. He also purchases the team jerseys. He works as a real estate agent. He has only been a Suns fan for two years. He brought some clients from Vancouver, British Columbia to Scottsdale to purchase some condominiums. One of the Canadians was a Memphis Grizzly fan. The Grizzlies were for a time situated in Vancouver. So the real estate agent took them to a game. They loved it. He was hooked. For two years he deducted his Suns games as a business expense. Guess what? The IRS came calling. He lost the battle. He purchased Suns' season tickets, and he challenged the IRS ruling and won.

Angelo is sixty. He has slicked back hair, he purchases ten games a year and he comes to Phoenix from Hammond, Indiana. He lives on 137th street in Hammond in a brick house that his parents bought in 1948. If you could find a person who looks like a mobster sent from central casting, it is Angelo. Why does he come every year for ten Suns' games? The answer is that he loves a local gentlemen's club Babe's. In the 2012 season he purchased ten seats near the floor at $225 a ticket. After four games, he was tired of the first part of the season. The Suns weren't winning, and he was getting weary of travel. The last six games had two of the best looking young ladies coming to the Suns' games. One wonders is Angelo coming back during the next season?

Milo is a Suns' fanatic. He is an airline pilot, he is single, he is forty, and he is a consummate ladies man. He is not a season ticket holder, but he has a distinction that few fans can match. He brings the best looking young ladies to a game and they provide the tickets. They are all blonde and the live in Scottsdale. I have no other information but next year's book will have the goods on Milo. He also looks like Brad Pitt. Stay tuned.

Carmel California is an Oceanside town next to Monterey. Hal is a Suns season ticket holder who flies in for at least thirty of the forty-one games. He is also writing a book on cheeseburgers. He boasts that he has dinner before each game at a different Phoenix restaurant. He always orders the same thing, a cheeseburger with fries. This turned out to be a problem at a couple of high-end Scottsdale resort restaurants that don't have cheeseburgers on the menu. When Hal went into the Camelback Inn, he wandered into the wrong restaurant. The matre'd informed him that they did not have a cheeseburger. Hal said bring him a ground chuck steak, a piece of cheese and two pieces of bread. He made his own cheeseburger. At another restaurant they now have a Hal Burger. He keeps a notebook describing each hamburger, the restaurant and he rates each cheeseburger one to thirty. He is finishing a book **Cheeseburgers In Paradise Valley**, Jimmy Buffet's legal team has filed a cease and desist order. And I thought that I was weird.

Howard: "Claude, what do you think of my analysis."

Claude: "Are you nuts? I can't go back to El Sereno because I know you."

Peter: "Who cares, the guy with the cheeseburger sounds like you. A person with no life."

The Suns fans are not only fanatics but, like the owner, they are civic minded. You have a group of people who love the Suns, and they could care less what anyone else thinks.

Perhaps the most intelligent, incisively critical and handsome young man from Medfield Massachusetts is Sidney Glick. He is thirty-five years old, and he has been a Boston Celtics fan for thirty years. Sidney said: "I am the number one Boston Celtics Jewish fan. I even take my rabbi to road games." The truth is that Sidney's wife won't let him go to any Celtics games on Friday, so he flies his rabbi to Phoenix with the idea of going to the services. Somehow he always seems to wind up at the Suns game. On Friday, Sidney says so long to his wife for services but he is really going to a Celtics game. On Friday night women are generally do not attend services in the Synagogue. Here is where it gets strange. Sidney's friend often sees him in Logan Airport on early Friday afternoon. The Boston Celtics are out of town and Sidney is off to a Synagogue in another city. There is a rumor that he also attends the Celtics' road games.

As he was traveling to Logan Airport, a friend hollered: "Sidney you are going to miss the service."

Sidney: "No, No, I am off to Phoenix. I have business there but I will be in the synagogue. I need to worship in the Valley of the Sun."

That night Sidney was seen at courtside watching the Suns. He was sitting a row behind owner Robert Sarver. Outside the U. S. Airways Arena a scalper looked very happy.

The next weekend Sidney was in Chicago for services but he was spotted at a Celtics-Bulls game. He is famous in his sports bar for his travels. That night in Medfield, Massachusetts, the local sports bar, the Noon Hill Grill, was the scene of a raucous crowd cheering" "Sidney, Sidney, Sidney." Finally, a patron walked over and asked: "Who in the hell is Sidney?" The waiter looked at the television and there stood Sidney in his Celtics shirt. "That's our Sidney," Bill said. When Sidney returned to the Noon Hill Grill, the owner sent free drinks to the table. It was an iced tea as Sidney doesn't drink. His only vice is paying big bucks for tickets to a Celtics road game. He often takes the local rabbi. "I am a religious man first, and a Celtics fan when they are in Phoenix," Sidney remarked. Then he returns and people ask him about the free iced teas at the Noon Hill Grill. Sidney had the last word: "Those free drinks only cost me nine hundred dollars."

Tom Ambrose's book **WACKO! Files And Tales From the Madhouse On McDowell** is a mirthful look at the Suns by a thirty-seven year employee. When Garfield Heard made the marvelous shot against the Boston Celtics in the 1976 NBA finals, Ambrose was sitting near announcer Al McCoy. A fan passed out in McCoy's lap as the announcer continued to call the game.

One of Ambrose's best tales is when Kareem Abdul Jabbar pinned the Gorilla against a wall and threatened him if he said anything. The humor behind this tale is that the Gorilla doesn't talk. As Ambrose concluded his book. he suggested that the "Madhouse on McDowell" was not only raucous but also fun.

MR ORNG: THE UTLIMATE FAN

By day Patrick Battillo is a quiet, unassuming, shy marketing director for Target. Then basketball season starts and he dyes his hair orange, he douses himself with orange body paint, and he comes to the games as Mr. Orng. He is normal. When you talk to him, he is self-effacing but he is the ultimate Suns fan.

The character known as Mr. Orng was born in 2006-2007 when the Suns were running deep into the playoffs. He travels to ten games a year, and he comes to the visiting arenas as Mr. Orng. "I haven't had any trouble from the fans, but the Chicago Bulls mascot, Benny the Bull, sprayed me with two cans of confetti. I had a back to back and I was in New York the next night as Mr. Orng with confetti."

The players love Mr. Orng and they go out of their way to talk to him. "Steve Nash was always supportive of me and I got to hang out with him." Hey that is reason alone to be Mr. Orng. In terms of Suns fans, Mr. Orng, he is a normal fan. He is on Twitter, he has a web site and he is accessible. Talk to him, e-mail him, text him and you will be in for a treat. He knows the game better than anyone except my wife, and he is a passionate Suns fan. He is also normal, despite the orange body paint.

The Suns are a team that inspires fan loyalty. Stay tuned. Next year will include some of the best, if strangest, Suns' fans tales.

Claude: "Howard, You nailed it. The Suns' are a great team and the Gorilla has more fun than you do. Maybe you need a life."

Peter: "Claude, the Gorilla looks, dresses and acts better than Howard."

chapter

EIGHT

THE ALLEGED WEASAL WHO COST THE SUNS A TRIP TO THE NBA FINALS: THE TIM DONAGHY SCANDAL

"I'M NOBODY TO JUDGE ANYONE." TIM DONAGHY

Tim Donaghy was a veteran NBA referee who was investigated by the FBI, convicted of calling fouls that were non-existent to help gamblers, and he was sent to prison. The irony is that Donaghy didn't see himself as doing anything wrong. He didn't believe that he was fixing games. He was simply providing gamblers additional information. When he was informed that one of his business associates, Danny Biancullo, was convicted in 2004 in a Federal Court, Donaghy replied, "As long as it wasn't molesting kids." Donaghy continued, "I'm nobody to judge anyone." Timmy needs to go to college, and take an English course. He also needs to learn that the truth is not a country in Eastern Europe.

On July 20, 2007 **New York Post** columnist Murray Weiss reported that the FBI was investigating allegations of a corrupt NBA referee. Soon it was revealed that the investigation centered on a thirteen-year NBA referee, Tim Donaghy. It was rumored that he had a gambling problem.

THE PHOENIX SUNS AND THE WEASAL REFEREE

In 2007, the Phoenix Suns were on a roll. Coach Mike D'Antoni's team finished 61-21 and won the Pacific Coast Western Division. They beat the Los Angeles Lakers four games to one in the first playoff series, and then they lost to the San Antonio Spurs in the conference semifinals.

The Suns were the best team in the NBA in the spring of 2007. Donaghy says that they were unbeatable. He does have a point. When the Spurs beat the Suns in 2007, Donaghy claimed that the other referees were steering the series in San Antonio's favor. He cited Robert Horry's hit on Steve Nash as proof that his bogus calls weren't the only reason for the Suns' loss. Donaghy commented to a **New York Times** reporter that his actions were: "No different than Wall Street insider trading." He continued: "Except I didn't affect the economy." These are sad comments as integrity and the willingness to admit you have committed a crime are not part of Donaghy's personality. The irony is that when he went to prison some of the inmates screamed; "Rat! Rat! Rat!" And then he was whacked on the knee with a long handled paint roller. He needed an operation, and he paid for it himself. It is alleged that the check was written on a Grand Cayman Island account to pay for the operation.

How good were the 2006-2007 Suns? They were virtually unbeatable with Amare Stoudemire averaging twenty plus points a game, Steve Nash chipping in eighteen plus and Leandro Barbosa coming off the bench to average eighteen points. Shawn Marion's seventeen points a game and. Raja Bell's almost fifteen points a game provided a defense-scoring tandem. They fit beautifully into the Suns' run and gun and shoot in seven seconds offensive system. Bell embraced and celebrated Mike D'Antoni's coaching philosophy. The Suns seemed destined for the NBA finals. It didn't work out. Why? A weasel was in the works. His name was Tim Donaghy, and he was an NBA referee. He also became a convicted felon who he went to jail. He influenced NBA games. He helped gamblers. He confessed. He accepted a plea bargain. Now why would I label this guy a weasel? The answer is a simple one. In all his confessional diatribes, Tim Donaghy has never accepted the full blame for his behavior. It is the NBA's fault, it is the other referees fault, it is David

Stern's fault, and it is the gamblers fault. This is why Big Boy Roberts suggested that "he is an alleged little greasy haired weasel."

Peter: "What do you mean alleged weasel?" Remind me to fire Peter.

ANDREW THOMAS: HE GOT IT RIGHT

Andrew Thomas, the former Maricopa County District Attorney, was a voice of reason in the scandal. Thomas pointed out that there were two games in the 2007 season that he believed that Donaghy influenced. The games that Thomas alleged that Donaghy shaped were two road playoff games. In a letter to commissioner David Stern and FBI director Robert Mueller, Thomas alleged that Donaghy's conduct might have violated Arizona criminal law. Thomas also had evidence.

Nothing came of Thomas' charges. There was little press attention paid to Thomas' allegations. After Thomas made his charges against Donaghy, he faced a state probe for abuse of power. Thomas lost the probe. In 2012, when the Arizona Ethics Panel disbarred Thomas, his complaint remained an obscure one. Had Thomas not had his own legal difficulties, one wonders how state charges against Donaghy might have progressed.

As Thomas pointed out, Donaghy became known as "the rogue ref, the fixer ref, the disgraced ref, the ratted out ref," but to hear Donaghy tell it he didn't do anything wrong.

TIM DONAGHY IN HIS OWN WORDS: HOW DO YOU SPELL WEASAL?

Tim Donaghy wrote a book about his criminal activity. Eventually, he sued the publisher, and he won a 1.3 million dollar judgment. They failed to publish the book and live up to the contractual agreement. With the money he was awarded, Donaghy self-published his memoir. When his book **Personal Foul: A First Person Account of the Scandal That Rocked The NBA** came out the sales were at best mediocre. That said it tells us a great deal about Donaghy. Most of which you wouldn't want to know or you would really see what a little weasel he is in all aspects of his life.

He informs the reader that he had a secret life for four years and it ruined his career. (p. xv) Is this guy self-indulgent? No, he is a narcissistic personality. He breaks the law, he blames other people and he talks of mingling with Spike Lee and Jack Nicholson. But his life is ruined. Wake up Tim! Who ruined your life? You did! Donaghy n about integrity, responsibility, ethics or honesty. He is still trying to look up those words in the dictionary.

He began his road to fixing games through friendship with James "Ba Ba" Battista and Tommy Martino. They were old high school friends. Tim's buddy "Ba Ba" was heavily into gambling. It wasn't long before Donaghy was betting. He considered himself a sports gambler. (p. 3) As he lost money, Donaghy remembered how he covered his bets. Donaghy recalled: "I did exactly what they wanted me to do. I told them that Allen Iverson was gone from the 76ers and that because it was still early in the season the underachieving Boston Celtics would be competitive." (p. 9) He did this illegal act for a two thousand dollar cash payment. Is the word stupid appropriate? You are making a quarter of a million dollars a year as an NBA referee, and you jeopardize your life for two grand. I guess if you hang out with "Ba Ba," that is the price you pay for stupidity.

DONAGHY ATTACKS A FEMALE OFFICIAL AND OTHER WEIRD COMMENTS

If you really want an insight into Donaghy, here is his view of the respected NBA female official, Violet Palmer. Donaghy writes: "Palmer had trouble with the NBA game." (p. 49) He continues: "Palmer came pretty much out of nowhere." The truth is that Violet Palmer has a longer career as a referee than Donaghy. She also officiated in the WNBA. She was its highest rated official. In 1997, she joined the NBA and when Charles Barkley said: "I don't think women should be NBA refs." He later apologized and said: "She does one hell of a job." I think that is Sir Charles only apology in history. Her accomplishments are untainted and her record is a strong one. When Donaghy has an opinion, it is an ill-formed and unintelligent one, Hey, you hang out with Ba-Ba that's what happens. There is no need to wonder how he got into the betting scandal.

Donaghy makes his case that he was abused by spilling dirt on every other referee. His so-called dirt is nothing more than sour grapes. His dirt is that they had opinions, they had a drink, and they didn't like him. They sound like my kind of people. Donaghy quotes Dallas Maverick owner Mark Cuban as saying that he wouldn't hire the NBA Director of League Officiating, Ed Rush, "to manage a Dairy Queen." (p. 52) Then Donaghy comments: "Cuban had it right. Rush did think he was King of the NBA." (p. 52) Is this beyond gratuitous? He was your boss Timmy.

If Donaghy wants to make Suns fans more infuriated than they already are with him; he did so by continually talking about Charles Barkley's betting. Let me see if I understand this. Barkley bet on games after he left the league, Barkley paid his losses, Barkley quit gambling and Barkley never broke the law. Now I know what is wrong with my neighbor, Charles Barkley, he is an honest man. Charles is also not only one of the more intelligent persons who played in the NBA, but he tells it like it is. I would like to thank Tim Donaghy for pointing out Charles' failures. I won't mention any of this to Barkley. He might want to use the word "weasel" to describe Donaghy. I have already copyrighted it.

THE BAD GUYS IN THE NBA AND DONAGHY'S BOOK

It gets worse Donaghy identifies Gary Peyton, Stephen Jackson, Rasheed Wallace, Antoine Walker and Chauncey Billups as the five most "belligerent, selfish, profane, self absorbed spoiled brats…." (p. 67) The reason for this judgment is that they knew he was blowing calls. I wonder did he look in the mirror when he used the words.

My hero in this group is Rasheed Wallace, who not only confronted Donaghy about blown calls but also threatened him. It also cost him more than a million dollars in fines, which Wallace was more than happy to pay. Weasel money. Rasheed Wallace gets my highest compliments.

Donaghy's book gets worse. "What room are you in at the Marriott, Timmy," (p. 85) a young girl giggled on the telephone. He actually writes this crap with a wife and four girls at home. Yet, he sees Gary Peyton as "self absorbed." The tragedy to the Donaghy book is that he describes his fellow referees, particularly Dick Bavetta, as honest, but they have tendencies that allow other teams to capitalize on their calls. Think about this for a moment. What Donaghy is intimating is that he also has tendencies. He probably doesn't realize that his tendencies break the law. Oh well, a little bending of the law shouldn't get in the way of the truth. (pp. 95-97)

One thing that this book did was make me love Joey Crawford. There are so many Crawford stories that are hilarious, but the best one is when he threw Golden State Warrior Coach Don Nelson out of a playoff game for staring at him. Nelson never said a word and Crawford sent him to the showers. Crawford did this before the game started. "Nelson was trying to intimidate me," Crawford remarked. "It wasn't going to happen." Crawford is a no nonsense referee with impeccable integrity. Timmy, integrity is not a country in Eastern Europe. Even Ba Ba knows that. What integrity means is that you do your job in a professional and unbiased manner. Don't worry Timmy I am waiting for you to look up the words in your dictionary. There is no such thing as integrity bets.

Peter: "When I go to Vegas I make integrity bets."

When the FBI catches Donaghy he writes: "The only concern I had was saving my own sorry ass." (p. 136) Remind me not to strike up a friendship with Donaghy. He didn't have to worry, Tommy and Ba Ba rolled over for the FBI and Tim went off to jail. He was supposedly the smartest of the three gamblers. He was the only one to go to jail. So maybe I should rethink smart.

DONAGHY GETS READY TO GO AFTER THE SUNS

What Phoenix Suns fans can't forgive is Donaghy's vendetta. He targeted the Suns while telling everyone that they were the best team in the NBA. But this is a great pick up line in Phoenix bars. On January 5, 2007 Donaghy was in Phoenix to referee the Suns Miami Heat game. He checked into his plush Biltmore area hotel, the Ritz Carlton, and he greased his hair with pomade. He looked in the mirror, and he was in love. Then he caught a cab downtown to collect ten thousand dollars from an eastern gambler. The FBI was on the case.

That night the Suns beat the Heat 108 to 80. There wasn't much money bet on that game. One wonders did the gamblers attempt to make a killing later on in the playoffs. Just a thought! Don't send Bruno and Luigi to talk to me.

One wonders why Donaghy didn't describe all the Suns' games that he influenced. He called them the best team in 2007. There is no evidence concerning how many, if any, other Suns games that Donaghy influenced. Only David Stern knows that little fact, and he is not talking.

Peter: "What do you mean Howard, 'games that he influenced,' are you a writing weasel? Tell it like it is." Unless I hear from the fans, Peter is fired.

The Suns fans believe that Donaghy fixed game three of the play-offs against the San Antonio Spurs. There were some questionable calls. Then a fan put the calls on You Tube. Look at it and you decide.

Peter: "Come on, Howard, don't be a weasel. What do you think?"

Howard: "I think that you are done as a critic, Peter."

In game three, San Antonio won 108 to 101 to give them a 2-1 lead. If you believe in conspiracies the NBA doesn't have the box score for those games on the Internet. No one knew that there was a scandal.

SEAN PATRICK GRIFFIN ON THE DONAGHY SCANDAL: THE PROFESSOR HAS IT RIGHT

When the scandal broke, Sean Patrick Griffin's **Gaming The Game: The Story Behind The NBA Betting Scandal and The Gambler Who Made It Happen**, published in 2011, pointed out that Donaghy smoked pot with a friend, and then he had a night of fun with his girl friend. Why is this important? It's significant because Donaghy never accepts full blame for his actions. It was David Stern's fault, he lamented. It was due to his frenetic schedule. It was due to the low pay. It was due to lack of respect. What Donaghy never realizes is that his problems were due to hanging out with criminals.

QUOTES FROM SEAN PATRICK GRIFFIN
1. "I, OF COURSE, HAD NO IDEA THAT DONAGHY WOULD LATER WRITE SUCH A DUBIOUS ACCOUNT OF THE SCANDAL." ON DONAGHY'S BOOK
2. "I FIND STRIKING PARALLELS BDETWEEN DONAGHY'S BOOK/CLAIMS AND HOSE OF JAMES FREY...." FREY HAD A BEST AN AUTOBIOGRAPHICAL BEST-SELLER THAT WAS FICITONALIZED. GRIFFIN SUGGESTS THAT THS IS DONAGHY'S SIN
3. "DONAGHY SPLITS HIS TIME WORKING FOR AN ONLINE GAMBLING SERVICE AND LECUTRING OTHERS ON PROBLEM GAMBLING." AS PATRICK GRIFFIN POINTS OUT THIS DOESN'S MAKE SENSE
4. "THE FORMER NBA REFEREE IS MENTIONED IN THE NEW STODAY AS HAVING MADE THREATENING CALLS AGAINST AN ADVERSARY-AGAIN."
5. SEAN PATRICK GRIFFIN ALLEGES THAT DONAGHY WAS A WILLING PARTICIPANT IN THE BETTING SCANDAL. DONAGHY'S BOOIK SUGGESTS OTHERWISE. THIS IS ONLY ONE OF HUNDREDS OF ALLEGATIONS OF IMPROPER USE OF FACTS THAT GRIFFIN ARGUES THAT DONAGHY USED IN HIS BOOK.

Who is Sean Patrick Griffin? He is a PhD. And he is an associate professor at Penn State University. His field of expertise is in the Department of Criminal Justice. He studies career criminals, their psychosis and their patterns of behavior. His website www.seanpatrickgriffin.net/about contains more material on Donaghy.

THE VARIOUS RING LEADERS IN THE DONAGHY SCANDAL

Tommy Martino, one of the ringleaders, turned informant for the FBI, and he detailed the Donaghy meeting with a woman that Griffin identified as Cheryl Wolf-Ruiz. Cheryl must be ok, a tabloid featured her wearing a Rolling Stones t-shirt, the one with the tongue and a headline in the **New York Post** read: "Dirty Ref's Sideline Gal Eyed By Feds." The **Post** story is an interesting one. They alleged that: "Tim Donaghy has a busty, blonde gal pal in Arizona, and federal investigators want to speak to her as part of their probe of his illicit gambling" Wolfe-Ruiz's attorney said she knew nothing. Most people who knew her agreed. So knew nothing. She had been a friend with Donaghy since 2003. They just probably liked to play checkers or Parcheesi. There were rumors neither one of them could learn to play chess. But checkers was another matter.

Robert Robinson, Wolf-Ruiz' lawyer, commented from his Glendale, Arizona office: "She and Donaghy did not have a sexual relationship." Like I said, they both liked to play checkers.

The forty one year old Wolf-Ruiz is gorgeous and divorced. She is the mother of two children. She allegedly owns a share in a Phoenix sports bar, Callahan's. Her lawyer continually denied an intimate relationship with Donaghy. She agreed to be interviewed by the **New York Post,** and she withdrew from the interview when they presented her with a list of questions.

Her attorney explained: "Donaghy did provide tickets to games for her and her boyfriend. I know she went to dinner with Donaghy on numerous occasions. There were many times when there were other people there." They probably needed a threesome for bridge or maybe Parcheesi. Then again maybe it's dominoes. She is beautiful and innocent of all charges. Me! I am not so sure.

Peter: "Did you check to see if she could read or play skilled card games?" Remind me to fire Peter.

Donaghy also took her to a strip club, according to the **Post**. I like Tim Donaghy's class, he is my kind of guy.

Peter: "You and Tim Donaghy are the same guy, Howard, you should use the M word. I don't mean mature." Peter has the word copyrighted.

At times, according to the **Post**, Donaghy was lonely so he rented Ms. Wolfe-Ruiz a room at the Marriott. I called the Marriott asking what price range Donaghy paid. They told me to get a life. Peter then told me to get a life. Claude then told me to get a life. My wife told me to get a life. I am still thinking about getting a life.

Why is this important? It highlights the behavior of an NBA official who cost the Suns a playoff game that would have advanced them to the finals. In game three of the Western Conference semi-finals, Donaghy came out with his hair greased back. I looked at him and he looked like he had the janitor's broom somewhere. He also looked nervous. Maybe Ba Ba was in the crowd. Donaghy worked alongside two excellent referees with integrity, Greg Willard who called nine fouls on the Suns and Eddie F. Rush who called six fouls on the Suns. Donaghy called ten fouls. Not even his fellow referees could believe some of his calls. Amare Stoudemire was furious and Donaghy knew it. Ed Rush calmed Amare down, while silently agreeing with the Suns' star and validating his complaints. A smile from Rush told Amare all that he needed to know about Donaghy. Rush whispered in Donaghy's ear to be more consistent. No wonder Donaghy skewers Rush in his book. Ed had the nerve to point out to the pompous little bastard was screwing up the game.

Peter: "Howard, tell us you true feelings, don't sugar coat it."

The other referees had nothing to do with Donaghy. He was thinking about Ba Ba and Ms. Wolfe-Ruiz. What kind of person uses two names?

Peter: "The modern liberal kind Howard, you're a moron."

This May 12, 2007 game was one of the worst officiated in NBA history. The bad calls, the no-calls and the lack of explanation even bothered the Spurs who won the series. The league should have investigated but no one was listening to the fans' complaints.

Things got even weirder four years after the series when Tim Donaghy explained his actions. The little weasel sat down for an interview in Chicago, and he defended his officiating. Timmy couldn't afford to make Ba Ba unhappy. As Donaghy made a series of questionable calls, the Suns protested. Coach Mike D'Antoni screamed incessantly at Donaghy, and the little weasel ignored him. You can't throw a coach out when you, as the referee, are shaving points. It doesn't look good.

In 2011, he had a book to sell. So the little weasel with the greased back hair sat down for an interview. It doesn't get any stranger than his statements. Here are some excerpts from an interview with **Chicago Now**. It is a strange interview that causes Sigmund Freud to roll over in his grave. Or for that matter it explains why psychoanalysis fails.

126

TIM DONAGHY'S QUOTES FROM THE CHICAGO INTERVIEW

When Donaghy sat down for an interview with **Chicago Now.com**, he made some curious remarks.

Tim Donaghy: "Tommy Nunez was supervisor of officials in that series. And he had a dislike for the Suns owner Robert Sarver, and he enjoyed the lifestyle in San Antonio, and liked to get back in the next round of playoffs...." What is even more bizarre is that Donaghy claims that Nunez watched tape so he could call certain fouls. What am I missing? Donaghy, not Nunez, got caught making illegal calls.

Then Donaghy claimed that the Suns-Spurs series was poorly officiated. Tim Donaghy: "So that was just a poorly officiated series from game one all the way until the last game." How lame is this quote?

Peter: "Does Donaghy get any stranger in his comments?" He does.

Tim Donaghy: "There is no doubt I feel the Phoenix Suns were the best team in the league." Then the little weasel suggested that Tommy Nunez helped to throw the series so he could eat dinner in San Antonio on the Riverwalk. Why didn't Nunez take Donaghy to court for slander? Maybe he couldn't serve him in jail. Nunez is a man of integrity. He had nothing to do with the Suns losing the series. It was Donaghy who was indicted, convicted and sent to jail. The only person who doesn't recognize this is Tim Donaghy.

One of the ironies of this scandal is that Donaghy, in his own words, acts like he was not involved in the betting scandal. He sounds at times like he is an innocent bystander.

Tim Donaghy:" People don't realize that at that time we weren't even betting any more because the guy who was involved in the scheme ended up going into rehab, so we were done betting at that time for about a month." Gee, Timmy there is no doubt in my mind that you are innocent.

He also justified the fracas between Robert Horry and Steve Nash Here it is in Donaghy's own words.

Tim Donaghy: "Certainly that was mishandled with the subjectivity of the league office as to whether to suspend somebody for doing what they did. Look at what happened with the Miami-Dallas game. Do you think they would have suspended all those players for a game 7? Had there been a game 7, with all those players leaving the bench area the way they did. The rule clearly states you can't leave the bench area to get involved in an altercation, whether the time out exists or not. In all reality, I doubt they would have suspended all of those players for a game 7 and I don't think it was handled properly with Phoenix in 2007."

Let me get this straight, Timmy, you are influencing the outcome of the game with bogus calls, and you don't think the league handled it properly.

Peter: "Howard, what part of stupid don't you understand." I am going to have to call Ba Ba to shut Peter up.

The FBI did handle the investigation properly, and, as Murray Weiss reported in the **New York Post**, Donaghy controlled the spread in key NBA games. He did this for at least two seasons. His guilt is beyond recognition; his penance needs to be forthcoming.

Stephen A. Smith's Show on ESPN suggested that Donaghy was in debt to gamblers, and he attempted to make up his bad debts with the point shaving. Smith showed undue restraint and great intelligence commenting on the Donaghy scandal.

When Tim Donaghy pleaded guilty to charges that he affected the point spread of NBA games, he blew the whistle on the gambling scandal. R. J. Bell, president of a sports betting service, tracked the games Donaghy worked from 2003 to 2007, and he concluded that during the two seasons that the FBI investigated there was evidence of some tampering. Bell also showed that games that Donaghy officiated had the odds change in Las Vegas at the last minute. He concluded that there was "an outside factor." This is a nice way of saying that Donaghy allegedly was influencing the scores.

Peter: "What do you mean allegedly?"

The odd thing is that as the evidence mounted, Donaghy was like a peacock that didn't think he was at fault. He blamed NBA Commissioner David Stern. This is ridiculous. Stern is a lot of things, but he is a man of integrity. He blamed those who supervised the referees. This is of course ridiculous. He was such an inept official that Portland Trailblazer, Rasheed Wallace, confronted Donaghy leaving the arena. Wallace knew he was up to something. Wallace was suspended seven games for confronting a future criminal, and he lost 1.7 million dollars in salary.

Brandon Land, an ESPN handicapper, labeled Donaghy a "rogue official." U. S. Congressman Bobby Rush, a Democrat from Illinois, asked Commissioner Stern to hold a hearing to make the public aware that the sport hadn't been damaged. It got worse when two of Donaghy's high school friends, were exposed as the bookies. They allegedly had ties to the mob. Ba Ba didn't seem to notice that they were in trouble. He was too busy lifting weights and chasing the young ladies.

Peter: "What do you mean allegedly had ties to the mob?"

How did Donaghy react to these charges? He turned on his sprinklers when the media showed up at his home to ask questions. He wife filed for divorce. As Donaghy saw it, he wasn't to blame. But he did have enough brains to plead guilty, and he magnanimously accepted a reduced sentence.

Peter: "Did Rasheed Wallace get a refund on his 1.7 million dollar fine?"

Claude: "Howard, can you fire Peter, he asks too many questions?"

On August 15, 2007 Donaghy appeared in court to answer to two federal charges related to the investigation. He was sentenced to fifteen months in federal prison on July 29, 2008. He served eleven months in a country club prison camp in Pensacola Florida. The word is that his tennis game and physical fitness regime helped Donaghy stay in shape. He served the remainder of his sentence in a half way house. He was sent back to prison in August for violating his parole.

DAVID STERN EXPLAINS THE MESS AND HE CLEANS IT UP

Whether or not you like NBA Commissioner David Stern, he did a good job investigating, defusing and reforming the referee situation. He also strengthened the NBA pool of officials by hiring younger, more diverse and experienced referees. Things have gotten better in the officiating department.

David Stern: "We would like to assure our fans that no amount of effort, time or personnel is being spared to assist in this investigation, to bring to justice an individual who has betrayed the most sacred trust in professional sports, and to take the necessary steps to protect against this ever happening again. We will have more to say at a press conference that will be scheduled for next week."

The NBA officials, none of whom were linked to shaving points, reacted to the situation. Gary Benson, a seventeen-year NBA official remarked, "Those are people that you work with and that you literally— you spend more time with those people than you do with your family." What Benson alleged was obvious-he was betrayed.

The irony is that Donaghy, the little weasel, criticizes the NBA for not handling it properly. Gee, Tim, maybe your officiating had something to do with it. Please don't send Angelo, Ba Ba and Bruno to talk to me.

DONAGHY'S TARNISHED LEGACY

Donaghy was in prison and out of the spotlight. Then in the 2012 playoffs, Tim Donaghy emerged once again as a villain. As the Boston Celtics made a run for the 2012 NBA finals the fans showed up with Tim Donaghy masks. This was a promotion from a Boston radio station, and the disc jockeys handed out the masks charging that the league wanted the Miami Heat in the NBA finals. It was a hilarious promotion. Only one person didn't find it funny. That person is David Stern. The last time I looked the Miami Heat won it fair and square. The legacy and tarnished legend of Tim Donaghy continues to haunt the NBA. This guy needs to go away. Just don't send Bruno and Luigi to see me Tim. Or for that matter Ba Ba.

Donaghy's book **Personal Foul: A First Person Account of the Scandal That Rocked The NBA** is not worth reading. It gets strange. In the copyright page, Tim gives you his fax number 941-358-3344, just in case you want to fax him a picture of your derriere. To cover his admitted criminal activity, Donaghy wrote: "In other words, even the referees' union understood the problem was bigger than one 'rogue' referee." (p. 237) That is great Tim, blame your colleagues for your behavior. You certainly aren't at fault.

Here are some excerpts from the book. "There were times I was so flush with cash that I didn't know what to do with it." (p. 40) Tim, I think Yale wants to offer you a scholarship to attend their business school. "I tell you who my first choice would be for a new commissioner: Mark Cuban." (p. 244) I think Saturday Night Live will come calling after this revelation. One more statement will tell you that Donaghy needs to conquer his narcissism problem. "At one point during my court proceedings, a newspaper published my home address. As a result, I received hundreds of letters of support." (p. 240) What is strange is that he complains about his home address being published and in his book he lists his fax number 941-358-3344. That is if you want to fax him a compliment. He goes on to claim that one came from a minister who was critical of Commissioner David Stern. Does the phrase "narcissist manipulator" come to mind?

THE JUDGE TELLS TIMMY NO

Just when you think the Tim Donaghy incident is over, it hits the news. In mid-August 2012, after we had forgotten about Donaghy, he petitions a New York court for an early release from his supervised probation. He argues that his court supervision should come to an end due to good conduct, and he argues that it is difficult for him to find work under court supervision. After taking thousands of dollars from gamblers for inside tips on games he worked as an NBA referee, Donaghy wanted out of his last three months of supervised probation. He completed thirty-three months of supervised probation, but he said that he couldn't do another 90 days. Donaghy's probation officer recommended that he couldn't begin a job as a paid radio talk show commentator. He could secure work once his probation was completed. Donaghy still doesn't realize that he is a convicted felon. A Brooklyn no nonsense Judge made it clear to him that he wasn't getting special privileges.

Brooklyn Federal Judge Carol Amon ruled that Donaghy could not receive paychecks as a radio talk show personality. He was working with host Danny Berrelli on "The Sports Connection" on a Philadelphia radio station. Judge Amon agreed with Donaghy's probation officer, who denied his request to work on the radio show. Donaghy continues to be self-absorbed. Also, why would a convicted felon, due to sports betting, be hired for a sports talk show? Ratings! Probably! Am I missing something here? Is this beyond stupid? His probation ended November 3, 2012, hopefully, we will never hear the name Tim Donaghy again. I hope he finds employment. Is there a market for greasy haired, ego driven former felons? Where is Ba Ba when you really need him?

The minute that his probation ended, Donaghy went to a basketball game at New York's Madison Square Garden. Then Donaghy posted a comment on a gambling site, Linemakers on Sporting News, defending his right to go to an NBA game.

"Tim Donaghy: "I don't think there is any reason why they'd remove me from the stadium. I'm there to take in a game and look at some live action and do a bit of scouting. I'm not even too sure that anyone is really going to notice me, to be honest with you."

Tim Donaghy signifies everything that is wrong with professional sports. He is spoiled. He is arrogant. He is pompous. He is clueless. Those are his positive points, you don't want to know the negative ones. Fortunately, he is not typical of NBA referees. He is an anomaly.

Peter: "That sounds better than saying he is an asshole.' Remind me to fire Peter.

Howard: "Tim, please don't send Ba Ba around to see me. Send him to see Peter."

Peter: "What do you really think about Tim Donaghy, Howard? Ba Ba should come around to end this lousy writing. Not to mention your sophomoric analysis."

Claude: "I am going to install a ceiling, this is boring me."

Tim Donaghy has paid his debt to society and he should be left alone. His friends say that he is a good guy. I would never disagree with Ba Ba.

chapter

NINE

ROBERT SARVER: THE MANAGING PARTNER IS A GREAT GUY

"WHAT IF THE OWNERS OF THE SUNS DISCOVERED THAT HORDES OF PEOPLE WERE SNEAKING INTO GAMES WITHOUT PAYING? WHAT IF THEY HAD A GOOD IDEA WHO THE GATE-CRASHERS ARE, BUT THE USHERS AND SECURITY PERSONNEL WERE NOT ALLOWED TO ASK THESE FOLKS TO PRODUCE THEIR TICKET STUBS, THUS NON-PAYING ATTENDEES COULD NOT BE EJECT-ED." ARIZONA GOVERNOR JAN BREWER

There is a persistent liberalism and respect for the underdog in Robert Sarver's personality. When he criticized SB 1070, Arizona's strict immigration law, he received the rueful wrath of Arizona Governor Jan Brewer. This is a Sarver trait. He goes against the grain. He does it his way. He has a way of making people angry. This is a trait that often pro-duces the cry "Sarver you suck" during a Suns game. He doesn't suck, and, in fact he is not only a good businessman, Sarver cares about the franchise. He also cares about equal opportunity, as his protest against Arizona SB 1070 demonstrated. He is as much for the little guy as he is for the millionaire. This is unique in sports ownership.

When Robert Sarver was growing up, he became a dedicated sports fan. In 1969, the eight-year-old Sarver tuned in regularly to Phoenix Suns games. He graduated from Tucson's Sabino High School in 1979 and three years later he earned a BA in business from the University of Arizona. The following year he became a CPA.

His interest in basketball continued while in college. His first date with his wife, Penny, took place when he took her to a University of Arizona NCAA basketball game. That is the good news. The bad news is that she had to come over to his house to watch it on television. He has since made up for this grievous faux pas.

At the University of Arizona, Sarver watched as the Wildcats had little national success. Then in 1983 Lute Olson was hired as the head coach and the University of Arizona developed into a national power. By this time Sarver was beginning his business career, but he was still a fan. It is in Sarver's formative years that the groundwork was laid to purchase the Suns. Sarver also became good friends with Olson and this was in later years an important influence upon his purchasing the Suns.

THE UNIVERSITY OF ARIZONA AND ON TO BUSINESS

At the University of Arizona, Sarver was a typical student who enjoyed college life. He was having so much that he barely passed his freshman year. He was seen regularly at the Green Dolphin enjoying a beer. Then his dad passed away, and Sarver became a serious student who evolved into an entrepreneur. He graduated in three years with a strong interest in banking. As Sarver studied business administration, he became interested in banking. When he graduated in 1982, he founded the National Bank of Arizona. He was only twenty-three, but he already had a solid and expanding business portfolio. In 1994, Sarver sold the bank to the Zions Corporation. It was the largest independent bank in Arizona. Then Sarver took his money to San Diego, where he purchased the Grossmont Bank. This was one of Southern California's largest community banks. In addition to banking, Sarver made large sums of money purchasing raw land and developing real estate.

Some of the early fiscal lessons he learned came from watching his father. Sarver's father built the Aztec Inn, and Tucson's Plaza International Hotel on his way to a great deal of wealth. When his father died of a heart attack at an early age, it was up to Robert to make his own fortune. He did it very well, as he became a respected business figure at the ripe old age of twenty-three.

Sarver's business career began when he borrowed $150,000 from his mother after his dad died and founded the National Bank of Tucson. This was only the beginning. He soon purchased four million square feet of commercial office space, 3500 apartments, 700 hotel rooms and a few thousand acres of raw land. As Sarver paid attention to business, the empire continued to grow. He is also the chairperson of the Western Alliance Bancorporation. This is a leading bank holding company in the Southwest with banking and financial services in Arizona, California, Nevada and Colorado.

It is with his investments, support from his family, good relations with the community, a bevy of local supporters, and a strong work ethic that made Sarver a multi-millionaire. It didn't happen overnight, as he spent twenty plus years amassing his fortune. Sarver had a dark secret. He was a born again sports fan. He wanted to purchase an NBA team, so he asked University of Arizona's legendary basketball coach, Lute Olson, for his advice. They talked. Olson recommended that a former University of Arizona basketball standout and a long time NBA player, Steve Kerr, as an advisor and eventually an investor. Kerr played for fifteen seasons in the NBA, and along the way won five championships, three with the Chicago Bulls and two with the San Antonio Spurs.

Steve Kerr was an integral part of Sarver's education concerning the NBA. He gave Sarver good advice, and he helped him navigate the basketball waters. He also joined the investment group that purchased the Suns.

Did Robert Sarver purchase the Phoenix Suns so he could have lunch with Al McCoy? The question may seem like a crazy one. But Sarver told Jerry Colangelo there was no need to introduce him to McCoy, because the new owner had been listening to him since he was eleven years old. At this point, Sarver was enjoying the NBA experience. Then a **Sports Illustrated** writer asked for a chance to spend a year with the Suns and write a book.

SARVER ACCORDING TO JACK MCCALLUM

For some reason Sarver gave Jack McCallum total access to the Suns in 2005-2006 for a book. The result was **:07 Seconds Or Less: My Season On The Bench With The Runnin' and Gunnin" Phoenix Suns**. It was a mistake. McCallum was nasty toward Sarver at every opportunity. He also detailed, at that time, Sarver's wealth.

The McCallum book has some positives. He loved the coaching staff and his description of Coach Mike D'Antoni highlighted the run and gun genius of the Suns. Amare Stoudemire is not treated very well. McCallum accuses him of "dogging it in rehab." He also criticizes Shawn Marion for not playing hard every night and James Jones for not being prepared. It is the owner, Robert Sarver that McCallum continually skewers, and he claims that Sarver is literally looking for some one to criticize. This is, of course, absurd, but it makes for good sales. The bottom line is that McCallum is jealous of Sarver's success.

One of McCallum's writing ploys is to compare Sarver's thoughts to those of his coaches. When the coaches explained to Shawn Marion that he needed to get more physical, they did so gently." Marc Iavaroni, an assistant coach, explained it to Sarver: "A guy will go into an absolute funk if he feels you're beating him up." (p. 70) McCallum suggested that Sarver is "stupefied" by this explanation. He also has a section in the book where he quotes Sarver using the F word five times in two sentences. (p. 79) This is unnecessary and inaccurate.

The McCallum book pictured Sarver as "a distracted owner..." (p. 46) For some reason, McCallum took Sarver to task for some strange reasons. He wrote: "The game is not everything to Robert Sarver and never will be." (p. 69) This is a strange conclusion. This is followed by the author's statement that Sarver does not interfere with the team. Some of McCallum's sentences are ugly as when he writes: "An exuberant Robert Sarver busts into the room like a stripper...." (p. 152) This is a bit nasty. McCallum's book is a fun read but the truth is missing. Stay tuned for the real story.

ROBERT SARVER'S ROAD TO OWNING THE SUNS

In the spring of 2004, Robert Sarver purchased the Phoenix Suns from Jerry Colangelo. Sarver was in his early forties, and he was taking over a beloved franchise from a man who was even more adored than the Phoenix Suns. He also negotiated an eight-year contract with Jerry Colangelo to advise with the Suns. This was a smart move as Colangelo was the business face of the franchise, and he could smooth the way for Sarver's acceptance. Over the years this didn't mollify some of the fans.

Like many owners, Sarver has had to endure indignities. "Sarver you suck." This was a comment from a guy sitting near me who had one of the worst potbellies I have ever seen and a rancid mouth to match. This doesn't faze Sarver. It is the cost of doing business. This is the price one pays for owning an NBA franchise.

Where Sarver gets in trouble with the fans is by running the Suns as a business. He cut costs by attempting to negotiate smart player contracts. He didn't cut costs on training rooms, equipment, a top-flight medical staff and the Suns continue to host fan events.

When Sarver purchased the Suns, he attempted to avoid long-term player contracts that financially hampered the franchise. Sarver was aware that other teams had players like the New York Knicks Jerome James who averages 1.9 points a game while making an exorbitant five point four million salary in 2006-2007. Sarver realistically realized that this was not the road for the Suns. He made many business moves to avoid financial loss. Some of his business moves were positive. Others were a mistake. He sold the rights for Rajon Rondo to the Boston Celtics, and Rondo became a franchise point guard. The Suns had Steve Nash under contract, and they weren't about to cut him loose for an unproven rookie. Even if that rookie went on to become an All Star. The Suns were stabilized financially, but Sarver's critics pointed out that he didn't spend his salary cap money. The Suns had financial cap space, and, as the critics screamed for the team to use it, there was an acrimonious atmosphere. Sarver didn't want to go over the salary cap. He is a businessman, not a hobbyist. The Rondo sale is one that he was criticized for, but Steve Nash responded with two NBA MVP awards. Where would Rondo play? He is not a shooting guard. He can't play small forward. He is a point guard. There was no room for him on the Suns.

Under Sarver's management the Suns had a chance to sign, trade for or draft Luol Deng, Nate Robinson and Rudy Fernandez. They didn't select these players for a variety of reasons. In retrospect, it looks like the right decision. Sarver is charged with not paying Joe Johnson what he wanted and letting Amare Stoudemire walk away to free agency. Sarver is tired of these tales but he endures them.

THE CASE FOR SARVER'S MANAGEMENT STYLE

There is a case for Sarver's management style. He has made the Suns a fun team with the run and gun style that has characterized his eight plus years as an owner. The U. S. Airways facilities are first rate, the food is good, the music is great, the Gorilla is a legendary mascot and while some complain about the music, D. J. Dizzie does keep things going. Then there are the Suns' dancers. They all look like they could use an In And Out burger but they put on a great show.

The cost of season tickets is among the best bargains in the NBA. The complimentary parking, the special events and the player's presence in the Valley of the Sun make for a positive experience. Sarver and his management support liberal causes, and they oppose anything attached to sexism, racism or discrimination. In hiring practices, the Suns are an example of affirmative action in its ultimate form.

ROBERT SARVER'S SECRET: HE IS A FAN

Robert Sarver has a secret. He is a fan. He loves the food in the Blue Moon Club, and he is a prime mover in the gourmet food that is provided under the stands near the team dressing room. As the fans in the more expensive seats eat, the Suns run out onto the floor with high fives for these fans. It is the ultimate fan experience. The fans that pay for this call it a bargain. The Suns also care about the budget conscious fan, and they provide affordable seats. There are ten to twenty five dollar tickets. This is a rarity in the NBA.

There is a dollar fifty menu; there are food franchises with different ethnic dishes. The Suns make sure that the average fan has a menu that includes half a dozen dollar and a half food items.

The nice thing about Sarver is that he is a regular guy. When he is in the arena, there are no bodyguards, no entourage; there is a no bullshit approach to the Suns. He wants the team to win. But he won't bankrupt the franchise. Another problem is that Sarver wants good citizens. He sees the Suns as an extension of the community. The lack of strip clubs in and around Phoenix keeps some players off the roster. Tim Donaghy, the disgraced NBA referee, loved the few strip clubs in the dark recesses of Phoenix. Suns' players are guilty of certain vices. They like to go bowling. They have normal families. The single guys have long-term girl friends. There is no domestic violence and no one is arrested for drunken driving. Jared Dudley has been caught with a hot fudge sundae at a Dairy Queen. Coach Alvin Gentry is in Paradise Bakery purchasing muffins. The rumor is that they are the fat free muffins.

The local and national media is also critical of Sarver. Bill Simmons, an ESPN writer, took Sarver to task for not upgrading his roster to assure more playoff wins. The Phoenix press is also on him at times. The issue is invariably money and Sarver's refusal to spend it. He attempts to explain what he is spending, and why he is not spending on other items. No one seems to listen.

THE PRESS AS A CONSTANT CRITIC

The press is a constant critic, but that is the cost of doing business. The **Arizona Republic** has two excellent writers, the columnist Dan Bickley and the beat writer, Paul Coro, and their reporting goal is to irritate Robert Sarver. They do a good job of it. They are also good writers and not company reporters like others in the NBA.

On June 25, 2011, **Arizona Republic** columnist, Dan Bickley, suggested that Sarver was among the worst owners in professional sports. This is of course utter nonsense. Sarver is a businessman, and he is a no nonsense guy. Bickley is an excellent writer who thinks he is Lon Babby. That is the general manager. The **Arizona Republic** writers are excellent, but they have it in for Sarver. They love Steve Nash and Grant Hill who are gone to other teams. Stay tuned.

SOME THOUGHTS ON THE SUNS FRANCHISE

The Phoenix Suns are a multi-layered business organization. There are clear lines of authority. Lon Babby is the chief operations officer. Since Robert Sarver's business decisions are for profit ones, there is a consistency to the Suns' operation. **Arizona Republic** columnist Dan Bickley constantly criticizes the present business model. Unlike, Mark Cuban you won't see Sarver on Dancing With the Stars. Unlike Jerry Buss you won't see Sarver with ten Playboy bunnies in a lounge that seats 8. Unlike Donald Sterling, you will see Sarver spend some money.

Basketball is headed in the money ball direction. This is a concept formulated by Oakland A's general manager, Billy Beane, for baseball. It has spread to all sports. In simplest terms, moneyball is a system where you sign players who have an upside due to statistical evidence. Is this a way of saying that you discover nuggets or gems in the player category? The Suns have many secret weapons. The best weapon is not a person; it is the organizational structure. From top to bottom, the Suns attempt to maximize their product with research and development. There are mistakes but generally speaking the concept works.

CRITCIZING SARVER AND WHY HE IS A GOOD OWNER

The primary criticism of Robert Sarver is not spending enough money. This is a fallacious argument. The Suns aren't winning, and this is the primary reason for continual criticism. The Suns have had under Sarver from the seventh to the tenth highest payroll in the league. They have the most expensive locker room, they are top of the line in technological equipment, and the training staff is the best in the league. In terms of facilities there is a first class feel to the Suns. There are enough expensive medical instruments to pay Kobe Bryant's salary. The front office is loaded with talented basketball brains, think Lon Babby, Mark West and Lance Blanks. The overall fiscal management guru and director of basketball operations, Lon Babby, is experienced in budget matters. None of these folks come cheap. They are salaried employee paid well due to their expertise. So forget the argument that Sarver is not spending money. He wants to win as well as the next owner, and he realizes that talent puts you in a position to go to the NBA finals. You don't find the talent without the right management structure. The Suns have a good corporate plan. They just don't have Dwight Howard, Dwyane Wade or Lebron James. (Sorry Kobe)

Robert Sarver is an excellent owner for another reason. He has set up a fan friendly management style that begins with the 6th Man, many of whom are women, and it continues with the people who let you in the door and seat you. In other words, the Sarver philosophy is that he has more people working to keep the season ticket holders happy than any NBA owner. The 6th man, a group of young male and female executives, handle any problems with season tickets. They also schedule special events. So Sarver does spend money.

What's wrong with Robert Sarver? In the early years of owning the Suns, he was much too slow running up the court with the finger. He was once on the trampoline and that didn't go well. That was during the first few seasons. He also locks up the cookies on the plane when the team doesn't win. Rumor has it that Garret Siler was upset with this ploy. To Sarver's credit, he no longer runs down the court with a finger, unfortunately the cookies are still locked up after a loss. For years Sarver sat center court. Last year, he moved his seats to the end of the first row. One suspects his wife had something to do with this strategic move. He is a financially experienced owner who loves the NBA game. He is also a businessman running the Suns as a for profit company. That doesn't always work out but the notion is that you don't buy a franchise to lose money. Are you listening Mark Cuban?

CAN FAN BLAME DONALD DIAMOND FOR SARVER OWNING THE SUNS?

When he was eight years old young Robert Sarver had a birthday party. His father was a big time Tucson businessman. The party was filled with important local entrepreneurs. One of them was Donald Diamond, an original Sun's owner, who talked at length with young Robert about the Phoenix Suns.

It was thirty-five years after his eighth birthday that Sarver purchased the Suns. He also listened to the radio and when he heard the mellifluous voice of Al McCoy, Sarver was hooked.

As he watched the Suns through high school and college, he saw the manner in which the franchise carried itself. He had a dream. He told people that one day he would own the Suns. No one took him seriously. After all he was a teenager, and when he entered the University of Arizona he looked for a major that would help him make the money to purchase the Suns. He chose business. So you can blame or praise Donald Diamond for putting Sarver on the road to owning the Suns. His background is unique and it helped in his march to franchise ownership and its defined organizational structure.

SOME THOUGHTS ON THE SUNS FRANCHISE

The Phoenix Suns are a multi-layered business. There are clear lines of authority. Lon Babby is the chief operations officer. There is a consistency to the Sun operation. **Arizona Republic** columnist Dan Bickley constantly criticizes the present business model, because he believes that it is a cost cutting device. But that is not the case. The Suns are building a team for the future, and that will take at least five years.

The Suns business plan includes 280 full time employees and more than a thousand part time workers. Kyle Hudson heads a program known as the 6th Man. This allows season ticket holders to have eyes and ears on the franchise. My favorite past sixth men are Melissa Fender and Khalif Fortune. She has since been promoted to the suites. My present 6th Man, Khalif Fortune, goes out of his way to provide good service, information about the Suns and he handles any problems. There is no information in this book from Khalif. What is strange is that Khalif and I grew up in Washington. Of course, I was there many years before him. He also played basketball professionally in the Philippines and I have written four books on Filipinos and spoke at the 1996 centennial in Manila.

Peter: "You are boring me Howard. Does any need to know this? Does anyone care?"

The Suns have many secret weapons. The best weapon is not a person; it is the organizational structure. From top to bottom the Suns attempt to maximize their product with research and development. There are mistakes but generally speaking the concept works.

TEN REASONS WHY SARVER IS TRYING TO KEEP THE FRANCHISE LEGENDARY

You want a bad owner, travel to Los Angeles and hang out with Donald Sterling. You want an owner who can dance, go to Dallas and hang out with Mark Cuban, You want an invisible owner hang out with the New York Knicks. You want an owner who is in Las Vegas playing cards or hanging out with nineteen-year-old girls, go see Jerry Buss and the Los Angeles Lakers. You want an owner who is a good guy, go to New Orleans and look up Tom Benson. You want a casino owner who treats the Sacramento Kings like a slot machine. See the Maloof brothers.

Peter: "Is there a point here?"

Claude: "Don't ask me any questions, I need to wash the car."

There is a point. Here are the Top Ten reasons to love Sarver as an owner. Or at least like him.

1.) **FAN FRIENDLY:** He puts together programs for the fans. There are special events with food, there are parties during the year to make the fans feel welcome, and the club holds meetings that educate the fans. The Suns also feed the fans. Sarver has a 6th man who is sometimes a woman. That is a young person in his or her twenties who helps you with tickets, special favors and other requests. Getting a Steve Nash autograph is difficult. Most everyone else if open to talking or a signed picture. There is no better fan experience.

2.) **THE PLAYERS:** The Suns attract good guys. They play well and they have a great deal of character. There are no Jalen Rose's calling future Hall of Fame players like Grant Hill, a bitch. Rose is a good guy but when the Lord asked him if he wanted brains or trains, he opted for a choo choo.

3.) **THE RESTAURANTS AND BARS AROUND THE ARENA:** You can't give Sarver credit for the good restaurants in and around the arena. I do. The newly christened, Legends, is a great sports bar with terrific food and inexpensive Happy Hour drinks. Legends used to be Coach and Willie's, and the new venue has good food at a reasonable price. Legends' new menu includes a make your own pasta, there is a special Monday night seven dollar burger. The flatbreads are great and a glass of Happy Hour wine is three dollars. Legends' is located at 412. S. Third Street. Don't miss it; the food and service is great. Ask for a free appetizer coupon, and get the meatballs, they are outstanding. Don't miss Burger Monday, it is a steal for the best burger downtown.

At 2 South 3rd Street, Kincaid's has one of the best Happy Hours from four to closing with good prices on wine and the appetizers are incredible. The crab and artichoke dip, the country fried calamari, the Buffalo Chicken wings and the Kobe meatloaf sliders are a bargain.

Cooperstown is a restaurant full of TVs and good bar food. It is my choice for great looking young ladies who are great servers. You might even get Alice Cooper to wait on you. The food is good and priced fairly. My favorites are the Al McCoy Crispy Chicken salad, the Charles Barkley chili and the Shaq stack burger. Cooperstown is behind the arena and a great sports and music bar.

Majerle's, yes the former Sun player, Dan, and now assistant coach has a great sports bar. The Sir Charles Chicken sandwich is my favorite. Since Charles Barkley went on weight watchers the sales of their excellent Charles Barkley hamburger is down. Maybe a Charles Barkley Diet Salad is on the horizon. The Jared Dudley grilled chicken sandwich is excellent as is Colangelo's Choice, which is half a club sandwich with your choice of any side in the place. Majerle's has great food at a good price. Now Dan needs to give his brother a raise.

The Arrogant Butcher at 2 Jefferson Street is a Fox restaurant downtown. The Happy Hour at the bar from 3 to 6 is great with appetizers like artichoke hummus, crispy shrimp and a series of low priced toasts. The local beer is three dollars and the wine is four dollars. It is a Fox restaurant, and it is a bargain with great food and drink.

The Starbucks inside the arena is a great place for a coffee or a quick sandwich. Tell the manager, I sent you. The cappuccinos are to die for. Enjoy. There is no better place to have a quick snack before the game. I take that back the Blue Moon Club inside the arena is the best. I can't afford the tickets for it. But it is wonderful. Now and then a friend feels sorry for me and take me for a sumptuous Blue Moon Club buffet. Who said it was just about basketball? It is also about food and drink. More information will be provided on the restaurants later in the book.

4.) **SUNS EMPLOYEES:** It doesn't matter what gate you come into the U. S. Airways Arena; an employee greets you warmly. My favorite employee manning the front gate, Sol, always has a ready smile and encouragement for the game. The ushers are just as good. Mitzi gives us a program and remembers our names. My 6th man has been a woman and my other two 6th men were great guys. My present sixth man, Khalif Fortune, is an Arizona State University graduate, and he played professional basketball for a year in the Philippines. He is a fountain of knowledge. He is gracious, answers all my lame questions, and he is the conduit to the special events that Robert Sarver and the Suns hold from time to time. Not only have Khalif Fortune and Melissa Fender treated me well, my first 6th Man was so good that he runs a similar program for the Oklahoma City Thunder.

5.) **FAN GATHERINGS:** Each year the Suns have season ticket holders in for a number of celebrations. You get to see the locker room, hangout with the players, the coaches and the staff. You get to see the training room. Last year the Suns had four separate areas of the arena for special events, and you rotated to the rooms to find out everything that you needed to know about the Suns. Definitely fan friendly.

6.) **THE BROADCAST TEAM:** With Al McCoy leading the way the TV and radio crew is knowledgeable and they aren't homers. When criticism is needed they go after the team. The rest of the crew is great. Scott Williams has a gregarious personality and he knows the game inside out, but he is not broadcasting this year due to his business interests. On radio, Tim Kempton gives you the blue collar working man's view of the game, and he is a perfect partner for Al McCoy. Eddie Johnson with his quiet, but articulate, delivery is able to delve into the games subtle points on television with the articulate newcomer Steve Albert.

The high profile Suns' broadcaster is Al McCoy. When the Suns win, McCoy will exclaim: "You can put this one in the old deep freeze." There is more to come in a subsequent chapter. There are some new faces in the broadcast booth. Stay tuned. Tom Chambers provides inside information on the NBA before the games, at halftime and after the games. He is a veritable fountain of knowledge. On the road, Eddie Johnson provides television color commentator. Johnson's analysis is among the best in the game.

7.) **THE UPGRADE COUPON:** This coupon allows season ticket holders to upgrade to a better seat. How many teams give up a $225 seat in exchange for a $10 seat? Not Donald Sterling of the Los Angeles Clippers. The Suns' Sixth Man, some of whom are great looking women, will help you with an upgrade any night.

8.) **THE SUNS' CHARITY WORK:** If this book makes any money a portion of the profits will go to a Suns charity. The charity work suggests that the players, management and the owner have a commitment to share their profits with the community. The Suns also awarded $35,000 in scholarships to sixteen students bound for college.

Phoenix Suns charity work is a sophisticated, ongoing program. On October 26, 2012 the Suns announced grants to various schools and charities. The grants range in size from $1,000 to $10,000 and they are intended to help children and facilities realize their potential. There is also an annual Playmaker Award of $100,000 to be used for specific programs.

The Playmaker grants began in 2005 when donors pledged $100,000 for four years. They are 37 playmakers working with the Phoenix Suns, and this charity work is largely directed toward schools and youth potential.

9.) **THE FORMER SUNS' PLAYS WHO RETURN:** Nothing is better than standing next to Connie Hawkins. The Hawk returns to Phoenix to show his appreciation for a team that made him an NBA Hall of Famer. When he is in Phoenix, Hawkins is warm and accessible. The Van Arsdale brothers are seen at games. Alvan Adams is around. He should be as he manages the arena. You can't miss him, he stands out in a nice suit.

10.) **THE GORILLA, THE SOL PATROL, DJ DIZZIE AND THE CHEERLEADERS:** The Gorilla is the Suns mascot. The first mascot was a Sunflower. You got it. A sunflower! Suddenly the Gorilla looks normal. The Gorilla and the Suns' cheerleaders should be number one on the list, but I have been married for more than forty years. So they are relegated to number ten. Why do I like the Gorilla, the Suns cheerleaders and lets not forget the Sol Patrol? What is the Sol Patrol? It is a group of young kids who are former gymnasts or should have been who dunk with the gorilla, dance and entertain. At times DJ Dizzie is shown playing music from a special spot in the arena. The conclusion is that this is great over the top entertainment. It makes the games interesting. Fun is the operative word with the Suns. Don't forget Mr. Orng. He isn't part of the Suns' official entertainment. But don't tell Mr. Orng that, as he is a fan who is a marketing director at Target, and he shows up with his skin painted orange and wearing an orange suit.

The Gorilla is my favorite. Some years ago, before we moved to Scottsdale, the Gorilla was giving Los Angeles Lakers center Kareem Abdul Jabbar a hard time. As he walked down the hall way to the locker room at half time Abdul Jabbar charged the Gorilla and pinned him against the wall. Where is Mark West when you really need him? Or for that matter where is Moses Malone?

Mr. Orng is increasingly becoming my favorite. He not only wears all orange outfits, but he is regularly featured on the Jumbotron TV. When he goes on the road, no one can believe it. In San Francisco they think he is weird. Funny, I thought in San Francisco he would appear normal.

SOME OF SARVER'S PROUDEST ACCOMPLISHMENTS

Although Sarver is a well-known philanthropist, there are some accomplishments that he holds dear. The Sarver Heart Foundation at the

University of Arizona is a tribute to his late father. Not only did Sarver personally fund the early years of the heart foundation, but also he has remained a prime mover in raising funds for its open heart and heart transplant surgery. The Sarver Heart Foundation is recognized as one of the top ten such facilities in the world.

The Children's Museum of Phoenix is another Sarver charity favorite. The one million dollar donation to the museum allowed its construction and the Sarver's remain heavy contributors to this innovative museum. Sarver also serves on the board of the Well Foundation, which is a leader in integrative medicine.

THE SUNS OWNERS YOU NEVER MET

The Phoenix Suns are a large and complete organization. There were some key people on top who make not only a fiscal contribution but they help the franchise achieve its status as a model sports team. The Suns' Vice Chairmen are an interesting group of investors who add a great deal more than money to the tem.

Andrew S. Kohlberg, the founder, President and CEO of Kisco Senior Living LLC, is an investor. His career is in real estate with an emphasis upon senior living. He has purchased his properties in a timely fashion to build his fortune.

He is a graduate of the University of Tennessee and he has advanced degrees from the University of California, San Diego in real estate economics. In 2002 Kohlberg was awarded the SAGE Person of the Year for his work in senior housing. The following year the National Association of Home Builders recognized his work with a special award.

Why would a real estate tycoon, like Kohlberg, get involved with the Suns? The answer is that he was not only a ranked tennis player, the NCAA Collegiate Player of the Year and an All-American at the University of Tennessee. He was on the Junior Davis Cup and Sunshine Cup teams. He was a successful professional tennis player and he competed at Wimbledon. Kohlberg won a gold medal at the Pan American games, and it sounds like he is now chasing an NBA ring.

Jahm Najafi is a key investor, and he is an important banker and fiscal guru. He is CEO of Najafi Companies since 2002. In banking from 1986 to 1990 he worked with Salomon Brothers Investment Bank. He also was the COO of the Pivotal Group from 1990 to 2002. His masters in business and economics form Harvard University and his B. A. from the University of California, Berkeley in economics and political science prepared him for the business world.

In addition to amassing a fortune, Najafi remained interested in philanthropy. He founded Social Ventures Partners Arizona to help non-profit organizations. He is a major investor and one of the Suns' vice chairmen. He is also a member of the National Basketball Association's Board of Governors.

Najafi is a prominent figure in Phoenix philanthropy working to aid in the growth of Arizona State University, and he is a benefactor to the Phoenix Symphony. He is a busy man but he still has time to attend Suns' games.

Sam Garvin has served as a Suns Vice President since 2004. He made his fortune in the rebate and mail order business. By the late 1980s, Garvin's Scottsdale based Continental Promotion Group had a one billion dollar annual gross. He is a huge Suns fan, and he spent eighteen years as a season ticket holder before he became a Vice Chairman. His initial seats were in the upper deck at the old McDowell arena. Do I break it gently to Garvin that purchasing season tickets is less expensive than ownership? No, I think I will keep that opinion to myself. Garvin is also a lawyer and he might take issue with my analysis.

Garvin's education at the University of Pittsburgh in political science and German studies, and later at the Thunderbird School of Global Management prepared him for international business. In 1998, he was named as one of the Phoenix area's Top 40 Under 40 businessmen. He is so busy in business I wonder if he has time to go to the games? Maybe this is why Garvin became a Suns' investor. He gets a free seat.

Prior to becoming active with the Suns, Garvin was a member of the Presidential Commission for the German American Tri-Centennial in the Reagan Administration.

Since 2005 Garvin has been an active member of the Suns' inner management team. He has enormous skills inside the NBA game. In 2007 Garvin was appointed an alternate NBA Governor to represent the league.

Jason Rowley is in his first year as the Suns' president and his sixth overall season working with the team. He manages the business operations, the Blue Moon Club and the US Airways Center.

A graduate of the University of Arizona in 1994, Rowley went into the U. S. Navy and he returned to law school at the U. of A. graduating in 2001. He joined the law firm of Snell and Wilmer in Phoenix and a few years later moved on to the Suns. He was named Phoenix Father of the Year in 2011. He is seen at Suns' games with his daughters Abigail and Lucille. They love the gorilla and Goran Dragic. They sound like smart young ladies.

SOME SARVER QUOTES

When Sarver and his partners purchased the Suns they had no idea that there would be some strange occurrences. While playing the Los Angeles Lakers, Sarver noticed that actress/director Penny Marshall was standing near the Suns huddle talking to some of the players. "This L. A. bullshit has got to stop," Sarver commented. There is a feistiness and determination to Sarver, and he doesn't like to be taken advantage of in his business dealings. The Suns are a business, and he lets everyone know it.

When Marc Iavaroni, an assistant coach, informed Sarver that a player sometimes goes into a funk if he is criticized, Sarver looked surprised. "It's the exact opposite of how things work in the business community," Sarver told Iavaroni.

Some of Sarver's best quotes come when key players get injured as this influences the results, the attendance and the whole future of the franchise. When Amare Stoudemire's knee gave out, then assistant coach, Alvin Gentry, was almost knocked down by Sarver as he ran into the arena. "Hey Robert I could own the franchise if I am injured." Sarver looked at him dumbfounded. "No you wouldn't Alvin, it is no fun when an almost one million dollar player goes down."

ROBERT SARVER: SOME CONCLUDING THOUGHTS

The Súns remain an interesting team and Robert Sarver is committed to winning. When the strike began, Seth Pollack accused Sarver of turning the "Phoenix Suns into a forgotten franchise." He complained about letting Joe Johnson go to the Atlanta Hawks, and he speculated that Sarver's "real estate and business interests have suffered with the Wall Street created financial meltdown." What does it have to do with the Suns?

According to another source, none of what Pollack said is true. One of Sarver's close friends pointed out that he purchased real estate at the right time. "Sarver purchased residential lots at a perfect time. Recently, he bought La Paloma Hotel and Resort in Tucson, as well as other resort interests. In addition to which his timing on purchasing real estate was perfect. The Alliance Bank stock is up, he is the chairman and he is doing fine financially." Another of Sarver's friends, who requested anonymity, said: "Robert is not taking money out of the Suns, they are probably costing him money."

The **Arizona Republic** on December 16, 2012 reported that Sarver is paid a quarter of a million dollars as director of Ameritage homes. That is just one of blips of his steady income stream.

Seth Pollack is also unaware of the Suns' financial structure. The Suns are a partnership and Sarver would not be allowed to take money out of the franchise. He is allowed to lose money. "Robert can afford it," his friend remarked.

The constant criticism from **Arizona Republic** writers Dan Bickley and Paul Coro is something that Sarver faces constantly. "The media has no idea how Robert works," his friend remarked, "he knows the rules and regulations of business. Whoever has these issues with Robert is crazy, they should leave him alone."

Sarver ignored this criticism and along with Lon Babby they planned a roster makeover after the 2011-2012 season. Everyone thought they were blowing smoke. In retrospect, they did exactly what they stated. There are now seven new, key players on the Suns roster. People are still upset that Steve Nash and Grant Hill are gone. That is to be expected. To blame Sarver for the Suns decline is natural. Perhaps in sports another view is that you have to retool the team.

In Phoenix there are more right wing political nuts than anywhere in the U. S. There is one website that attempts to link Sarver with Arizona's political problems. If you want a good laugh go to Politico Mafioso for the strangest links attacking Sarver. This website is a joke. See http://politicomafioso.blogspot.com/2012/06/liberal-loser-robert-sarver-drafts_28.html for the most offensive post I have ever seen. If you look purchase my book **Obama's Detractors: In The Right Wing Nut House**, available from Amazon, to really understand the radical right.

Peter: "Howard this is a shameless plug for your book." It is.

During his first twenty-three months owning the Phoenix Suns, the team went to the Western Conference Finals twice. The Los Angeles Clipper owner, Donald Sterling, is approaching thirty years as a franchise owner, and his team has never reached the conference finals. So Sarver is doing something right.

Whether you like or dislike Robert Sarver, he is doing his best to return the Suns to an elite NBA level. He is trying to build a winner. It doesn't happen overnight. Just look at Donald Sterling it took him thirty years to build a team.

chapter

TEN

COACH ALVIN GENTRY: THE QUIET FORCE BEHIND THE SUNS

"WHEN YOU LEAST EXPECT IT, SOMEONE MAY ACTUAL-LY LISTEN TO WHAT YOU HAVE TO SAY," ALVIN GENTRY

Coach Alvin Gentry is a unique individual. He comes into Paradise Bakery, and he is just an average guy. That is an average guy who is at the top of his profession. He jokes and talks with the regulars with a smile and words of encouragement. He epitomizes the Suns organization. He is committed to the community, he is an excellent coach and he is a great person.

ALVIN GENTRY: THE FORMATIVE YEARS

When Gentry was born on November 5, 1954 in Shelby, North Carolina, he grew up in a typical Southern town. This was a town with a thriving fabric mills and a small town atmosphere. The church was important. The calm local atmosphere, and the presence of strong church-family influences were important in developing his character. Gentry loved Shelby as a kid; he had other thoughts about his adult life. He didn't want to work in a factory, and he didn't want to become a farmer.

His first cousin, David Thompson, also grew up in Shelby, and he attended Crest Senior High where he was a star on the basketball team. Then Thompson attended North Carolina State where he led them to a National championship in 1974. After three years in college, Thompson was the number one pick of the Virginia Squires in 1975, and after the ABA-NBA merger; he went on to star with the Denver Nuggets. Thompson was not only friendly to Alvin, but he did everything he could to further his basketball career. He would be the reason that Gentry got into NBA coaching by getting him a tryout with the Denver Nuggets. He didn't make it as a basketball player, but his knowledge of the game brought Gentry to a head-coaching job in the NBA. But it was Shelby, North Carolina that formed his character.

THE SHELBY YEARS

His father, B. H. Gentry, was a fiber worker and his mother, Beulah, had to run a tight ship at home as the family lived a quiet life sitting down to dinner in a bucolic town. There were six kids in the Gentry family and two adults in a three-bedroom home. Early on Alvin learned diplomacy and compromise.

Alvin's mother, Beulah Mae, was a hard workingwoman who was employed at a grade school cafeteria. When one of Alvin's sisters, Loretta, came to a Suns game she remarked: "Look at Alvin doing his best Mama impersonation." She was referring to his habit of folding his arms to show his discontent with a scowl on his face. His mother had a tough, competitive attitude about life and Gentry has that persona in the NBA.

When he talks to NBA officials this is apparent. School was important for the Gentry family. In his early years, Alvin loved to run through the woods with his friends, and he would sneak behind the local drive in theater to watch a movie. He spent a great deal of his time on the linoleum floor of a gym at Holly Oak Park. He was a gym rat, and he also played for the Shelby High football team. They were one of the best football squads in the state. The Golden Lions were state champions in 1970 defeating Salisbury 13-7 and in 1972 defeating Mooresville 26-21. He was a receiver on the football team. He was a top-flight student and vice president of the Shelby Student Council. Alvin also was a member of the Monogram Club, the Octagon Club, the Spanish club and he was the School Marshall. He did all this while playing basketball day and night.

One day Alvin's basketball coach called him into the office and told him that he was starting as a sophomore. The coach also mentioned one other thing, he would guard his cousin, David Thompson, when they played rival Crest High School. Looking back on this experience, Gentry recalled: "Thompson only had thirty nine points that game. I really held him down." By the time that he was a senior, Alvin led his high school to the conference title. He was a solid player averaging fifteen points a game. A college scholarship was on the horizon.

He also had a normal family life. "We had food every night. We sat down as a family. When Christmas came, we had presents under the tree. On Easter, everybody had a new outfit. My parents were married sixty three years before my mom passed away (this was 2005) ... I came from a loving, very disciplined home," Gentry remarked. Why did Gentry make this comment to **Arizona Republic** beat writer Paul Coro? The answer is complex. Unlike many NBA players he didn't come from the ghetto. He also hates it when people describe him as articulate, insightful and intelligent. In other words he hates stereotypes and condescending people.

Alvin's father, G.H. Gentry, was respected in Shelby. He was a deacon for sixty-seven years at the Maple Springs Baptist Church. "I never met anyone who disliked by father," Gentry told Paul Coro. "My dad was truly a saint." G. H. once went eleven years without missing a day of work. The Gentry family included six children and the town was one that embraced family values. Alvin has always had a warm spot in his heart for Shelby, North Carolina.

While in high school, Alvin had a facility for mathematics. He also had a secret. He wanted to play in the NBA. He loved basketball, but he also had an interest in management. This would be his degree choice in college. Gentry also has another secret. His sister, Loretta, is better at mathematics and she is presently a senior employee with the United States Information Agency in Washington D. C.

It was a strong Christian childhood that prepared Gentry for the NBA. When you look at what referee Tim Donaghy did to the Suns, you have to be a Christian to forgive that little weasel. Stay tuned there is a chapter on that little greasy haired weasel. Gentry's personality is one that is stoic. He doesn't seem bothered by anything. There are times when he is unhappy. That usually occurs when a defensive rotation is missed, a player fails to hustle down the court or his coffee is cold at Paradise Bakery.

There is a humility and gentility to Gentry that comes from his small town roots. The journey to the head coaching position for the Phoenix Suns was a long and complex one. When Gentry grew up in Shelby, North Carolina, he looked up to his first cousin, North Carolina State and future NBA star David Thompson. When Clemson University came calling, Gentry considered going there, but he loved the coaching style of Pistol Pete Maravich's father Press. He attended Appalachian State University playing for Press Maravich and later Bobby Cremins. They contributed a great deal to his coaching style.

AT APPLACHIAN STATE AND ON TO COACHING

At Appalachian State, Gentry started twenty games, and he was a tough, blue-collar player. In his varsity career Gentry scored 489 points during his four years at Appalachian State. Unlike many basketball players, Gentry paid attention in the classroom. He left Appalachian State with a management degree. Professor Mike Moore, in the history department, remembers Gentry as a polite and serious student. Moore also remembers Gentry as a gym rat and a library regular. He later attended graduate school at the University of Colorado in 1977-1978. One of his friends in Shelby remarked: "Alvin's school work was most important and that came from his mom and dad."

When he graduated from college, an NBA team didn't draft him, but he still hoped for a tryout. His basketball knowledge was A plus, and he did have some skills. His cousin, David Thompson, secured a tryout with the Denver Nuggets. While working out with the Nuggets, Gentry impressed Coach Larry Brown with his knowledge of the game. Brown told some of his friends about Gentry's high basketball IQ.

The result was that in 1980, Gentry signed as an assistant coach at Baylor University for one year. He assisted Gene Iba. Then Larry Brown recommended Gentry to University of Colorado Coach Bill Blair, and he continued his coaching career on a team that struggled.

From day one, Gentry helped the Colorado program. He recruited future NBA guard Jay Humphries and forward Matt Bullard. When Bullard graduated from the University of Colorado, he was undrafted. By that time Gentry had left the program, but he outlined a training regime for Bullard. By 1991, Matt began a thirteen-year career in professional basketball and he played nine seasons for the Houston Rockets. While Bullard came to Colorado as Gentry was leaving, he credits the Gentry inspired work ethic, the inspiration and the belief in Bullard's career. Matt said that this kept him going.

While at the University of Colorado, Gentry worked with his star recruit Jay Humphries, a guard, who was Colorado's all time assists leader, and he learned a great deal about playing defense from Gentry. When the Phoenix Suns, as the thirteenth pick in the 1984 draft, selected Humphries, Gentry had his first interaction with the Phoenix Suns management.

The years from 1981-1985 were important ones for Gentry at Colorado. These were losing and not winning seasons, and they helped Gentry adjust to both wins and losses. It was under Gene Blair that he learned more about the college game. His knowledge of film sessions, scouting, game preparation and managing players led to others recognizing his skills. His input was important to Colorado's minimal successes. In 1985, Gentry became an integral part of Larry Brown's staff at the University of Kansas. In 1988, when Kansas won the national collegiate title, Brown was hired away by the NBA. Brown became the San Antonio Spurs coach, and he took Gentry with him.

THE SAN ANTONIO CONNECTION AND LARRY BROWN

It was in San Antonio that Gentry learned to refine his game substitution strategy. No one handles NBA players better than Larry Brown. As Gentry watched the San Antonio coach, he slowly developed his own system. Gentry realized that the fragile egos, the pumped psyches and the competitive drive for playing time needed to be continually readjusted and egos managed. A coach has to do all this and still win at least fifty games to keep his job.

It was while coaching in San Antonio that Gentry met his wife, Suzanne, who was the Spurs corporate sales director. In 1989, Gentry was officially an NBA coach. It was a long journey from Shelby, but he made it with dedication and hard work. He was still a decade away from becoming the Suns fourteenth head coach.

There is one obvious conclusion. That is that Alvin Gentry is a continual student of the game. He was now in a profession where success is measured by wins and little else matters. A combination of discipline and a defined offensive system helped Gentry move up in the NBA coach ranks. It was Larry Brown's philosophy, combined with his own touch that made Gentry ready for the NBA head coaching ranks.

THE NBA COACHING JOURNEY TO THE SUNS

The NBA coaching journey has been a roller coaster ride for Gentry. While an assistant under Larry Brown at San Antonio, he learned how to put the pieces together. That is Brown's unique substitutions and creative game plans taught Gentry a number of things about the pro game.

After two seasons with the Spurs, the Los Angeles Clippers hired Gentry as an assistant. It was the 1990-1991 season while he worked under head coach Mike Schuler, who was a former NBA Coach of the Year that Gentry was thrown into an adversarial situation. The owner, Donald Sterling, did what he could to cut costs. It showed on the team's record. The Clippers were 31-51. Then Gentry signed with the Miami Heat joining Kevin Loughery's staff in 1992.

The Miami Heat was a new franchise in disarray. Ron Rothstein, who coached the team in its first two seasons, had a 42-122 record. The Heat experience was an important one for Gentry, as he learned to turn adversity into success. He spent 1992-1994 as an assistant coach. When Kevin Loughery was fired with a 17 win and 29 losses in the 1994-1995 season, Gentry was named the interim head coach. He finished the season with a 15 and 21 record. The Heat looked for a big name to resurrect their sinking franchise. They found the perfect candidate in Pat Riley, who came in to take the head coaching position. Riley had won four NBA championships with the Los Angeles Lakers, and he had a legendary resume.

HEADACHES AND SUCCESS WITH THE DETROIT PISTONS

Gentry headed to the Detroit Pistons in 1995 to become an assistant coach working with Doug Collins on a team that many believed would advance to the Eastern Conference Finals. There was trouble from day one with the Pistons. Jerry Stackhouse and Grant Hill had arguments over where the ball should go. The Pistons center, Bison Dele, wasn't interested in playing. He had a lucrative and guaranteed contract, and he quickly lost interest in NBA basketball. The Pistons lost five games in a row, and there was something wrong with team chemistry. The use of players in a constant rotation and an inability to finish games, in the last few minutes, cost the Pistons any chance for success. When the team bus let the players out they went twelve separate ways. This was another lesson for Gentry. He learned to build team chemistry.

The Detroit Pistons were a team with a personality the opposite of Alvin Gentry's. They were defiant, they were fiery, they were unpredictable, and they were as likely to fight amongst themselves as with their opponent. This doesn't means that Alvin Gentry isn't fiery. He is, if you miss a double team, he is if you miss a defensive assignment, he is if you don't execute the pick and roll properly. The head coach, Doug Collins, was not only hot headed, but he had an unpredictable personality. If you didn't get it right away, you had a chance to hear some nasty words about your game. The players tuned out Collins early in the season. He is one of the finest coaches in the pros. He just wasn't right for the Pistons. It was a veteran team. He needed young kids that he could teach. The players had trouble adjusting to his often demeaning, and demanding style. Gentry is just as demanding but in a quiet, studious manner. It was only a matter of time before Collins was fired.

On February 2, 1998 Gentry took over as the head coach compiling sixteen wins and twenty-one losses. The Pistons missed the playoffs. It was as the Detroit Pistons head coach that Gentry's formidable coaching skills were exhibited. As an interim coach for the Pistons, Gentry had some big wins. His strategy sessions and free flowing offense led the Pistons to defeat the Sacramento Kings 111-85 on February 23, 1998, and then the Pistons upended the Indiana Pacers 122-91 on March 11. In five weeks, Gentry's coaching turned the Pistons into a defensive minded team that could score at will. The players wanted him back for the next year.

African American head coaches were few and far between in the 1990s. The Pistons interviewed a number of candidates. Joe Dumars and Grant Hill went to management and elicited support for Gentry. He was named the head coach, and the Pistons presented a contract worth one million dollars a year with incentives that could double the salary.

Things were looking great for Alvin Gentry. Then disaster struck. The Pistons lost a total of 126 man-hours to injuries, a number of the team's stars had mediocre scoring years, and it looked as if the season was lost. Gentry didn't give up on his team. They turned it around and made the playoffs. The lost in the first round to the Atlanta Hawks.

In the Fall of 1999, Gentry entered his second season as the Pistons' head coach realizing that he had to go deep in the playoffs to retain his job. He also was in the final year of his contract.

The 1999-2000 Detroit Pistons season was not what Gentry expected. The star-studded team went 42-40 and finished fourth in the NBA's Central Division. The fans also didn't show up on large numbers as the Pistons ranked fifteenth in attendance. Grant Hill averaged 23.6 a game. He was the lone bright spot in an otherwise chaotic season.

The problem with the Pistons is that they were twenty-first in defense. After 58 games with the Pistons 28-30, Gentry was fired. It was Grant Hill's final season, and he was once again an All Star. He was headed to the Orlando Magic signing a ninety plus million dollar contract. But Hill wasn't enough to keep the selfish and underachieving Pistons from helping Gentry's exit. There were other problems. The Pistons' temperamental and highly overpaid center Bison Dele, retired.

Peter: "Who the hell is Bison Dele? I think you are making stuff up."

The middle of the Pistons line up was a disaster. The Pistons also had a soft forward in Christian Laettner and an aging 6-10 center in Terry Mills. The interior Pistons' defense was so weak that opponents simply passed the ball into the paint and every big man in the league had a double double. It didn't make for a winning combination. George Irvine took over for Gentry with twenty-four games left and he went 14-10.

THERE IS A COACHING HELL: ON TO THE LOS ANGELES CLIPPERS

Then it was on to the San Antonio Spurs for a brief stint before he was hired to coach the Los Angeles Clippers. If there is a coaching hell, it is the Los Angeles Clippers. The owner, Donald Sterling, knows how to make lots of money. When it comes to basketball, he doesn't know how to spend his money. This is the quagmire that Alvin Gentry dropped into and his coaching was a high point for the franchise. That is saying a lot.

From 2000 to 2003, Alvin Gentry did was few coaches could accomplish. He made the Los Angeles Clippers look and play like an NBA team. His record of eighty-nine wins and one hundred thirty three losses doesn't tell the whole story. In the 2000-2001 season Gentry's Clippers beat the Los Angeles Lakers 118-95 and the Phoenix Suns 98 to 88, and this seemed to mollify Donald Sterling. The team finished with a 31-51 record and the following year the team improved to 39 wins and 43 losses. The next year was a disaster as the Clippers finished with 28 wins and fifty-four losses. Gentry was fired during the season and interim coach Dennis Johnson finished with an eight and sixteen record. The first thing Gentry did after he was fired was to thank owner Donald Sterling for the chance to coach the team. He left as a class act. One wonders if Sterling allegedly consulted a hooker for the next coach. The next coach, Mike Dunleavy, was in for a rough ride.

During his last year with the Clippers the team had nine young players playing for long-term or contract extensions. "I couldn't blame those young players for attempting to inflate their statistics, they were what twenty three years old and going after big money. We just sort of fell apart," Gentry concluded.

The road to the Suns' head coaching job began when Gentry was the lead assistant for six years under Mike D'Antoni and Terry Porter. Gentry had great knowledge of the game and Terry Porter listened intently to his ideas.

HOW TERRY PORTER SCREWED UP THE SUNS

The Phoenix Suns were a mess in February 2009. The players were unhappy. The owner was perplexed. It was a bad situation. When the general manager, Steve Kerr hired his friend former NBA player Terry Porter, it was to bring toughness and defense to the Suns. It was Porter's journey to the NBA from the small University of Wisconsin, Stevens Point basketball program to a lengthy career that impressed Kerr. Porter played for seventeen years in the NBA, and this attests to his tenacity. Porter was tough, disciplined and he never accepted excuses for failure. He also lacked personality, as well as common sense, and he had a frightening look.

During training camp, Raja Ball, the Suns' shooting guard and premier defensive specialist, remarked: "Everything is different." Porter took this as a challenge to his system and to his manhood. When Bell asked what was expected of him, Porter got angry. While Coach Mike D'Antoni couldn't take Bell out of the game because of his defensive prowess and three point shot, Porter decided to teach him a lesson. He benched Bell for no reason. This was not a smart move as Bell is as tough as Porter and worked long and hard in the basketball minor leagues before starring in the NBA. There is no greater respect for Bell than Kobe Bryant's comment: "Raja is one of the NBA's premier defensive guys." So Porter cooked his own goose with his attacks on Bell.

Porter only lasted four months as the Suns coach. The reason for his firing is a simple one. He employed a tough defensive minded style that Suns' personnel were incapable of playing. He never did adjust to the players, and they never tried to meet his demands. Everyone failed. When Alvin Gentry was promoted he said: "We are who we are and I think, we have to go back to trying to establish a breakneck pace like we've had in the past." Invariably, beat writers said that this was a return to the Mike D'Antoni system. This is not true. It was the Alvin Gentry system. In other words it was a blend of the seven-second and shot system that was D'Antoni philosophy, and the Gentry style, which included new defensive alignments.

THE FIVE REASONS FOR PORTER'S FAILURE

Why was Terry Porter a disaster? There are five main reasons. First, he didn't use All Star point guard Steve Nash effectively. Second, he didn't employ Grant Hill's defensive skills. Third, his substitutions made little sense. He had trouble making game time adjustments. Fourth, he tried to get the players in such great shape that he overworked the veterans. Shaquille O'Neal is the perfect example. Fifth, he argued with players and if they disagreed he offered to fight them. Raja Bell is the poster boy for Porter's character malfunction. He also didn't fit the profile of past Suns' coaches.

Porter was the thirteenth Suns' head coach. "I hired Terry," Kerr remarked, "because I believed in him. He's got a ton of integrity and dignity and class, and he's got a great work ethic." What Kerr didn't understand is that Porter could not handle people well, and his xs and os education was not a strong one.

The Suns' players were outraged with Porter's in your face attitude. Raja Bell, the Suns' premier shooting guard, almost came to blow numerous times with Porter. The trouble with the Suns began in training camp when the coach had his players take long runs, which was like a form of punishment from a youth summer camp. He also spent most of his time coaching defense. The October training camp was one where the players grumbled and some, like Raja Bell, openly wondered if Porter knew what he was doing. Amare Stoudemire later complained that Porter held his game back. Boris Diaw was openly critical of the coach. It was Diaw who wondered if the offense would crumble. When Diaw approached the coach about his concerns, Porter told him to get in shape. Porter's set play offense is what drove the players crazy. This offensive style took away the creativity and individual initiative of Steve Nash that led to the Suns' success. To his credit, Nash only said good things about Porter. One wonders what he really thought.

When Porter tried to slow down the Suns' explosive offense, he was demeaning to the players. They resented him. The Suns were 28-23 when Porter was fired, but it wasn't about their record. Porter didn't understand the Suns' culture. The run and gun and shoot in less than ten seconds was a carryover from Mike D'Antoni.

When the Suns acquired Shaquille O'Neal, Porter had trouble integrating him into the offense. "You can't keep that style and then go say we are going to get Shaq," Porter commented.

Personally, Terry Porter is defiant. In the eighteen games prior to the All Star game the Suns lost ten. When Porter was fired, he didn't understand the reason for his dismissal. He remarked: "How many coaches have got just 51 games into a shot?" Terry is a smart man. He just didn't know how to manage his players. If you want him to coach a defense he can. If you want him to teach toughness he can. If you want him to prepare a game plan he can't. Then Porter went on to blame his dismissal on the players. "I would have done some things different from the roster standpoint…there was some difficulty with the personnel we had…." To the end, Porter didn't understand his failings. He also didn't comprehend that when you are in ninth place and eight teams qualify for the playoffs your job is in trouble. He refused to take his hands off the reins. As a result, he lost the reins.

The bottom line is that Porter couldn't coach. He couldn't get along with his players. He had no idea how to use O'Neal and he was clueless about other teams.

Peter: "Any areas of success for Porter?" No!

SHAQ AND COACH ALVIN GENTRY

When Shaquille O'Neal arrived in the Valley of the Sun things were a mess as the franchise reeled under Terry Porter's inept leadership. The coach had lost control of the ship. Raja Bell wanted out. Steve Nash wasn't as productive. Rookie point guard Goran Dragic lost his confidence due to Porter's berating. When O'Neal made his debut with the Suns on February 20, 2009 against his former team the Los Angeles Lakers, Shaq scored fifteen points and had nine rebounds. The Lakers won 130-124 and Shaq acknowledged that he needed to turn the Suns around. For the remaining twenty-eight games Shaq averaged 12.9 points a game and 10.6 rebounds. There was still some gas in the tank. Much of this was due to the training staff and the new coach Alvin Gentry.

It was the following season that O'Neal was once again a force. He was the co-MVP in the All Star game, and his Suns statistics improved to 18 points a game and nine rebounds. He also had 1.6 blocks a game. Then O'Neal was traded to the Cleveland Cavaliers and ownership informed him it was a cost cutting measure.

While in Phoenix Shaq hung out at the Cheesecake Factory, and he lived near the Biltmore Hotel. He loved Phoenix. "I went to Phoenix in peace, arms up in surrender. I went from punking Penny to fighting with Kobe all the time chilling out with DWyade and banging heads with Pat Riley. I was burned out. I didn't want to fight nobody. So I wasn't about to punk Steve Nash," O'Neal concluded. By all accounts Shaq was happy playing with Nash and the Suns. He also had only good things to say about Coach Gentry. He loved playing with Grant Hill. "I have never met a single person who doesn't like and respect Grant Hill," Shaq remarked.

It took some time for Shaq to adjust to Nash's pick and roll and once he did there was no stopping his offensive rolls. He also loved playing with Amare Stoudemire. "Amare was a hardworking kid, very friendly," Shaq recalled. "He had a lot of offensive weapons."

Shaq weighed in on Coach Terry Porter. "Terry Porter got a raw deal in my opinion," Shaq continued. "He wanted to put the brakes on a little…get it inside now and again, but Steve and Grant couldn't really do that." As Shaq reflected on the inability of the Suns to adapt to Porter's system, he had empathy for the coach. The Suns also hated Porter's two-hour practices. A long practice under Coach Mike D'Antoni was half an hour and there were sometimes only a fifteen-minute run through or practice for the game. Alvin Gentry made mental notes. If he had to take over for Porter, he would return to the D'Antoni system.

O'Neal also liked General Manager Steve Kerr, and he believed that the Suns were on the right track for future success. Despite the turmoil surrounding the changes in the Suns' roster, Shaq loved his time in the Valley of the Sun. It was a vacation and he played well. He kept a low profile and liked his teammates. He had a great deal of respect for Coach Alvin Gentry and he sympathized with the Suns plight. Shaq thought the ship was sinking, and the Suns needed to be rescued.

ALVIN GENTRY TO THE RESCUE

When the Suns named Gentry to replace Porter there was a sign of relief not only among the player but also among the fans. Gentry's twenty years of coaching in the NBA, his knowledge of the players, his familiarity with the run and gun system, and his pattern of substitutions is a key to his success.

Alvin Gentry gets upset when you label him smart or intelligent. He considers the term condescending. A better way to explain Gentry is to suggest the he is shrewd. What this means is that he employs the players strengths. Gentry uses a small line up as well as anyone in the league. It is this unpredictable substitution pattern that helps the Suns high-octane offense.

There was also some drama attached to the Suns job. They were trying to trade All Star Amare Stoudemire when the All Star game was in Phoenix. The Suns were also nervous about announcing Porter's firing. Stoudemire wasn't happy that the Suns were shopping him. Porter claimed he was fired for no reason. Anyone who watched the turmoil surrounding the Suns disagreed.

Amare Stoudemire: "If my last home game is as an All Star starter here, that would be a great way to go out."

ALVIN GENTRY TURNS THE SUNS AROUND

The first game that Gentry coached was a breath of fresh air. One of his first substitutions was to put newly acquired point guard, Goran Dragic, into the game. Gentry whispered to him: "Relax, you're a pro." Porter was too hard on Dragic and had little faith in his ability. Dragic was struggling. The first thing that Dragic did when he went into the game under Coach Gentry was to turn over the ball. Coach Gentry smiled and remarked: "You're a pro now." Dragic smiled and went on to a great season.

When the Suns signed Dragic in September 2008 they brought in one of Europe's premier point guards. He began his pro career at seventeen, and he had five years of European league experience. The irony is that Dragic was drafted in the second round by the San Antonio Spurs and traded to the Suns. Had Porter not been fired, Dragic would not have blossomed. This is Alvin Gentry's gift. He can work with people.

Amare Stoudemire on Gentry: "It's his character, his aura. It's hard not to get along with him. He's a funny guy. He's smart. He knows the game of basketball."

In November 2009, Alvin Gentry was NBA Coach of the Month. In March 2010 Gentry once again was named the NBA Coach of the Month.

Gentry has a staff second to none in the NBA. It is the unseen and often-underappreciated assistant coaches that have made the Suns run and gun system a popular one.

COACHES UNDER GENTRY: IGOR KOKOSKOV AND NOEL GILLESPIE

Igor Kokoskov is in his fifth season as a member of the Suns coaching staff. He has been in the NBA for thirteen seasons He began his NBA career with the Detroit Pistons and then moved on to the Suns. He is the first full-time, non-American assistant coach in NBA history. The Suns recognized the importance of the international game before any other NBA team, and they brought Kokoskov in for his basketball knowledge. He also coached at the college level at the University of Missouri.

A native of Belgrade, Serbia, he was an assistant with the Serbian national team in the 2004 Olympics. In European competition, he has coached teams that twice qualified for the European Championships. He is also a key participant in the NBA's Basketball Without Borders program.

As an x's and o's coach, Kokoskov is a master and he is an important cog in the Suns coaching machine.

Noel Gillespie is an his tenth season with the Suns, and his interest in an athletic career began at the University of Wisconsin-Whitewater

He acts primarily as an advance scout. His scouting reports and pre-game preparation are important to the Suns' success. He also was an assistant coach to Dan Majerle in the Las Vegas Summer League since 2006 and along the way he has helped to develop a number of the younger Suns.

When he began his career with the Indiana Pacers in 2001, video production and scouting developed his reputation and when he came to the Suns in 2002 he brought along a reputation for carefully defined scouting reports.

ALVIN GENTRY: HOW DOES A NICE GUY LAST 600 GAMES INTO 2012?

In January 2012 T. J. Simers, a **Los Angeles Times** reporter, caught the essence of Gentry's personality. While interviewing Gentry, the coach recalled something his dad said; "It's hard work to be a jerk." That statement from Gentry's father describes many NBA players, and early on Alvin learned to work with people.

The question is how does a nice guy like Gentry work in four different decades as a coach with success in more than 600 NBA games? Simers doesn't approach the question, but the answer is an obvious one. First, Gentry has deep knowledge of basketball. Second, he has great people skills. Anyone who has worked for Donald Sterling has to have superior people skills. Third, he can manage players. Fourth, he was an unflappable personality. He only gets upset if there is no help on the weak side. Fifth, he is a student of the game past and present, and he can adjust to any style. Sixth, he can manage personalities and even work with jerks. Seventh, he relies on precision scouting, intuition and heavy preparation for games.

When he coached the Los Angeles Clippers, he remarked to Simers: "If you want to survive you can't take anything personal." **Los Angeles Times** sports writer T. J. Simers was surprised when Gentry told him that his favorite athletes were Tim Tebow and Kobe Bryant. "Why?" Asked a befuddled Simers. The answer was typical Gentry: "I love an athlete who goes beyond the call of duty to maximize his talent." Then Gentry went out to coach the Suns against the Lakers. Kobe scored seventeen of the Lakers' first twenty-five points. Maybe Coach you want to save those comments for the Paradise Bakery. It might be better to praise Pau Gasol, he doesn't have a killer instinct.

T. J. Simers is a jackass. He went after Lakers Coach Mike D'Antoni after a Lakers loss in December 2012, and the Lakers coach remarked: "You're starting to piss me off because you said something that's not factually correct." This dispute came when Simers suggested that the Lakers didn't practice defense. D'Antoni just held a press conference, Simers was there, and he explained the Lakers' defensive practices. Simers later went on Twitter and apologized. The point is that the sports writers often want to write a story with facts that are untrue. So D'Antoni should be congratulated for letting T. J. Simers have a taste of his own medicine. That is undue criticism.

Peter: "Howard is there any chance T. J. Simers and Dan Bickley are brothers?"

GENTRY'S YEARS WITH THE SUNS

Just when I truly believed that Alvin Gentry wasn't going to ever be a critical and vocal coach, he proved me wrong. He turned angry. In late February 2012, he ripped his team in the press. As a season ticket holder, I was on Gentry's side. The Suns looked awful. Unlike the perpetually complaining season ticket holder, New York Ernie, who went to the 6th Man booth and asked when he was getting his money back, Coach Gentry took a tough love approach. Practices emphasizing defense made the necessary impression. After losing to the lackluster Golden State Warriors 106-104, Gentry blew his stack. When the Suns fell behind 36 to 17 early in the game, Gentry pointed out that it is difficult to win these types of games. "The game was lost in the first ten minutes," Gentry continued. "When we got an opportunity to do something good and we come out like that, it's just ridiculous." He talked about the season ticket holders. He intimated that they might want their money back. I wonder was he talking to Ernie?

At the press conference after the Golden State game, Gentry even swore. I am not sure I can forgive the coach for that. Then the team went on a winning streak. There was a message to Gentry's anger, he woke his team up and they finished with a 500 record, and they almost made the playoffs. While Gentry is a nice guy, he is capable of being critical, he is also capable of excellent coaching.

THE 22 THINGS THAT ARE INTERESTING ABOUT ALVIN GENTRY

1. He once worked for six months selling shoes. This fact came from Los Angeles Lakers Coach Mike Brown.

2. His son is still mad over the Suns trading point guard Goran Dragic. Now that Dragic is back everything is fine at home.

3. His sister is better at mathematics. She works for the federal government.

4. He sometimes eats a Blueberry muffin with extra frosting at Paradise Bakery.

5. His birthday cookie from Paradise Bakery is with purple frosting. He does not have purple socks or a purple tie.

6. "Brian's Song" is Coach Gentry's favorite movie.

7. John Grisham is Coach Gentry's favorite writer.

8. In April 2012 Coach Gentry visited Graceland. The Suns were playing the Memphis Grizzlies. He took a picture of Elvis' $1200 Microwave that Presley bought in 1958.

9. He is a two time NBA Coach of the Month in October/November 2009 and March 2010.

10. He is the fourth fastest coach in franchise history to reach 100 wins.

11. Gentry's ten wins in postseason play is second among Suns' coaches.

12. On February 7, 2012 he reached the three hundred-win milestones as a Suns coach.

13. After he took over as the Suns head coach on February 17, 2009, the Suns scored 140 or more points in the next three games. The old run and gun offense was back.

14. He is the fifth Suns head coach to earn a playoff berth in his first full season as the head coach.

15. On May 9, 2009 the interim head coach designation was removed and Gentry became the 14th head coach in franchise history.

16. During the fifth game of the 2010 season, in a playoff game with the Los Angeles Lakers, Gentry threw up on national TV. Food poisoning was the reason for his illness. Source: Alvin Gentry

17. Alvin Gentry has a 13D-shoe size.

18. When Gentry went to Graceland, he took along the Suns video coordinator. The video coordinator's name: Elvis Valcarcel. So Gentry took Elvis to visit Elvis. Then they went to the gift shop where Elvis went wild buying memorabilia. That is Elvis Valcarcel.

19. Shelby North Carolina, Gentry's hometown is also home to David Allan Coe, Rodney Allen Rippy, Don Gibson and Earl Scruggs.

20. Alvin Gentry was born on November 5 as was UCLA and NBA legend Bill Walton and musician Ike Turner.

21. When Gentry was the Detroit Pistons head coach, the **Detroit News** nicknamed him "the Stabilizer."

22. In his first three seasons as the Suns head coach Gentry's team finished second in the Pacific division. In two of those three years they missed the playoffs. The year that they qualified for the playoffs, 2009-2010, they went to the conference finals after beating San Antonio in four straight games. In the conference finals, they lost to the Los Angeles Lakers 4 games to 2 games. The Lakers went on to beat the Boston Celtic for the NBA championship.

Peter: "Howard, you desperately need to get a life."

Claude: "No comment. Peter is a sage."

COACH GENTRY'S 2012-2013 CHALLENGE

During the 2012-2013 season, Alvin Gentry's job is to take a new roster and bring the team back into the playoffs. He is one of the most underrated coaches in the NBA, and he relishes the challenge of bringing together a new and diverse roster. He is in the last year of his contract and Coach Gentry deservers an extension. Stay tuned.

The Phoenix Suns have the best head coach in the NBA. They are having him work the last year of his contract without any serious discussion about an extension. In his office, Gentry has all the accoutrements of a successful head coach. He has plaques on the wall, he has scouting reports on his desk and the book **50 Shades of Grey** is prominently displayed on his desk. Remind me to talk with Coach Gentry about his reading selections.

As the 2012-2013 season began, he had a budding superstar in Michael Beasley. The problem is that there are two Michael Beasley's, the one who shows up with a ten point night and the other one was scores thirty. Unfortunately, the ten point Beasley has been the one to come to the fore. When Beasley is not at the small forward position, P. J. Tucker takes up the remainder of the minutes. Tucker is exactly the opposite of Beasley. He is a tenacious rebounder, he is a frenetic defender and he can shut down the opponents top front line scorer. He can also score. Because of these skills, Tucker is in the game at crunch time, and this isn't good for Beasley's confidence.

Dan Bickley, the **Arizona Republic** columnist, summed up Gentry: "He was the model assistant, supremely loyal to Mike D'Antoni. He took over when Terry Porter flamed out, guiding the team on an improbable journey. His coaching drew rave reviews from Steve Nash and Grant Hill." What Bickley concludes is that the Suns need to win now to save Gentry's job. I don't think so. Robert Sarver and Lon Babby are fair-minded men, and they will judge Gentry on the entire season. The Suns do not look like a playoff team. Alvin Gentry deserves an extension, a pay raise and some loyalty. Time will tell.

The best part of Alvin Gentry is that as the 2012-2103 season progresses, is that he is focused on his team not on a contract extension. "I don't really worry about that," Gentry said. "No one really coaches to lose." That said, Gentry is one of the fiercest competitors in the NBA. His teams are prepared and he is a class act.

A good indication of Gentry's coaching talent is to look back on the last season. In 2011-2012, despite all the issues with the strike, Gentry's team came roaring back from a poor first half to salvage the year and a 33-33 record.

chapter

ELEVEN

THE FIRST HALF OF THE 2011-2012 SEASON: JANUARY TO THE ALL STAR BREAK, HELP

"I THINK THE WHOLE TEAM HAS BEEN ENCOURAG-
ING...THEY'VE BONDED TOGETHER, THEY PLAY HARD
AND THEY TRY TO PLAY UNSELFISH AND DO THE
RIGHT THING. WHEN THAT'S THE CASE, THE YOU HAVE
TO FEEL GOOD ABOUT IT." COACH ALVIN GENTRY, OC-
TOBER 8, 2012

As the 2011-2012 season began, the Phoenix Suns had a positive schedule. They weren't in line to play many of the top teams. The Suns weren't scheduled to play the Miami Heat, the Chicago Bulls, the New York Knicks and the Orlando Magic at home. This meant that marquee players Dwight Howard, Carmelo Anthony, Derrick Rose, LeBron James, Chris Bosch, Dwyane Wade and Amare Stoudemire would not be playing in Phoenix. This isn't good for the box office, but it was great for the Suns win-loss percentage.

As the Suns prepared their roster for the 2012-2013 season, the previous year provided a road map for a roster blow up. Change was necessary. The Suns were old, stagnant and not going anywhere. They needed to rethink and restock with new players. This would be a painful process as Steve Nash and Grant Hill left for Los Angeles.

Peter: "After reading this book, I think that you should go to Los Angeles."

THE IRONY OF THE 2012 SEASON

The irony of the 2012 season is that the Suns played much better against the good teams. The schedule was a problem as there were too many games in too few days.

Once the season concluded, the problem with the 2012 schedule was the large number of back-to-back games. Suns management realized that the tired and aging Suns needed a makeover. The aging superstars Grant Hill and Steve Nash theoretically were supposed to wilt under this schedule. By the time the season concluded, Nash and Hill were in better shape, playing at a higher level than almost anyone in the league. You can credit the Suns training staff, as well as the lack of nightclubs and discos in Phoenix, and the intensity of the team. Character, as well as talent, wins games. The Suns had plenty of incentive to win, as they hadn't made the playoffs in two years.

The sixteen games in the first month of the season were not inspiring. The six wins and ten losses indicated that the Suns were having some internal problems. With six of the ten losses by more than ten points there was concern for the future. There was also concern for my future, as I needed the NBA season. Otherwise I would be condemned to drinking coffee, watching the Scottsdale Barbies and writing books. No one I had coffee with wanted me solely writing books. They could only take so many of my stories. When the NBA season was announced, I walked into Paradise Bakery and there was a cheer from the table. They wouldn't have to listen to me talk about my books the Beatles or President Barack Obama. I could bore them with my tales of the Phoenix Suns. As I looked back on the first part of the Suns' strike shorted season, I didn't have a positive feeling.

THE FIRST MONTH OF THE STRIKE SHORTENED SEASON

The January 23, 2012 game with the Dallas Mavericks was an indication that thing were not going well. The Mavericks won 93 to 87 and the Suns sunk to 6-10 with a 3-6 record on the road. There were some high points. Marcin Gortat scored nineteen points and grabbed seventeen rebounds against the Mavericks. He couldn't match former Sun Shawn Marion who torched his former team for twenty-nine points. The only non-starter to play well, Shannon Brown, had fourteen points. The Suns were not in sync and Alvin Gentry looked for remedies. None came quickly.

The next night the Suns returned home and lost to the Toronto Raptors 99-96. The Raptors star player, Antoni Bargnani, returned from injury to score thirty-six points and a 31 to 19 third quarter run put the Raptors in the lead for good. Paul Coro, the best writer for the **Arizona Republic**, speculated that there were jobs on the line. Perhaps the low point was January 30 when the Suns lost to the Dallas Mavericks 122-99. To add insult to injury, it was a home loss. Steve Nash had a hip contusion but Sebastian Telfair filled in very well with thirteen points and six assists. It was obviously early, but it was also apparent that Sebastian Telfair was an excellent moneyball signing. He could do it all off the bench and with great consistency.

At the end of January 2012, the Suns won seven and lost thirteen games. The home record was four wins and six losses. The team was struggling. This was unacceptable to Coach Alvin Gentry, and he was not smiling on the sidelines. There were signs of hope as they beat the New York Knicks in Madison Square Garden and the Boston Celtics in their arena. They also defeated Memphis. The point is these were all playoff teams. The Suns lost to some lesser teams, the Cleveland Cavaliers, the New Jersey Nets and the Toronto Raptors.

What was wrong in January 2012? The answer is a simple one. The players and the coaching staff were getting used to each other. There were some new players in the mix. The Polish hammer, Marcin Gortat, was still getting used to Steve Nash's pick and roll. Then Nash departed to the Los Angeles Lakers and the freelance offense ended. Ronnie Price was great defensively, but he never fit into the offense. Coach Alvin Gentry never gave up on his team and the new defensive minded assistant coach, Elston Turner, began to work his magic. The rookie power forward, Markieff Morris, had some great games and then he struggled. His play was generally excellent, but he hit the rookie wall in the middle of the season. In the first month, Morris was playing about twenty minutes a game. Morris surprised everyone with a deadly three point shot. Something he didn't have in his arsenal at Kansas. He also gives the Suns a toughness that they haven't previously experienced on the boards.

By the end of January 2012, there was grumbling from the fans. New York Ernie took his friend Jasmine to her seat. "I am going to find out what happened to the team," Ernie remarked. He then went to the Sixth Man desk and asked for free tickets to another game. He had just scammed his way into free parking across the street from the U. S. Airways Arena by saying that he was eating at Kincaid's. Then he walked over to Legends, and he used coupons for two free meatball appetizers. He ordered an iced tea to save money. He did leave a two-dollar bill as a tip. He told his friend, Jasmine: "It looks like a five." Who said that New York Ernie isn't the greatest freebee artist in the Valley of the Sun? He is also the first person to get a free hotel room at the Ritz Carlton when he told the manager that he was Mike Miller's cousin. The manager scratched his head and asked: "Who is Mike Miller?" New York Ernie opened a large file of Miller pictures with autographs. The manager comped New York Ernie and put him on the same floor as the Miami Heat. I shudder to think what happened. Then New York Ernie sold the pictures on EBay.

New York Ernie's freebies with the Suns have got him to order Phoenix Cardinal tickets. He had them for one year and didn't get one freebie. He called the Cardinals in the season that they had lost eight straight games and cancelled his tickets. The Cardinals gave him a refund for the full season. But New York Ernie had a scam. He was friendly with one of the ticket takers and they let him into to the last four games as he said that he had misplaced his tickets.

The Suns were losing home games that in the past they won. Home losses to New Orleans, Cleveland and New Jersey had the press complaining about the rotation, defense and the players. The Suns quasi-general manager, Dan Bickley, wrote in the **Arizona Republic** that there needed to be some changes. This may be the one time that Coach Alvin Gentry agreed with Bickley.

The worst January 2012 loss was to the Toronto Raptors. The Suns had not lost to the Raptors since Canadian point guard Steve Nash returned to the Valley of the Sun in 2004. Former Suns General Manager Bryan Colangelo smiled from his seat in Section 101, as the watched the Raptors win. Nothing seemed to go right by the end of January. But head coach Alvin Gentry and the quiet, but efficient, Elston Turner were working on a plan. It was to make the bench a more defined and prominent factor.

There were some problems. Channing Frye seemed to lose his three point shot. He hit only thirty nine per cent in the first month. Shannon Brown was still adjusting to the Suns style, as was point guard Sebastian Telfair. The rookie power forward Markieff Morris and former Milwaukee Buck Michael Redd also had their moments. Ronnie Price played great defense at the shooting guard, but he didn't score enough. So Gentry and Turner had their work cut out for them. An emphasis on defense slowly entered the Suns' practices.

One of the highlights of the 2012 season was watching Michael Redd's return to the NBA. Once one of the most prolific scorers in the league, Redd worked through two knee surgeries to return with a vengeance. He averaged 8.2 points a game, but, in some key games, Redd's deadly three point shooting brought the Suns to victory. On January 14, Redd made his Suns' debut with fourteen points. On March 18, he scored twenty-five points in a win over the Houston Rockets. He was a valuable bench player all year.

ENTER ELSTON TURNER

When Coach Alvin Gentry lobbied to bring in Elston Turner, as a defensive coach, few people paid attention. Turner was a finalist for the Suns head-coaching job in 2008, and he is a fourteen year league coaching veteran. Turner's defensive specialist two-year contract was one of the Suns' smartest, if unheralded, moves in the off-season. Turner is a quiet, intelligent intense coach who has a difficult job. Most of the Suns thought defense was a country in Eastern Europe. It took Turner to the All Star break to get through to the Suns, when he did they had among the best second half defensive efforts.

As a student at the University of Mississippi, Turner was a 6-5 guard-forward who helped Ole Miss to the NCAA tournament during his senior year. He demonstrated key skills in the NBA that made him a natural coaching choice. Turner always had a sense of his role. When he played with the Chicago Bulls, it was defense that kept him on the roster. His time in Chicago prompted the Bulls to interview him in 2010 for their head-coaching job. By that time he had been an assistant with the Sacramento Kings, the Houston Rockets, the Minnesota Timberwolves and the Portland Trail Blazers.

The irony to Turner's hiring is that he was a finalist for the head-coaching job when Terry Porter was hired. Unlike Porter, Turner sought out the players and convinced them that his forty-minute defensive sessions would help the team. It took until the All-Star break but Turner did get results.

It was Turner's eight seasons in the NBA as a player, and his fourteen years as an assistant coach that honed his skills. He was a role player during his NBA career, and he fought to remain in the league. Defense was his forte. This experience created a competitive intensity. He was a second round draft choice in the 1981 NBA draft, and he quickly became an adept student of the game. But his pro basketball career didn't end with the NBA, he spent a year playing for the Rockford Lightning in the CBA and four years in Spain, Italy and Greece and then he came home. He played in the CBA for the Wichita Falls Texas team and in 1994-1995, he began his coaching career with the Chicago Rockers in the CBA. Turner was thirty-five years old and ready for a new career. By the time that he arrived in Phoenix, Turner had an impressive resume. Would it translate for the Phoenix Suns? It did. The former Swiss cheese defense vanished by the later part of the season. The main change was that Channing Frye became the focus of a collapsing defense. Not only was Frye a more active defender, his rebounding improved, and the team by March 2012 was in a stronger defensive mode. Once Turner convinced Frye to move inside for defensive rebounding and to post up on offense, his game improved. On offense, Frye suddenly had new moves and they were due to his new defensive alignments and Dan Majerle's help with the offensive end.

Elston Turner's impact is a positive one. "When you give up points off turnovers, 90 percent of the time it will lead to layups," Grant Hill remarked. He then pointed out that Coach Turner had a defensive scheme, and he approved of it.

In the off-season, the Suns didn't renew Coach Bill Cartwright's contract and Turner was elevated to the lead assistant. Cartwright's pro career was a great one with three championship rings with the Michael Jordan led Chicago Bulls. He also had a three-year head coaching stint with the Bulls that resulted in fifty-one wins and one hundred losses. He was the New York Knicks first pick and the third overall in the 1979 NBA draft.

Cartwright is a quiet student of the game, and the players referred to him as "teach." He helped Robin Lopez re-emerge in the second half of the 2012 season. Cartwright, like the other coaches, is a quality human being. Elston Turner was brought in for defense and Cartwright was a hire of former general manager, Steve Kerr. This wasn't the reason for not renewing his contract. The Suns were going in another direction, and Turner could coach the entire bench.

In November 2012 **Arizona Republic** beat writer Paul Coro weighed in on Turner's successes. It is not a pretty picture. The Suns have the worst defensive schemes for preventing three point shots, but with the present roster it didn't work in the early part of the season. By December 2012, the Suns were the third worst NBA field goal percentage defensive teams. Despite these statistics, the Suns' defense has improved. When Turner found P. J. Tucker on the roster, he had the prototype stopper. They also have two interior stoppers in Gortat and O'Neal. Things will get better in time.

The Suns allow teams to shoot too many three pointers as 43% of a visiting teams shots are from the three-point line. This is due to soft outside defense. Yet there are positives as the Suns are one of the least publicized team in the NBA.

DAN MAJERLE: THE COACH WITH THE BIG SHOT

Dan Majerle is what I call the secret coach. That is he is able to impart his shooting skills and NBA knowledge to a team that is constantly evolving. He is a quiet, but a studious, piece of the coaching puzzle. He can also still hit a shot during warm ups.

During his years in the NBA, Majerle learned a great deal about positioning for a shot. He was big, but slow, and as a dead shot he needed his place on the floor. There is no better coach to demonstrate how and where to take a shot. He also played for a number of teams and in different systems. So he can acquaint players with the rigors of different lifestyles in the NBA.

In the first half of the 2012 season, Majerle was working with a new group of players. It took him some time to impart his experiences. After the All-Star break, the Suns shot selection improved. Dan Majerle, the coach with the big shot, had a lot to do with the offensive improvement.

When the Suns opened the season 12-19 there was concern about the future. There was no need to be worried as the bench took over the slack. During the season the Suns played better against winning teams than they did losing teams. In March, the Suns won eleven games to help salvage the season. This was due to Shannon Brown, Sebastian Telfair and Markieff Morris coming off the bench with solid games.

THE NEW PHOENIX SUNS: THE BENCH FACTOR

Coach Alvin Gentry worked hard on developing a solid second unit. It was tough to play just five-second unit performers, as the Suns had seven excellent bench players. By the end of the year, the second unit was one of the best in the NBA. Some newcomers dominated the second unit. Shannon Brown, a free agent signed when the Los Angeles Lakers refused to pay him a fair salary. He could play the small forward, the shooting guard and he could fill in at point guard. Sebastian Telfair developed into a premier back up point guard and with his newly acquired three point shot, he became an offensive weapon. It was defense that was Telfair's new calling and he excelled at it. Somewhere Elston Turner is lurking in the background.

The rookie, Markieff Morris is a monster on the boards. He also developed an efficient three point shot. His 36% three-point average was the highest among those coming off the bench. When he came out of the University of Kansas, few people realized that he had a three point shot. While playing for the Suns, he developed into a deadly outside shooter. The best is yet to come.

There is a new bench as the 2012-2013 season opens. Time will tell if they jell. There is a good chemistry and Coach Gentry continues to shuffle the lineup.

Phoenix Suns' X Factor: Newcomers In The 2011-2012 Season

Statistics of first-year Suns Players

Shannon Brown: 10.8 PPG, 2.6 RPG, 1.1 APG, 41% FG, & 35% 3PT

Sebastian Telfair: 5. 9 PPG, 1.5 RPG, 2.3 APG, 40% FG, & 32% 3PT

Michael Redd : 7.9 PPG, 1.5 RPG, 0.7 APG, 40% FG, & 31% 3PT

Markieff Morris : 7.5 PPG, 4.4 RPG, 1.0 APG, 40% FG, & 36% 3PT

THE SUNS FIRST HALF SEASON: A SUMMARY

As the first half of the 2011-1012 season concluded, the Suns were 12-19 in their first thirty-one games. But there were signs of improvement on defense and there was a much better shot selection. For the first time since the 2003-2004 season, the Suns held their opponents to under a hundred points a game. The bad news is that the Suns averaged fewer points in the first half of the seasons than at any time in the last decade.

During the All Star break there were a series of practices that further helped the Suns to jell. "We had a situation where we had three really good practices and as a coaching staff we made some decisions as far as rotations and what we're going to stick with and live with when it came to those guys in the rotations," Gentry said.

One of the things that the Suns worked on was increasing field goal percentage. Since Steve Nash returned to the Suns they have been amongst the leaders in field goal percentage. This was the case in 2011-2012, as they finished sixth in the league.

TO THE ALL STAR BREAK: FROM FEBRUARY ONWARD

As the Suns rolled into the second month of the season, I was depressed. Things were not going well. Coach Gentry looked depressed. He has more to worry about them I did. He was still trying to figure out his rotation. He had twelve's guys, all of whom could play, and he wanted a nine or ten man rotation. Gentry worked it out in the weeks before the All Star game. The second half of the season was an unqualified success. Alvin Gentry should have gotten his contract extension. Stay tuned.

chapter

TWELVE

LANCE BLANKS: THE GENERAL MANAGER AND THOSE AROUND HIM INCLUDING BRAD CASPER NOW GONE

"IT'S MY DNA TO ACCEPT EXTREME CHALLENGES AND I EMBRACE THAT...I LOOK FORWARD TO MAKING THESE TOUGH DECISIONS." LANCE BLANKS

On August 5, 2010 Lance Blanks joined the Phoenix Suns as their general manger. As a former player in the NBA, he had a great deal of experience. He is a shrewd student of the game. He can deflect a question with a smile better than anyone in the NBA.

Blanks grew up in Del Rio, Texas. He was born on September 9, 1966, and at the age of forty-six he is one of the youngest executives in the NBA. He also comes from a family of noted athletes. His father, Sid, was a running back for the Houston Oilers in the AFL in the 1960s. His uncle, Larvell, was a professional baseball player with the Cleveland Indians in the 1970s, and his older daughter, Riley, is a promising star on the junior tennis circuit. Lance's daughter is also a junior at the University of Virginia, and her best tennis years are in the future. Blanks athletic career is a storied one, and his attention to detail and business makes him one of the NBA's rising executives.

BLANKS IN COLLEGE AND GETTING READY FOR THE NBA

Blanks began his college career at the University of Virginia, and then after two years, he transferred to the University of Texas. He left the Longhorns program as the eighth leading scorer in school history. He was also the schools steals leader.

During his junior year, Blanks had an immediate impact upon the Texas team scoring 19.7 points a game while leading Texas to a 25-9 season, and he won the Southwest Conference Newcomer of the Year award. His steals record, 111, and minutes played, 1,295, still stand as University of Texas records.

His senior year was even better as he was the Longhorns second leading scorer at 20.3 points a game. That year the Longhorns advanced to the Elite Eight and the backcourt of Blanks, Travis Mays and Joey Wright was christened the Texas BMW. Mays was the fourteenth pick in the 1990 NBA draft by the Sacramento Kings, and the Phoenix Suns selected Joey Wright in the second round of the NBA draft. Wright never appeared in an NBA game, playing overseas before beginning a successful coaching career. In Texas real estate circles, Wright is known as a savvy investor who has done well. For a few years, Wright coached the Brisbane Bullets and then the Gold Coast Blaze in the Australian professional league. The Australian team went bankrupt, and he headed home for Texas real estate. The excitement of the BMW Texas backcourt remains the stuff of Longhorn legend.

The BMW backcourt for the University of Texas provided not only excitement, but also when the famed backcourt made the Elite Eight in the NCAA basketball tournament, it established Texas basketball. There was no room in the Texas gym as they were the most exciting team in the Southwest Conference. When UT inducted Blanks into the Texas Athletics' Longhorn Hall of Fame, he remarked: "I feel honored to come back and be recognized for my effort....It means a lot that my time at UT mattered...."

At the University of Texas, Blanks was instrumental in the Longhorns going deep into the NCAA playoffs. He also was an excellent student, and he earned a bachelor's degree in radio/television. He also was selected during his senior year as a member of the NCAA All-Midwest

Regional team. At the University of Texas, Blanks left with not only school records, but he was recognized as an over the top student. The best was yet to come.

THE UNDER THE RADAR PERSONALITY OF A GM

There is no one under the radar more than Lance Blanks. He is the Suns general manager. What does that mean? It means that when you meet Blanks, he wants to know what you think. At a Suns' function, I asked Blanks if they were going to trade Steve Nash? He smiled. He should have called me a moron. Instead Banks said: "What do you think?" I searched for an answer. I looked at my lovely wife Carolyn and said: "If my wife divorced me she would want some money." Blanks smiled. He probably hadn't heard anything so stupid. He smiled. I smiled. My wife frowned. Blanks said: "Interesting!" He smiled. He left.

The point of the story is that as the General Manager you have to listen to nonsense. This is why they pay him the big money.

BLANKS AS A PLAYER

As the twenty-sixth pick in the 1990 NBA draft, Blanks played in three NBA seasons. His first NBA team, the Detroit Pistons, was one where Joe Dumars was a key player. It was in the Pistons culture that Blanks learned the ins and outs of the NBA game.

He also played for the Minnesota Timberwolves for two seasons. It was in Minnesota that Blanks logged enough minutes to be considered a defensive stopper. He was learning the subtle nuances of the game.

LANCE BLANKS NBA SALARIES

1990-1991 DETROIT PISTONS $365,000

1991-1992 DETROIT PISTONS: $415,000

1992-1993 DETROIT PISTONS: $490,000

Then he took his game to the Quad City Thunder and the Oklahoma City Cavalry in the CBA. He ended his pro career with five years in Germany and Greece. Along the way, Blanks was one of the more astute students of the game. The way that Dumars played the game, his high level of integrity and his brains on the court and off led him to the Piston's chief executive since 2000. Blanks watched and obviously learned from Dumars' example.

BLANKS' TRAINING FOR A GM POSITION

Before he was hired as the Suns general manager, Blanks was the Cleveland Cavaliers assistant general manager for five years. He was previously the director of scouting for the San Antonio Spurs, prior to joining the Cavaliers. When Blanks worked with the Cavaliers their overall record of 272 and 138 made his job an enviable one. Then James left to sign with the Miami Heat. Blanks faced the media. He remarked: "Lebron is 25 years old. My guess is, like us all, if we go back to that age there are things that we may or have not have done differently." Blanks went to say that he wasn't about to judge James. Blanks was not asked the question in Cleveland, but on the day that Blanks was introduced as the Suns new General Manager. His skill as the Vice President of Cleveland's basketball operations brought other job offers. He shrewdly waited for the right fit.

While with the Cavaliers, Blanks sat down for an interview with **Sports Nation**. He remarked that his time working for the San Antonio Spurs were years in which he did more "draft work and college scouting." With Cleveland he was part of the entire front office. He was now an assistant general manger working with Danny Ferry. It was a training ground for a gm position. Blanks remarked: "It is a dream to work in the NBA." He then went on to suggest that knowledge and hard work is the key to success.

When Lon Babby came to the Suns, as the director of basketball operations, one of his first tasks was to hire a general manager. Babby's choice was Lance Blanks. There were a number of success indictors in Blanks resume. He has deep knowledge of players, he understands contracts and labor negotiations, and he has a willingness to try different avenues to NBA success.

He worked for the Cleveland Cavaliers as they were in the process of losing Lebron James to Miami, and the subsequent firing of head coach Mike Brown. He witnessed General Manager Danny Ferry resign. The Cavaliers were a sinking ship, and Blanks worked well in the midst of controversy. He is a perfect fit for the Suns. The Suns planned to blow up their roster and Blanks would be in the middle of the process.

Cleveland Cavalier General Manager, Chris Grant, remarked: "Lance has been a key part of the special group that has helped establish a culture of success in our organization....We wish Lance the best as he moves on to the Suns."

The Blanks-Babby duo replaced Steve Kerr. It was a tough job as the fans loved Kerr, and he had NBA credibility with a long career and championship rings. As a former player and local college icon at the University of Arizona, Kerr was one of Arizona's most popular players. Like all the rumors that flew around the Valley of the Sun, no one knew if Kerr left due to disagreements with managements direction, or if he simply wanted to live in San Diego and work as an ESPN analyst. It doesn't matter. What is important is what Lance Blanks brought to the Suns. He brought a hard-core work ethic and a deep understanding of what makes an NBA team successful.

THE GREGG POPOVICH FACTOR

It was in San Antonio that Blanks learned most of what is important in the NBA. He is the fifth former Spurs employee to become a general manager. While working alongside Gregg Popovich, Blanks learned from the best teacher in the NBA. When the Los Angeles Lakers, the Oklahoma City Thunder and the Los Angeles Clippers reached the 2012 playoffs, they all had one thing in common. They had people in their organization trained by Popovich. The Thunder's general manager, Sam Presti, got his start working for Popovich. The Lakers coach Mike Brown was an assistant with Popovich and Clipper coach Vinny Del Negro played for him. Suns coach Alvin Gentry is also a Popovich protégé. So Lance Blanks is in good company. "You learn a lot about coaching from Pop," Mike Brown continued. "You also learn a lot on the front office side."

In Cleveland, Danny Ferry is another Popovich trainee attempting to turn a non-Lebron James team around. What Popovich's former students say to a man is that the Spurs can alter their roster, modify their playing style, and redo their substitution patterns while never losing a step.

Popovich values the organizational structure first and the players second. He has taken some of the biggest head cases in the NBA and turned them into steady players. He also took a couple of rookies, Tony Parker and Manu Ginobili, and turned them into All Stars. When Parker got off the plane after a ten-hour trip from Paris, Lance Blanks was waiting to conduct a workout. "I was terrible," Parker recalled of that day in 2001. "Lance was beating me up He was playing no defense, just fouling me like crazy. I didn't play well. They almost didn't draft me." But Popovich saw an intangible in Parker and his intuition led to an All Star point guard, who is now in the second decade of an illustrious NBA career. Lance Blanks was there to judge his talent and he had a lot to do with the Spurs decision to draft Parker.

POPOVICH'S DECISIVE NATURE: IT'S CATCHING

Popovich is decisive. When Coach Bob Hill started out 3-15 in 1996, Popovich, then the General Manager, fired him and took over the team. His secret is to integrate veteran players, like Tim Duncan or David Robinson, with the younger players. The Spurs are also famous for picking up players and turning their career around. Robert Horry was done in the NBA, and when Popovich brought him into the fold he became "Big Shot Bob." Another Popovich strength is to coach all twelve players. Everyone on the roster feels he is helping the team. Lance Blanks watched this and learned from it.

When the Spurs get ready to pick up a released veteran, Popovich will consult with the veteran players. Tim Duncan gave thumbs up to signing Stephen Jackson and Boris Diaw toward the end of the 2012 season. One is a head case and the other eats too many croque monsieur's. At San Antonio they played well and never gave Popovich any trouble. They are still there in the 2012-2013 season.

When Popovich's alumni discuss the Spurs, they all say the same thing. " I think everyone that has had a chance to work for Pop...would tell you that a lot of things that have the greatest impact are not necessarily basketball-related," Sam Presti remarked. When Presti took over the Oklahoma City Thunder, he used the Spurs model to take the franchise to the NBA Finals.

BLANKS APPOINTMENT AND PROGRESS

In 2010, as Lon Babby hired Lance Blanks to head the basketball side of the operation, there were the usual press questions. Who was Lance Blanks? Why was he hired? What would his philosophy be in terms of the roster? What Babby saw was the talent evaluator in Blanks' personality. He is a person who will take the Suns roster and over time restructure it. The Suns also wanted someone with a winning background. Blanks had it.

The media recognized that Blanks had a strong scouting background. He was also a player. What did the media miss? They didn't spend enough time pointing out that one of Blanks' beliefs is that some players need a fresh start. Because of that philosophy the Suns signed Michael Beasley, Jermaine O'Neal and Wesley Johnson. Beasley and Johnson are young players looking for a second chance to establish themselves as dominant players, while O'Neal is a crafty veteran, a born leader, and a player who can mentor the young roster. He can also dominate in the middle as a scorer and rebounder.

The aggressive move to bring Luis Scola to the Valley of the Sun added another big man. Blanks also believes in taking a chance on players who improve, hence the signing of P. J. Tucker who is a hard line competitor who has earned his minutes. When Tucker came off the bench to score fifteen points and grab seven rebounds in a come from behind victory over the New Orleans Hornets on Thanksgiving weekend 2012, Blanks decision looked good. It was Dan Majerle, coaching in the Las Vegas NBA Summer League, who alerted Blanks to Tucker's hidden talent.

As the 2012-2013 season began, the irony is that Dan Majerle discovered the best defensive addition to the Phoenix Suns. That came with the signing of 6-6 P. J. Tucker who looks like a motorized version, if a bit smaller, of the old power forwards like Karl Malone or Charles Barkley.

THE OTHER SIDE TO LANCE BLANKS: COMMUNITY AND THE ROSTER

There is another side to Lance Blanks. He is active in the NBA's Basketball Without Borders program that supports positive social-educational change through basketball. This program began in 2003, and it provides a continual commitment to charitable causes.

One of the things that Blanks learned from working with Gregg Popovich was to bring the team into the community. He has done that very well. He also is excellent at working with others in the Suns front office.

As the 2011-2012 season concluded, with the Suns 33-33, Blanks talked about revamping the roster. Most people didn't pay much attention to his comments. They were in for a surprise, as the Suns exploded the roster, and Blanks created a new team. He is one of the architects, who has completely changed the Suns' makeup.

Lance Blanks generally keeps a low profile. After the Suns changed their roster in the summer of 2012, Blanks told Paul Coro of the **Arizona Republic** that the goal was to build a roster that was good for some years to come. Blanks remarked: "The first goal was to be able to put a team out there that would handle the new era of the organization....A transition like that is not always seamless. We wanted to make sure we had people to weather the ups and downs entering the next era...." This sounds to me like Blanks was explaining why Steve Nash and Grant Hill were no longer with the team.

Blanks expects a great deal from Luis Scola, who is viewed as a key to a strong defense. Scola, who has been playing professionally since he was fifteen, is a veteran who can score and defend.

OTHERS IN THE FRONT OFFICE

There are a number of people in the Suns front office who are important but somewhat anonymous. John Treloar is the Director of Player Personnel, and he is in many ways the most experienced Sun insider. When he joined the suns on September 15, 2010, Treloar assisted Lon Babby and Lance Blanks with the overall basketball operation.

He has been a head coach in the NBA Development League with the Erie Bayhawks who were affiliated with the Cleveland Cavaliers and Toronto Raptors. With thirty-three years of experience in professional basketball, Treloar is a valuable addition to the Suns. He has not only coached but he has evaluated players and handled management duties. Treloar also coached at the college level as an assistant coach at Louisiana State University and Indiana University. His time working under legendary Indiana coach Bobby Knight was important to evaluating players and systems. He has a B. A. in business communication, and he is recognized as a top-flight player assessment individual.

Brad Casper is a President of Business Operations. As the former head of the Dial Corporation, Casper is concerned about the Suns being fan friendly. He also has the best haircut in the front office. Casper promotes the Suns "members-only opportunities." This is a program to allow season ticket holders to receive gift cards, autographed Suns jerseys, meet with players, tour the arena and generally feel like they are inside the Suns organization. There is also access to select speakers and personal events. Casper is also responsible for the Suns excellent Internet presence. There is always something building on the Internet for the Suns, and this makes it fun for the tech savvy.

How did the Suns land Brad Casper? He was running a company ten times the size of the Suns organization. The answer is simple one. He is a fan with a passion for the NBA. In private, someone told me the Cincinnati Reds are his favorite team. I suspect were his favorite team, the Suns, were on his radar. Casper spent sixteen years with Proctor and Gamble and his forte is marketing. He was an important addition to the Suns, because he understands the consumer. To get Casper to sign with the Suns there was a secret strategy. In 2010, Casper resigned from Dial and he attended the preseason game near Palm Springs at the Palm Desert, California tennis court. There he saw the Suns play in beautiful, if a bit hot, summer weather, and Casper was hooked. He signed with the Suns.

Casper was immediately put in charge of Project Refresh. This sounds like a Dial soap commercial. Clean up the fans and scrub them clean. Sarver and his top management were concerned about fan defection. He shouldn't have any concerns, while season tickets dipped a bit, the fans were still there. It became Casper's job to make sure they returned in large numbers. The Suns are not only fan friendly but they are accessible beyond any other team. That means they are working hard to make things smooth for the fans. They are also spending Robert Sarver's money. Not a bad way to go.

As this book was completed, Casper left the Suns to return to a mainstream business career. He will be missed.

LANCE BLANKS SUNS ROLE

Lance Blanks looks at his role as one where he has a three to five year window to turn the team around. On player selection, Blanks remarked: "It not about the contract. It's getting up and doing the best you can with what's in front of you, and facing the challenges you're faced with." Blanks has two years left on his contract to achieve his goals.

He spent a great deal of time preparing for the 2012 draft. The rumors of Steve Nash leaving, the twenty three million in cap space, the restive fans who complained about the Suns missing the playoffs for two straight years brought the Suns brain trust out with step one. That is finding a player in the draft that would fit into the system and do well. Blanks is spending a great deal of time looking at the possibilities. He did his homework as the Suns drafted well. The top pick, Kendall Marshall, is a moneyball selection. That is he has more value than meets the eye. He is a diverse and well-rounded player who fits the Suns' system. He doesn't come cheap, as he is the thirteenth pick in the 2012 draft. As the season began, Sebastian Telfair played so well as the back up point guard that Marshall by December had Bakersfield on the back of his jersey. The Suns NBA farm team could help him continue to develop his game. He only played in two of the first eight Suns' games and that did nothing for his development.

Who is Kendall Marshall? He is twenty years old and he averaged an ACC record 9.8 assists, which was second in the nation. He is a gifted passer, and, like Steve Nash, he has eyes in the back of his head when passing. The knock on Marshall is that he is not athletic. This is the same knock on Jared Dudley and it was the word on Steve Nash when he left Santa Clara for the NBA. Marshall is a shrewd decision maker who will fit into the Sun's pick and roll offense. Lance Blanks commented: "We didn't get Kendall for his athleticism and Kendall knows that…We got him for his brain and his ability to make people better…." Marshall put his feelings into perspective: "I feel there is no pass I can't complete."

Marshall was not penciled in as an immediate rotation player, but who knows the NBA is a strange league. Goran Dragic can mentor the young Marshall. Where this puts Sebastian Telfair's stellar play made it difficult to use Marshall, and he spent the first nineteen games on the bench. He did get in a few times for mop up minutes.

In December 2012, Marshall was sent down to the D-League to play for the Bakersfield Jam. He showed immediately that he was an NBA player. In his debut with the Jam, Marshall played for only eighteen minutes, and he scored twenty-one points with eight assists and only two turnovers. Marshall's performance was so strong that Lance Blanks attended some later Jam games. The experience and seasoning with the Bakersfield Jam is an important step in Marshall's evolution as an NBA point guard.

LANCE BLANKS AND THE MEDIA DANCE

One of the problems of an NBA executive is that the media is a constant presence. Whether you like the questions or not, you have to look at Blanks ability to handle the press. He is a master at it. When Lance held a luncheon for the media, he discussed draft prospects. It was early June 2012, and the Suns were still considering their draft choices. One writer asked him if the Suns were going to get more defense minded. In the media dance, Blanks gave the perfect answer. He remarked: "We want to add other ways to win ball games. By no stretch do we want to take away what has been so successful…." I am not sure what that means but it is the media dance that NBA executives must execute.

The Suns roster for 2012-2013 places more emphasis upon youth and player development. "The one thing I've learned through this process over the years is that Phoenix is relevant in players minds," Blanks concluded.

There is no doubt that Blanks has done a good job recreating the Suns' roster. He recognized that Josh Childress, Robin Lopez, Ronnie Price and Hakim Warrick didn't fit into the Suns' system. They are now gone. It was agonizing to lose Steve Nash and Grant Hill, but to rebuild the team it had to get younger. Blanks talks of building continuity between the front office, the coaches and the training staff.

When Blanks talked to the press, he said that the Suns' word for the future was commitment. That is how he defined the attempt to return the team to playoff status. "I've surveyed the land, and I got it and I understand it from ownership all the way down," Banks continued. "My hands are on it in a different way now." This translates to Blanks believing that the old run and gun system was no longer important, and he crafted the roster with two big men, Luis Scola and Jermaine O'Neal, and an inside banger P. J. Tucker. This is Blanks way of retooling the roster. Now it is time to see if it works. Stay tuned.

chapter

THIRTEEN

LON BABBY: FROM YALE TO THE VALLEY OF THE SUN

"GENIUS IS FORMED IN QUIET, CHARACTER IN THE STREAM OF HUMAN LIFE," GOETHE

Lon Babby went to Yale Law School. He was on his way to a career as a fancy New York or Washington lawyer. Then sports got in the way. He loved basketball and baseball. He grew up watching the New York Knicks and the New York Yankees. This was his downfall; he couldn't get the fan out of his life. So he gravitated to sports management.

What makes Babby right for the Suns' job? There are a number of things, but it begins and ends with Yale Law School and what he learned about compensation, deal making and fairness.

BABBY'S TRAINING FOR THE SUNS JOB

He was a player agent representing Tim Duncan, Hedo Turkuglo, Grant Hill, Shane Battier, and Ray Allen among others. His sports agency negotiated player contracts, marketed its clients and created business opportunities. Along the way he has made his clients a lot of money. Babby was considered one of the best negotiators in the sports management business. He is an under the radar type of guy. Although he is essentially shy, once he opens up you realize how smart he is, and he also has integrity. He also speaks his mind. What is he doing in NBA sports management? The answer is providing his clients with services that free them up to concentrate upon basketball.

He has also worked in professional football and baseball. His experience in every part of the professional sports world made Babby a natural choice to run the Suns. How did he get to the Phoenix Suns? His background is not only interesting, but it is a high level one that prepared Babby to run a professional basketball team. There is a great deal in the years before he came to the Valley of the Sun that helped him to run the show.

It is Babby's thirty-five years of practicing law that set him up for his position with the Suns. As the President of Basketball Operations, he is the brain behind the organizational structure. For many years, he was a practicing attorney in Washington D. C. with Williams and Connolly negotiating sports contracts. The road to the Suns was a long and interesting one. It was also a surprise to many of his friends, but once he negotiated Grant Hill's contract, the managing partner, Robert Sarver, knew that he had a franchise director.

On Tuesday July 20, 2010, the Suns formally announced that Lon Babby was the new President of Basketball Operations. The fifty-nine-year-old New Yorker came with an impressive resume. "This is truly a dream come true for me," Babby remarked at a press conference. "It allows my career to come full circle." He is only the fourth Suns' President of Basketball Operations. After thirty-five years in various sports management positions, and at a number of important administrative, court and contract levels, Babby has the unenviable task of turning around the Phoenix Suns. What prepared him for success?

BABBY'S EARLY BACKGROUND PREPARED HIM FOR SUCCESS

As a kid growing up in New York, Babby went with his father to Madison Square Garden and watched the Knicks. He was only 5-7, but he loved basketball. It was while living in Valley Stream on Long Island that Babby's sports interest flourished. His dad, who managed a clothing store, would take Lon on the train into the city for a sandwich at the Carnegie Deli and a Knicks game. Babby was hooked. He loved sports.

Since he wasn't going to be the point guard of the future, Babby concentrated on school. He went to Lehigh as an undergraduate, where he was an outstanding student. He was admitted to Yale Law School. This was this his crowning achievement as a young man. The best was yet to come.

He met his wife at a summer camp when he was sixteen, and they have been married for thirty-seven years. Their son, Ken, is a senior executive at the **Washington Post** and their daughter, Heather, is a marketing specialist for New York's Saks Fifth Avenue. After law school, Babby clerked for a federal district judge while his wife, Ellen, completed her PhD in French at Yale. Babby likes to say he is the second smartest Yale grad in the family.

In 1977, when he went to work for Edward Bennett Williams' Washington D. C. law firm, he was just another lawyer. It didn't take long for sports law to become a big part of his life. That same year Babby began working for the Washington Redskins, as one of their attorneys; he educated himself on sports management. Since Williams owned the Redskins, it was a natural move.

This began his rise to professional sports. As he worked under Edward Bennett Williams, who also owned the Baltimore Orioles as well as the Redskins, Babby learned the ins and outs of the sports business. He also worked with Jack Kent Cooke, another Redskin owner. It was with Cooke that he learned some of the subtle nuances of professional sports world. In the Washington D. C. business culture, Babby was a busy man.

When you meet Babby, he is friendly and open. There is no pretension. He is generally a very happy person with a warm handshake, and he indulges fans with photos and conversation. One wonders if the last two seasons has dulled his happiness quotient. He doesn't look like there has ever been a moment of controversy in his life. He is well adjusted, he has a great family and he loves his job. To quote Grant Hill: "He is the smartest man I know." Hill's mother might take issue with that statement.

ENTERING THE PROFESSIONAL SPORTS WORLD

When he began his sports career in 1977, representing the Washington Redskins, he was hooked on sports law. In 1979, he went to work for the Baltimore Orioles, and he was with this baseball franchise for fifteen years in various legal capacities. While working in baseball, word got around that Babby appealed to elite good guy athletes who signed top end contracts.

As a sports agent, Babby pioneered the concept of charging athlete clients an hourly fee rather than a percentage of their total contract. He also pioneered the business model of front loaded contracts for players. One of Babby's best contracts was a $122 million dollar agreement for Tim Duncan with the San Antonio Spurs in 2003. For sixteen years, Babby negotiated some of the best contracts in the NBA.

One of Babby's pet peeves is that restricted free agency takes away some of the best years of a player's earning career. While he is in management with the Phoenix Suns, he has always been a player's advocate and this attitude comes from working in sports other than basketball.

It was while working in baseball and football that Babby became a specialist in sports contracts. As general counsel, he negotiated the team contracts and later, when he opened his own sports agency, he was effective in representing players due to working both sides of the sports world.

Babby's company, Home Team Marketing, is one of the premier sports management businesses. Now that he is with the Suns, he is no longer active in the company. But there is a clear picture of Babby's expertise from his clients.

How do his clients describe Babby? They use the four p's: preparation, poise, perseverance and performance. He has modeled his career after that of Edward Bennett Williams, the founder of Williams and Connolly, and his chief thrust is to combine sports knowledge with a great deal of legal and fiscal skill. He can also think out of the box. It was Babby who convinced his client, Shane Battier, to sign a shoe deal with a Chinese company. He also negotiated a mega million-dollar salary deal for another client, Josh Childress, to play in Greece.

He sounds kind of boring and not very controversial. He isn't. There is one incident in his life that provides enough controversy for the rest of his life. In 1981, Babby represented John Hinckley, the man who shot President Ronald Reagan. "Our defense was the correct one," Babby continued. "Hinckley was not criminally responsible because he was mentally ill." Babby believed that Hinckley needed to be treated fairly by the justice system. This speaks to his high level of integrity. He is also not afraid to take on a controversial subject.

At thirty years of age, Babby was on his way as a big time Washington D. C. lawyer. Why did he do pro bono work? Babby has always spoken of a sense of justice and fair play. He also specialized in First

Amendment and civil rights law. I think Josh Childress needs to hire him to get more playing time.

THOSE IN THE SPORTS WORLD BABBY REPRESENTED

Babby's list of major clients has included some very famous names:• Tim Duncan• Ray Allen• Grant Hill• Shane Battier• Chamique Holdsclaw• Tamika Catchings • Josh Childress

When he worked as the general counsel for the Baltimore Orioles, he demonstrated not only leadership but also an eye for equalizing the competition. He had no thoughts of going into sports management. Then in 1996, former Dallas Cowboy Hall of Fame running back, Calvin Hill, called Babby and asked him to represent his son Grant. After interviewing a number of agents Grant wasn't impressed. Then he met Babby. The contracts that Babby negotiated for Grant with the Detroit Pistons, the Orlando Magic and the Phoenix Suns were among the best in NBA history. Babby contacts with Suns owner Robert Sarver led to his hiring as the President of Basketball Operations.

WHY DID BABBY COME TO THE PHOENIX SUNS?

Why did he want to come to the Phoenix Suns? This is a good question. Since I didn't interview Babby, I can only speculate. I talked to him twice during the season. He is unusually friendly. He is unusually honest and straightforward. If you ask him a question, he will answer it. He has a ready smile and a cherubic look. Beneath that beats the heart of an excellent businessman, a shrewd attorney and one gets the impression that Babby is still a fan. He is also one of the brightest minds in the NBA.

Babby's thirty-five years of experience in sports management, at one level or another, makes him a great addition to the Suns. He has deep basketball knowledge and the owner, Robert Sarver, is concerned about the fiscal bottom line. This is why Sarver hired Babby. It was to keep the finances straight. He had done that very well as the Suns have almost forty million dollars in cap space.

The **Sports Business Journal** named Babby as one of the 100 most powerful figures in sports. The **Sporting News** suggested how well regarded Babby was as he was only the fourth basketball president in

Phoenix Suns history. After spending sixteen years representing players, Babby knows how to spend money, as well as how to conserve it.

Since Lon Babby came in to run the show there are some changes. There is a sign in the locker room. "No Excuses." Babby sees this as cultural enhancement. He also vows to make better use of the draft. Who can forget Earl Clark? He is now a Los Angeles Lakers, but time will tell if he sticks. It is the attention to detail at the pre-draft camps that is important to NBA teams seeking to rebuild their roster.

It was at the Chicago Bulls Pre-Draft combine that the Suns' front office and scouts converged for a look at some under the radar players. Babby, along with John Treloar, the Suns' Director of Player Personnel, carefully scrutinized a crop of prospects, and this led to Kendall Marshall becoming the thirteenth pick in the 2012 NBA draft.

As the Suns prepared for the 2012-2013 season, there is a complete roster makeover with eight new players. The Suns have $7 million for an in-season signing. So the roster overhaul may have a few more additions.

WHAT LON BABBY BRINGS TO THE TABLE

Because he has worked on both sides of the table, as management and as a sports agent, Babby's key accomplishment since 2010 has been to guard against large contracts that bear no results.

When he was hired it was a move designed to strengthen the business side of the Suns. He has succeeded in this aspect. The quasi-general manager, Dan Bickley, doesn't think so and the **Arizona Republic** is constantly critical. What they miss is that Babby or perhaps Lance Blanks and Mark West have dumped some bad contracts. Think Hedo Turkoglu, Hakim Warrick, Mickael Pietrus and Josh Childress.

By trading Robin Lopez and Hakim Warrick, the Suns escaped not only what were bad contracts but players with mediocre contributions. Under the Babby-Blanks-West leadership other out sized contracts, notably Vince Carter's, was terminated

In May 2012, Lon Babby held a media luncheon. He informed the press that major spending was no longer in the works. One reason for this was that the Suns hoped to spend some of the money on resigning Steve Nash. That didn't happen, as Nash moved on to the Los Angeles Lakers. "Besides if he doesn't come back we will have ten million dollars in cap space," Babby remarked of Nash.

BABBY'S PLAN FOR THE FUTURE

During the summer of 2012, Babby talked about signing a top scorer. That didn't happen. What did happen was that the Suns brought size and strength inside with Luis Scola, good shooting outside with Michael Beasley and more depth at every position with the additions of Wesley Johnson, P. J. Tucker and Kendall Marshall. The roster is deeper, and it has versatility. So Lon Babby still has his work cut out for him. The talk of a "dynamic scorer" highlights one of the Suns problems. That is to find a go to guy. It will probably be Goran Dragic or Marcin Gortat. Michael Beasley is in the mix but only time will tell if he can elevate his game.

The question of rebuilding the team was one Suns management faced in December 2010, when they traded Jason Richardson to the Orlando Magic. This began a restructuring of the roster. The problem is that the Suns' two most popular players, Steve Nash and Grant Hill, were still playing well in their late thirties. Any thoughts of trading either player or not signing them to a contract extension was a difficult decision. They were simply too popular, they could both still play, and they were well respected in the community. "As much as we hated to admit it because we loved what this team represented, it was like watching the sands fall through the hour glass," Lon Babby said. It was a difficult decision but the Suns made plans as early as December 2010 to blow up the roster. It was accomplished with careful planning. There was still a strong and highly negative public reaction. The Suns weathered it.

The move to getting younger, financially more flexible and tougher inside began with the hiring of Elston Turner. It continued as John Shumate was brought on as an assistant coach in September 2012 to work with the younger players.

On Steve Nash, Babby remarked to **Arizona Republic** beat writer, Paul Coro: "We spent many hours with him on the topic of 'How could we bring you back what combination of players would work for you?" Babby paused and remarked: "We want it to work for us to give us the financial flexibility to play you and pay the players we're interested in." As he continued, Babby stated that the point guard ran the Suns' offense. Babby knew that they had a good run at a replacement. This was an indication why Goran Dragic was signed to a long-term contract. Babby was of the opinion that stability at the point was difficult because Sebastian Telfair was signed for only another year. This is the reason that Kendall Marshall was drafted. The Suns speculated that Telfair will have some serious free agent offers.

In order to attract free agents, in the summer of 2012, Babby had life sized cut outs made of the players the Suns were pursuing. These photographic images were put up in hotels where the prospective players stayed and outside the U. S. Airways Arena. The Suns staff made a DVD of each player's day in the Valley of the Sun. Some players, like Wesley Johnson, when he was traded to Phoenix, he told the press that he was taking his wife on a date in the Valley of the Sun. He loved the place from the time he set foot on Phoenix soil. After he visited Phoenix, Michael Beasley didn't listen to other offers. He signed with the Suns.

Babby revealed that Robert Sarver pushed for the signing of Goran Dragic and the acquisition of Luis Scola. Dragic agreed to a salary that was more than a million dollars less than Portland offered, because he wanted to live in the Valley of the Sun.

Trennis Jones, a basketball operations special assistant, was one of the Suns' secret weapons in Dragic'a acquisition. Babby sent Jones to Houston and to New Orleans to help in the signing of Dragic and the contract offer made to Eric Gordon. They signed Dragic and New Orleans matched the Gordon offer.

As Babby pointed out, Michael Beasley was a number two draft pick in 2008 and Wesley Johnson was the number four pick in the 2010 draft.

BABBY SHOWS HIS CAUTIOUS SIDE: CAP SPACE

As the Suns revamped their roster and worked on crafting a new team, Babby met with reporters. He told them that he was cautious about using cap space. He pointed out that there were no shortcuts to creating a better team. It would take a roster shake up and some time. The Suns would use their cap space, Babby told reporters, only "if it was prudent." He reiterated the need for flexibility.

When Babby said that the Suns would match any offer for center Robin Lopez, he put the Suns in the enviable position of trading Lopez and getting something in return. When the Suns traded him to the New Orleans Hornets they received the Minnesota Timberwolves Wesley Johnson and a future first round draft choice. Not bad!

There have been some pains for Babby in the rebuilding process. Babby suggested in 2012 that it might be another two years before the franchise is rebuilt as a playoff contender. This comment not only suggests his analytical intelligence but he is realistic.

BABBY'S ACCOMPLISHMENTS AND THE FUTURE

After the **Sports Business Journal** named Babby as one of the 100 most powerful figures in sports, he had a number of teams interesting in hiring him. The Suns are fortunate to have him. Babby provides a level of continuity to the franchise. He will attempt to continue molding the Suns into a winning playoff team. After spending sixteen years representing players, he has a feel, and the experience for how to turn around a franchise.

As the 2012-2013 season began, the question was: Would the Suns new roster be a ticket back into the playoffs? That question is being answered. There are some other Babby positives. Along with Mark West and Lance Blanks, Babby has acquired ten draft picks over the next three years. They may also have some hidden stars. Former Syracuse Coach Jim Boeheim believes that Wesley Johnson is underrated. Dwyane Wade talks about Michael Beasley's impending stardom. If one of the players works out, it will be fine.

The knock against Babby is that he is a numbers guy. There are only a few people who recognize that this is a positive and not a negative. Then moneyball concept should reap rewards in 2012-2013. Time will tell.

TOP TEN LON BABBY FACTS OF IMPORTANCE

1. ON WORKING: I HAVE AN EXCUSE TO WATCH AS MANY GAMES AS I CAN WHILE SAYING I AM WORKING.

2. ON FANS: THE PASSION THAT WE SHARE AND THE JOY WHEN OUR TEAM WINS, EVEN THOUGH WE NEVER SET FOOT ON THE FIELD.

3. ON PRESS CONFERENCES: I WOULD LIKE TO SEE FEWER PRESS CONFERENCES TO OFFER APOLOGIES FOR INEXCUSABLE CONDUCT.

4. BABBY'S DEEPEST AND DARKEST SECRET: PEOPLE ARE SURPRISED TO KNOW THAT I AM TAKING PIANO LESSONS.

5. FAVORITE QUOTE: "NO MAN STANDS SO TALL AS WHEN HE STOOPS TO HELP A CHILD," ABRAHAM LINCOLN

6. FAVORITE AUTHORS: DORIS KEARNS GOODWIN AND RICHARD RUSSO

7. FAVORITE MUSIC: THE BEATLES, BACH AND TONY BENNETT

8. HIS HEROES: MICKEY MANTLE, Y. A. TITTLE AND MORRY STEIN.

PETER: "WHO THE HELL IS MORRY STEIN?" HE IS THE FOUNDER OF THE SUMMER CAMP WHERE BABBY MET HIS WIFE.

9. FAVORITE CITY: BARCELONA
10. FAVORITE TRIP: A CRUISE TO THE BALTICS
PETER:"LON BABBY HAS A LIFE HOWARD, NOW YOU NEED TO GET ONE."
WHERE BABBY STANDS IN DECEMBER 2012

After the Suns won seven and lost nineteen to start in the 2012-2013 season, Babby gave a vote of confidence to Coach Alvin Gentry. "I think Alvin has pushed the guys and got them playing hard," Babby said. As Babby observed Gentry's record of 152 wins and 128 losses is an indication of his success. Babby also let the media know that the Suns were not adverse to a trade early in the season. He doesn't want to wait for the trade deadline to change the roster, which includes eight new faces.

In a December 2012 meeting with the press, Babby reiterated the franchise goal to take its time placing Michael Beasley in a position to be successful. The critics are harsh about Beasley's passing mistakes, his inattention to defense but they laud his offensive skills. Time will tell if the Beasley experiment will work.

What is obvious is that Lon Babby is remaking the roster and he is doing it with young, energetic players who need a fresh start.

chapter

FOURTEEN

AFTER THE ALL STAR BREAK: THE SUNS ARE ON A TEAR, ENTER ALVIN GENTRY IN 2011-2012

"THERE IS NEVER ENOUGH BASKETBALL FOR ME," ALVIN GENTRY

Alvin Gentry lives, breathes and obsesses over basketball. One wonders if this was the case as the Suns opened the second half of the 2011- 2012 season. There is no need to worry as Coach Gentry was up to the challenge. He never met an obstacle he couldn't attack and conquer. It was bringing the Suns back to NBA respectability and perhaps making the playoffs that was Gentry's mission in the second half of the 2011-2012 season.

By the All Star break it looked like the Phoenix Suns were headed for a losing season. The fans were unhappy, the owner Robert Sarver was scratching his head, and the media gurus predicted doom. The players were still trying to mesh. Enter Alvin Gentry. He devised a series of special practices, and the team meshed in the second half of the season.

The fans were disgruntled. The team needed some sort of spark. No one knew what was wrong. Alvin Gentry and his staff spent some time refiguring the second unit and players like Sebastian Telfair, Shannon Brown and Ronnie Price brought a defensive intensity that rubbed off on the starters.

When the Suns returned from the All Star break they were in fourteenth place in the NBA's Western Conference standings. Things did not look good as only eight teams make the playoffs. Coach Gentry laid down the law. They had to play hard and play defense. No mention was made of offense that was taken are of, and it was up to Elston Turner's defense sessions to help turn the team around.

GENTRY'S ROAD TO TURNING THE SEASON AROUND

Gentry hates to be called intelligent or smart. So my take is that Alvin Gentry is smooth, motivating, articulate, ready and tough. So that spells SMART. I guess that is the same as intelligent.

The Phoenix Suns coach is quiet, studious and a very nice guy. He is also the most under rated coach n the NBA. He is a brilliant basketball mind, but he is quiet and self-effacing. I forgive him for these sins.

When the second half of the season began there was a new and fiery Alvin Gentry. He made substitutions on the basis of good play. Suddenly the bench took notice, and they gave the starters a run for their money. At home, after the All Star break, the Suns won twelve games and lost only five. They also won twelve of their last twenty games against teams with a wining record. They had nineteen one hundred point games in the second half of the season compared to six in the first. The coach was angry, and he let his players know it. They responded. Now it's time for a contract extension.

I suspect that the first half Suns record of 14-20 went a long way toward Gentry's decision to push his players. A .500 season appeared impossible and the Suns were better on the road than at home. The Suns played so poorly during the first half of the season that they had a worse record than the Cleveland Cavaliers, the New Orleans Hornets, the Golden State Warriors and the New Jersey Nets. This was an embarrassment. Things did turn around quickly.

Coach Gentry took charge. He had three tough practices following the All Star Break. When Mike D'Antoni coached the Suns, the practices were often fifteen to thirty minutes. The players loved it, as D'Antoni ran offensive sets and the practices didn't tire anyone out. During Gentry's practices the Suns emphasized fundamentals and concentrated upon defense. A former Sun player told me that Coach Gentry probably felt his players, with the exception of Grant Hill, couldn't understand the word defense. They did after these three practices. Gentry also established a firm rotation The result was that Robin Lopez became a more effective back up center, Sebastian Telfair emerged as one of the best back up point guards in the NBA. Shannon Brown played so well the Suns brought him back for a three and a half million-dollar salary. They may not be able to afford either Brown or Telfair in 2013-2014, as they have turned into premier players off the bench. The toughest decision that Gentry made was to attempt to use Josh Childress in the rotation while Hakim Warrick spent more time on the bench. In retrospect, that was a mistake and Childress was waived in the contract amnesty period. Warrick was also traded. They just didn't work out. The Suns' were relieved of Childress cap space hit but they still had to pay him twenty one million dollars Ronnie Price, a back up shooting and sometimes point guard, saw little action during the last half of the season. He is now a member of the Portland Trail Blazers. Warrick, Childress and Price never complained. They are seasoned pros.

THE NEW MID-MARCH SUNS

By March 17, the Suns improved to 22-22, and point guard Steve Nash had a season high seventeen points to lead the Suns to a 109-101 victory over the Detroit Piston. This put the Suns outside the playoffs but they still had a chance. The victory over the Pistons made it three in a row, and the Suns looked like they were making a run for the last playoff spot.

On March 25, the Suns were in Cleveland to play an awful Cavalier team. The Cavaliers coach, Byron Scott, said it best: "We are just not a very good team." The Suns won 108 to 83 and Marcin Gortat had a monster game with twenty-two points, eight rebounds, an assist and two blocks. The Cavaliers outstanding rookie Kyrie Irving was held to sixteen points The Suns were now 25-24 and they had quickly turned around a bad season. In the next fourteen games they would win eight and lose six. The Suns were back on the road to the playoffs. Then they lost the last three games of the season.

As the Suns took the floor at the U. S. Airways Arena against the Los Angeles Clippers on April 19, they defeated them. The Suns were 33-30 and 19-12 at home and things looked good. That night they beat the Clippers with Marcin Gortat scoring fourteen points and grabbing as many rebounds. Sebastian Telfair came off the bench in sixteen minutes to score thirteen points, and he was a marvelous floor general. The rest of the Suns bench scored eleven points. Telfair also had three assists. This was one of the keys in the second half of the season, as one player after another took up the slack. Shannon Brown was one of the keys, as he replaced whoever was injured in the starting lineup. Both Telfair and Brown played better as starters.

As things looked good for the Suns making the playoffs disaster struck. They lost their last three regular season games and didn't make the playoffs. A series of key injuries hurt them. For the first forty-nine games the Suns had the fewest injuries in the NBA. That changed with Channing Frye hurting his shoulder and Grant Hill going down with a knee injury. Steve Nash's back acted up after forty-nine games in a shortened season. Hill's injury took place before an important road trip, and he missed fourteen of the Suns' last fifteen games. But the second unit, particularly Sebastian Telfair and Shannon Brown, picked up the slack by playing tenacious defense and running a high scoring offense. The Suns were 19-11 thus far in the games after the All Star contest. They needed two wins to get there but it didn't work out.

IN APRIL THE SUNS GOT IT TOGETHER

By April 2012 the Suns jelled. They were fighting for a playoff berth and they won eight games and lost six. They were 4-2 at home, and they were the best NBA team in terms of improving their record after the All Star break. With the Suns seven games under .500 at the All Star break, they not only played exciting basketball, but they beat teams with winning records consistently. Only a rash of late season injuries kept the Suns from the playoffs. During the last eighteen games in which they were behind, the Suns rallied to win eight of those games.

When Grant Hill went down with an injury Shannon Brown filled in for 15.6 minutes, Michael Redd for 10.5 minutes and Sebastian Telfair for 9.8 minutes. The late season 18-13 Suns record indicated that the team not only came together, but they had a strong nucleus for the next season.

WHAT WENT RIGHT AND WHAT WENT WRONG

One of the ironies of the 2012 season is that the Suns lost a number of games to inferior teams. "We were playing teams that we were better than, but we weren't ready to play them, and guys weren't in great shape at the beginning," said president of basketball operations Lon Babby. Shannon Brown took a different view. He argued that a full training camp, and an eighty-two game schedule would have blended the Suns into a playoff team.

Gentry put an end to this confusion in the second half of the season with a stifling defense and a firm rotation. The change came during a twelve game stretch over fourteen days in February when the Suns won ten games and beat some of the best NBA teams. The Suns' Polish center, Marcin Gortat, turned into a key defensive player, while maintaining his offensive efficiency, and he was a team leader. Gortat also ran the pick and roll with Steve Nash and this brought the crowd to its feet as Gortat slammed the ball.

It was the changes in the bench that brought the Suns to the .500 level, as Sebastian Telfair, Markieff Morris, Michael Redd and Shannon Brown morphed into a strong bench. The Suns were having fun and winning. Brown down the stretch displayed an athleticism and high basketball IQ that brought him a 2012-2013 Suns contract. It was while playing for Coach Gentry that he found his A game.

Coach Alvin Gentry is quiet, reserved and a gentleman. He may not be this way in the locker room, and he isn't always quiet on the floor. He instills a fury and the game plans were ones that kept the Suns' competing.

Statistics are boring, but they tell a great deal about the Suns. The Suns went from 29th to 22nd in rebounding and the defense ranked sixteenth with the Suns holding opponents to just over 40% shooting. Not only did the defense improve but also defensive coach Elston Turner created simple double teams and defensive rotations that caused other teams problems. It was a new Suns defense, and it jelled after the All Star break.

When the season ended the Suns were 33-33, they didn't make the playoffs. But it was a good run. During the last home game, the players threw t-shirts into the stands. It was the player's way of thanking the fans. Steve Nash was accorded one ovation after another and no one knew that it was his last hurrah. The Suns fans and players had a mutual feeling. It was a good, if not a great season. It was as much about the experience, as it was going to the playoffs.

HOW THE PLAYERS AND TEAM FARED AFTER THE ALL STAR GAME 2012

Although the Suns finished 33-33, there was a great deal of improvement among the players. Jared Dudley averaged a career high in rebounding at 12.7. He also shot a career high .485 percent. Channing

Frye, after a slow start, averaged 12.1 points after February 1. He had the second most three pointers of any NBA player. He also had nine double doubles during the abbreviated season. Marcin Gortat had a career high 15.4 points a game, and he is only the eighth player in Suns history to average double digit rebounds for the season. Shannon Brown was in the starting lineup for seventeen games, and he scored in double digits in thirty-three Suns games.

Grant Hill was a terror after the All Star break. He shot .500 from the field, he had double figures in nine of fourteen games and his defense shut down key players from other teams. The examples are Miami's Dwayne Wade holding him to 6 of 17 shooting, Atlanta's Joe Johnson 8 of 23, Memphis' Rudy Gay 7 of 20 and the Clippers Chris Paul 6 of 15.

From March 1 to 10 the Suns came back from double-digit deficits in five straight home games. This is the only time that has been done in the NBA since the Portland Trail Blazers did it in 1998.

SOME STATISTICAL FACTS ABOUT THE SECOND HALF OF THE NBA SEASON

The Suns had eight games where they were down by double digits at half time, that they came back and won. When the Suns were guaranteed a .500 record, it was the thirtieth time in the franchise history that they were a winning team. By going 12-4 at home since the All Star break the Suns had one of their most successful post All Star game runs.

When the second half of the 2011-2012 season opened, Coach Alvin Gentry emphasized that they had a favorable schedule, they had worked on cutting down turnovers and performing better at home. The energy off the bench that Gentry talked about emerged and had it not been for Grant Hill's injury in the last few games, the Suns might have made the playoffs. It was still a great season and 33-33 was not a bad finish.

chapter

FIFTEEN

THE SUNS BROADCAST TEAM: AL MCCOY, TOM CHAMBERS, SCOTT WILLIAMS, EDDIE JOHNSON, TIM KEMPTON, ANN MEYERS DRSYSDALE AND THE NEW TV GUY STEVE ALBERT AMONG OTHERS

"YOU CAN PUT THIS ONE IN THE OLD DEEP FREEZE,"
AL MCCOY ON A SUNS' WIN

In 1966, Al McCoy, a Phoenix broadcaster, read that the Philadelphia Warriors and the St. Louis Hawks were coming West for an NBA exhibition game. McCoy called the Hawks General Manager, Marty Blake, and asked him if his radio station, KOOL, could broadcast the game. "No charge," the indefatigable McCoy remarked. Blake agreed instantly.

The broadcast went well and McCoy loved the experience. He also wondered if the NBA was coming to the Valley of the Sun. The operative wisdom was that Phoenix was too small a market, too remote and the fans were too disinterested to support professional basketball. McCoy knew better. He became one of the earliest supporters of an NBA franchise. McCoy also wanted to be the Suns broadcaster. It took him a few years, but his persistence paid off, and today he is a broadcasting legend.

He had to wait his turn as a run of broadcasters paved the way for McCoy. He was finally in the booth for good in 1972. Until that time there were some interesting changes in the broadcast booth.

BOB VACHE AND HOT ROD HUNDLEY: THE FIRST VOICES OF THE SUNS

The first voice of the Suns, Bob Vache, was the sports director for KTAR radio and television. For the first year and a half of the Suns franchise, he was the team voice. He also covered Arizona State University sports for twenty-five years. As he broadcast the Suns games, Vache was known as a humble guy with few opinions. Then he was killed in a tragic automobile accident leaving a sponsors party.

Vache was only forty-five and he was the sports director for KTAR radio and television. He was a native Arizonan born near Tolleson and he stated in broadcasting at age twenty. His sports car went out of control on a curve and crashed into a power pole. It has been less than two hours since he finished his final sports program on KTAR.

Jerry Colangelo hired former NBA player Hot Rod Hundley to do the play by play. Hundley was Vache's color analyst. "I was in bed asleep when Jerry Colangelo called and woke me up. I couldn't believe it when told me Bob was dead," Hundley said. When Hundley found out that he had to take over the play-by-play duties, he did extensive research and he was a great broadcaster. But Hundley was viewed as a color man.

The Suns coach, John "Red" Kerr was fired about the time that Vache died and so Colangelo offered Kerr a spot in the broadcast booth. He moved on to become the voice of the Chicago Bulls and one of the most legendary broadcasters in NBA history. Hundley was relegated back to the color man position.

Then the Suns brought in Joe McConnell from 1970 to 1972, and he proved to be a popular local choice. McConnell, a Purdue graduate, was also a football announcer. In Phoenix, he was competent, but he lived in Indiana. He took a job with the Pacers in 1972 paving the way for Al McCoy to take over the microphone. McConnell wasn't an exciting announcer, but his play-by-play partner, Hot Rod Hundley, lit up the Valley of the Sun with his personality and partying.

It was Hundley who was an over the top guy who loved the local nightclub scene, and he was always the life of the party. There are still legendary stories of his exploits. One of Hundley's favorite stories was to tell people that Alfred Hitchcock used the Jefferson Hotel on South Central Avenue for the opening scenes in his 1960 movie Psycho. The hotel became a focal point for the partying Hollywood elite. Hot Rod Hundley was in the middle of it, and one night at about one in the morning Hundley and Paul Newman were walking down Central Avenue, each one was carrying a bottle of scotch. They were talking politics. The Phoenix police showed up and had pictures taken with the two and they signed autographs. Then the police took the two to Durant's for a late nightcap and Hundley had a gigantic bacon cheeseburger. Newman had a salad. It was still the Wild West. Hundley was the perfect drinking partner.

In 1972, when Paul Newman, who was filming The Life And Times of Judge Roy Bean, threw a television set out of the 4th story balcony of a Westward Ho hotel room; it was Hundley who bet him a hundred dollars that he couldn't throw the TV set out the window.

One night Hundley and Lee Marvin walked into the hotel bar, and they laughed about Paul Newman's exploits. That night Marvin and Hundley wandered up to the fifteenth floor of the Westward Ho, they proceeded to buy drinks for everyone in the bar until closing time. It appears there was a lot of good will for the Suns. When Marvin left Hundley, he asked: "Who in the hell are the Suns that you are talking about?" Basketball still needed some recognition in the Valley of the Sun.

"The Suns had a lot of talent my first year in Phoenix," Hundley continued. "The fans at the airport were unbelievable." J. Walter Kennedy, the NBA commissioner, pointed out that the Valley of the Sun had more positive fan support than any NBA team. So much for the antiquated idea that Phoenix couldn't support professional sports. Soon the Arizona Cardinals and the Arizona Diamondbacks brought professional football and baseball to the Valley of the Sun.

HOT ROD HUNDLEY: THE BAR BILLS WERE HIGH

When Hot Rod Hundley took over he loved the job. He did some play by play and more of the color commentator. In his book, **Hot Rod Hundley: You Gotta Love It Baby**, published in 2008, he said he quit smoking to sound better on the air. As a former NBA star, Hundley brought excitement to the Valley of the Sun. He spent five years broadcasting with the Suns, and he also was in the booth for the Utah Jazz and the Los Angeles Lakers. When he was in Phoenix Hundley worked primarily as a color man.

While living and broadcasting for the Suns for five years, Hundley owned a Phoenix bar, the Court Jester. He gave the players a 50% discount and the place was filled. He named one of his draft beers "DBush" after New York Knick Dave DeBusschere. Things definitely became more sedate after Hundley.

"When I was broadcasting for the Suns I owned a bar in Phoenix call the Court Jester," Hundley remarked and he went on to point out that the bar was filled with young women. On the NBA players, Hundley observed: "Everywhere you go people treat them special...the women want your company and the men want to buy you drinks."

Hundley's observations on the Suns are important. He documented the love between the fans and the team. "There was a big-time love affair with the Suns in Phoenix," Hundley wrote. (p. 67) Hot Rod Hundley spent five years broadcasting with the Phoenix Suns, and when he left in 1974 the bar tabs in such establishments as the roof top bar at the Westward Ho Hotel and other watering holes such as Navarre's and the bar at Durant's became normal places once again. Hundley ate dinner regularly at Durant's, and he loved to sit at the bar. He also told everyone who would listen that walking in the back door and through the kitchen was a Phoenix tradition. Hundley left town but the tales of his partying remains. But did the Suns have fun with Hundley? You bet!

On the road, Hundley and Connie Hawkins loved to party. One night while playing the New York Knicks they went drinking in Harlem and Hawkins introduced Hundley to his friends as "my adopted brother." Another night in Harlem, Hawkins said that Hundley was "his valet."

He went on to become the Utah Jazz' voice in Salt Lake City. He retired in 2009, and he is presently in good health enjoying himself in Salt Lake City.

AL MCCOY FORMALLY JOINS THE SUNS

As a radio guy, Al McCoy spent a lot of time making tapes of his broadcasts. He listened to a playback and decided that he would edit the first NBA exhibition game that he broadcast. He took out his mistakes. The result was a ten-minute broadcast that highlighted his future Hall of Fame credentials. At the time, McCoy was broadcasting Pacific Coast League Phoenix Giants baseball games. Jerry Colangelo loved the tape, and made a mental note to give McCoy a chance when he could. Bob

Vache's tragic death brought McCoy into the booth, and he is still the voice of the Suns.

From 1968 to 1972, McCoy stayed in touch with Colangelo. What Jerry observed was that McCoy was a steady guy. Hundley and Vache were drinkers and they loved to party. McConnell was a distant sort of person who would not be a permanent voice for the franchise. Colangelo realized that Al was the guy for the job.

The pieces in a broadcast team are many, varied and they must mesh for radio-television coverage. This didn't happen until McCoy came on full time. On September 27 1972, he formally joined the Suns. He soon became not only the voice of the Suns, but he employed certain phrases that brought instant recognition. He screams "shazam!" when a three point shot is made. When the Suns win he remarks: "You can put this one in the old deep freeze." He also is prone to giving players nicknames, Steve Nash became the Nash Rambler, and Jason Kidd was Captain Kidd. Shawn Marion was christened the Matrix. It is McCoy's use of phrases that makes him a descriptive broadcaster, and while he is not a color guy, his comments are much like the great color broadcasters.

The Suns broadcast teams present radio and television coverage that is among the best in the NBA. The interesting part of the coverage is that they are not homers. There are no excuses made for poor play, and there is a type of coverage that makes the fans want to come to the U. S. Airways Center. Al McCoy is the dean of radio broadcasters and his right hand man Tim Kempton works with him with style and grace.

While the Suns have great pre-game, halftime and post game analysts, they also have the only "Giant Teddy Bear" in the NBA, and this is Al McCoy's partner, color man Tim Kempton, who has created on air personality that no one can match.

TIM KEMPTON: THE GIANT TEDDY BEAR WHO ENTERTAINS

The first thing that you notice when you met Tim Kempton is that he is like a giant, friendly teddy bear. He smiles. He jokes. You love the guy the first time you meet him. He is also one of the most knowledgeable radio color men. Tim compliments Al McCoy with humor and insight.

As a color guy, Kempton knows a bit about the NBA, as he played for eight different teams in an eight-year career. He was the 124th pick in the 1986 draft, and he played with the Suns in 1992-1993. Kempton is the perfect sidekick for McCoy; he is knowledgeable, funny and very well educated.

As a University of Notre Dame graduate, Kempton is pleasant and fun loving. To the fans, he is friendly and approachable and full of great stories. He is a great partner, as he tells tales about Al McCoy playing the piano in the lounges of their hotels.

It is Kempton's NBA career that makes him a walking encyclopedia of NBA lore. He pays attention to detail, and his sage comments suggest humor and insight. Unlike many color commentators, he is not full of himself. There are no Chris Berman phrases that sound like nonsense, Kempton knows the game and makes it fun for the fans.

TOM LEANDER: A PRO ON THE TUBE

Tom Leander is an excellent and knowledgeable television announcer whose comments are carefully structured. That is he is professional but not exciting. But he knows the game so well he is a fountain of knowledge. He has worked in broadcasting for the Suns for twenty years and the last nine he has been one of the television play-by-play announcers. He grew up listening to Al McCoy and Los Angeles Lakers announcer Chick Hearn. He attempts some McCoy type phrases like "elevate and detonate." That phrase is too intellectual for the fans; they prefer a hard dunk. He is skillful in employing nicknames and strange phrases for Suns' fans, and he will remain in the booth as the back up guy to newly hired play-by-play announcer Steve Albert.

It is Leander's job to handle all the Suns' games in the 2102-2013 season as Gary Bender has retired. "I grew up listening to Al McCoy and Chick Hearn and they were famous for catch phrases." This quote suggests why he is an excellent analyst. He has also worked well with Tom Chambers, Eddie Johnson and Scott Williams.

GARY BENDER: A PRO TO THE MAX

Gary Bender has been a Suns broadcaster for eighteen years and in 2011 he announced his retirement. He will return to the University of Kansas to work with the alumni association. His years with the Suns were exciting ones. He called the Suns TV games with class, and he is a high character person. Bender worked for five pro football, basketball and baseball teams. "I have often said I'm kind of an ordinary guy who really experienced some extraordinary things," Bender remarked. He remains an icon and a wonderful voice for the Suns.

As Bender retired, he looked back upon his career. He loved living in the Valley of the Sun, and he formed permanent friendships with Eddie Johnson, Al McCoy, Tom Chambers and Dan Majerle. He will miss Phoenix.

SCOTT WILLIAMS: THE BIG MAN WHO COULD AND DID

As he grew up in Los Angeles, Scott Williams was a dedicated Los Angeles Lakers fan. Kareem Abdul Jabbar led the Lakers and with James Worthy, Magic Johnson and Byron Scott they were not only fun to watch, but the play of the big men inspired Williams to improve his game.

In 1986, Scott led Los Angeles' Glen A. Wilson High School from Hacienda Heights to the 1986 C.I.F. State Championship. North Carolina coach Dean Smith recruited him, and Scott was an excellent student as well as a basketball player who had a complete inside game. At 6-10, and almost two hundred thirty pounds, he was a formidable inside presence.

When Williams completed his degree and his playing days for the University of North Carolina Tarheels, he was ready for a career in broadcasting or business. He went undrafted in the NBA. But his size and skill prompted the Chicago Bulls to bring him into their training camp. He had skills as a big man, and he was a smart player who learned the finer points of the game from Coach Smith. He made the Bulls roster.

After he signed as a free agent with the Chicago Bulls, Williams took a look at the Bulls roster. Michael Jordan led a team destined to win sixty one games with a roster that included Bill Cartwright, Scottie Pippen, Horace Grant, John Paxson and B. J. Armstrong. They were loaded and the Bulls went on to become NBA champions. Against all odds, Williams made the roster and this began an NBA career that went from 1990 to 2005. He also won three championship rings in his first three NBA seasons.

The first thing that Williams did was to demonstrate his intelligence by asking Michael Jordan to define an NBA professional. He listened and emulated the traits that Jordan believed defined a winner. Every day Williams showed up early for practice, and he was the only rookie and undrafted free agent to make the Bulls roster. He signed for $150,000 dollars and this was a good rookie salary as John Paxson was making only $385,000 in his eighth NBA season.

Williams played four years with the Bulls winning three championships, and then in 1994 he signed with the Philadelphia 76ers. He had four and a half injury riddled seasons before he was traded to the Milwaukee Bucks in 1999. It was with the Bucks that his scoring 7.6 a game and rebounds 6.6 a game were career highs.

As he continued his NBA career in 2000, Williams played for the Phoenix Suns for one and a half seasons, as well as the Denver Nuggets, the Dallas Mavericks and the Cleveland Cavaliers. He was a power forward-center who defined the essence of professionalism. With a degree in broadcasting, an ingratiating smile and a mellifluous voice, he was a natural for the broadcasting booth.

It was while Williams played for the Suns for a year and a half from 2002-2004 before ending his career with the Cleveland Cavaliers, that he was hired as a color commentator. In 2005, when Williams became a color commentator for the Cavaliers, he was a natural. His infectious smile, deep knowledge of the game and camera friendly appearance made him a fan favorite in the television booth. He had a great run with the Cavaliers describing Lebron James' game. He also worked as a color commentator for the Milwaukee Bucks. From 2008 to 2012, Williams was a Suns television analyst.

SCOTT WILLIAMS ON NORTH CAROLINA AND DEAN SMITH

Looking back on his days at the University of North Carolina, Williams reflected on the values, the education, the training and the ability that Coach Dean Smith brought to his character.

> MY EXPERIENCE IN BASKETBALL AT EVERY LEVEL HAS TAUGHT ME THAT THE MOST SUCCESSFUL TEAMS ARE THE ONES THAT HAVE THE BEST TEAM CHEMISTRY. THAT WAS TRUE ON MY TEAMS AT NORTH CAROLINA...AS WELL AS IN THE NBA WITH CHICAGO. IN BOTH THOSE PLACES THE PLAYERS PULLED SO HARD FOR ONE ANOTHER THAT IT ENERGIZED THE TEAM. THINGS DIDN'T OCCUR BY HAPPENSTANCE AT NORTH CAROLINA. THERE WAS AN EDUCATIONAL VALUE ATTACHED...IT WAS EDUCATIONAL FOR A YOUNG MAN WHO HAD GROWN UP IN LOS ANGELES TO GO TO THE DEEP SOUTH TO PLAY BASKETBALL....COACH SMITH NEVER TOOK CREDIT FOR OUR WINS BUT WENT OUT OF HIS WAY TO TAKE THE BLAME FOR ALL THE LOSSES, CLAIMING HE HADN'T PREPARED US PROPERLY. COACH SMITH HAS BEEN A FATHER FIGURE TO ME. WHEN THERE'S A MAJOR DECISION TO BE MADE IN MY LIFE, I DON'T HESITATE TO CALL...."
>
> SOURCE: DEAN SMITH WITH GERALD D. BELL AND JOHN KILGO, THE CAROLINA WAY: LEADERSHIP LESSONS FROM A LIFE IN COACHING, PP. 157-159.

Williams is a well rounded and multi faceted person. His degree in broadcasting, success in business and personal speaking make Williams a much sought after person. His post basketball career is a busy one. This is an indication of how hard he works and his native intelligence and personality. With a mellifluous voice, he sounds like he has been on television his entire life. He is a student of more than the NBA game, he is a consummate observer of life.

"When I look at some of the guys who didn't make it in the league," Williams told me when I met him in a German airport, "I wonder why." I told Scott. It was drive, patience, practice and intelligence that they didn't possess. He has those traits.

There is a sense of being inside an NBA game when you listen to Williams. He has a quick delivery on television, and his smile is one that suggests a warm personality. He has other interests and it appears that Williams has moved on pursue those interests.

THE BROADCAST TEAM 2012-2013: Television Steve Albert: Play-by-Play, Eddie Johnson, color analyst

Radio: Al McCoy: Arizona Sports 620, Play-by-Play: Tim Kempton:

Color Analyst Ivan Valenzuela: KSUN 1400 AM (Spanish), Play-by-Play: Arturo Ochoa: Color Analyst

Ann Meyers Drysdale, new in 2012-2013, color analyst

EDDIE JOHNSON: INTEGRITY AND DEEP KNOWLEDGE AND HE IS STILL FUN

Eddie Johnson epitomizes the Suns. I ran into him at A. J's, a yuppie super market in Scottsdale. I introduced myself and he wanted to talk about my history books. He told me he has a degree in history. I insisted that he talk about him. He did play seventeen years in the NBA; he did score 19,202 points and had a career scoring average of 16.0. When I told him that I scored 80 points in one year at Lincoln High School, he agreed that we should talk about his exploits. The point of the story is that Eddie Johnson is a gentleman, a thinker and he loves the Valley of the Sun. He also looks like he can still play the game. He is also an astute broadcaster with deep knowledge of the NBA game.

He arrived in Phoenix in a trade in 1987, and he was the 6th Man of the year as a Sun. From 1987 to 1990 Johnson's scoring was 17.7, 21.5 and in his final Suns year he scored 16.9 points a game. He was a prolific scorer who also played solid defense. In 1990-1991, he was with three NBA teams, including the Suns, and he still averaged in double figures.

As a broadcaster, Johnson is an expert analyst. He has not only deep knowledge of the game, but he can explain the small details, the intricacies and the mysteries of basketball. Johnson is a humble person who credits Al McCoy with much of his success. He also admits that he can't play the piano as well as McCoy but he is one of the best analysts in the NBA. Maybe McCoy can give him some piano lessons.

TOM CHAMBERS AND THE POST GAME TV ANALYSIS

Tom Chambers was one of the best big men in the NBA. He is also one of the more insightful post game television personalities. With Fox Sports Arizona and Fox Sports Arizona Plus broadcasting eighty Suns games, Chambers will analyze the Suns in his usual literate post-game summary.

In the pregame, half time post game segments with Tom Leander, Chambers does an excellent job dissecting what is right and what is wrong with the Suns.

The Tom Chambers segment of the pre, half time and post game home shows is a television treat as it broadcast from an open-air studio located outside the U. S. Airways arena. Chambers works alongside Kevin Ray in an informative and entertaining segment of the Suns' broadcasts.

ANN MEYERS DRYSDALE AND STEVE ALBERT JOINS THE BROADCAST BOOTH

The Suns are a team of firsts. They hired Ann Meyers Drysdale to broadcast games. This is the first time in thirty-three years that an NBA team will feature a woman in the broadcast booth. As Ann Meyers she was the first woman to try out for a men's pro basketball team. In 1979, she participated in six games with the Indiana Pacers. Then Meyers went on to become the first high profile star in women's professional basketball. She married former Los Angeles Dodger pitcher, Don Drysdale, and she began raising a family. But basketball was still in her blood. In 2007, she joined the Phoenix Mercury management team. She has served as a Vice President for both the Suns and the Mercury. She is primarily a public relations person but Mike D'Antoni had her scout when he was the coach.

Steve Albert comes to the Suns with a distinguished resume. He has served as a play-by-play announcer for the New Jersey Nets, the New Orleans Hornets, the Golden State Warriors, the New Jersey Nets and the Cleveland Cavaliers. He signed a five-year contract after calling Showtime boxing for twenty-four years. He was last in an NBA booth when he called the New Orleans Hornets games in 2005.

Basketball is in his blood. He was a ball boy for the New York Knicks and his broadcasting credentials include being the voice of the New York Mets, the New York Jets and the New York Islanders. He also called some games for the New Jersey Devils. He is also taller and better looking than his brother Marv, and he has better hair.

SUMMING UP THE BROADCAST TEAM

The Suns' radio and television personalities are a varied group of broadcasters. With three high-end professional athletes balancing the on air talent there is a critical, but supportive, approach to the Suns broadcasts.

There are no other NBA radio-television teams that have as much fan support as the Suns' broadcasters. The Suns television and radio broadcasts generally outdraw the national TV ratings and this suggests the professionalism of the Suns media.

chapter

SIXTEEN

STEVE NASH: THE FACE OF THE FRANCHISE IS GONE

"HE HAS TO BE MAYBE CONSIDERED THE GREATEST SUN OF ALL TIME," REX CHAPMAN, FORMER TEAM-MATE

Victoria British Columbia is a cold, beautiful English faux type city on Canada's extreme western coast. It is a small town and somewhat boring. In 1991, Ian Hyde-Lay, the basketball coach at St. Michael's High School, a Victoria school noted more for academics than athletics, began preparing for the basketball season. In Canada, high school basketball's popularity is similar to America's interest in curling. Hyde-Lay was an old-fashioned basketball coach. He hated fancy passes, there was little dribbling and a behind the back pass earned you a seat on the bench. He taught a slow, methodical basketball game that stressed patience and banging the ball inside for the big guy. But there was one thing that everyone recognized about Hyde Lay, and that is that he knew basketball. His deep knowledge of the game prompted him to revamp his coaching style and adjust to Steve Nash's game. Hyde-Lay had never seen a young kid with the court sense and vision that Nash possessed.

NASH AT ST. MICHAELS AND IAN HYDE-LAY

When Nash initially attended Mount Douglas Secondary School, his parents were concerned about low grades. They spent the money to send Steve to the St. Michael's University Prep School, a private boarding institution. He played basketball, soccer and rugby at St. Michaels, and he honed his basketball skills under the best high school coach in British Columbia.

When he transferred to St. Michael's, Nash had only been playing basketball for three years. He was twelve when he picked up his first ball in the Mount Douglas Secondary School playground; he passed it behind his back to a friend and went out the play soccer. No one could believe his innate skill.

In 1991, Hyde-Lay found a transfer on his basketball team. The kid, known as Steve Nash, dribbled too much, he loved to pass the ball behind his back and he didn't like to shoot. "When I first saw Steve, I realized that he saw the court different from other kids," Hyde-Lay recalled. "He was always in the gym. I decided that I would leave him alone, he had skills that I hadn't seen in any Canadian player." Since Nash was a gifted soccer player, he saw the basketball court different than other kids. He anticipated plays, and he taught players the pick and roll.

Hyde-Lay was intrigued by Nash's willingness to pass. "I couldn't believe the number of shots that he passed up," Hyde-Lay commented. Although he was an adjustable coach, Hyde-Lay had a system that he wanted Nash to fit into for the team. There was no problem, Steve did, but things did not go well.

The irony is that the coach, Ian Hyde-Lay, did change his concept of the game. He continually lectured Nash on being more traditional. To Hyde-Lay's surprise, Nash accepted the criticism and the two strong post players on the St. Michael's team led this seemingly small and relatively insignificant athletic high school to a 50-4 record and the British Columbia High School title. Long before he entered college and the NBA, Nash had everyone involved. He made all the players feel equal.

Hyde-Lay was an interesting influence. He told Steve to become a complete player. While Nash has never been noted for his defense, he does play it. Unlike many Canadian coaches, Hyde-Lay played basketball at a high level. From 1975 to 1980, he was a star player. He also captained the first Canadian Inter-University National Championship team in 1979-1980.

NASH'S TIME PLAY AND PERSONALITY

While Nash was a backcourt wizard at St. Michael's, he took the blame for team losses. He was hyper critical of his performance. Why he did this remains a mystery. Coach Hyde-Lay suggested that in the process, he built unity and a brotherhood. In high school his teammates wanted to play with Steve Nash. After more than twenty-five years, players still echo that sentiment.

At St. Michael's there were multiple signs of Nash's future greatness. The coach noticed that when Steve had an open drive to the basket he would circle under it and making a floating shot. This is a much more difficult maneuver and the shot was a crowd pleaser. Then Hyde-Lay realized that Nash had difficulty leaping off his left foot. He was a gym rat and in his sophomore year in high school he sprained his ankle. He could hardly move off his left foot. For some reason coming off his left foot for a lay up was something that Nash avoided. Even after his ankle healed, Nash loved the under the basket floater shot. It remains in his NBA arsenal. In the NBA, he rarely goes off his left foot. What looked like a weakness turned into a crowd-pleasing strength for Nash as his unorthodox shot is featured on television highlights.

While he was competing for the British Columbia AAA basketball title, Santa Clara coach Dick Davey showed up to watch Nash. He offered Steve a scholarship. This was Nash's only American scholarship offer; he accepted it. No one knew that Syracuse and Washington State were Nash's first choices.

When Nash finished his high school career in Victoria, Hyde-Lay made a series of impressive videos and mailed copies to over fifty colleges. No one was interested. Steve wanted to go to school at Syracuse or Washington State. At Syracuse, Jim Boeheim didn't have his recruiter go into Canada. What's the point! No one played division one ball out of Canada. At Washington State, Kevin Eastman, ignored the tapes sent by Coach Hyde-Lay. It was a strange time as recruiters had little knowledge of Nash's game.

Hyde-Lay recalled: "Steve had everything. He had charisma, intelligence, great leadership skills, sound moral values, unbelievable raw skill and a work ethic second to none. Other players had some of these attributes but only a very select few possess all of them."

A small Catholic college near San Jose, California, the University of Santa Clara, saw something in Nash. The coach, Dick Davey, while playing golf in San Jose remarked to me of Nash: "He is such an unbelievable talent. You looked at him and he carried himself like a little kid. Then he took the basketball court. I knew we had something special, I thought about the NCAA post season, I said to a friend: 'here we come." When Davey went out to talk to other coaches he failed to mention Steve Nash as his prize recruit. "I just didn't want to tip anybody off and we got him quietly into the freshman class. I was worried that we would lose him," Davey said.

When he arrived at Santa Clara, Nash loved the school. It is small, private, Catholic and the student body is one that is diverse and interesting. There was more to Nash than basketball and his business interests, notably those in the entertainment industry, have been helped by his superb college education. But it is basketball that had taken him to Hollywood in his last few years in the NBA. When his career began at Santa Clara, no one predicted his Hall of Fame success. That is no one but Steve Nash.

NASH AT SANTA CLARA AND DICK DAVEY

`In the 1990s, I was continually in the Santa Clara University gym watching their basketball team. I lived a few miles from Santa Clara in Fremont, where I was a history professor. I was still playing in an over fifty league in San Jose, and I had the opportunity to see Nash play. I also had a number of conversations with Coach Dick Davey. He is two years younger than I am, so I always felt like I could give him advice. After all I am the older icon. He was a long time assistant to the Broncos legendary coach Carroll Williams. Then upon William's retirement, he took over the Broncos head-coaching job.

The problem was that Davey was head coach at a school that didn't have a large basketball budget. The good news is that the academics, and the proximity to San Francisco brought a number of future NBA players to the campus.

Santa Clara requires that its players go to class and earn a degree. Williams had done well recruiting players who went on to the NBA. There were thirteen former Santa Clara players who had been in the NBA when Steve Nash showed up in 1992. They all have degrees.

Davey told me that he had this point guard from Canada that no one looked at, and he was a real find. I told Davey that I had played a year of high school basketball and a point guard from Canada was a stretch. I asked Davey: "Is he also going to organize a curling team?" Boy, was I wrong!

When Nash showed up at Santa Clara the starting point guard was a senior, John Woolery. He was competitive, and he was not about to give up his job to a young kid from Canada. In the early preseason scrimmages, Woolery hounded Nash so badly he had trouble getting the ball up court.

Woolery had a mission. He wanted to destroy Nash's confidence. It didn't happen as Woolery and Coach Davey witnessed Nash' tenacious approach to the game. The only newspaper to pay any attention to the Santa Clara basketball team, the **San Jose Mercury**, constantly praised Nash's development but no one else seemed to listen.

Davey talked to the press constantly about the talented point guard from Canada. The press yawned; they were bored with Davey's tales about some obscure point guard from the middle of nowhere. Most people thought Davey had lost his mind. The first time I saw Nash in the Santa Clara gym, I thought this guy is in for trouble. Boy, I was wrong. He looks like a junior high kid. He had the worst body I had ever seen for a college basketball player. He was skinny and he didn't look like a basketball player.

Peter: "Howard what do you know? You looked like a basketball player, but you couldn't play."

When Woolery took the ball away from Nash repeatedly in practice, Steve took him aside after practice, and he asked him how he did it. Rather than give up, Nash went to the gym late at night and set up a dribbling drill. You could hear the basketball bouncing around at midnight. Maybe this was why Nash graduated with B plus rather than an A average.

Sitting around the dorm with Woolery and his teammates, Nash talked about being drafted into the NBA. He was the hardest working player on the team, and if he had a weakness he worked on it. When Davey gave Nash a key to Toso Pavilion, and he went in night after night to work on his game, the coach checked on him and couldn't believe his work ethic. Steve was also an hour or more early for practice.

Steve Woolery: "Nash worked harder than me. He was the hardest working player I have ever seen." Woolery, who lives in Antioch California, works as a pharmaceutical representative, and he coaches a junior high school basketball team.

In Nash's last two years at Santa Clara, they won the West Coast Conference title, and went on to NCAA tournament berths. The Broncos were giant killers with Nash at the point guard. They beat the second ranked University of Arizona Wildcats and also knocked off the Top Ten perennial power the University of Maryland.

There were a lot of people who took note of Nash's developing skills. The NCAA tournament was filled with pro scouts and Nash was once again under the radar. He still had to prove himself to the pros.

Kareem Abdul Jabbar was retired and a basketball analyst when he saw Nash play for the first time. Nash was a skinny freshman with a bad haircut and Abdul Jabbar described his game with superlatives. He couldn't believe Nash's court sense. A report went to the Los Angeles Lakers, and they ignored it.

The Broncos play by play announcer, Steve Physioc, looked at Abdul Jabbar and remarked of Nash: "He's a baby faced assassin." Abdul Jabbar turned to Physioc and wondered: "Is Nash a foreign ringer?" Santa Clara was picked to finish last in the West Coast Conference, and then they beat Pepperdine 73-63 in the spring of 1993 to advance to the NCAA tournament. It was Nash's twenty-three points that made the difference. A week later, they beat second seeded Arizona. In Las Vegas the bookies took a beating, as the Broncos were 7 to 1 to beat the University of Arizona.

By the time that he graduated from Santa Clara, Nash was the Western Conference Player of the Year in two seasons and the Broncos three NCAA tournament trips were due to his point guard play. But Nash also had a social life and a good one. The Hut may be Santa Clara's secret recruiting tool.

THE HUT AND STEVE NASH

Santa Clara University retired Nash's jersey in 2006, and he nervously praised the school. Everyone was surprised when Nash talked about having a party at the Hut. The Hut is the student bar just across the street from the new Santa Clara University business school. Nash let Santa Clara fans know that he was a big fan of the Hut. I spent many a night in the Hut while I taught at Ohlone College, after Broncos games it was time for a burger and a large beer. There is nothing like a college bar with cheap burgers, beer in a bong and peanuts. On some nights my neighbor, Terrell Owens, was sitting in the Hut telling everybody he was Terrell Owens. I had one of my female students ask me: "Who is Terrell Owens?" I granted her an A. Don't worry she earned it.

Peter: "Right! Sure! No problem."

The Hut is located at 3200 The Alameda in Santa Clara and is known as a dive bar. I beg to differ as it has a back patio, when I was doing research for my other books at Santa Clara, the Hut was just a few steps from the library. I always did my research on Tuesday nights as the drinks were two for one, and I was the oldest guy in the bar. So people in the Hut bought me drinks.

Peter: "As a taxpayer, I want my money back."

I also went there after watching Santa Clara basketball games, as it is near Toso Pavilion. What is even more interesting in 2006, as I was vacationing in San Francisco, I met a friend at the Hut and Steve Nash was having a drink on a Sunday evening in a bar filled with college students. It was a coke. I was disappointed. The previous year Terrell Owens was in the bar weekly. Maybe he went elsewhere, as the girls didn't seem to know him. Neither Steve nor Terrell knew that they were in the presence of a famous writer. The best part of the Hut is that a gin and tonic comes in a ten ounce plastic cup. They have a beer bong. They only clean the women's room. It is truly bizarre but fun. There are dollar bills stuck on the wall with peoples names on them. A beer pong table and a funky basketball game accentuate the Hut. Why did Steve Nash ever leave the University of Santa Clara? I was still having drinks there in my mid-fifties. I guess Steve had a life.

Peter: "How about you, Howard, I don't think you have a life."

NASH: ON TO THE NBA IN THE VALLEY OF THE SUN

Steve Nash is the face of the Phoenix Suns franchise since he returned to the Valley of the Sun in 2004. Of course, that ended in 2012 when he signed with the Los Angeles Lakers. His road to the franchise face was a long and circuitous one. There were still doubts about Nash's ability to transition to the NBA as he left Santa Clara.

As the Phoenix Suns fifteenth pick in the 1996 draft, the crowd at the Suns draft day booed. No one could believe that this baby faced Canadian who didn't appear to jump more than a foot of the ground could play basketball. The fans went nuts. The Suns had a premier point guard in Kevin Johnson. Had the Suns lost their mind?

It was in the Suns first training camp that Nash demonstrated his competitive spirit. He was guarding Kevin Johnson, and the premier ball handler stumbled as Nash pressed him. Johnson got up and threw the ball at Nash. Steve defiantly threw it back. Rex Chapman, the outstanding three point shooter, remarked: "It showed me there was something more to Steve than met the eye."

When Nash arrived in the Valley of the Sun, he played a supporting role to Kevin Johnson, Sam Cassell and later Jason Kidd. They were three key mentors who helped Nash refine his game. He wasn't expected to get much playing time. He learned from his early experiences, and by the second year in the league his playing time dramatically increased. He played almost twenty-two minutes a game in his second Suns' season. Donnie Nelson, the Dallas Mavericks General Manager, believed that Nash's potential was greater than the Suns realized. After two seasons in the Valley of the Sun, he was traded to the Dallas Mavericks.

Donnie Nelson is one of the NBA's most astute executives. Nelson began his career as a scout in the Golden State organization. Donnie wasn't a traditional thinker. He saw basketball talent out side the U. S. When he went to Europe, he came back with Sarunas Marculionis, from Lithuania, who became one of the NBA's earliest high profile European players. The Lithuanian played for eight years in the NBA and Nelson became a respected scout bringing European players into the fold. Then when his father, Don Nelson, was hired as the Dallas Mavericks coach, Mark Cuban brought Nelson in to run the front office. After his father left, Nelson continued as the general manager, and he remains one of the NBA's more astute gm's.

The Nelson's had some knock down and drag out discussions over Nash, and the son won the father over. Donnie Nelson has as good, if not better, knowledge of the game, than his father. Donnie convinced dad to spend some time letting Nash's talents mature. Don listened to his son grudgingly. Then Mark Cuban had to be convinced that he wasn't wasting his money.

When Coach Don Nelson left the Mavericks, former point guard Avery Johnson took over, and he saw Nash's play and leadership skills. Coach Johnson tried to get Cuban to extend Nash's contract. The Mavericks owner refused citing Nash's back and age as the reasons for not resigning Nash. Cuban told everyone that Nash was an old point guard and not worth the money. Almost a decade later Nash remains a star. Cuban has been eliminated from Dancing With The Stars and Donnie Nelson is still running the show. Sort of as Cuban continues to meddle with a franchise slowly slipping into oblivion.

The six years that Nash spent in Dallas were important ones. His best friend, Dirk Nowitzki, provided a formidable scoring punch along with veteran Juwan Howard and hot shooting guard Michael Finley. In 2000-2001, for the first time in a decade, the Dallas Mavericks went to the playoffs. The trip was not an auspicious one as the San Antonio Spurs beat them in the first round four games to one. As Nash became a two time All Star, the Dallas Mavericks "Big Three" brought another trip to the playoffs where they lost in the first round to the Sacramento Kings.

DON NELSON AND THE NASH RULE

After the loss to the Kings, the mad genius, Coach Don Nelson, implemented the Nash rule. That is Steve would have to take a specified number of shots each game. Nelson wrote on a blackboard "the Nash Rule." This was a minimum of ten shots for the point guard. It was under Don Nelson that Nash learned not only patience, but also he brought his shot under control.

The Nash Rule was the first tribute to his point guard genius. Looking back from the vantage point of 2012, Coach Don Nelson was asked if it was a mistake for the Mavericks not to resign Nash. Nelson replied: "Yeah, that was a huge mistake when they didn't resign him. It's proved out-he's still playing at 38, for crying out loud. The best player I ever coached-basketball player-was Steve Nash."

RICK CELEBRINI AND THE PHYSIOTHERAPY REVOLUTION

Sometimes athletes find an edge. That is a legal edge without performance enhancing drugs. Steve Nash hired a retired Canadian soccer defender who had a second career as a physiotherapist to train him for the NBA. The irony is that Celebrini is ten years younger than Nash, and he is working him out.

Celebrini played soccer in Canada with Nash's brother, Martin, at the University of British Columbia. Celebrini was on four collegiate soccer championship teams. He went on to play for the Edmonton Brickmen and the Vancouver 86ers. By the time he retired in 1996 a rash of injuries prompted Celebrini to study and become a well-known physiotherapist. What does this have to do with Steve Nash? Plenty!

In 2001, Nash hired Celebrini for workouts. The one-hour sessions with Celebrini were important ones. It is the science of body mechanics that makes the physiotherapist important. What Celebrini pointed out was that Nash's shot mechanics were off due to the excessively physical play.

Nash told **Sports Illustrated** writer, Jack McCallum, "I didn't become a real player until I started to work with Celebrini." He changed Nash's approach to the game, as well as his conditioning regime.

Celebrini pointed out that Nash's right hip was injured and that altered his shot. When Nash appeared on the PBS Show, hosted by Charlie Rose, he pointed out that he emphasized the strengths of his game. His one-legged running body floating shot came partially from the workouts with Celebrini and his experiences in Canadian basketball. Nash argued that balance, quickness and flexibility allowed him to play over thirty-five minutes a game. Celebrini helped him to conquer his well-known back problems. Nash pointed out that he lacked speed, as well as quickness. He compensated with his moves.

The impact of Celebrini's training is obvious. When he is in Phoenix and working Nash out, he has his best games. It is not a coincidence that when he began worked with the physiotherapist in 2001, he was on his way to back-to-back MVP awards. The restorative ice tub soakings after practice or a game has a great deal to do with Nash's ability to remain a top point guard. As he approaches his fortieth birthday, Nash continues to be a premier NBA point guard. A small amount of his growth is due to NBA head coach Don Nelson, who developed and instituted the infamous Nash rule.

COACH DON NELSON AND THE NASH RULE

It was in Dallas that Nash came under the watchful eye of Don Nelson. Not only was Nelson the most unorthodox coach in the NBA, sorry Phil Jackson, he was a master motivator that got his players to accept the notion that Nash wasn't taking enough shots. He went nuts over Nash's unselfish play. Nelson complained to Nash and told him to take more shots. Nash ignored Nelson. The other players laughed. In the NBA there are not enough shots for each player. That is simply the way the league operates.

No one ignores Don Nelson. Not only did the mad scientist, that is how Larry Brown referred to Nelson's coaching, love Nash's game, but also he wanted him to diversify it. So Nelson implemented the "Nash Rule." That was a requirement that Nash take ten shots a game. As the team statistician kept track that first year in Dallas, Steve shot 7.9 times a game and the players chuckled over the Nash rule. Nelson didn't complain as the Mavericks were winning. Nash was also averaging nine assists a game. Nelson knew enough not to tinker with success.

Was there a need for the Nash Rule? No doubt about it. Steve was basketball's most unselfish player. His college roommate, Randy Winn, who went on to play major league baseball, remarked that he passed in casual games in the gym rather than shoot.

While with the Dallas Mavericks, Nash was famous for his work ethic and conditioning. One hot and unusually muggy summer day in 2003 Nash was out to lunch with Dallas trainer, Al Whitley, and Nash was asked to have a beer. He didn't like beer, and he didn't like to drink. The others began kidding him, and Nash responded that he would have a couple of beers if they ran between bars. Then Nash proceeded to run Whitley and those working out for six miles from bar to bar. The group finally stopped in exhaustion and Dirk Nowitzki jokingly remarked: "I'm going back to Germany."

As a point guard, Nash early on became a passer, a team player, a facilitator, and he was the ultimate team player. It was never about individual statistics, even though he had some of the best in the league. It was about winning as a team.

FREE AGENCY AND BACK TO THE VALLEY OF THE SUN

After the 2003-2004 NBA season, Nash became a premier free agent. There was a great deal of interest among NBA teams. The only team was that wasn't interested was the Dallas Mavericks. In one of the strangest personnel decisions in NBS history, Mavericks owner Mark Cuban refused to pay Nash. Cuban went on a number of national television shows stating that he was a businessman, and it was not good business to pay millions of dollars to a point guard with a beat up body. In retrospect, Cuban looks like a jackass.

Peter: "Howard, what are your real feelings about Mark Cuban?"

The danger of making too much money while still in college, as Cuban had done, blinded him as far as basketball decision-making is concerned.

Peter: "You don't understand, Howard, Mark Cuban thought that market value was a country in Eastern Europe."

Cuban commented that the thirty-year-old Nash couldn't take the physical beating, and he was not worth a long-term deal. The Suns offered $65.6 million dollars. Cuban in his infinite wisdom talked about Nash's body breaking down from his fitness routine. The Maverick owner went even further suggesting at age thirty Nash had maybe one or two good years. The Mavericks owner did offer a nine million dollar annual deal for four years with a fifth year partially guaranteed. It was a weak

NBA contract, and it showed no respect for what Nash had done for the Mavericks franchise.

What made the contract so ridiculous was that Nash could collect no more than thirty-six million dollars. It was a no brainer, and he explored free agency. The Suns came in with a fully guaranteed six year sixty-five point-six million dollar contract. Cuban gloated publicly, and he let the press know that the Suns had made a huge mistake. The country bumpkins in the Valley of the Sun, Cuban told the press, understood neither the financiers nor the intricacies of the NBA. How does Cuban look a decade later after back-to-back Nash MVP awards?

Mark Cuban's lack of foresight was demonstrated on The Late Show With David Letterman when he remarked "Steve Nash is a great guy, but why couldn't he play like an MVP for us." Because you didn't pay him enough money! Much to Nash's credit, he took the high road and wished his former owner and the team well. Nash is a class act.

On the Letterman show, Cuban's reference to Nash being named the 2004-2005 NBA MVP was that it was an accident. Nash was only the third point guard to receive the award, Bob Cousy and Magic Johnson sere the previous recipients. He repeated the next year, and Cuban had no comment.

Once he returned to the Valley of the Sun, Nash was the face of the Phoenix Suns. In 2005, the Sun met the Dallas Mavericks in the Western Conference semifinals, and the Mavericks strategy was to cover the rest of the Suns defensively and make Nash beat you with his scoring. Cuban was all over radio and television telling anyone who would listen that Nash couldn't score in the important games.

The Suns beat the Mavericks four games to two and Nash scored 48 points in game 4, 34 points in game 5 and 39 points in game six. Cuban should have fired himself as a coach. He would have done well to go back to selling computer equipment. Or maybe do another season on Dancing With The Stars. No! Not that, he dances as well as he describes Nash's game. He knows how to look in the mirror and loves what he sees.

What does Steve Nash think about the idea of being a scorer? I don't know, but I think that he prefers to pass the ball. Always the consummate team player, Nash pointed out it was wiser to pass up some shots early to get the whole team going. When players signed with Phoenix they told the press that they wanted a Hall of Fame point guard. To a man they said it was Steve Nash because of his unusual, unselfish passing.

When Nash inked a contract with the Suns, it brought in a number of players who loved the point guards passing. Grant Hill, Marcin Gortat, Hakim Warrick, Vince Carter and a host of others talked about coming to the Valley of the Sun, it was to get the ball from Steve Nash.

THE CRITICS ON THE SUNS AND NASH

One of the problems running a sports franchise is that the critics often tell the owners how to run the team. There is only one person who can tell Robert Sarver how to run the team that is Mrs. Sarver. She is a quiet, intelligent woman from the middle west and so far she has show her intellect by staying out of the mix. She also demanded privacy. So you won't hear about her in this book. This is not so with a number of critics.

Much of the criticism surrounding the Suns franchise is directed toward Robert Sarver. That is fair, he owns the team. But he also has made some good decisions. He did sign Nash. He also runs the Suns as a business. This is his greatest sin. Even Steve Nash thinks it is fine, as he discussed the business side of his trade to the Los Angeles Lakers with Sarver and his management team.

Bill Simmons, one of basketball's best writers, argues that the Suns from 2004 to 2008 made some of the most "perplexing moves" in the NBA. He charges that when they traded the seventh pick in the 2004 draft to Chicago they lost the chance to take Luol Deng or Andre Iguodala. The reason they did this was to sign a more seasoned player. The signing of Quentin Richardson to a $42.6 million contract was unfortunate. Hindsight is 2020. At that moment Richardson looked like a player who could help the Suns reach the NBA finals. Simmons also argues that trading Joe Johnson to Atlanta was a mistake. He fails to mention Johnson's exorbitant salary demands or that Boris Diaw proved to be an excellent replacement. Again Steve Nash is in the mix as Diaw's scoring was the direct result of Nash's pinpoint passing.

Simmons is typical of the informed critic. He never fully analyzes the reasons why a trade, failure to match another teams offer or simply not signing a player, is to the Suns advantage. Whether right or wrong, management does assess these things. There are mistakes and there are good decisions. It is all part of the game.

But some trades are open to criticism. When Simmons complained that the Suns traded Rajon Rondo's rights to Boston, he neglected to mention Steve Nash's long-term contract. The Suns could have traded Nash and saved money by bringing Rondo into the fold. They didn't.

Didn't Simmons recognize that they had Steve Nash and the $5 million helped the salary cap. When the Suns paid Diaw and Marcus Banks large contracts they did make a mistake. Banks' $21.3 million dollar contract didn't bring results at the shooting guard position. In his two seasons with the Suns, Banks averaged five points a game, and he was traded to the Miami Heat. What this move should have done was to squash the rumor that Sarver and the Suns were too thrifty. There was nothing thrifty about signing Diaw to a $45 million contract. Bill Simmons ends his comments on the Suns writing: "Note to the Phoenix fans: You can now light yourselves on fire." What a mature guy. Simmons really knows how to tell it like it is, and he not only has a warped judgment, he has a bit of hostility toward the Valley of the Sun.

The worst part of Simmons' writing is labeling Nash's MVP awards "a baffling choice." Maybe playing like Bob Cousy is what made Simmons mad. Like most writers, who can't explain themselves, Simmons argued that Nash got the award because he is white. He beat out Shaq by thirty votes and Nowitzki by 717 votes. Last time I looked Nowitzki was white and he was third in the voting. Does Simmons see a conspiracy here of talented white guys? He should stick to his ESPN columns and forget about books. They only cloud the issue, and they don't make sense.

WHAT HAS NASH MEANT TO THE SUNS

It is Nash who tells his teammates to keep digging. Nash dribbles and probes and attempts to find a glitch in the other teams armor. He also asks Coach Mike D'Antoni if the officials have something against the Suns. No Steve. That is except for the weasel, Tim Donaghy. It is his playmaking ability that has the Suns on a roll. Nash is able to dish the ball out to his teammates and keep the Suns scoring momentum intact. He is one of the most prolific assist leaders in NBA history.

In ten seasons with the Suns, Nash was the brand name that identified the product. He is popular in the Valley of the Sun, and his skill set is amongst the best in the NBA. As a playmaker, he is unparalleled and he turned average performers into better players. Boris Diaw, Joe Johnson, Shawn Marion and marginal players like James Jones benefitted from playing with Nash, because he could distribute the ball so effectively. They scored in higher numbers than at any time in their careers. They received overvalued contracts due to Nash's contribution to their game.

STEVE NASH'S HIDDEN MOMENT

In the 2012 season, Nash went into Scottsdale's AJ's Market to purchase take out dinners. AJ's is a fine gourmet market with great food. Nash's friend, Dirk Nowitzki, was with him and the ladies behind the take out counter, Linda, Janet and Shari vied to wait on Nash. The manager stepped in and Nash bought two fish dinners with double vegetables. Dirk looked on disappointed. He was looking at the German potato salad, the bratwurst and the strudel. Nash lectured Nowitzki on the fattening nature of the potatoes. Dirk didn't look happy. One of the ladies said: "Steve you should try to get that big guy with you to play basketball." Nash responded: "He's a German, he doesn't know anything about basketball." That night Nowitzki's Mavericks won 122 to 99. Steve Nash didn't play against the Mavericks, because he was injured. Nowitzki was still trying to get himself back into NBA playing shape, and he scored only ten points. Former Sun Shawn Marion scored twenty-one points. Maybe Nowitzki should have had the potato salad. The Suns were also 7 and 13 at the time Nowitzki was in town. It was a tough time for Coach Gentry.

The first half of the Suns 2011-2012 season was a nightmare. Friends like Dirk Nowitzki helped Nash to weather the storm. In the second half of the 2012 season, Nash was one of many catalysts who helped turn the team around. No one imagined that he would sign with the Lakers in the off-season. The drama was constant in the ten weeks after the season ended. No one knew it at the time but Steve Nash's Suns run was over. It was a great time for the fans, and it seems that Nash enjoyed the accolades and praise. He will receive a much warmer reception than Kobe Bryant when he enters the U. S. Airways Arena.

```
┌─────────────────────────────────────────────────────────────┐
│                                                               │
│           STEVE NASH'S PHOENIX SUNS STATISTICS                │
│                                                               │
│   1996-1997: PPG: 3.3 APG: 2.1 THREE PT %: 41.8 FT%: 82.4     │
│   1997-1998: PPG: 9.1 APG: 3.4 THREE POINT %: 41.5 FT%: 86.0  │
│   2004-2005: PPG: 15.5 APG: 11.5 THREE POINT %: 43.1 FT%: 88.7│
│   2005-2006: PPG: 18.8 APG: 10.5 THREE POINT %: 43.9 FT%: 92.1│
│   2006-2007: PPG: 18.6 APG: 11.6 THREE POINT %: 45.5 FT%: 89.9│
│   2007-2008: PPG 16.9 APG: 11.1 THREE POINT %: 47.0 FT%: 90.6 │
│   2008-2009: PPG: 15. 7 APG: 9.9 THREE POINT %: 43/9 FT%: 93.3│
│   2009-2010: PPG: 16.5 APG: 11.0 THREE POINT %: 42.6 FT%: 93.8│
│   2010-2011: PPG: 14.7 APG: 11.4 THREE POINT %: 39.5 FT%: 91.2│
│   2011-2012: PPG: 12.5 APG: 10.7 THREE POINT %: 39.0 FT%:89.4 │
│     ppg= points per game----apg=assists per game ft%=free throw %│
│                                                               │
└─────────────────────────────────────────────────────────────┘
```

NO, NOT THE L.A. LAKERS: NASH DEPARTS

The Valley of the Sun received an unexpected July 4th present. The face of the Suns franchise, Steve Nash, announced that he was signing a three year 27 million dollar Los Angeles Lakers contract. The cries went out: "It is Sarver's fault." In fact, it wasn't, as the Suns were prepared to offer Nash about thirty million, give or take a million.

After the shock wore off, it was obvious that Nash and the Suns were still friendly. He could have signed with the Toronto Raptors for thirty six million or the Suns could have worked a trade with the New York Knicks. The Lakers deal was the best one for the Suns. They received two first round draft picks, two-second rounder's and three million dollars. Not bad. Robert Sarver can go to a number of dinners at Dominick's.

During his last eight-years with the Phoenix Suns, there was a love affair with Steve Nash. It was good for both sides. He was the face of the franchise and sold a lot of tickets. The last two seasons, as the Suns dealt some top talent and had trouble making the playoffs, were average ones. Personally, Nash had stellar years. He is a consummate team player, and he never complained about the constant movement of personnel.

When Nash signed with the Lakers many were surprised. In retrospect, it should have been expected. He is an hour's plane flight to visit his three children. He has a production company and the film industry is Nash's next career. His parents live in Gainey Ranch, a toney part of

Scottsdale, where the well to do and most intelligent Scottsdale folks live.

Peter: "Howard are you going to let the readers know that you live in Gainey Ranch?

Howard: "No."

What did the Los Angeles Lakers do to acquire Nash? They began by using the nine million dollar trade exception they acquired when they traded Lamar Odom to the Dallas Mavericks. That trade exception was on the books for eight months and by acquiring Nash the Lakers are more attractive to Dwight Howard. Guess what, Howard signed with the Lakers after they acquired Nash. "I finally have a real point guard," Howard comments. The four draft choices that the Lakers gave up may or may not be important. The two first rounders and the two-second round picks will be low ones. The Nash acquisition also takes the pressure off the Lakers Kobe Bryant. He is no longer required to handle the ball, score and play defense. Now he has to do only two of those things.

In the 2012 season, Nash made eleven point seven million dollars. He talked at length with team owner Robert Sarver and President of Team Operations Lon Babby, and they listened to Nash's notion that he wanted to play for the Los Angeles Lakers. Nash pointed out that money and draft choices would help the franchise. They granted his wish for a Lakers trade.

The Lakers had too many offensive struggles last year. When they brought in what they called the point guard of the future, Ramon Sessions, he was terrible in the Oklahoma City playoff series. Then Sessions declined his $4.55 million dollar team option in June, and he entered the free agent market. There was no rush to sign him. Then along came Mark Cuban who knows all about point guards. Cuban announced that he was going to sign Sessions. Ironically, Cuban missed out on Session's, as he signed a two year ten million dollar deal with the Charlotte Bobcats. When Cuban's veteran point guard Jason Kidd signed for three years with the New York Knicks for the paltry salary of three million a year, it was an indication of desperate changes in Dallas. As Cuban made a pitch for premier point guards, he wasn't willing to pay the going rate. The Maverick's salary, the working conditions and the fringe benefits didn't fit with the premier point guard's talent. The Mavericks now have O. J. Mayo as the designated shooting and point guard, but this is not an upgrade from either Jason Kidd or Steve Nash.

236

Clearly, the Lakers needed an upgrade at the point guard position. In January 2012, the Lakers went thirteen consecutive games without breaking the one hundred-point barrier. Ramon Sessions had trouble getting the ball inside to Andrew Bynum or Pau Gasol. Kobe had too much pressure on him, the bench was weak, Pau Gasol was pouting, Andrew Bynum was so immature that he ignored Coach Mike Brown and said that he was "into his Zen." He is now into the Philadelphia 76ers, and he is no more mature. His inner Zen is in hiatus. Metta World Peace showed up out of shape and hardly resembled Ron Artest. He couldn't dance, as his Dancing With the Stars appearance demonstrated. He is also a bad actor. They blame Coach Mike Brown for this circus. The truth is that it is Los Angeles that is the circus. It won't be the same with Nash in the Lakers' fold; he will demand accountability, as will Kobe. They will be a tough team.

The day of the trade Suns' fans were screaming for Robert Sarver's head. This is crazy. He did what he could to facilitate Nash's wishes, and the trade took place after Nash called Kobe. I asked Sarver at a party the team sponsored for season ticket holders the following question: "What are the three things he needed to do to make the Suns' fans happy." He commented: "Win, win, win." I think I even understood his dilemma.

After Nash's agent, Bill Duffy, flew from New York to meet with Suns Managing Partner Robert Sarver, he made a case for Nash's trade to the Lakers. "I'm calling it the family values deal," Duffy continued. "Steve was adamant about being close to his children." What is amazing is that Nash wanted the Suns to benefit from his departure. But Sarver had to agree. He did. Duffy said that he was grateful to Sarver, as was Nash. The Suns also wanted to establish a new brand at point guard. That new brand turned out to be an old one as the Suns welcomed Goran Dragic back to the fold. The dragon returned, and he is the Suns' starting point guard. His cousin lives in Phoenix, and he returns to play for his favorite coach Alvin Gentry. Dragic is all smiles. Gentry is all smiles. In the publicity surrounding Nash's departure, Dragic signed a four year 30 million dollar deal with an annual bonus of one million dollars if he made the NBA All Star team, the fans are buzzing with excitement. Dragic asked for $10 million annually but he had to settle for $7.5 million. He loves playing for Gentry. Maybe the coach should kick in a little of his salary

Steve Nash suggested some of the reasons that made him want to be a Los Angeles Lakers. He wanted to play with Kobe Bryant. He emphasized that his children and championships were his main concerns. "The idea to be close to my son, my daughters, who will be in Phoenix was the number one priority," Nash told ESPN. Pau Gasol tweeted: "It will be a huge honor to play alongside Steve." That means Pau realizes there is someone to pass him the ball. Something that wasn't happening last year and only time will tell about the future. Pau might even get the ball down low.

The bottom line is that Robert Sarver was reluctant to trade Nash. He did so to honor his former point guard's wishes. This is to Sarver's credit. I won't boo Nash when he returns in a Lakers Uniform. I will cheer the ultimate good guy. Is there life after Steve Nash? I hope so.

In two separate stints with the Suns, Steve Nash may be their greatest player. His impossible no look passes, his one handed lay ins, his finger licks between dribbles, his soft arching jump shot and his cross over dribble excited fans for a decade.

"It was the most successful time of my career personally and as a team," Nash continued. "Those are the defining years of my career."

QUOTES FROM STEVE NASH

WHEN ASKED IF HE WATCHES REPLAYS OF GAMES
"I NEVER DO, I JUST GO HOME AND BEAT MYSELF UP."

STEVE NASH TO REFEREE LEON WOOD WHEN RAJA BELL HARD FOULED KOBE BRYANT
"YOU LET THINGS GET OUT OF HAND AND THIS IS WHAT HAPPENS."

"MY IDEAL DAY WOULD BE TO GET A GOOD WORK OUT IN, LISTEN TO MUSIC, TALK TO MY FAMILY AND FRIENDS ON THE PHONE, READ AND GO TO A GOOD MOVIE."

"PEOPLE HAVE ALWAYS DOUBTED WHETHER I WAS GOOD ENOUGH TO PLAY THIS FUCKING GAME AT THIS LEVEL."

"MY HEROES WERE ISIAH THOMAS, MICHAEL JORDAN, MAGIC JOHNSON. I THINK THEY WERE JUST SO COMPETITIVE AND CREATIVE."

chapter

SEVENTEEN

GRANT HILL: THE OTHER FACE OF THE FRANCHISE IS GONE

**I'VE DONE A LOT OF BASKETBALL DRILLS, NOT A WHOLE LOT OF COMPETITIVE STUFF. I HAVE BASICALLY BEEN IN THE GYM EVERYDAY WORKING ON MY GAME, WORKING ON THE TIME OFF THAT I'VE HAD FROM THE GAME, JUST GETTING MYSELF PREPARED MENTALLY AND PHYSICALLY FOR THE SEASON.
GRANT HILL**

Grant Hill is that rare combination of an athlete who is brilliant in an academic manner, and he is even better on the basketball court. How would one describe Hill? Integrity! Perseverance! Ethics! Skill! Talent! Awareness! Philanthropic! Family! Kindness!

These are some of the words included in descriptions of him. If Steve Nash is the face of the Suns, Hill provides the gritty determination that made them one of the best teams in the second half of the 2012 season. Then, without warning, the Suns decided to get younger, and

Hill was off to the Los Angeles Clippers. The second face of the Suns was gone.

The rumor is that Grant Hill is the oldest player in the NBA. This is patently untrue. He is one day younger than Kurt Thomas. At age thirty-nine, Hill is a medical marvel. The Suns conditioning and medical staff can take a good deal of the credit. Grant still gets most of it for overcoming a potential career ending set of injuries to continue his Hall of Fame career in the Valley of the Sun.

HILL'S FORMATIVE YEARS

When Grant Hill was born on October 5, 1972, his father Calvin was on his way to the first one thousand yard rushing year by a Dallas Cowboy running back. The bad news is that Grant Hill was born in Dallas. The good news is that Mark Cuban hadn't arrived. Grant grew up in Reston Virginia. He was a star at South Lakes High School, and in 1990, he was selected for the McDonald's All American team.

When the Dallas Cowboys drafted his father, Calvin, in 1969 a number of scouts were worried. He graduated from Yale. Calvin not only had a degree in history, but he was a person who had opportunities outside of football. The Cowboys told people they were taking a chance on Calvin. It wasn't much of a chance, as he led Dallas to one Super Bowl title and two NFC championships in six years with the team. He also played in the World Football League for the Hawaiians, as well as the Washington Redskins and the Cleveland Browns. When Grant's mother, Janet, graduated from Wellesley College, where Hillary Rodham Clinton was her roommate, she was an honor student. She graduated with a degree in math in 1969 and the she received a master's degree in math from the University of Chicago. Then Janet worked as a teacher and later she opened a consulting business.

Hill's mother made her mark in corporate consulting when she advocated hiring practices that didn't depend upon affirmative action. She considers diversity to be divisive, and her ideas on hiring qualified people led to many corporate board appointments. She sits on the boards of the New York Cotton Exchange, the McDonald Dental Lab, the Duke University School of Business and the Rand Corporation Drug Policy Institute among others.

In 1997 the Dallas Cowboys hired the Hills to improve the team's player development program. This appointment was the result of some ugly off the field incidents involving drugs, rape and drinking. The Hills helped to clean up the Cowboy's culture.

In Reston Virginia, Grant's father, Calvin, who suffered serious knee injuries, would not let his son play peewee football. Calvin told him to wait until high school. As Grant grew up in an affluent suburb, he demonstrated early athletic ability. When it came time to play high school football, Grant declined. He found his passion. It was basketball.

He blossomed early and the high school basketball coach wanted him to bypass the junior variety and start in the ninth grade on the varsity. He didn't want to do it. The coach and his dad had a meeting and Grant cried. He wanted to be with his friends. His dad and the coach had the last word. Grant was a starting small forward on the varsity. As a freshman he averaged eleven points a game.

When he was a high school junior, Grant visited the Georgetown campus, and he talked at length with Coach John Thompson. Grant had every intention of enrolling at Georgetown. Then Thompson introduced Grant to Mary Fenton, Georgetown's academic adviser. She placed a book in Grant's hand and told him to read it. He started reading. She rudely hollered: "Read it out loud." Grant couldn't believe this rude woman. "I was a little startled, but I took the book and started reading." Then she hollered again: "I meant out loud." He still couldn't believe it. What Miss Fenton didn't realize is that Grant qualified academically for Georgetown, as well as Duke. He was off to Duke, after this nasty slight from the Georgetown academy adviser. Miss Fenton didn't realize that his SAT scores were off the charts.

It was after he attended a Georgetown-Duke game that Grant's love affair began with the Blue Devils. He watched Duke play, he saw how Coach Mike Krzyzewski directed the team, and he was amazed at the athletic prowess of the Blue Devils. He decided on the spot to attend Duke. His parents had no idea that he would enroll at Duke. There was more to Grant than basketball and Duke's academics, as well as Coach K's integrity, brought Hill's game to Duke. He also loved the campus. College life was something Hill enjoyed; he wasn't just there to play basketball.

His parents sat down with Hill and made their wishes known. Calvin wanted his son to attend the University of North Carolina and play for Dean Smith. His mother wanted Grant to enroll at Georgetown University. A Fox Sports documentary on Hill's career suggests that he was a good son who made up his own mind. He was off to Duke University.

At South Lakes High School the average SAT score was 1588 and Hill had a score that exceeded that. He was not only a good student, but his advanced placement tests were good enough to earn him some college credit while still in high school. The recruiters didn't always see this side of Hill. They were too interested in his athletic ability to recognize that he was a brilliant student.

When Jalen Rose criticized Grant Hill for going to a "white high school," he neglected to do his research. South Lakes High School also graduated Big Pooh an MC from the Hip Hop group Little Brother, Spookey Ruben, a pop musician and Aron Kader the first Palestinian comedian. Kader was featured in Michael Moore's film Fahrenheit 9/11. The school is almost twenty percent African American. The diversity of South Lakes High was an influence upon Hill. The strangest thing about his high school is that the mascot was a Seahawk.

Every major university recruited the six foot seven and a half inch Hill. He harrowed his choices to North Carolina, Michigan, Georgetown, Duke, the University of California, Berkeley and the University of Virginia. It was Coach Mike Krzyewski's system, as well as the superior academics at Duke, that brought him to the Durham campus.

HILL AT DUKE

A reporter asked Hill if he regretted not leaving Duke early for the NBA money. Grant replied: "I wanted to stay an extra year I loved it so much." In his four years at Duke, Hill played on teams that won national titles in 1991 and 1992. This was the first time a team won back-to-back titles since UCLA did it in the early 1970s. In his senior year, Hill led Duke to the NCAA championship game where they lost to the Arkansas Razorbacks. Hill was voted the college defensive player of the nation in 1992-1993 and the following year he was the ACC Player of the Year.

Hill's statistics at Duke were impressive. He became the fist ACC player to amass 1900 points, 700 rebounds, 400 assists, 2000 steals and 100 blocked shots. He averaged 14.9 points a game with six rebounds and 3.6 assists in his 129 games at Duke. His Duke number 33 jersey was retired, and he was a member of the bronze medal U. S. team in the 1991 Pan American games in Havana, Cuba.

One of Hill's proudest college moments came in 1992 when he threw a pass seventy five feet to Christian Laettner who dribbled once and hit a game winning jump shot against Kentucky with 2.1 seconds remaining in the game.

National recognition for his Duke career included a first team All America award, and the designation as the ACC Player of the Year during his senior season in 1993-1994. He was ready for the NBA.

His B. A. in history from Duke gave him a life long appreciation for African American art, and he learned about the subtle nuances of American history. He also had some interest in business matters, and this direction would make him a fortune.

MAKING DOCUMENTARIES ON DUKE

Hill's experiences at Duke were so positive that he has produced two documentaries on his experiences at Duke University. The first one had nothing to do with basketball, but it whetted Hill's appetite to look deep into the Blue Devil's basketball culture.

He did this in a documentary about the two national championship teams that he played on while at Duke. It is the 1991 and 1992 Blue Devil basketball season that is the focus of Hill's best work. In cooperation with Amy Undell, the second documentary "Duke 91 & 92: Back-To-Back" is a Turner Sports first film that explores the Duke basketball culture. The difficulty of repeated national college basketball championships is the focus of the second Hill documentary. He spares no one in this personal look at the Blue Devils. The personality differences between big man Christian Laettner and point guard Bobby Hurley are explored, and he points out that these differences led to a strong team with more cohesion.

It was the honesty that made the Hill film on the Duke experience so positive. By looking with candor at Christian Laettner's brusque personality, the documentary suggesting how strong Coach K was in integrating diverse personalities into the program. Overall the documentary suggests why combining a college education with elite basketball produces character and integrity.

LIFE AFTER DUKE

After a storied college career at Duke, the Detroit Pistons drafted Hill as the third pick in the 1994 draft. The Hill's also knew the pitfalls of a professional career. So his father, Calvin, called Lon Babby who negotiated Grant's rookie contract. Grant's rookie contract was a forty five million deal for eight years. Then Babby negotiated a ninety three million dollar sign and trade contract, and the Pistons traded Hill to the Orlando Magic. The irony is that Babby now runs the show for the Suns. After six seasons with Detroit, where Grant was not only one of the best NBA defenders but a prolific scorer, he broke the bank.

He played so well in his rookie year that he topped the All Star game voting. Not even Michael Jordan, Magic Johnson and Larry Bird achieved this distinction. But the Pistons were only 28-54 in his first NBA season.

This led Piston Coach Doug Collins to pressure Hill to score more. "He can dominate the game more subtly, by getting the ball to open people," Collins remarked to **Sports Illustrated**. The Pistons had a "Be Like Mike" campaign, and in 1996 they went to the playoffs.

Hill's six years with the Pistons saw him share the Rookie of the Year Award with Jason Kidd. He also played in five NBA All Star games by 2000.

When Hill was said to be the next Michael Jordan, he took exception to the comparison. "Being hailed as an heir to Jordan didn't seem fair to me." Who could disagree? He told **USA Today** that: "No matter what I did, if I didn't score as many points as Michael or win a title in as many years as him, I would be a failure. Besides I was never a scorer...."

On August 3, 2000 Hill signed a deal with the Orlando Magic but the years in Orlando were tough ones. He sustained an ankle injury that required complicated surgery, and than he picked up an infection that almost killed him. He sat out the fourth season with the Magic. By the 2006-2007 season Grant was back in top form averaging 14 points a game and 3.6 rebounds, while playing solid defense. Rumors were that he was about to retire. He was also a free agent. He wanted to continue playing.

Lon Babby, still Hill's agent, worked out a deal with the Phoenix Suns on July 11, 2007, the first day of free agency guaranteeing Hill 1.83 million dollars for the first year with a $1.97 player option. Recognizing his leadership, Hill was named co-captain with Nash.

Alvan Adams, a Sun legend and Ring of Honor member, allowed Hill to wear his number 33. From day one, Grant Hill was a productive Sun.

GRANT HILL: THE COMMERCIALS AND MOVIES

Because he is so handsome and articulate, Hill is a favorite of advertisers and movie people. His humorous and long running commercial "Grant Hill Drinks Sprite," as well as commercials for the watchmaker TAG Heuer and the sportswear company, Fila, prompted some ribbing from teammates. Adidas and Nike also signed him to lucrative endorsement deals. He is also a spokesperson for McDonalds. Amare' Stoudemire wanted the commercials, but Hill was more photogenic.

On television, Hill showed up with cameos on Living Single, not surprisingly portraying himself. His girl friend in this episode was

Queen Latifah. He also appeared on Tim Allen's Home Improvement. The musical group, Nickelback, featured Hill in one of their music videos. In 1995, he appeared with Ricki Lake on the MTV Music Awards. Throughout his career, Hill has been a much sought after spokesperson, pitchman and celebrity guest. He has always held himself well with the public, and he is the envy of his teammates. Then the roof fell in. It didn't fall in on Grant Hill. The victim was the articulate, well-dressed, suave and personable former NBA player and now a respected TV analyst Jalen Rose.

JALEN ROSE AND THE SORRY TALE OF THE FAB FIVE

When Jalen Rose made a derogatory comment about Grant Hill, he ignited a controversy. Rose inappropriately called Hill "My bitch." This comment resulted from an ESPN 30 Minute Documentary on the University of Michigan's Fab Five. This film focused on the five talented freshmen that enrolled at Michigan and announced that they were ready for an NCAA championship. They became the first lineup of all freshman starters in NCAA history. They left behind a program at Michigan that was under probation, and three of the Fab Five went on to lengthy NBA careers. The other two failed in the pro game. The focal point to the controversy, Jalen Rose, is intelligent, well read, and by all accounts a good person. He lacks the sophistication to realize how hurtful and inaccurate his remarks were as they were directed to Hill.

One of the persistent arguments inside the NBA is whether or not a college education helps the player's maturity, their ability to handle money and their public persona. The answer from virtually everyone is that a bit more college would add to player sophistication. A controversy that broke out from comments made by ESPN analyst, Jalen Rose, provides a good example of why a college education is important. Rose may look articulate, and he is on sports. On life, he doesn't have a clue.

The ESPN 30 Minute film on the Fab Five focused on the 1991-1993 University of Michigan basketball team that started five freshmen. It is the top rated ESPN TV program in that genre. The Fab Five are considered one of the greatest college teams. For their talent, trash talking and show time play the University of Michigan team was a top television draw. They also never won a national championship, and when the Fab Five left the university they created so many problems that Michigan was placed on probation.

The road to the recruiting of the Fab Five began when Steve Fisher replaced University of Michigan Coach Bill Frieder who moved to Arizona State University. Because of his low-key approach, Fisher was considered an interim coach. Then in 1991 he won an unexpected NCAA champion on a team led by future NBA star Glen Rice. The school signed him to a long-term deal, and in 1991, Fisher signed the most talented incoming freshman class in Michigan history.

During their freshman year, the Fab Five led Michigan to the NCAA title game losing to Duke. As sophomores, the Fab Five reached the title game once again losing to the University of North Carolina. In that game, Chris Webber called time out with eleven seconds remaining. Michigan didn't have a time out, and this is considered one of the biggest bonehead plays in college history. Webber entered the NBA draft after the NCAA tournament and Rose and Howard followed the next year. Ray Jackson and Jimmy King played for four years, but they lacked the talent, dedication, personality and discipline for professional basketball.

Mitch Albion's book **Fab Five: Basketball, Trash Talk, The American Dream** was hard on the team and its coach Steve Fisher. The coach was chastised for the team's baggy shorts, as well as their infatuation with hip-hop and rap music. Albion suggested that Michigan's pronounced swagger brought a new interest to college basketball.

The irony of Rose's criticism is reflected in Albion's book. He points out the Duke not only respected the Fab Five and the University of Michigan, but point guard Bobby Hurley remarked that they were luck to beat them. (p. 91) Grant Hill publicly spoke out on their amazing talent. (pp. 91, 126) Why almost two decades later would Rose continue to tirade? The reason is a simple one. During one of the Duke-Michigan games, Grant put on a clinic scoring on the last twelve possessions and Hill had five of those baskets.

To his credit, Fisher was an excellent mentor. He was fired because of the Fab Five. The firing took place when it was revealed that Fisher had given complimentary tickets to Ed Martin. A Federal Court charged Martin with conducting an illegal gambling place and money laundering. He also allegedly loaned Chris Webber $280,000. These allegations sent Fisher on to San Diego State. An NCAA investigation resulted in vacating the Final Four games from the 1992 tournament, as well as vacating victories in the 1992-1993 season as well as every game from 1995-1996 and 1998-1999. The Fab Five was long gone, but the money given players continued. Finally, the University of Michigan stepped in and cleaned up the program. This was the culture that produced future NBA stars Chris Weber, Jalen Rose and Juwan Howard.

Most of the Fab Five came from single-family homes in the ghetto. They were not only celebrities at the University of Michigan, but they had so much fun that there was no emphasis on degrees. Grant Hill got his degree, he has endorsements, he has a NBA Hall of Fame career, and he has respect. These are accomplishments that the Fab Five missed.

What was sad about the Fab Five was the level of hostility. Jimmy King, who failed to make it in pro basketball, talked openly of his dislike for Christian Laettner. One wonders where that hostility developed. In 1992, Laettner was the only college player selected for the U. S. men's Olympic Dream Team. That is probably the reason for King's comments. Much to their credit the Fab Five had no drug issues. There were also no violent explosions, and they did their best to make the University of Michigan a championship basketball school. They were simply immature kids who were celebrities. It was their disdain for rival players, which is puzzling to onlookers. Basketball is a game where players have a fraternal feeling. Chris Webber had enough sense not to cooperate for the film, as he knew that a controversy was brewing. When he was being recruited, Webber spent a night at the Hill household. He ate with Grant's parents, and he was a friend. So Webber escaped Rose's demeaning and unsavory comments.

Rose made some of the most egregious and outlandish remarks calling Grant Hill "his bitch." As a savvy student of the media, Rose made this comment to promote the 30-minute Fab Five film. It played on ESPN and the film analyzed recruiting, the Fab Five's years in at the University of Michigan, their failures to win an NCAA title and the subsequent years after college. The Fab Five television show was a great one, as it showcased the successes and failures of the players. By 2011, they were all successful in one-way or another, but they were still bitter about their years at Michigan. Some of this bitterness was taken out in comments about Grant Hill.

When it was broadcast on March 13, 2011 on ESPN it became the highest rated sports documentary. Jalen Rose, an ESPN analyst, displayed a venal hatred toward Grant Hill. He also hated Duke.

Jalen Rose: "Schools like Duke didn't recruit players like me," Jalen Rose commented in the video. "I felt that they only recruited black players that were Uncle Toms...I was jealous of Grant Hill. He came from a great black family. Your mom went to college and was roommates with

Hillary Clinton. Your dad played in the NFL as a very well spoken and successful man. I was upset and bitter that my mom had to bust her hump for 20 plus years."

Can you imagine such vitriolic criticism? It was a normal family with normal parents. Boy do I feel sorry for Grant Hill. What Rose fails to recognize is that Hill's parents went to work every day and not only made a good living, but they raised a normal family. They also had college degrees, numerous businesses, they consulted for major firms and they were on the board of directors for many corporations.

Rather that criticize Rose, Grant Hill felt sorry for him and he reached out to his friend. Rose commented about the Fab Five at the University of Michigan: "We are who the world hates." It is sad to read Rose's comments, as he is a wonderful analyst and a great person. It is awful that he can't put the past behind him.

When Rose commented that because Grant Hill grew up in a home with a mother and a father, he was not truly African American, the press attacked Rose. The **New York Times** and every other major newspaper skewered him. The **Washington Post's** Jason Reid noted that the documentary went out of its way to highlight inappropriate racial comments by Jalen Rose. To their credit, the **Washington Post** defended Rose's right to his comments. When pressed to explain his comments in detail, Rose dug a deep hole. He stated that he referred to Hill as "his bitch." Rose also suggested that perhaps Hill was an "Uncle Tom." This is the most vicious stereotype. It was an overstatement as all Rose attempted to say is that he could shut down Hill in a game. It didn't turn out that way. Jalen Rose didn't look good.

When Grant Hill answered these charges, he did so in a thoughtful and intelligent manner. He pointed out to Rose that he was engaging in stereotypes. As I watched the 30 Minute special, my take was that Rose's comments were more appropriate to white bigots. Rose is not a bigot but his language is ill chosen. The irony is that Hill didn't call Rose what he was, a nasty, spiteful, hateful, venal young man.

In a thoughtful response in the **New York Times**, Hill pointed out that he felt pride when he watched the Fab Five. Hill remarked of the Fab Five: "The idea of a Fab Five elicited pride and promise in much the same way that Georgetown teams did in the mid-1980s." Hill continued: "The Fab Five represented a cultural phenomenon that impacted the country in a permanent and positive way." Rumor has it that Jalen Rose felt like he was 5-2 after reading the **New York Times**.

Hill continued: "It was a sad and somewhat pathetic turn of events...
to see friends narrating this interesting documentary...and calling me
'a bitch' and worse, calling all black players at Duke 'Uncle Toms.'" The
sad thing is that Rose got a pass from the media. He should have been
harshly criticized. He wasn't. Grant Hill made it clear he didn't want
Rose torn to pieces with criticism. Word has it that Rose now feels like
a midget.

JALEN ROSE SOFTENS HIS COMMENTS

Jalen Rose tried to soften his comments. The result was much like
stepping in cow manure. He said that he "respected Duke's program,"
and his comments were taken out of context. But Rose is a professional
broadcaster, and a good one, even he understood how weak his defense
was in the face of the evidence.

What Jalen Rose did, unintentionally, was to stereotype Grant Hill
and Duke University. As Hill pointed out, not everyone at Duke came
from a Leave It To Beaver family. His mother raised Nolan Smith, who
plays for the Portland Trail Blazers. He also plays in the memory of his
late father Derek Smith. His dad had a distinguished nine-year NBA
career. The articles on Nolan Smith fail to mention that his mother,
Monica, has a law degree from the University of Louisville. When he was
a kid, Nolan grew up with Michael Beasley and they remain friends. It
would be fun to see their pick up games. I wonder if Jalen Rose could
compete? Just a thought!

After four years at Duke, the Portland Trial Blazers selected Smith
as the 21st pick in the 2011 draft. Hill remarked: "I caution my fabulous
five friends to avoid stereotyping me and others they do not know in
much the same way so many people stereotyped them back then for
their appearance and swagger. I wish for you the restoration of the bond
that made you friends, brothers and icons." Hill continued: "I am proud
of my family. I am proud of my Duke championships and all my teammates. And I am proud I never lost a game against the Fab Five." There
is the heart of the matter. Hill won championships, he had big time NBA
contracts and he is a lock for the Hall of Fame. Hill took the high road.
Jalen Rose took the low road.

Jalen Rose's thirteen-year NBA career proved that he was an All
Star, and he will one day enter the Hall of Fame. The question is: "Did
he feel that he should apologize to Grant Hill? Imagine coming from a
normal family. That was Grant Hill's sin. Rose is also intelligent, as he
majored in communications at the University of Michigan, and he is one

of ESPN's top analysts. He is bright, he is handsome, he is analytical, and he is well dressed. What possessed Rose to attack Grant Hill? Only he knows the answer. My thoughts are that a degree would have helped. Rose did explain himself in April 2012 when he stated: "I have a lot of respect for Grant. We spoke after the piece was published. Unfortunately, it was taken out of context by the media...last time I checked Grant and I are both black. I was an ignorant high school student when I said those things." This is as close to an apology as Rose could deliver. He seems incapable of recognizing stereotypical attitudes.

There were some positive comments. "I'm running a charter school so the student can be more like Grant," Rose remarked. Jalen Rose is a good guy. It took the Grant Hill controversy for people to realize that he is really a sweet guy. Stay tuned. There is more greatness to come from Jalen Rose. He should send a thank you note to Grant. The weird end of this controversy is that Hill sent a sizeable check to Rose's Detroit charter school. Thank you Grant and Jalen for patching up your differences. You are my second and third favorite players. Pat Burke, Sebastian Telfair, Goran Dragic and Steve Nash are tied for number one.

Grant Hill is a wonderful and fully rounded out person. Are you listening Jalen Rose?

CHRIS BROUSSARD WEIGHS IN ON ROSE-HILL

Chris Broussard is my favorite ESPN analyst. He is thoughtful, he is witty, he is insightful and he writes well. He also had some thoughts on the Rose-Hill controversy. He suggested that the exchange between the two was an example of a larger problem in the African American community. According to Broussard, being educated means selling out your people. Broussard defended Rose by suggesting that his type of language went on every day in the black community.

What Broussard argues is that athletic achievement is viewed as being dominated by African Americans and academic achievement is a white domain. He suggests that this is a stereotype that needs to end. As Broussard pointed out, African American achievement is a part of every major university, but there is too much attention paid to athletics. What Broussard failed to mention is that Grant Hill is a great athlete, but he was an equally good student at Duke. Grant's first strength is academics as witnessed by his African American art collection, his grades in college, his thoughtful comments to the media and his business models. He continues to have deep intellectual interests.

Yet, Broussard is right. Grant is a storyteller, as is Jalen. They both work to keep youth in line. Rose founded a charter school to help inner city kids achieve. Hill puts money to work for youth groups. The bottom line is that Rose will be more careful with his comments in the future. Chris Broussard did a service pointing out that Rose and Hill want to help America's youth get off the streets. That is the positive development from this controversy.

Hill's career by 2007 was already a legendary one. He was a multiple All Star, he had two long-term NBA contracts that hade him financially secure, and he still loved to play the game. There was no reason to continue playing. The problem is that he loved the game. So he came to the Phoenix Suns and reinvented his game. He is now finishing his career with the Los Angeles Clippers and there is still a great deal of fire in his gas tank. So he came to the Valley of the sun for an interview. How and why Hill signed with the Suns is an intriguing tale.

GRANT HILL WITH THE PHOENIX SUNS

On July 1, 2007, Grant Hill became an unrestricted free agent. He wanted to live in the Valley of the Sun, and his wife, Canadian born singer, Tamia, also loved the area. Hill had something to prove. He would come back from his ankle injury to play as well as ever.

When Grant Hill signed with the Phoenix Suns, his agent, Lon Babby, met with Robert Sarver, and the two-year contract called for $1.8 million and first year and an almost two million dollar salary the second year. After some injury plagued years, some skeptics wondered if Hill could still play. He soon proved he could.

"Obviously money wasn't the biggest factor here," Babby continued. "He had offers for a lot money. Grant wants a chance to win a championship, and he wanted to go to a place would give him a chance to contribute. Phoenix was the perfect fit."

What the Sun received was a seven time All Star and some defensive help at the small forward. When Hill joined the Suns the defense was like a sieve. He soon changed that perception. But it wasn't until Alvin Gentry took over as the coach that the Suns' defense came together. Mike D'Antoni encouraged Hill to continue his offensive prowess. He minimized Hill's defensive skills, but when Gentry took over Hill became the Suns' defensive stopper. The point is that Hill is a complete player.

The decision to leave the Orlando Magic was not an easy one. Hill had been there since 2000, and he earned ninety-three million dollars in six seasons. He also had injury problems, and he played in only 200 of the 492 Magic games while he was under contract. The Magic training staff had no awareness of Hill's medical problems. Hill wanted to come to the Suns as much for the medical staff as the right to play with Steve Nash.

Hill was selected as a Suns' co-captain, and he wore his familiar number 33 jersey. This is thanks to Alvan Adams allowing his old number to once again hit the floor. The up-tempo Suns style with Steve Nash running the point was the perfect fit for Hill. He had some injuries with the Suns during his first year but Hill still averaged 13.1 points a game, 5 rebounds and 2.9 assists. The next season, 2008-2009 was one in which he appeared in all eighty-two games, and this was the first time he had done this in his career. He also averaged 12 points a game, as well as 4.9 rebounds and 2.3 assists. The Suns medical staff got credit from Hill weekly.

In his final season with the Suns in 2011-2012, Hill reached the 17,000 career point total and he was 798th in all time NBA scoring, 79th in assists and 66th in steals. Not bad for a small forward. Some point and shooting guards didn't have these gaudy statistics. On July 18, 2012 Hill signed a 6.5 million dollar contract with the Los Angeles Clippers. The second face of the Suns' franchise was gone.

GRANT HILL: SOME 2012 STATISTICS
1. AFTER THE ALL STAR BREAK HILL SHOT 50% FROM THE FIELD AND HE AVERAGED 11.1 POINTS PER GAME
2. HILL HAS APPEARED IN 363 OF 392 GAMES SINCE JOINING THE SUNS
3. ON APRIL 14 HE HAD A CAREER HIGH EIGHT OFFENSIVE REBOUNDS AGAINST THE SAN ANTONIO SPURS
4. HILL'S 22 POINTS ON MARCH 23 AGAINST THE PACERS WAS HIS SEASON HIGH
5. FROM MARCH 7-20, 2012 HILL HAD EIGHT STRAIGHT DOUBLE DIGIT SCORING EFFORTS

GRANT HILL'S CHARITY WORK
It is in the area of charitable work that Grant Hill has made a huge contribution. He was Vice-Chairman of the Special Olympic World Summer Games in 1999 held in Durham, Raleigh and Chapel Hill, North Carolina. Along with his mother and grandmother, he established a

scholarship at Dillard University in New Orleans. His grandmother supported the school, and the Hill family made its commitment to education in the post-Katrina era.

As a strongly academic young man, Hill is a voracious reader. He was instrumental in popularizing the READ program, which supports libraries, advocates literacy and promotes reading. His father, Calvin, set up a day care center in New Haven to help those who go to school in the local community. Grant is a financial benefactor of this day care center. In his hometown of Reston, Virginia, Hill funded an organization to help students fund their education.

THE AFRICAN AMERICAN ART COLLECTION

If Grant Hill didn't play basketball, he would be a Professor of African American History and Art. He has had a lifelong fascination with art. In the process he has assembled one of America's best collections of African American art. His collection went on tour for three years, and it was featured in seven cities. Hill labeled his collection: "Something All Our Own: The Grant Hill Collection of African American Art." (Are you listening Jalen Rose?)

The works of Romare Bearden, Elizabeth Catlett, Hughie Lee-Smith, John Biggers, Phoebe Beasley, Malcolm Brown, Edward Jackson, John Coleman and Arthello Beck, Jr., highlight Hills' collection. Hill set up the Something All Our Own Scholarship to assist students who lack the funds to pursue a degree in visual arts. It is Hill's view that African American art is a neglected aspect of history. He is filling in that void with his collection and deep knowledge.

GRANT HILL: THE ENTREPRENEUR

In the business world, Hill is involved in eight high profile real estate ventures. Like most of his business, he has set up real estate units that promote the concept of affordable homes with luxury apartments. It is the Grant Hill brand that is most important to his life and career. When he endorses a product Hill makes sure that it is one that he can identify with and that be believes is a product with integrity.

His endorsement deals with McDonald's, Nike, Nestle and Fila fall into that category. When FILA signed him to a seven year eighty million dollar endorsement deal, the sneaker and apparel company considered it money well spent. The Fila ad featured Hill jumping in a tuxedo with basketballs swirling in the background. The ad emphasized the Grant Hill 11 shoe. Because of Hill's prominence, FILA went from the seventh best selling athlete footwear company to the third in its first two years with Hill as a spokesperson. Their sales increased by 52% the year that the Grant Hill 11 shoe was released. This led to the Grant Hill 4 shoe, which was released with a new endorsement deal. Television spots promoting the slogan "Change The Game" highlighted the Hill shoe. As one FILA spokesperson remarked: "Grant Hill allowed us to challenge Nike, Adidas and Reebok." Without Grant Hill as a spokesperson, FILA would have been just another shoe company. The Grant Hill 5 continued FILA's drive for commercial success, as they signed Hill to a lucrative second contract.

The Hill endorsement deals prompted FILA to move into third place in the lucrative athletic shoe market behind Nike and Reeboks. Nike paid Michael Jordan twenty million a year to help maintain its number one position.

One of the more interesting endorsement deals came in 2009 when Hill signed to endorse Sam's Choice Cola. This cola sells in Wal-Mart and it did very little for the large retail chain. Since Hill came aboard Sam's Choice Cola is now a big seller.

Where does Grant Hill fit in the pantheon of athletes who are rich from endorsement deals? While he was still playing for the Orlando Magic, Hill was number ten in endorsement deals, according to **Sports Illustrated,** as he brought in over ten million dollars a year. The **Sports Illustrated** article suggested that while Hill was injured and not playing his squeaky clean image had a large number of endorsement deals on the table.

Peter: "How does Grant Hill have time to play basketball? He is too busy making money."

GRANT HILL'S NBA EARNINGS

Season	Team	Lg	Yearly salary
1994–95	Detroit Pistons	NBA	$2,750,000
1995–96	Detroit Pistons	NBA	$4,050,000
1996–97	Detroit Pistons	NBA	$5,025,000
1997–98	Detroit Pistons	NBA	$5,850,000
1998–99	Detroit Pistons	NBA	$6,675,000
1999–00	Detroit Pistons	NBA	$6,939,000
2000–01	Orlando Magic	NBA	$9,660,000
2001–02	Orlando Magic	NBA	$10,865,250
2002–03	Orlando Magic	NBA	$12,072,500
2003–04	Orlando Magic	NBA	$13,279,750
2004–05	Orlando Magic	NBA	$14,487,000
2005–06	Orlando Magic	NBA	$15,694,250
2006–07	Orlando Magic	NBA	$16,901,500
2007–08	Phoenix Suns	NBA	$1,830,000
2008–09	Phoenix Suns	NBA	$1,976,400
2009–10	Phoenix Suns	NBA	$3,000,000
2010–11	Phoenix Suns	NBA	$3,324,000
2011–12	Phoenix Suns	NBA	$6,500,000
Career	(may be incomplete)		$140,879,650

NICE GUYS DO FINISH FIRST

Mike Lupica, writing in **Esquire**, remarked that Grant Hill is a "hope for sports heroism." Lupica continued: "He conducts himself with an elegance that seems more uncommon in sports than a collective bargaining agreement." He is also one of the few high profile athletes to be featured in **Esquire**. When fans voted for their favorite player in the 1995 and 1996 All Star games, Hill received the highest number of votes. His picture on the front of a Frosted Mini Wheaties cereal box was a favorite, and it was the best selling cereal of the mid-1990s.

Former Detroit Piston Coach Don Chaney remarked to **Time** magazine: "Grant is headed for stardom." Then ankle injury came and he demonstrated that he was not only a star, but also one who could overcome adversity.

Hill has homes in Orlando and the Phoenix area and his wife Tamia is a four time Grammy nominated R & B singer who is best known for her 2001 hit "Stranger In My House" and the 2003 hit "Into You." Grant and his wife have two daughters MylaGrace and Lael Rose. At forty, Grant Hill can still put the ball in the basket and his character driven career heads him to the basketball Hall of Fame in due time. The best in Hill's life is yet to come.

chapter

EIGHTEEN

CHANNING FRYE: MR. INSIDE AND MR. OUTSIDE

"SET YOUR SIGHTS HIGH, THE HIGHER THE BETTER. EXPECT THE MOST WONDERFUL THINGS TO HAPPEN, NOT IN THE FUTURE BUT RIGHT NOW. REALIZE THAT NOTHING IS TOO GOOD. ALLOW ABSOLUTELY NOTHING TO HAMPER YOU OR HOLD YOU UP IN ANY WAY," CHANNING FRYE

Channing Frye is the epitome of a Phoenix Suns player. He can shot outside, he can shot inside, and he is deadly at the three-point line. Frye is as close to a local as the team could get. He grew up in Phoenix and attended St. Mary's High School, and he starred at the University of Arizona. At six feet eleven inches, Frye is a skillful a big man as there is in the NBA. As a center or power forward Frye is quick to the basket and a fearsome competitor.

CHANNING FRYE: THE EARLY YEARS

When he was born Channing Thomas Frye in White Plains, New York, his family moved to New Hampshire when he was a baby and then on to Phoenix when he was seven years old. Channing's father, Thomas, is co-founder and co-president of Education Solutions and Services, which offers office support to public and private charter schools. The constant presence of books, music and culture in the Frye household created a level of education that didn't depend upon basketball.

Frye and his father are the second and third most famous people in the family. His grandfather, John Mulzac, was a member of the legendary Tuskegee Airmen. In the Frye household it was about school and accomplishment. Somewhere along the way, basketball came into the mix.

While growing up in Phoenix, Channing Frye liked to take a nerf ball and dunk it in a makeshift hoop in his backyard. He was recognized for his basketball talent early at Hendrix Junior High, and he went on to St. Mary's Prep where he was an All State and All Metro selection. At St. Mary's in his senior year, Frye averaged 22 points brought down 15 rebounds and he had six blocks a game. He also led St. Mary's to the Class 5A state championship and the team posted a 30-3 record. He was a fourth team Parade All American and the Arizona player of the year while a senior.

When his high school career ended, Fry was rated the number ninety-eight recruit in the nation by **Hoop Scoop** and the thirteenth best center in the country by the Fast Break Recruiting Service. His slight build suggested that he was a natural small forward or an undersized power forward. A hard worker, Frye developed his outside shot with the idea of moving into one of the forward slots when he entered the NBA.

He accepted a scholarship offer to the University of Arizona, and he starred for Lute Olson's teams for four years. While at St. Mary's, Frye was an excellent student. He would have qualified academically for any university.

CHANNING FRYE AT THE UNIVERSITY OF ARIZONA

At six feet ten inches and 235 pounds, Frye was a center on a team that featured future NBA players Luke Walton, Andre Iguodala and Salim Stoudamire. In his first season at the University of Arizona, Frye averaged 9.5 points a game and brought down 6.3 rebounds. In the NCAA tournament, Frye was the Wildcat's second leading scorer. He also added twenty pounds to his frame and this helped his inside play.

In 2002-2003, Frye's sophomore year saw him bulk up, and the result was that he led the Wildcats in blocked shots, and he was second in the Pac Ten in that category. He averaged 13.5 points a game and he had 10.5 rebounds. After two years at the University of Arizona, Frye was a top NBA prospect. But he wasn't an early draft entry. The result is that he had some great career moments at Arizona. He also refined his game shooting a remarkable .595% percent during one of the Pac Ten seasons. In 2002, he connected for twenty-five points against USC. In his senior year he blocked seven shots against Oregon, and he had sixteen rebounds against Mississippi State.

Channing Frye loved attending the University of Arizona. He had a wonderful time there, and with friends like Richard Jefferson, his game continued to develop. By the time he was a senior, Frye became one of the most decorated University of Arizona basketball players. He was first team All Pac Ten for the second straight year. He was the Sapphire Award winner. This is the trophy given annually to the school's outstanding student athlete. He also won the 2004-2005 Pac Ten Sportsmanship Trophy. He was eighth his senior year in Pac 10 scoring, and he was an all around player with an over fifty percent shooting average. He shot 83 percent from the free throw line. He had twenty-five consecutive double-digit scoring games, and he played solid defense. He was co-captain of the Wildcats during his final two seasons

CHANNING FRYE IN THE DRAFT AND BEYOND

In the 2005 draft, the New York Knicks selected Frye in the first round, and he was the eighth overall pick. When he was drafted, Frye remarked: "I think with the tools and the veterans we have here in New York, we can definitely have a winning team. I feel like I definitely can contribute."

That year Frye was named to the rookie All-Star team. It was with the Knicks that Frye learned about the quirks of the NBA. Coach Isaiah Thomas replaced Frye in the starting lineup with Jerome James, and Thomas defended his action as a change made for defensive purposes. James is a stiff on defense as well as offense. Coach Thomas was soon unemployed. This was Frye's first lesson that at times the coach doesn't know what he is doing.

Much to Frye's credit, he took the high road. He didn't criticize a coach like Isaiah Thomas who didn't belong on the bench. Frye simply continued to work hard on his game and the best was yet to come.

The second year with the Knicks, Frye averaged almost ten points a game, and he continued to display accurate outside shooting. Then surprisingly on the night of the 2007 draft, Frye was traded to the Portland Trail Blazers, along with guard Steve Francis in exchange for Zach Randolph, Fred Jones and Dan Dickau. It was in Portland that Frye found a community that he loved, and he still lives there in the off-season.

THE PORTLAND TRAIL BLAZERS IS NOT A REBIRTH

The trade to Portland led to a new social and personal life connected with the Pacific Northwest. Frye has interests outside of basketball, and the culture of the Portland community was important to a tranquil life. But he was still first and foremost a great basketball player. The Portland Trail Blazers were not the perfect fit, but unwittingly they became the last stop before Frye's rebirth in the Valley of the Sun.

In Portland, Frye's minutes decreased, and his point production fell. He never complained. The Trail Blazers style was more physical and Frye had a finesse game. So it was off to sign a free agent deal. In his first season with the Suns, Frye averaged 6.8 points a game, and the next year he was down to 4.2 points a game. The Trail Blazers were going in another direction. Frye looked around for a new team.

In July 2009, he signed a two-year contract with the Phoenix Suns. "I felt it was a good situation for me and a good opportunity....It's a chance to play with two or three All-Stars," Frye commented to **Portland Oregonian** beat writer, Mark Hester. It was a prophetic statement.

Frye's Suns contract was reworked after the first year and he signed for six years with a total salary of around $30 million dollars. His contract includes a Player Option for $6.8 million for the 2014-2015 season.

FRYE COMES TO THE SUNS

When Frye signed his Suns contract as a free agent on July 14, 2009, he was working five days a week in a Portland gym. The free wheeling offense of Coach Mike D'Antoni was a perfect for Frye's game. He had four years of NBA experience, and his outside game had grown dramatically.

In 2009-2010, Frye was a top free agent signing as he averaged 11.2 points a game with 5.3 rebounds and a career high 0.9 blocks. He also had a team leading number of three point shots made, 172, while showing an increased shooting efficiency. The next season, 2010-2011, saw Frye average 12.7 points a game with 6.6 rebounds and 1.2 assists. It was against the Minnesota Timberwolves when he made nine straight three pointers on the way to a 33-point night that Frye's game reached its high point.

His three years with the Suns have made him one of the new faces of the franchise. He scored in double figures, this is something he hadn't done since his first year in the league, and he played tougher inside while continuing to drain the three pointer. In the strike shortened 2012 season, Frye averaged 10.5 points a game with 5.9 rebounds. His shooting percentage was a career low 41.6% but by NBA standards it was more than acceptable.

In April 2012, Frye injured his shoulder and the partial dislocation made it difficult for him to perform during the playoff run. He had surgery in the off-seasonAt twenty-nine, Frye is at the peak of his game. The shoulder dislocation derailed a decade of hard work. His doctor, Lewis Yocum, viewed Frye's surgery optimistically. Rudy Gay had a similar operation and he continues to play at a high level. When he is in Phoenix, Frye is seen with an expensive chauffeur, Grant Hill, who drives Frye to practice. Robert Sarver needs to kick in a little more money to pay for Hill's service.

It is off the court that Frye is a star. His foundation supports youth activity centering on basketball and nutrition. The Channing Frye Foundation sponsors a kickball tournament in Portland, and he is active with his charity in Phoenix.

The 2012 season was an up and down affair for Frye. He did some things that the fans didn't recognize. His most significant improvement was on the defensive end of the court. He has had the bad rap that he is not a good defender. This simply isn't true. He was more aggressive on the boards, and he defends the power forward as well as the small forward. It was when Frye was placed at the five or the center position that he struggled. Who can guard Andrew Bynum or Dwight Howard?

CHANNING FRYE: SOME CONCLUSIONS AND THOUGHTS ON FOOD

In the off-season, Frye lives with his wife, Lauren, in Portland. His son is named Hendrix after his junior high school and not Jimi Hendrix.

He set up the Channing Frye Foundation in 2007, and this organization has the goal of pointing youth in a positive and healthy direction. He sponsors a charity kickball tournament every year in Portland. He also donated ten thousand dollars to the Randall Children's Hospital. When he has money left over, he is often seen in Portland's Powell's Book Store.

When he is in Portland, Frye eats at John's Landing, where there is a dish named after him. It is a plate of French fries topped with cheese, ground beef and jalapenos with some tomatoes, guacamole and sour cream. He also loves the Buffalo Gap. Frye went online to rate his restaurants. Pok Pok is one of his favorites because it is different. He also likes Stanich's. He is often seen standing outside the restaurant waiting to get in for breakfast at the Screen Door. He loves the Screen Door's chicken and waffles. It is a good thing Steve Nash is with the Los Angeles Lakers. Nash is the food police and Frye would be in trouble.

In Phoenix, Frye frequents Fleming's Steak House, and he loves the Mexican food at Tia Rosa. Just as he was about to enter what might have been his most productive Sun season, Frye was sidelined by a heart ailment.

THE UNEXPECTED MEDICAL PROBLEM

Channing Frye is a dedicated, hard worker. He even cut his honeymoon short to work on his game. He is twenty-nine years old and at the peak of his game. The shoulder injury suffered at the end of the 2011-2012 season was a minor set back. There was another problem.

In a routine physical prior to the start of the 2012-2013 season it was discovered that Frye had an enlarged heart. He will miss the 2012-2013 season in which the Suns have a revamped roster. He has a problem with a heart muscle that will take some time to heal. The prognosis is that Frye will be up and shooting three pointers within a year. Stay tuned Mr. Inside and Mr. Outside still has a lot of game left.

The NBA in recent times has been plagued with heart problems. The Boston Celtics have two players, Jeff Green and Chris Wilcox, who have had heart related problems. Sacramento King Chuck Hayes had to delay his long-term contract for a brief time, while he was cleared to play. The medical staff for the Phoenix Suns has every intention of bringing Frye back into the rotation. It's only right that Channing Frye should have the last word.

Channing Frye on twitter: "Thanks every for your support. I will be ok. It will pass and I'll be back we have the best staff in the NBA helping me out."

CHANNING FRYE'S SALARY HISTORY

2005-06	New York Knicks	NBA	$2,162,880
2006-07	New York Knicks	NBA	$2,325,000
2007-08	Portland Trail Blazers	NBA	$2,487,240
2008-09	Portland Trail Blazers	NBA	$3,163,769
2009-10	Phoenix Suns	NBA	$2,000,000
2010-11	Phoenix Suns	NBA	$5,200,000
2011-12	Phoenix Suns	NBA	$5,600,000
Career	**(may be incomplete)**		**$22,938,889**

IMPORTANT CHANNING FRYE FACTS

CHANNING FRYE'S FAVORITE PORTLAND RESTAURANTS: 1.) JOHN'S LANDING. HIS FAVORITE DISH: CHANNING'S FRIES TOPPED WITH CHEESE, GROUND BEEF, JALAPENOS, TOMATOES, GUACAMOLE AND SOUR CREAM. 2.) NOBLE ROT. SEE FRYE'S BLOG FOR A DESCRIPTION OF THIS EATERY. 3.) POK POK IS AN ASIAN FUSION RESTAURANT WITH A VARIED MENU AND YOU WAIT AN HOUR AT TIMES. 4.) THE BUFFALO GAP IS ONE OF FRYE'S FAVORITE RESTAURANTS IN PORTLAND.

CHANNING FRYE'S PORTLAND HOME: IT IS LOCATED JUST SOUTH OF TOM MCCALL WATERFRONT PARK, A LARGE EXPANSE OF LAND POPULAR WITH CYCLISTS, WALKERS, RUNNERS AND PEOPLE WHO ATTEND THE CITY FESTIVAL. FRYE'S HOME IS ALMOST MID-POINT BETWEEN THE ROSE GARDEN WHERE THE BLAZERS PLAY AND TUALATIN WHERE THE TEAM PRACTICES.

CHANNING FRYE HAS A KICKBALL TOURNAMENT FOR CHARITY IN PORTLAND AS WELL AS HIS SUN CHARITY EVENTS.

CHANNING FRYE MET AND MARRIED LAUEN LISOSKI, A TUALATIN HIGH SCHOOL GRADUATE, WHEN HE JOINED THE PORTLAND TRAIL BLAZERS IN 2007.

THE FRYE FAMILY FOUNDATION IS A NOT FOR PROFIT ORGANIZATION THAT'S GOAL IS TO EMPOWER A NEW GENERATION OF PHILANTROPISTS. HE IS ALSO A SUPPORTER OF MYMUSICRX WHICH DONATES MONEY TO HELP CHILDREN WITH CANCER.

CHANNING FRYE'S FAVORITE ATHELE AS A YOUNG MAN: MICHAEL JORDAN.

CHANNING FRYE'S FAVORITE VIDEO GAME: WORLD OF WARCRAFT OR HALO

CHANNING FRYE'S FAVORITE MUSICIAN: N.E.R.D. OR JIMI HENDRIX

CHANNING FRYE'S FAVORITE BAND: OUTKAST

CHANNING FRYE'S FAVORITE REALITY TV SHOW: THE BIGGEST LOSER

CHANNING FRYE'S FAVORITE TV SHOW: GAME OF THRONES

FAVORITE BOARD GAME: RISK

FAVORITE CARD GAME: TEXAS HOLD EM

FAVORITE MOVIE: KILL BILL 1 AND 2

FAVORITE VACATION SPOT; OAHU, HAWAII

FAVORITE SUBJECT IN SCHOOL: HISTORY

FAVORITE SNACK FOOD: HOSTESS CHOCOLATE DONUTS
Peter: "Howard have you considered getting a life?"

Official Website: www.channingfrye.com **Facebook**: www.facebook.com/channingfrye **Twitter**: www.twitter.com/channing frye **Tumbler**: channingfrye.tumblr.com **Foundation**: www.fryefamily-foundation.org

chapter

NINETEEN

MARCIN GORTAT: IT'S HAMMER TIME

"PEOPLE ASKING HOW OLD I AM AND I SAY, 'FOR REAL OR JUST FOR PASSPORT,' BECAUSE I'M ACTUALLY 34, I JUST HAVE MADE PASSPORT FOR NBA...." MARCIN GORTAT

Marcin Gortat is a joker. He loves to use poor English to make a point. The reality is that he speaks perfect English. But why not have some fun with the press. Marcin doesn't want to find out if Dan Bickley has a sense of humor. He doesn't. What Gortat wanted was a shot at an NBA career and it was a long and difficult task to get there. He is now a premier starting center in the NBA. Not a bad feat for a player who had to sit and wait for his chance.

SITTING BEHIND DWIGHT HOWARD
If you are a professional athlete the worst punishment is sitting behind a superstar. This turned out to be center Marcin Gortat's job with the Orlando Magic. He sat at the end of the bench behind Dwight Howard. The player known as the Polish Hammer, practiced diligently and

waited his chance. It didn't come in Orlando. Then the 6-11 240-pound center was traded to the Phoenix Suns. No one seemed to know anything about Gortat. He is European, he was 24.7 in the gym, and he has a high basketball IQ. He simply hadn't been given a chance. While he was sitting behind Orlando's superstar Dwight Howard, Gortat learned the subtle nuances of the NBA game. But basketball wasn't Gortat's first love.

He was an excellent soccer player and the world of professional soccer was one that he embraced. Basketball came later and it was almost accidental that he got into the American game. When he did, he loved it.

When he arrived in Phoenix the first thing Gortat did was to change his workout routine. Gortat remarked: "I change my warm up I change my practice routine, my lifting program. I change everything... My status change back in Poland. People are writing about me more, people talking about more things...My whole life turn 180 degrees since I'm here. It's nothing bad, I love it." The road to the Valley of the Sun was a long and arduous one. It all began in Poland.

GORTAT'S EARLY YEARS

Marcin was born in Lodz, Poland on February 17, 1984, and he began to play soccer at age ten. He began his professional basketball career at eighteen. His family had a big influence upon his athletic career. From an early age, Gortat was called "the Warlock." Where and how he got this nickname remains a mystery. Perhaps it was his family who saw him as a basketball sorcerer.

Peter: "Are you writing nice things about Gortat because his birthday is the same day as yours?" No!

His father, Janusz, was a Polish boxer and bronze medalist in the Munich 1972 Olympics and he returned to Montreal for the 1976 Olympics. His mother was a member of the Polish national volleyball team. As he grew up in an athletic family, Marcin graduated from a technical school where he also acquired fluency in English, German and Serbian as well as Polish.

As a young man, Gortat played soccer, and he was also a high jumper. Along the way, he became of Poland's best basketball player. It was only six months after he started playing basketball that he was selected to the Polish National Under 22 Team. He came by the game naturally, and he was a presence in the middle the first time he stepped on the court.

In 2005, the Suns drafted him and traded his rights to the Orlando Magic. The Magic saw a raw talent and they sent him off to play for two plus seasons in Europe. He played for Rhein Energie in Cologne, which is a team in Germany's basketball Bundesliga.

Since his introduction to the game, he has had an unstoppable worth ethic. He works out twenty-four seven on his game. There is a quiet tenacity to Gortat, and he remains focused. It took some time to get his career off the ground. He bounced around for a time in the basketball minor leagues.

In Germany, when Gortat played for the Koln 99ers, who were also known as the afore mentioned Rhein Energie, he spent four years from 2003 to 2007 developing his inside game. In 2006, he led Rhein Energie to the German domestic championship. He was not only able to define his skills, but it was not long before Gortat attracted NBA scouts. Orlando had offers for Gortat, and they constantly turned a deaf ear to those inquires. Yet, the Magic front office didn't believe that he was ready for the NBA, as a result he went through a torturous apprenticeship. The journey to the NBA was not an easy one.

GORTAT'S JOURNEY TO THE NBA

When he arrived to play for the Orlando Magic, they added him to their active roster. He was also placed on the Pepsi Pro Summer League roster where he was on the Magic's active roster. In 2007-2008, he played five games for the Anaheim Arsenal averaging 9.8 points a game. The Orlando Magic General Manager Otis Smith, a former NBA player, saw an upside in his game, and he did what he could to keep him. The rumor was out that their franchise center, Dwight Howard, was not going to stay around in Orlando. So Smith reasoned that Gortat would be his replacement.

It is due to the tenacity of the Sun's front office that they were able to trade Jason Richardson, as well as Hedo Turkoglu and Earl Clark, to Orlando for Gortat, Vince Carter and Mickael Pietrus. It was Gortat who became the centerpiece for the Suns. Carter was playing on one leg and Pietrus couldn't comprehend the Suns' system even if he had it in French. The problem for the Magic is that Otis Smith believed that if he put enough pieces around Howard he would sign a contract extension. Fortunately, for the Suns, that logic didn't prevail. Carter and Pietrus soon were gone.

The reason for Gortat's recall was to back up Dwight Howard. It took some time but Gortat finally began to get some minutes on the floor. It was when All Star center Dwight Howard was injured that Gortat showed off his skills. On December 15, 2008, subbing for Howard, Gortat scored sixteen points and picked off thirteen rebounds. Then it was back to the bench. On April 30, 2009, subbing once again for Howard, who was suspended, Gortat made his first playoff start in Game 6 against the Philadelphia 76ers. He responded with eleven points and fifteen rebounds. The NBA scouts realized that Gortat was a diamond in the rough. The Suns took note.

The NBA was aware of Gortat's skills. Dallas Maverick owner, Mark Cuban, sent an offer sheet in July 2009 with a five year $34 million dollar contract offer. The Orlando Magic matched it and Gortat was back on their bench. He was not happy. Then he was traded to the Phoenix Suns. He has blossomed in the Suns' system. The Suns took advantage of his Orlando strengths while continuing to polish his entire game. Before he left the Magic, Gortat did have some excellent games.

GORTAT'S BIG MOMENTS IN ORLANDO

Although he backed up Dwight Howard, while with the Orlando Magic, Gortat did have some good moments. Then on April 16, 2008, Dwight Howard's back acted up and Gortat came in for twenty-eight minutes and scored twelve points while grabbing eleven rebounds in a 103-83 victory over the Washington Wizards. The Wizards' performance was the best in Gortat's brief time with the Magic

On March 11, 2009 while playing only twenty-three minutes, Gortat scored thirteen points, and he grabbed fifteen rebounds. This helped Orlando clinch a playoff berth with a blow out 107-79 win over the Chicago Bulls. When the 2009 season ended, Gortat has averaged 3.8 points with 4.5 rebounds. His last salary with the Magic was $700,000, and he was ready for free agency.

MARCIN GORTAT'S PHOENIX SUNS DEAL

2009: $5,584,000
2010: $6,322,320
2011: $6,790,460
2012: $7,258,960
2013: $7,727,280

When he did get on the floor with the Orlando Magic, Gortat played well and he was a hot commodity in the free agent market. The problem is that as he sat behind the best NBA center Dwight Howard, he worried that his skills would atrophy. They didn't. As the 2009 season concluded, the Magic in July 2009 decided to trade him.

THE SUNS' GORTAT TRADE

In December 2010 the Suns traded for eight times NBA All Star Vince Carter, center Marcin Gortat, swingman Mickael Pietrus and they received a first round draft pick. Phoenix sent Jason Richardson, Hedo Turkoglu and Earl Clark to the Magic. "This transaction helps us now and in the future," Lon Babby remarked. The irony is that Gortat was the only player worth anything. They soon found out that he was a polished player ready for the NBA. Lance Blanks, Lon Babby and Mark West knew they had a long term and highly productive player in Gortat. They also realized that he was a bargain for less than seven million dollars a year.

MARCIN GORTAT'S SUNS' STATISTICS

In his first three years with the Suns, Gortat was an unusually productive player. In 2010-2011, his thirteen points a game and ten rebounds gave the Suns its first inside presence since Shaquille O'Neal exited the franchise. He played in fifty-five games the first year after coming from Orlando and his inside play allowed the wing players greater shooting freedom. The offense opened up as a result of Gortat's presence.

In his second season, his 15.4 points a game and ten rebounds helped the team, and by the third year he continued to develop with eleven points and almost ten rebounds a game. The point is that he was reliable and consistent; it had been a long time since the Suns had that option in their arsenal.

THE MARCIN GORTAT FOUNDATION AND HIS PERSONAL SIDE

In October 2009, Gortat established a foundation to help young people fulfill their sports dreams. Gortat's MG13 Foundation sponsors sports camps and there are numerous grants scholarships. He also purchases equipment and provides schools with what is needed to field teams. It is difficult in Poland to promote basketball, as soccer is the national sport. So Gortat is a native ambassador for the American game.

In Poland top athletes often don't have funds for schooling and international participation. Gortat is aiding in the recruiting, and training, as well as to send young Poles to international athletic events. It is an organization dedicated to increasing and perpetuating knowledge about basketball.

While growing up in Poland, Gortat talked about his sports family, his mom and his dad who were extremely athletic. His dad won two bronze medals in the Olympics and there were expectations for Gortat's own athletic prowess. "You can see my body language when you watch films of my father fighting in the Olympics," Gortat remarked.

He continues to represent the Polish National Basketball team in European games. Gortat is aware there are many expectations for him. He doesn't know were the Polish Hammer nickname came from, and he appears somewhat uneasy with it. Gortat is naturally shy despite his size.

His favorite food is naturally Polish food, and he shops at a local Polish super market in Phoenix. He loves the kielbasa and calls it "the true meat." Gortat continued: "You can splice in half with onions and it is delicious." A Touch of European Café in Glendale is among his favorite restaurants.

As Gortat pointed out, the Polish President will show up one day at the U. S. Airways Arena and he looks forward to celebrating Polish night. He works as hard off the court as on it. "The most important thing for me is to make plays," Gortat remarked, "and to make the playoffs." He is the consummate competitor.

"I am trying to use my skills to be a little smarter than I was a few years ago," Gortat observed. He is showing a new maturity with an increased number of double doubles, as the 2012-2013 season commenced. "I believe that I should be more of a leader," Gortat remarked. He spoke highly of Jermaine O'Neill's leadership. "I am one of the best players on this team and I am going to try to prove it," Gortat said. He also said his game has improved dramatically due to O'Neal's stewardship.

He also had a love affair with the Phoenix fans. "The Suns fans definitely deserve a playoff team," Gortat concluded.

As the younger and faster Suns emerged, Gortat was one of the older players and he provided as much leadership as possible. Tom Leander and Tom Chambers hosted a program that showcased Gortat's talent, and they agreed that he was a key factor in the emergence of the new look Suns. As Gortat looked back on his three seasons with the Suns, he has a vision of future success. When he arrived in the Valley of The Sun, Gortat began to change the Suns' culture with his strong inside presence. In the 2011-2012 campaign, Gortat averaged 15.4 points and 10 rebounds. For a big man he had 0.7 steals and 1.5 assists, which suggests the depth and quality of his game. Since Steve Nash has gone to the Los Angeles Lakers, Gortat hopes to continue these numbers with the new point guard Goran Dragic.

Marcin Gortat is a player on the rise. He finished the 2011-2012 season with his best statistics, and he is consistently rated as a top ten

NBA center. The reason is that he is a versatile big man. The best is yet to come.

MARCIN GORTAT: THE 2012-2013 SEASON BEGINS ROUGHLY

During the Suns first nineteen games in the 2012-2013 season, Gortat struggled. He no longer has Steve Nash with his feathery, pin-point passes and the Gortat-Dragic pick and roll hasn't been perfected. In a November 19, 2012 **Arizona Republic** article, Gortat said that he was frustrated with the Suns. Gortat lamented that he was no longer the same inside option. The additions of Michael Beasley and Luis Scola changed the Suns' inside game. It was for the better, and he had to adjust to the new play. He is down from twelve to nine shots a game and his numbers have declined from fifteen points a game to eleven.

Not only is Gortat is hard working player. He is an honest one. "I'm certainly not the player I was last season, I need to find my place in the new order. I'm still capable of helping this team, and regularly recording a double, double, but when the ball sticks to one person on offense, it hard to find a good rhythm."

Then Gortat pointed out that his two strongest offensive options the pick and roll and the post up have declined. Michael Beasley gets the ball outside and works methodically and with skill for a shot. Luis Scola works inside, and he is a terror on the boards. This changes in the Suns inside basketball culture, but, in the long run, it should help Gortat's game. But as the 2012-2013 season was in its early stages, Gortat was still finding his way in the paint.

Obviously frustrated, Gortat remarked: "Unfortunately, I don't think I'm even an option for (coach Alvin) Gentry. He doesn't even take me into consideration. The situation is critical. We're playing the same thing we've been playing last year, but the truth is we have a completely different set of players. I don't think it really works. I can't get frustrated now though, I have to stay positive." This is from the heart of a competitor. Coach Gentry knows how to use the roster, and for the remainder of the 2012-2013 season. Gortat's lack of touches will be discussed.

By Thanksgiving, 2012, Gortat was frustrated with his minutes on the floor and his performance in the first eleven games. He vented his feelings to a Polish newspaper. He also displayed his frustration to Coach Alvin Gentry, who said: "You try to make sure that he understands exactly what you're trying to do, and there's not a problem if you ask me." If everyone had Gortat's drive to get better and improve with each game, it would be great for any team.

Marcin Gortat is the premier unselfish NBA center and his presence is one, which guarantees that the Suns will turn things around and re-enter the playoff picture.

On a warm Wednesday night, November 21, 2012, Gortat dominated the game against the Portland Trail Blazers. He scored twenty-two points, he grabbed seven rebounds and he played with an intensity that made his mentor Jermaine O'Neal smiled. O'Neal also came in and scored seventeen points with five rebounds. The Trail Blazers never had a chance as the thirty-nine points from the Suns' centers brought a resounding win. Gortat was back and his mentor, O'Neal, was smiling with ready approval. Stay tuned; the best is yet to come from Gortat. Hopefully, Jermaine O'Neal will be around for another season, as his mentoring role is a key to the entire team.

The Suns offered Gortat a contract extension in November 2012, and he turned down the offer. "We just said we're going to wait," Gortat told Paul Coro of the **Arizona Republic**. Gortat continued: "I want to finish this contract, and we'll see where I go from there. It didn't even bother me or change anything in my attitude or performance."

Gortat is enjoying Jermaine O'Neal's mentoring and his game is benefitting from the tutoring. When asked about O'Neal's impact, Gortat said that he would pay for his next year's salary. "Playing with him has been my best experience from this year," Gortat concluded.

GORTAT'S YEAR ROUND BASKETBALL

When Gortat left Poland to arrive at the Suns training camp, he had played for Poland and led the national team to a qualifying berth for the 2013 EuroBasket championship. As the Suns 2012-2013 season opened Gortat was up and down as a scorer, rebounder and defensive specialist. This was due to constant practice and playing in Europe. "I think I lost the hunger of the game," Gortat continued. "I wasn't hungry enough to go and get it." The Gortat slump ended just before Christmas as he poured in twenty-three points against the Charlotte Bobcats.

To restart his game, Gortat lifts weights for two days, takes a day off and begins the cycle once again. To recharge his mental batteries, Gortat goes to a Phoenix bowling alley. He also uses his Playstation and reads. It is time away from basketball that Gortat uses to prepare himself. How now has a mentor, Jermaine O'Neal, and his game is improving.

As the Suns were having difficulties in the early part of the 2012-2013 season there were rumors that the Boston Celtics were interested in trading for Gortat. In the off-season, Danny Ainge, the Celtics General Manager, made overtures for Gortat. The Suns turned them down, but in the middle of January 2013 Alvin Gentry expressed his unhappiness with Gortat's play and his comments to a Polish newspaper. Whatever happens Gortat is a seasoned and skilled NBA center.

chapter

TWENTY

THE PERILS OF THE NBA: HAKIM WARRICK AND SEBASTIAN TELFAIR, TWO DIFFERENT SUNS

"IT SEEMED LIKE NIKE WAS IN CONEY ISLAND," SEBASTIAN TELFAIR COMMENTED ON THE PRESSURE TO ENDORSE PRODUCTS

In the 2011-2012 season, there were two players who were quick to the basket and exciting to watch. One was Hakim Warrick, who is the quickest big man in the NBA to the hole, and who was relegated to the bench in the second half of the season. The other is the premier back up point guard Sebastian Telfair. On many teams, Telfair would be the starter, but he has played behind future Hall of Famer Steve Nash and now the Slovenian sensation Goran Dragic. But without Telfair the Suns would be in trouble. He is the driving force behind the Suns' second unit and on some nights they outscore the starters.

The contrasts between Warrick and Telfair offer some sobering thoughts on life in the NBA. No matter how much of a star a player is in high school or college, the transition to the NBA is a difficult one. Why some players succeed and others are like Kwame Brown failed remains a mystery.

WHY IS HAKIM WARRICK GONE?

Hakim Warrick is gone but when he played he had some exciting moments. When Steve Nash got him the ball, he was in the lane with a thunder dunk. Because of his slight physical appearance, Warrick is nicknamed the helicopter or skinny. With his infectious personality and warm smile, he has fit in everywhere as a veteran presence.

The problem was that he didn't fit into the Suns' rotation. He was relegated to the bench, and in the off-season he was traded, along with Robin Lopez, to the New Orleans Hornets. Then it was off to the Charlotte Bobcats for redemption with the Michael Jordan owned NBA franchise.

While he was in Phoenix, Warrick never complained about the lack of playing time, and he performed admirably when called upon. He has a demeanor that coach's love and the Charlotte Bobcats will find a way to use him. Rod Higgins, the Bobcats President of Basketball Operations, remarked that Warrick's "athleticism allows him to play multiple positions, which will make for a smooth transition into our current roster and style of play under coach Mike Dunlap." The Bobcats won only seven games last year, so Warrick will be an experienced addition.

WHY SEBASTIAN TELFAIR IS THE PREMIER BACK UP POINT GUARD

The other exciting bench player, Sebastian Telfair, has had an up and down career. However, the Suns gave him the chance to show that he is a solid NBA player. He played the fewest minutes of his career with the Suns in 2011-2012, but he had his most productive year. He also won the Dan Majerle Hustle Award. This is important as it is voted on by his teammates. The two players are a contrast in styles and direction, and they show the problems of adjusting to the NBA game.

When he left New York's Abraham Lincoln High School, Telfair was the second highest scorer in New York history with a 27.1 per game average. Rick Pitino called him the best high school point guard he had ever seen. When he jumped directly to the NBA after high school, it was not an easy transition, as he went from team to team. He was in the league for seven seasons when the Suns signed him on December 9, 2011 as the NBA lockout ended. He had played for the Portland Trail Blazers, the Boston Celtics, the Minnesota Timberwolves, the Los Angeles Clippers and the Cleveland Cavaliers. He was well traveled but not properly used at the point guard. Alvin Gentry solved that problem, and Telfair is now the best back up point guard in the NBA.

THE CASES OF TELFAIR AND WARRICK: IT IS TOUGH IN THE NBA

The careers of Hakim Warrick and Sebastian Telfair suggest the difficulty of stardom in the NBA. Warrick with a slight build and great athleticism hasn't fit into any team. He is a tenacious worker and Warrick's new start with the New Orleans Hornets was off to a good start. When the Hornets general manager, Dell Demps, traded for Warrick he remarked that it was to acquire his veteran leadership as well as strength off the bench. Then without getting a chance to crack the Hornets line-up, Warrick was traded for a nine-year veteran shooting guard, Matt Carroll, who sits on the end of the Charlotte Bobcats bench. Carroll is a one-dimensional player while Warrick has an upside. Warrick's up side is that he can play center, power forward or small forward despite his lack of weight. He has the size, the leaping ability and the quickness to help a team's front line. He will do that well for the Bobcats.

Telfair came out of Brooklyn's Lincoln High School as one of the nations most publicized high school players. He was so exciting that his home games often had Lebron James, Derek Jeter, Jay Z and a host of celebrities in the stands. He has struggled as a pro, as has Warrick, but they both have enormous talent. They also have had to fight their way into the playing rotation and wherever they have played their teammates have embraced their play. After many years in the NBA, Telfair has become a proven back up point guard.

WARRICK: THE QUICKEST GUY TO THE WHOLE, WHAT WENT WRONG?

Hakim Warrick signed a four-year contract with the Phoenix Suns. When he arrived in Phoenix his contract was worth roughly four million dollars a year. He lived in the pricey Biltmore area off 24th and Camelback. At 6-9 and 219 pounds, he is a sleek and quick small forward. In the strike shortened 2012 season, he never got a chance to fit into the Suns' run and gun game. Although he got lost at time on the bench, Warrick did have a few break out games. Against the team that traded for him, the New Orleans Hornets, he scored eighteen points in a 93-78 win on December 30, 2011. In an April 24, 2012 game against the Utah Jazz, Warrick scored twelve points in a 100-88 loss.

In college, Warrick was a key player for Syracuse University. He was a strong low post player, and he could also shoot the three with proficiency. He was also a player who valued his education, and he left Syracuse with a degree in retail management and consumer studies. He is bright, and he is careful with his money. He never missed the Suns' free breakfast prior to practice. With 21 plus points a game and 8.6 rebounds as a Syracuse senior, Warrick was viewed as a potentially strong small forward. At Syracuse, Warrick was known for his spectacular dunks, and his seven-foot plus wingspan made him an exciting college player with a strong upside.

He was the nineteenth pick in the 2005 NBA draft by the Memphis Grizzlies. He played for four years with the Grizzlies and in his last three seasons averaged in double figures. As a cost cutting measure, the Grizzlies allowed Warrick to become a free agent. It was the best thing for his pocket book. He signed with the Milwaukee Bucks in 2009-2010, but he was traded to Chicago. In 2010 he signed a four-year sixteen plus million dollar deal with the Phoenix Suns, and it appeared that he would be in the Valley of the Sun for a long time. It didn't work out.

Of all the Suns players I like Hakim's twitter page the best. He wants to know how Usher's new album sounds, and he doesn't think that the Mentalist should replace Law and Order on TNT. He is bright and complicated. Warrick is also mentally tough.

He never mastered the pick and roll with Steve Nash and by the end of the season he was out of the rotation. He was always a professional. He continued to work and be ready.

In his eight seasons in the NBA, Warrick contracts provided for almost fifteen million dollars. In his last season with the Suns, he made 4.2 million dollars, and he leaves the Valley of the Sun with fond memories. He also leaves with a lot of money.

SEBASTIAN TELFAIR: THE EARLY FAME YEARS

As Sebastian Telfair grew up in Brooklyn, he was an immediate New York playground legend. He was born on June 9, 1985 and he became a sensation on local basketball courts. While playing in the street courts around the rough Brooklyn housing projects, Telfair developed extraordinary basketball skills. He was just over six feet, and he had lightning moves.

In his early career there was intense media interest in Telfair's career, and there was a great deal of pressure to help his family. The financial offers poured in while he was still in high school.

Telfair led Brooklyn's Lincoln High School to multiple state championships, and he seemed like a lock for NBA stardom. During his senior year at Lincoln in 2003, Telfair was followed around by a film camera crew working on a documentary "Through The Fire," which documented his time at Lincoln High School and the pressures upon him to go straight to the NBA. It was a professional basketball career that would financially help his family. This film featured University of Louisville Coach Rick Pitino and rapper-entertainment mogul Jay Z, and it is a brilliant look at the pitfalls, frustrations as well as the hollow fame of the sports world.

The documentary only added to the legend. Then there was a murder down the hall in the apartment building, where the Telfair family lived. That was only one of many things that made him go pro early. He was a good kid, and he decided to take care of his family. When he signed a lucrative Adidas shoe contract, he helped his family escape the Brooklyn tenements. Telfair's cousin, Stephon Marbury, lived on the fourth floor of the same building. By his senior year, Sebastian was drawing so much attention he caught the eye of documentary filmmakers, authors and sponsors. Soon he was besieged with endorsement contracts. He hadn't even graduated from high school.

In his senior year at Lincoln High School, Telfair was named New York State's Mr. Basketball. The fame was there and he believed that the fortune was on the horizon. The long and arduous road to fame and fortune was a tough one. But Sebastian Telfair is tough and talented, and he made it.

The film, "Through The Fire," documented the problems that young Telfair had as a rising New York basketball star. Telfair talked to Rick Pitino about attending the University of Louisville. The Adidas shoe contract was too lucrative and Telfair went pro. The Adidas contract was money he needed for his family. Soon he was working out for most NBA teams.

Telfair's agent, Andy Miller, who also represented Minnesota Timberwolves Kevin Garnett, remarked that the Adidas contract was worth more than fifteen million dollars over six years. The deal guaranteed Telfair six million and there is no word if they picked up his option for the remainder of the contract. It worked for Adidas and it worked for Telfair.

"I've been wearing Adidas shoes since I started playing basketball, but the bottom line is that for the past couple of years all the shoe companies have been interested in sending me pairs of their shoes," Telfair said.

Before he was eighteen years old, Sebastian Telfair was a million-aire. An Adidas executive, Ken Wulff, remarked that Telfair had "street cred." The Adidas advertising campaign centered on Telfair's size, they said he was 5-11 and they missed it by two inches. The ad for the Telfair shoe said: "Nothing is impossible." What that had to do with Telfair and his career remains a mystery. Telfair's contract with Adidas was one of the best and only Lebron James, Tracy McGrady, Kobe Bryant, Allen Iverson, Carmelo Anthony and Yao Ming have shoe endorsements worth more money. Tim Duncan's deal is worth only $350,000 a year, so Tel-fair's agent did a great job. He did all right financially before he entered the NBA draft.

ON TO THE NBA

Telfair was the Portland Trail Blazers thirteenth overall pick in the 2004 NBA draft. He began his pro career at the tender age of eighteen and he was the Portland Trail Blazers starting point guard. There is no player who has had as much media coverage, with the exception of Leb-ron James, than Sebastian Telfair.

In 2002 Telfair appeared in a DVD "Ballin' Out of Control" and it appeared that he was on his way to basketball greatness. The high point of the early hype surrounding Telfair came on March 8, 2004 when he was featured on the cover of **Sports Illustrated**. The cover shot showed a smiling Telfair dribbling and the headline "Watch Me Now" predicted big things. In 2006, Telfair was the subject of an excellent documentary about how he went on to the NBA while his older adopted brother, Jamel Thomas, bounced around the lower levels of professional basketball. This film does a superb job showing that Telfair was concerned about his family and their financial condition. This is the reason he skipped col-lege. The DVD shows the amazing leap from Brooklyn's neighborhood playgrounds to big time basketball. Along the way there was tension and heartbreak, but Sebastian Telfair has weathered the storm. He is now a well-respected and talented NBA player. The case of his brother, Jamel Thomas, suggests the warnings signs of failure in the professional ranks.

JAMEL THOMAS: THE WARNING SIGNS OF BASKETBALL

As Telfair worked on his game, he had an older brother Jamel Thomas. He as a 6-6 guard with skills that were well developed. He was a marvelous defender but only an average shooter. He played his college ball at Providence and he went on to a brief NBA career before taking his game overseas to Turkey and Italy. He is now thirty-nine and retired.

Thomas' book **The Beautiful Struggle** highlights the problems of a professional basketball career. It is a tough go. As Thomas recalled his three games for the Boston Celtics, his four games for the Golden States Warriors and five games with the New Jersey Nets there were the warning signs of failure in professional basketball. He also signed contracts with the Cleveland Cavaliers, the Portland Trail Blazer and the Utah Jazz, but he never played for these teams in an NBA game. He also played two seasons in the CBA and the ABA. In his book, Thomas provides some interesting insights in Telfair and his cousin Stephon Marbury.

The good news is that when he graduated from Providence with a degree, his literate book suggests there is much more beyond basketball for Jamel Thomas.

TELFAIR'S LONG AND CURIOUS NBA CAREER

At Portland, Telfair's career got off to a promising start and Coach Nate McMillan had him as the starting point guard. He played a great deal with another high school draftee, Martell Webster, and Telfair developed his game. Then he suffered a thumb injury and Steve Blake replaced him in the starting line up.

The two years at Portland was an up and down experience. On January 1, 2005, Telfair scored fourteen points as Portland beat the Golden State Warriors. For the next month his game steadily improved. Then interim coach Kevin Pritchard made him the starting point guard. He averaged 6.8 points a game and 3.3 assists. When the Trail Blazers lost twenty-three of their last thirty games, a new coach, Nate McMillan, came in to run the show. Things didn't go well. Telfair shot a low percentage from the field, and the Trail Blazers gave up on him. He was traded to the Boston Celtics. His one season with the Celtics was not a productive one. His shooting percentage continued to decline, and his ball handling skills were erratic.

When Kevin Garnett was shipped to the Boston Celtics in a blockbuster trade, Telfair wound up with the Minnesota Timberwolves. It appeared that Telfair was back as a Timberwolf. He had his best NBA season with a 9.3 points a game scoring average and 5.9 assists. Then there was a coaching change, Randy Wittman, was fired and Kevin McHale took over. The Timberwolves signed him to a three-year contract but Telfair never fit into McHale's system.

On July 20, 2009 Telfair was traded to the Los Angeles Clippers. He didn't last a season, and by February 17, 2010 he was send packing to the Cleveland Cavaliers. He was then traded back to the Minnesota Timberwolves. His contract expired and he was a free agent. When Telfair singed with the Phoenix Suns, after the NBA strike ended in December 2011, he was coming into a system that could use his talents.

He didn't disappoint as a Sun. His one-year contract, with a player option that he exercised, brought him back into a system that utilized his talents. He had some good games. He scored twenty-one points in the loss to San Antonio. When Steve Nash was out with a bad back, Telfair fill in nicely.

Telfair's life and career is examined in Ian O'Connor's **The Jump: Sebastian Telfair and the High Stakes Business of High School Ball** and in a documentary **Through The Fire**. As the 2012-2013 season opens, Telfair is only twenty-seven and he is making a salary of one point five million dollars. He has made fifteen million dollars in the NBA while attempting to find stardom. The best is yet to come.

The hype and pressure on Telfair has been enormous. In the Valley of the Sun, he can relax and no one will bother him. That is a blessing.

TELFAIR COMES OF AGE IN 2012

The mental toughness to compete in the NBA is essential. Telfair displayed that trait in 2012, and he had his best season to date. He demonstrated that he is a complete player with a strong upside. As the season wound down the Suns were driving for a playoff berth. In his last seven games, Telfair scored in double digits in five games and he averaged 11.7 points off the bench. He also gave the Suns solid defense.

On March 15, 2012, Telfair got his first start at point guard for the Suns, and he responded with eight assists and only one turnover in a 91-87 win over the Los Angeles Clippers. He had at least one steal in more than half the games, and his turnover to assist rate was among the highest in the NBA.

It is Telfair's maturity at the point guard position, which gave Coach Alvin Gentry's flexibility in substitutions after the All Star break. He also won the Dan Majerle Hustle Award, and it appears that Telfair is firmly entrenched with the Phoenix Suns. His talent is immense and he is finally getting his due in the NBA.

When Sebastian Telfair returned to New York in the summer of 2012 it was to his home in Westchester. He talked about remaining in

Phoenix to practice with the Suns a month after the season ended. The maturity and dedication of the twenty seven year old Telfair was evident in press interviews. Like many of the Suns players, he reflected that he played much better after the All Star break.

He credited Steve Nash and Grant Hill with adding to his professional stature, and he learned a great deal from the Suns' system. For years the critics suggested that speed and quickness were the reasons for Telfair's outstanding game. He pointed out that he worked on his shooting in Phoenix. "There's a lot of knocks about my shooting, but I can shoot the ball extremely well now," Telfair remarked.

Telfair said that he has been watching film of his last Suns' season and this suggests his commitment to the game. He is also working on business ventures outside of the NBA game. But Telfair remarked: "We're in Westchester...but you now wherever I live, I'm Brooklyn all day."

SEBASTIAN TELFAIR; CARRY THE DEFENSIVE LOAD

After twenty-five games into the 2012-2013 season, with the Suns at ten wins and fifteen losses, Telfair teamed with P. J. Tucker to give the Suns a defensive presence that is important to their late game comebacks. On December 17, 2012 the Suns were down nineteen points to a woeful Sacramento King team. Enter Telfair who played eighteen minutes and Tucker who played fourteen minutes and between them they had only nine points. What they did was to shut down the Kings defensively. Telfair took the ball away from Sacramento's tandem of point guards and Tucker shut down DeMarcus Cousins. P. J. Tucker remarked: "Bassy (Telfair) works so hard on guards to turn them over. When you see a guy working like that, you can't do anything but work as hard...." The second unit, which now includes Michael Beasley, is among the best in the NBA and it is due to the defensive load that Telfair and Tucker carry.

On his new role as a defensive stopper, Telfair remarked: "I'm out there denying the ball from guys where they aren't getting as many touches. I like to see that frustration." It is his newly found defensive mode that has kept Telfair in the rotation and the Suns frequently have Goran Dragic on the floor as the shooting guard for a brief time and Telfair runs the point. This suggests his importance to the Suns.

chapter

TWENTY ONE

THE DRAGON RETURNS: GORAN DRAGIC
POINT GUARD

**"I MEAN IT'S A FUNNY STORY, I STARTED FIRST WITH
SOCCER THEN WITH BASKETBALL. THEN I GOT MY LEG
INJURY AND MY MOM SAID NO MORE SOCCER...THEN I
WENT TO BASKETBALL." GORAN DRAGIC**

Goran Dragic arrived in Phoenix in September 20, 2008 and two days later he signed with the Phoenix Suns. He was unquestionably Europe's best young point guard. He was also a complete unknown. Could he compete? It soon became evident that he was one of the most accomplished foreign basketball players to enter the NBA. He could pass the ball behind his back, he seemed to have eyes behind his head and he loved the pick and roll. When the Suns describe him, it sounded like he was Steve Nash. He wasn't but he Is pretty good. He also had a chance to learn the NBA game by sitting behind the future Hall of Fame point guard.

With Steve Nash manning the point, Dragic was brought in to learn the point, as well as the shooting guard position. It was the early months of his initial season that were a nightmare. He played under the Fuhrer, Terry Porter, and he took some time to adjust to the American game. When he did, he was a lights out performer. Dragic's road to the NBA was a long and twisted one.

He is one of the best second round choices in NBA history. The irony is that the Phoenix Suns didn't draft him. He was the 46th selection in the 2008 draft by the San Antonio Spurs. Gregg Popovich and his staff saw a star in the making. They loved his ball handling and more importantly his decision-making. It was in Slovenia that he developed the skills for an NBA career.

DRAGIC'S DEVELOPMENT IN THE EUROLEAGUE

When he was seventeen in 2003-2004, Dragic played for the Ilirija Ljljana team in the Slovenian 2D league. After one year he was promoted to the Slovenian Premier A League performing for the Adriatic League team KD Slvan. By 2004, pro scouts from Europe and America were amazed at Dragic's vertical leap and court sense. At six feet three inches he played like a 6-5 guard. He is deceptively quick, and he has a marvelous court sense. Unlike most European players, he does play defense and he is not soft under the boards. In Europe he was one of the top rebounding point guards.

When he played in the Euroleague for Olimpija Ljubijana, in 2003-2004, his game reached a higher level. Dragic was a drive and dish point guard, and he was always pushing the ball down the court. His outside shooting in Euroleague was average. To be successful in the NBA, he needed an outside shot. As a result, he developed his perimeter shooting. His lateral movement and his aggressive point guard play made Dragic a natural for the NBA.

In Euroleague play, Dragic was one of the strongest defenders. He played in Spain for CB Murica in 2006-2007, and the high level of play helped his game. Then it was back to Olimpija Ljubijana in the Slovenian league. His play was so much better than other point guards that he was predicted as a second round NBA draft choice. He was drafted in 2008 in the second round as the forty-fifth overall pick and after San Antonio drafted Dragic, he was traded to the Phoenix Suns.

DRAGIC UNDER TERRY PORTER: HELP

When Goran Dragic showed up to play for the Suns, it was a dream come true. He was mentored by his idol Steve Nash, and he had supportive teammates. It looked like a match made in heaven. It soon turned into a match made in hell. Coach Terry Porter was the reason. He played Dragic about thirteen minutes, he scrutinized his shots, he complained about his ball handling, and he questioned his toughness. One wonders if Porter also complained about Dragic's aftershave lotion. He was after all a European and Porter didn't respect his game. Dragic is a blue-collar worker, and he simply continued to work hard. He shot less than forty per cent with the Suns and it looked like he was a mistake. The mistake was Steve Kerr hiring Terry Porter. The coach thought communication was an Island off the coast of Italy. He simply could not explain what he wanted to his players.

Hallelujah! Terry Porter was fired. The first game that Alvin Gentry coached, he brought Dragic in as one of his earliest substitutes. He smiled after Dragic had a turnover and looked at the bench. Coach Gentry said: "You're a professional now." He smiled once again at Dragic and clapped his hands. The rest of the 2008-2009 season was magic for Dragic. His confidence returned, his shot returned, his ball handling improved and he torched the San Antonio Spurs with a 23 point fourth quarter in the playoffs, and he finished with 26 points for the game. Things looked rosy for the future. The next season was a disaster.

The 2009-2010 Suns were a difficult fit for Dragic. He didn't play well with the second unit. He also cut his foot at home and he struggled. He did have his moments. On January 25, 2010, Dragic scored career high thirty-two points in a losing effort against the Utah Jazz. "It was beautiful," Steve Nash told the **Deseret News**.

The Suns traded Dragic to the Houston Rockets for Aaron Brooks, a former Sixth Man of the Year, and this proved to be one of the franchises biggest mistakes. The NBA strike took place. Brooks signed to play in China, and when the strike was over he was still in China. He became a free agent after the Suns released him. He signed with the Sacramento Kings and, at times, he is their starting point guard.

It was the final twenty-eight games of the 2011-2012 season that earned Dragic a contract approaching ten million dollars a year. When starter Kyle Lowry went on the injured list with a bad ankle, Dragic averaged 16.3 points a game and 7.3 assists after the All Star break. What was apparent is that he needed to be a starter. In the NBA lockout the Los Angeles Lakers, the Sacramento Kings, the Toronto Raptors, the New Orleans Hornets, the New Jersey Nets and the Charlotte Bobcats were interested in signing Dragic. He chose the Suns due to Alvin Gentry and his overall feeling for the organization.

THE NBA LOCKOUT AND DRAGIC

When the NBA lockout and prolonged strike took place, Dragic signed with Caja Laboral in Spain. He kept his skills alive in Spain as he prepared to return to the NBA. The Caja Laboral team was having trouble in-group A of the Turkish Airlines Euroleague regular season. So they signed Dragic to a short-term contract. The newspapers described Dragic as much like the Indiana Pacers Reggie Williams. Dragic had played for Caja Laboral in 2006 and he averaged more than ten points a game.

The Caja Laboral contract had an option out clause, as Dragic kept his skill level intact. He was also playing for a new contract as his 2011-2012 Houston Rocket agreement was for $2.1 million, and then he was an unrestricted free agent. He makes almost eight million dollars with the Suns.

It was during the lockout that teams jockeyed to see what Dragic was doing in Europe. Scouts showed up to watch some of his games. It was in Houston that he revitalized his career.

DRAGIC REVITALIZES HIS CAREER IN HOUSTON

In Houston, Dragic was the back up point guard to Kyle Lowry. When Lowry went down with a knee injury, Dragic not only filled in but he became a floor leader. When Lowry came back Dragic remained in the starting lineup.

In the 2011-2012 season, Dragic led the Houston Rockets to the playoffs and in April he was outstanding. On one of every four offensive possession, Dragic ran the pick and roll. He is such a good ball handler that he can take his time finding the big man. This drives defenses crazy. It is as a running point guard that Dragic is most valuable. He is one of the NBA's top players in the transition game. He can knife to the basket or send up a floating shot due to his extreme athleticism.

Dragic is a versatile player. He can come in at the shooting guard position. In Houston he was often on the floor with point guard Kyle Lowry. He is also an excellent shooter and can drive quickly to the basket. He is good on one on one or isolation plays. As a defender, Dragic is better than Nash. He has good hands, and he has the strength to stop quick drives. The teams that try to post him up fail.

Goran Dragic 2011-2012	G S	MP G	PP G	FG%	3FG%	FT%	AP G	RP G	SPG
Games Started	28	36.5	18.0	.490	.379	.839	8.4	3.5	1.8
Games in April	14	36	18.9	.464	.329	.842	7.7	3.5	1.8

GORAN DRAGIC REPLACES GORAN DRAGIC IN PHOENIX

When the Phoenix Suns signed Goran Dragic to a four-year contract worth thirty four million dollars, it was an agreement designed to replace Steve Nash. When he was originally drafted by the San Antonio Spurs in the second round and traded to Phoenix, it was Steve Kerr who believed that Dragic would replace Steve Nash. He has but the road back to the Suns has been a strange one. He was traded because a foot injury hurt his play. With the Houston Rockets he demonstrated that he was a starting point guard. The Portland Trail Blazers were ready to sign Dragic to a long-term deal. His cousin lives in the Phoenix area and he loves playing for Coach Alvin Gentry. So Goran Dragic signed with the Suns.

GORAN DRAGIC'S NBA CAREER STATISTICS

Year	Team	GP	FG%	3P%	FT%	RPG	APG	SPG	BPG	PPG
2008–09	Phoenix	55	.393	.370	.769	1.9	2.0	.5	.0	4.5
2009–10	Phoenix	80	.452	.394	.736	2.1	3.0	.6	.1	7.9
2010–11	Phoenix	48	.421	.277	.608	1.8	3.1	.8	.1	7.4
2010–11	Houston	22	.472	.519	.667	2.5	2.5	.6	.2	7.7
2011–12	Houston	66	.462	.337	.805	2.5	5.3	1.3	.2	11.7
Career		271	.444	.364	.737	2.2	3.3	.8	.1	8.0

GORAN DRAGIC'S PERSONAL BESTS

1. HE WON A GOLD MEDAL AT THE FIBA EUROPE LEAGUE UNDER 20 CHAMPIONSHIP TOURNAMENT IN 2004.

2. HE WAS THE SLOVENIAN LEAGUE ROOKIE OF THE YEAR IN 2005

3. HE WAS A SLOVENIAN LEAGUE ALL-STAR IN 2006.

4. HE WON THE SLOVENIAN LEAGUE NATIONAL CHAMPIONSHIP IN 2008.

5. HE WAS THE MVP IN THE BORIS STANKOVIC TOURNAMENT IN 2010.

6. HE WAS NAMED WESTERN CONFERENCE NBA PLAYER OF THE WEEK APRIL 2-8, 2012. LEBRON JAMES WAS THE EASTERN CONFERENCE PLAYER OF THE WEEK.

NBA: DRAGIC AND NASH COMPARED

Goran Dragic's signing with the Suns appears to continue a Steve Nash type point guard, and this bodes well for the future. Get ready for the Goran Dragic point guard style. Dragic averaged 11.7 points and 5.3 assists last season. It is Dragic's numbers as a starter that tells a quite different story about his efficiency and overall play. He started the Rockets final 26 games (28 for the season). In those 28 games, he averaged 18.0 PPG and 8.4 APG. It was his leadership on the court that brought the Houston Rockets into the playoffs.

Coach Alvin Gentry said: "He was here before and he really understands what I want in a point guard. I think his decision-making has gotten a ton better. I think his shooting is improving…I just want him to be himself…." You can see from this comment why Gentry is a successful coach. The Dragon is back and the point guard position is solidified. When he scored his first NBA triple double on April 13, 2011, against the Minnesota Timberwolves, Dragic signaled that he had arrived as an elite point guard.

As the 2012-2013 season was in its formative stage, Coach Gentry remarked that Dragic "really pressed and put himself in a position where he thinks he's got to do it." This comment may reflect on more than Dragic as the Suns are playing as hard as they can, but the results are not apparent in the victory column.

Stay tuned the best is yet to come.

chapter

TWENTY TWO

MARK WEST: THE BEST NBA CENTER IN AN NBA FRONT OFFICE (SORRY MITCH)

"VICE PRESIDENT OF PLAYER PROGRAMS MARK WEST'S OFF-COURT TOUCH WITH PLAYERS BECOMES MORE IMPORTANT...." PAUL CORO, THE ARIZONA REPUBLIC, AUGUST 14, 2012

The Paul Coro quote suggests Mark West's importance to the Phoenix Suns. After playing seventeen seasons in the NBA, West has a good grasp of the game. But there is more to West than just basketball, as he has a degree in finance as well as an MBA. When he was featured in **Fortune** magazine in 1999 the article emphasized that Mark West was managing fifty stocks and bonds portfolios in Phoenix. **Fortune** editorialized that he was a "classic buy and hold investor with an aggressive asset allocation...." That comment is a perfect example of how he played on the court. The only time that he had trouble was when he guarded Moses Malone. That was not a fun time for West.

The Malone story is a hilarious one. Moses went to the same high school as Mark, but he was five years older and he played pro ball for twenty-one seasons. In what was a friendly rivalry, Malone loved to give West trouble. Of course, Malone gave everyone a hard one. Malone often commented: "That seventh grader is tough." This humorous comment suggests the level of respect that Malone had for West.

MOSES MALONE AT ST. PETERSBURG HIGH AND WEST

Mark West no longer has to be beaten up in the paint by Moses Malone. He served as a role model of how to be tough in the paint. Fortunately for West the Malone era was five years prior to West's arrival at Petersburg High School. In this Virginia town, West honed his considerable basketball talents. West was selected as the **Richmond Times-Dispatch** 1979 player of the year.

The 1979 Petersburg High School team featured West' 6-10 physical presence and the top scorer Darell Stith who became a two thousand point scorer at Virginia State. They were the district champions and went on to lose in the finals of the state tournament. The only blemish on an otherwise great season was a loss in the state finals. St. Petersburg High School retired the jerseys of Malone, Stith and West. They didn't win the state championship, but West went on to a dominant career at Old Dominion University.

He was glad that he didn't have to face Malone. Guess what! When Malone retired from the NBA in 1995 West had been in the league for twelve years. West commented: "Moses was the toughest player I ever faced."

He remarked that the best shooter he ever guarded was Kareem Abdul Jabbar. As West watched Abdul Jabbar's skyhooks going in the hole, he tried to block the shot, as he appreciated the skill level of the Hall of Famer. What West did was to observe technique, and he was a master at defending against it. He considered basketball a scientific game, and this is why he is a formidable force in the Suns front office.

West is now in charge of player development. One wonders if he now has a different frustration. He still looks like he can play. West is also a highly personable and very open person. Asking him a question and you will get a straight answer. His road to the NBA began in Virginia.

THE FORMATIVE YEARS

While attending Petersburg High School in Virginia, West became a much sought after college prospect. At 6-10 and two hundred forty pounds he decided to attend college near his home. He enrolled at Old Dominion. Mark had a secret, he liked school and he was good at it.

But it was basketball not his finance major, that caught everyone's attention. By the time that he finished his career at Old Dominion, West was the school's top shot blocker with 446, second in career rebounds with 1,113 and he had the highest field goal percentage, .559, in the school's history. He was also a three-time honorable mention All American. As a first team All-Sun Belt Conference selection as a senior, West was ready for the NBA draft.

After West graduated from Old Dominion College with a degree in finance, he began his professional career. He was a strong inside player with a high basketball IQ. He was the thirtieth overall pick by the Dallas Mavericks in the second round in the 1983 draft. This began a long and illustrious NBA career. As a player who did the little things, he displayed an in-depth understanding of the game.

West also had some statistical evidence of future greatness. He led the nation in blocked shots in his sophomore and junior years. In his four seasons at Old Dominion the Monarchs sere 80-37, and they played in the NCAA tournament twice and the NIT twice. There were some other great moments in West' college career. In 1980, Old Dominion upset the top ranked DePaul team 63-62 in one of college basketball's most storied games.

There is more to West' life than basketball. His degree from Old Dominion was in business administration with an emphasis upon financial management. He also had a great deal of marketing classes. After Old Dominion, he became a licensed stockbroker and he remains a keen market analyst. He was featured in a July 19, 1999 issue of **Fortune** and they discussed his marketing, stock brokering, and financial career. He has worked as a licensed broker since 1992. He was a partner at Prudential Securities in Phoenix and in 2000 Old Dominion recognized him as a distinguished alumni. After seventeen seasons in the NBA, West looked to use his finance degree to invest his money and live a normal life. Fortunately, he couldn't get basketball out of his system. A look at West's pro career tells you a lot about him.

In 1982, West was a member of the U. S. national team that won a silver medal at the FIBA World Championship. Doc Rivers was the top scorer on this team, and the USSR won the gold medal. His career at Old Dominion was a storied one, but it was time to move on to the NBA.

MARK WEST'S NBA CAREER

With 6259 points and 5347 rebounds, West was a tireless NBA worker during his lengthy career. West ranks second to Artis Gilmore in career field goal percentage for his 58.03 average. He was a blue-collar guy who came to play every night. After the Dallas Mavericks selected him in the second round, he was ready for the NBA. The Mavericks realized that they had a strong inside player. During his rookie year, West sat and learned. He played in thirty-four games and his primary role was defending and rebounding. In limited minutes he learned the NBA game.

His first game in the NBA was against the Phoenix Suns, and he didn't score a point. The Mavericks Elston Turner, now the Suns' defensive coach, had four points and almost thirty years later West is in the front office and Turner is running the Suns' defense.

During his first three years he went from the Mavericks to the Milwaukee Bucks and then to the Cleveland Cavaliers. It didn't make for a feeling of job security. In 1988, he landed in Phoenix and for the next seven years he was a major Suns' contributor. He also loved living in the Valley of the Sun. In 1994, he wound up in Detroit for two years. The Pistons were a team in disarray, and while West never fit into their mix he was still as strong contributor. This is one reason that the Pistons finished 28-54 and they did have one player who dominated. That was Grant Hill who scored twenty points a game.

Then West finished his career in Cleveland, Indiana, Atlanta and his last twenty-two NBA games were played with the Suns.

When he entered the NBA in 1983, he had no idea that he would spend seventeen years banging the boards for key rebounds. He played for eight years with the Suns and in two of the Suns seasons he was a double figure scorer while playing solid defense.

As a player, West not only had a high basketball IQ, but he had the requisite intensity to survive in the NBA talent jungle. He was what some sports writers labeled a dirt player. This is, of course, nonsense, he was driven, talented and he survived. The 2012-2013 Suns have two dirt players like West, they are Sebastian Telfair and P. J. Tucker. They do the little things that win you games.

Of all the teams that West played for in his lengthy career, the Cleveland Cavaliers appreciated his talents. West was waived by the Milwaukee Bucks and joined the Cavaliers where he was considered an indispensible player off the bench. They did everything they could to avoid trading him to the Phoenix Suns. They relented and when he arrived in Phoenix, West became an important peace in the Suns front line. The Cavaliers front office remembers his playing skill and his role as a mentor to younger players.

West was a strong back up center who played well at both ends of the court. In Cleveland West's scoring went from 3.9 points a game to 8.5 pints a game. He also backed up center Brad Daugherty. West credits Cleveland Coach George Karl with helping him refine his game. Then he played for Coach Lenny Wilkins, and this was another learning curve that helped Mark make the transition to the Suns front office.

MARK WEST'S NBA TEAMS
1983-1984 DALLAS MAVERICKS
1984-1985 MILWAUKEE BUCKS
1985-1988: CLEVELAND CAVALIERS
1988-1994: PHOENIX SUNS
1994-1996: DETROIT PISTONS
1996-1997: CLEVELAND CAVALIERS
1997-1998: INDIANA PACERS SALARY
1999: ATLANTA HAWKS
1999-2000: PHOENIX SUNS

During the 1989-1900 season, West came into his own as a forceful front line player. During that season, he averaged ten and a half points a game and nine rebounds. He was firmly established as a defensive player who could score. By the 1990-1991 season, West's Suns' salary was $875,000. He was in his eighth year in the NBA, and he was already preparing for a financial career outside basketball or a management position in the NBA. But he had another decade of basketball and he took advantage of his talent to continue to make a name for himself in the pro game.

WEST'S MOVE TO THE PHOENIX SUNS FRONTS OFFICE

It was West's road to the NBA and his subsequent career that put him in a position to make key decisions on the Suns roster. As Vice President of Player Programs, West is no longer a basketball player. He is a businessman who evaluates basketball talent with an eye to the financial bottom line. The job includes player evaluation, roster development and player relations. He is also a specialist in community outreach. No one is better at his job. The good news is that Moses Malone no longer beats him up in the paint.

When he explains his job, West stresses that every team has a Vice President of Player Development. His job is to give the franchise advice on whom to sign and who not to sign. He has made some excellent decisions so far.

West's long NBA career helped him move to the Suns front office in 2001. The nice thing about Mark West is that he doesn't need the job with the Phoenix Suns. He is a licensed stockbroker and his business knowledge is first rate. He is a basketball person with a business mind, and he understands the players better than anyone in the league. That is not an easy task.

When he played for the Suns from 1988 to 1994 and again in the 1999-2000 season, he acquired not only a deep understanding of the community, but he was one of the few players to see the Suns long-term success. He brings that expertise to the front office.

At first glance, West appears confident, quiet, almost diffident, and he is a shrewd judge of character. He has a calm, friendly exterior. That is unless you are Moses Malone.

THE HONORS FOR MARK WEST AND THE ASSISTANT GENERAL MANAGER

There have been a lot of honors for Mark West. He was inducted into the Old Dominion University Sports Hall of Fame. He had his ODU number 45 retired. His NBA peers thought enough of his skills to have him take a high level position with the union. He has served on the executive board of the NBA Players Association.

As the Suns assistant general manager, he is in charge of analyzing talent and working with Lance Blanks on the future roster. As the Vice President of Player Programs, Mark West is in a position to advise and direct the Suns' roster. He is also very good at quietly going about his job as the new roster attests.

chapter

TWENTY THREE

THE SUNS TRAINING STAFF: THE BEST IN THE LEAGUE

"AARON HAS SHOWN IMMENSE DEDICATION TO THE LEAGUE AND THE SAFETY AND HEALTH OF ITS PLAYERS," WALLY BLASÉ, PRESENTING THE 2008-2009 TRAINER OF THE YEAR AWARD.

The first thing that players who are thinking about signing with the Suns hear is about the miracles worked by Aaron Nelson and the Suns' training staff. They have extended many career. It is the best training unit in the league. Jermaine O'Neal took less money to come to the Suns, because his sixteen-year old NBA knees needed the Suns training staff. In the first dozen games, O'Neal is the best backup center in the league, and he is playing like a frisky youngster. When the young centers from the Portland Trail Blazers and the New Orleans Hornets came into town, O'Neal has double-digit scoring nights and enough rebounds off the bench to insure victories. He quietly thanks the training staff.

After Shaquille O'Neal left the Suns, he returned periodically to get a physical tune up. When you walk into the training room you see the injury prevention methods famous to the Suns. Aaron Nelson is the headman, and Mike Elliott, who explains the nature and extent of the equipment, assists him. Such state of the art machines as a Cryosauna and the altitude Chamber help the players with injury recovery and conditioning. The Cryosauna is a sauna in which you are subject to cold to such a degree that your muscles regenerate. If I am not explaining this well, it is because I majored in history. Steve Nash loves to crawl into the Cryosauna. Weird! I am not sure what the altitude chamber does but it keeps everyone healthy. It also takes a lot of money out of Robert Sarver's pocketbook.

THE SUNS TRAINING STAFF IS SCIENCE NOT VODOO

The Suns training staff points out that it is science not voodoo that explains their success. The expensive machines, the measuring of the body for the purpose of creating a training chart, and the continual, re-designed workout programs bear witness to Aaron Nelson and his staff's success.

There is one story that bears testimony to the training staffs genius. They examined Stoudemire, and they said that his knees probably had a three-year life. Robert Sarver built Stoudemire's contract with three years guaranteed and the remaining two dependent upon his health. Stoudemire's agent shopped his client to other teams who had little knowledge of his health problems.

When Suns power forward Amare Stoudemire's contract expired, he began negotiating with the Suns and other teams on a long-term deal. The Suns were wary of his knees. The New York Knicks eventually signed him to a six-year maximum contract worth more than $120 million dollars. The Suns would only guarantee three years on a similar contract for Stoudemire as the training staff and doctors had doubt about his durability. Robert Sarver was heavily criticized for not matching the Knicks offer. In retrospect, it looks like a smart move. The Suns argued that Stoudemire had a three-year shelf life, as a top scorer. Guess what? They were right.

The best thing about the Suns training staff is the overall player physical. It is painful, it is a long and complex process, and the players learn more than they need to know about their bodies. Channing Frye is a case in point. He was in a miserable shooting slump. The training staff came in and analyzed his body. They found that his thigh and hamstring were out of alignment. It threw off his balance and hence his shot. They fixed this problem and during the last part of the 2012 season, Frye was once again a lights out three-point shooter.

When Shaquille O'Neal showed up the staff kept him so healthy that he played in more games in Phoenix at the end of his career than he did in his mid-career years. Shaq gave the Suns training staff the nickname YUMS. This stood for Young Unorthodox Medical Staff. It may be unorthodox to Shaq but to head trainer Aaron Nelson it is just good science. "It's regular kinesiology, physiology, functional anatomy." If you say so, Aaron, sounds good to me.

"As soon as I was traded to Phoenix, the training staff there fixed me up," O'Neal continued. "The Phoenix trainer-Aaron Nelson-was the one who solved it." Then Shaq began working with Michael Clark, the Suns' physical therapist, and the result was that Shaq was once again an inside force. The problem was his toe. It had arthritis and it hadn't healed properly.

Nelson uses a goniometer to evaluate flexibility in eight different body areas and the result is that treatment makes the Suns' players lose fewer games through injury than any team in the NBA. The program includes flexible muscle testing, visual assessments and a series of psychological tests. I am not sure what this means. It does keep the players healthy and happy.

This all sounds sort of boring, but there is a method to Aaron Nelson's madness. Each player is given a personal work out program. They call it a "corrective exercise program." The result is that Suns' players have fewer knee and ankle injuries. Grant Hill at forty is the poster player for the Suns training staff. The Los Angeles Clippers are now cashing in on the Suns' training staff, as Grant Hill ends his career in Southern California.

When Steve Nash left the Suns for the Los Angeles Lakers, he thanked the entire staff, not just Aaron Nelson. Nash worked with Tom Maystadt, Erik Phillips and Mike Elliott and he called the staff a group of guys that had "a huge impact on me." He also thanked Coaches Alvin Gentry and Mike D'Antoni for their positives rather than negatives.

THE TRAINING STAFF BREATHES NEW LIFE INTO OLD BODIES

The number of athletes who have had their careers revived lengthened and extended by the Suns training staff is legendary. Vince Carter looked like he was playing on one leg until he came to the Suns. Grant Hill revived his career and at forty he looks like he has discovered the fountain of youth. Steve Nash kept his back in order. Michael Redd had two knee surgeries and this former scoring machine was considered done in the league. He signed with the Suns, and he once again became a prolific scorer. He credited the Suns training staff for his return to form. Nash played an average of 77 games a season in his last eight years with the Suns, and this is a testimonial to the training staff. Over his first four seasons with the Suns, Hill missed only fifteen games. Now the Suns have a reinvigorated Jermaine O'Neal who looks more like a starting center than a back up.

Medical Staff Dr. Tom Carter: Head Team Physician (Orthopedist) Dr. Tim Byrne:

Cardiologist Dr. Monte Hessler: Chiropractor Dr. John Badolato: Dentist Dr. William Ko: Dermatologist Dr. Jay Schwartz: Ophthalmologist Dr. Ryan Rehl: Otolaryngology (ENT) Dr. Ryan Golub: Podiatrist Jay McCoy: Psychiatrist Dr. V "Bob" Evani: Surgeon

In 2012 the Suns were the fifth oldest team in the NBA, but they had the fewest players to miss games. The Suns don't have a problem with injuries. The scientific types who ran the show in the training room due to their training staff, as well as the methods employ this and the results are outstanding.

WHAT AARON NELSON DID THAT WAS RIGHT

Aaron Nelson studied with Michael Clark, a recognized physical therapist, and he was intrigued by the chronic injuries that professional athletes experienced. "I was looking for some way to change not only how we treat and rehab injuries but how we prevent injuries," Nelson commented. What Nelson did was to use the Goniometer and after a short process, Nelson and his staff begin manual therapy such as stretching and massage.

The physiology of the body is something that Nelson understands. He is also a believer in the weight room. The Suns staff sets up a weight room program, an exercise program, a nutritional chart, and they monitor the body. The staff also uses electrical stimulation, ice and ultrasound to treat the players. The results are outstanding. It is not a miracle, Nelson will say, it is simply science. There are fewer nagging injuries and more healthy bodies.

It also doesn't come cheap. It is expensive. The word around the NBA is that the Phoenix Suns have the best medical staff. The ultimate respect shown Aaron Nelson comes when Coach Alvin Gentry consults him on the number of minutes that the older players should have on the floor. While Gentry listens intently, he often asks for Nelson's opinions. This is the highest compliment.

When Jack McCallum's book **:07 Seconds Or Less: My Season On The Bench With the Runnin' and Gunnin' Phoenix Suns** was published in 2006, he described Nelson as attempting to convince the players to eat right. A few boxes of krispy kreme donuts were in the locker room next to the power bars, the nutritional supplements and the fresh fruits. Some six years later the krispy kreme's are gone and there is a full nutritional breakfast before and after practice. The multiple vitamins and power bars now take over the Suns locker room.

VOODOO TREATMENT IN GERMANY

When the Suns signed Jermaine O'Neal they got themselves a bargain. He is making about 1.3 million dollars, he is only thirty-four years old and he can still play.

Peter: "Didn't O'Neal get that voodoo treatment?"

I had no idea what Peter was talking about. It turns out that O'Neal had a respected, if not FDA approved, procedure on his knees. Kobe Bryant had the same treatment as has Grant Hill. The procedure is known as the regenokine treatment. It is a revolutionary non-surgical procedure. Its founder, Dr. Peter Wehling, conducts the five-day treatment that draws blood, incubates it and it is spun into a centrifuge that turns it into an orange serum. Then the serum is injected into the arthritic joint for five days. Everyone who has had the treatment swears by it. There are at least fifty pro athletes who have had the procedure. After the treatment, Jermaine O'Neal remarked that he felt five years younger. He also indicated that he signed with the Suns due to the training staff. They will have their hands full, but they are up to the task.

SOME SECRETS TO THE SUNS TRAINING STAFF

When Grant Hill showed up to play for the Suns, most observers considered him a shadow of his former self. Not true. When Shaquille O'Neal came to the Suns no one said he could run. Guess what? He did!

Now it is up to Jermaine O'Neal to keep the training staff legend alive and to highlight the secrets of the training staff.

The reason that Suns' players miss fewer games than any other team is a simple one. Medical expertise. Training schedules. Nutrition. There is a great deal of emphasis on the constant realignment of the body. When the Suns medical staff fixed Channing Fry's right butt cheek, he once again became a dead on three-point shooter. Am I missing something here? Fixing a right butt cheek! Most training staff would laugh at this concept. Not the Suns, they used science to solve Frye's shooting problems.

Peter: "I told you, Howard, it is voodoo." I deferred to the head trainer. It is science.

Aaron Nelson: "To us it is simply science."

Shaquille O'Neal not known for his intensive training gave Nelson and his staff credit for making his last few years in the NBA productive ones. With O'Neal the problems were feet and ankles as well as the knee and hip problems. All Suns rotation players receive four treatments a week to keep them healthy. The goniometer, which evaluates their flexibility, is in constant use.

There is also muscle testing. Leg squats are used to determine movement. By determining which muscles are tight or weak, which joints are not properly moving and what causes pain, the Suns have been able to remain relatively injury free.

RECOGNITION FOR AARON NELSON

In the 2008-2009, NBA season, Aaron Nelson was named trainer of the year. His fellow athletic trainers, who base their vote on the results of a year long training and the veracity of the program, vote this honor each year. It is named in honor of Joe O'Toole, the former Atlanta Hawks trainer. The National Basketball Athletic Trainers Association presents the award each year to the trainer who prevents injuries and provided rehabilitation. The system used by Nelson is part of the National Academy of Sports Medicine's Corrective Exercise and Optimum Performance Training Program.

What Aaron Nelson has done is to set a standard for sports medicine that most other franchises are emulating. Are you listening Donald Sterling and Mark Cuban? Probably not! Nelson was with the Suns for fifteen seasons, when he was named the best trainer in the NBA. It was a long road but one that he mastered. When players show up they can't wait to meet with the training staff. Sebastian Telfair commented that he had never had a full body evaluation. That is what players want to extend their careers.

chapter

TWENTY FOUR

THE DAN MAJERLE INFLUENCE

"OTHER PLAYERS SKIP THE MID-RANGE AND MOVE STRAIGHT BEYOND THE ARC, PERHAPS NO ONE SO DRAMATICALLY AS DAN MAJERLE." CHRIS BALLARD

In the lexicon of the Phoenix Suns, Dan Majerle holds many firsts. He is the first Suns' player to own a sports bar. He is the first friend to Suns' legend Charles Barkley. He is the first Sun to win a gold and silver medal in international play. That ends some of his firsts. But not the accolades, as he is a member of the Suns Ring of Honor, he is an assistant coach, and he is a successful businessman with numerous Majerle's Sports Grills. The Dan Majerle story is an inspiring one as is his nickname, "Thunder Dan," for his ferocious dunks. His good looks made him a matinee idol. He was also one of the best three point shooters in the history of the NBA. No wonder Charles Barkley hung out with him. It wasn't for his three point shot. It was about the ladies. He also had some unique experiences in international basketball. But Dan was always a team player, and he has great personal integrity

DAN MAJERLE AND INTERNATIONAL PLAY: THE SIGN OF HIS CHARACTER

While Dan Majerle is one of the Suns greatest players, he is also known for his sterling play at the international level. He was on the US national team that won a bronze medal in the 1988 Summer Olympics.

No one stood out more than Dan Majerle in the 1988 summer Olympics when U. S. supremacy took a beating due to a coach who didn't know how to do his job at the international level. The U. S. roster was a mishmash of players who didn't fit and they had a coach with an inflated reputation and little knowledge of the international game. That coach, Georgetown's Coach John Thompson, went on to international play with a U. S. team that didn't include a top-level point guard. He also had little knowledge of the nuances of the international game. It was a tragic story.

When Majerle was a member of the Olympic team that Georgetown Coach Thompson screwed up so badly, he never said a negative word about the coach. He played hard and he demonstrated that he understood the international game. This experience led to the selection of the original Dream Team for the 1992 Olympics. Majerle never said a word as Thompson picked his own guy from Georgetown as the point guard. The selection of Charles Smith and then Bimbo Coles over Tim Hardaway doomed the 1988 U. S. Olympic team. It made it difficult for the American team to compete in the slash and pick international game. The American team did win a bronze medal, but the arrogant and self-righteous Thompson defended his inadequate player selection and uninspired coaching. Fortunately, Jerry Colangelo was waiting in the wings to redeem the U. S. in the international basketball game.

When the U. S. team didn't get to the gold medal round, Coach Thompson appeared disinterested. In the game for third place, the U. S. beat Australia 78 to 49, and it was Majerle who led the team in scoring with twelve points. Mitch Richmond and David Robinson also chipped in twelve, and ironically the undersized Richmond was the leading rebounder.

Jerry Colangelo stepped in and convinced NBA players that it was their destiny to return basketball glory to the U. S. He made it clear that they could bring their families to the games, they stayed in five star hotels and they were provided with tickets to all the events. Not only did

U.S. basketball come roaring back, fans from other nations could be seen chanting: "USA, USA."

Majerle did win a gold medal with the U. S. team at the 1994 FIBA World Championship. He averaged 8.8 points a game, he pulled down 2.2 rebounds and he had 1.6 assists per game. In the championship game against Russia, Majerle played only fourteen minutes, and he scored eight points. This team was dominant with Shaquille O'Neal, Alonzo Mourning, Shawn Kemp and Larry Johnson providing an intimidating front line with Reggie Miller shooting from outside and Joe Dumars at either shooting guard or point guard. No one came close to the U. S. as Golden State Warrior Coach Don Nelson gave his team complete freedom on the court, and they destroyed the competition. The American's won the gold medal with a victory margin of almost thirty-two points a game.

His pro career began when he was the fourteenth pick in the 1988 draft. This was after a legendary career at Central Michigan. But things didn't start out well for Majerle with the Suns. At the draft, his name was called, and the fans booed. When Cotton Fitzsimmons took the public address system and announced Majerle's selection. Fitzsimmons remarked: "You'll be sorry you ever booed this young man." Fitzsimmons knew what he was talking about, as Majerle became not only one of the most popular suns, but he is one of the most prolific scores in Suns' history. He was a three time NBA All Star and twice he was selected to the All Defensive second team. For his playing expertise the Suns retired his number nine Suns jersey in 2003.

DAN MAJERLE: THE FORMATIVE YEARS AND ON TO THE NBA

While growing up in Traverse City, Michigan, Dan began a storied basketball career. After starring at Central High, then it was off to Central Michigan University where he starred for 1984 to 1988. Majerle CMU's statistics reveal that he is the second all-time scorer with 2,055 points. He was only sixteen points from the Central Michigan scoring leader. He is sixth in career field goals at .536. He also ranks second in career steals and third in career blocks. While at Central Michigan, Majerle was a three-time All Mid-America Conference All Star selection. While averaging twenty points a game in his final three seasons, Majerle also had time to earn a physical education degree. It is business sense that is Majerle's forte, as he has shown with his successful sports bars in the Valley of the Sun. The Majerle Sports Bars are consistently ranked nationally in the top ten.

After the Suns selected him with the 14th pick in 1988, he teamed with Kevin Johnson to inaugurate a series of perennial playoff teams. Majerle's initial five-year contract was reported to be for $2 million dollars. This is a bargain by any standard. In his NBA career, he scored over 10,000 points and had almost 1200 steals. His nickname," Thunder Dan," resulted from his quick and ferocious dunks. When the Suns retired his jersey on April 17, 2002 it was a fitting climax to his career.

There are many highpoints to Majerle's career. One in particularly took place in late February 1990, when Majerle held the Philadelphia 76er star, Charles Barkley, to twelve points and four rebounds while the Suns beat the 76ers 129-99. "Dan Majerle can't stop me, man," Barkley remarked. "I'm just tired." From that point on Majerle and Barkley were good friends. When Barkley was traded to the Suns on July 17, 1992, the first thing he did was to look up Majerle. The night that Barkley was selected as the NBA's Most Valuable Player for 1992-1993; he was sitting in Majerle's bar/restaurant eating a hamburger. It was later named for Barkley.

Barkley has been the victim of Majerle's sense of humor. In 1993, when the Suns beat the Los Angeles Clippers 111-105, Majerle had a terrible shooting night. Dan commented: "My best play was to throw up bricks letting Charles get all the rebounds and score his points." Majerle continued commenting on Barkley: "He never acted like a superstar." The compliments go both ways, as Barkley continues his friendship with Majerle.

IRON MAN MAJERLE AND THE END OF HIS FIRST SUNS CAREER

The 1993 season was an interesting one as Majerle played more minutes in the playoffs than was good for his health and career. In twenty-four post-season playoffs Majerle logged 1,071. He sat out only eleven minutes. Majerle said: "I think even my Upper Deck Dan Majerle sports card had a back problem." His production was still great in 1993-1994, as he averaged 16.5 points a game but in 1994-1995 a bad back and some chronic injuries led to a 15.6 points a game average. Then he was traded to the Cleveland Cavalier.

When Majerle was traded in 1995, Barkley's feeling for Sun management was never the same. In his first game against the Suns, Majerle scored twenty points. This pleased Charles Barkley. "I think I've said on occasion that Majerle, Joe Kleine and Danny Manning were the three guys I wanted on this team no matter what, and one of them is gone,"

Barkley concluded. It was less than a year later that Barkley was traded to the Houston Rockets. When Barkley was inducted in the Basketball Hall of Fame in 2006, his old friend Dan Majerle stood and applauded. "I wouldn't have missed Charles induction for any reason," Majerle concluded.

MAJERLE'S ROLE AS A SIXTH MAN

It was as a sixth man that Majerle found his role. With brutish force his dunks were fan favorites, and the cries of "Thunder Dan" roared from the Suns arena. When Majerle averaged 17.2 points a game in 1991-1992, he appeared to be a lock for the NBA's Sixth Man Award. He didn't win. The trophy went to Indiana forward Detlef Schrempf for the second straight season. Majerle was robbed.

There are many highlights to Majerle's career. In 1997-1998, he was the Suns third leading scorer, and the two previous seasons he averaged over ten points a game. When Charles Barkley joined the Suns, Majerle didn't get as many shots, but he continued to be a key player continuing his deadly three point shot. In 1992-1993, he led the NBA in three-point accuracy. He also played in all eighty-two games, and he was a key figure in the NBA finals losing to the Chicago Bulls.

When Majerle was traded in 1995 to the Cleveland Cavaliers, he was released and signed as a free agent with the Miami Heat. In Cleveland, he had back problems and his scoring declined to 10.6 points a game, which was his lowest since his rookie season. But in the playoffs, Majerle was the Cavaliers second leading scorer in the first round loss to the New York Knicks. Cavalier Coach Mike Fratello said: "Dan Majerle was our secret weapon off the bench." His final five seasons with the Heat saw his back act up, but he was still a strong contributor. His 444 three pointers with the Heat, and his popularity are what the post Pat Riley fans recall.

THUNDER DAN AND THE SOCIAL LIFE OF AN NBA STAR

Dan Majerle was for a time one of the most famous Suns. In his heyday, he wore his fame with good humor. When the Suns were the visiting team the ladies lined up at the hotels and Dan signed bras, breasts and thighs. Charles Barkley stood by in awe. There was the time in Chicago when a woman ditched her date, and she followed Majerle into a movie theater. She sat a row behind him watching the movie, as a date he didn't know that he had.

When Dan married his girl friend on Christmas Eve 1994, there was anguish. When he was traded to the Cleveland Cavaliers, Majerle put on a happy face but he was not ready to leave the Valley of the Sun. He didn't sell his home, and he vowed to return. The general manager, Bryan Colangelo, traded him for center John "Hot Rod" Williams and Majerle began his journey to the end of his career. When he left the Suns, he believed that he was a scapegoat for the team not going deeper in the playoffs.

MEET COACH DAN THE SHOT DOCTOR

When the Suns hired Majerle as an assistant coach in 2008, it was due to Robert Sarver's recognition of Majerle's historical importance, as well as his ability as a shooting coach. It was also a move that was designed to help the Suns execute their three point shot. Majerle has been an integral part of the staff and his coaching on shooting techniques helped Raja Bell become an outside threat. He also helped to develop Markieff Morris' three point shot.

His early coaching experience came under short term Suns head coach, Terry Porter, who seldom listened to his staff. Dan had to make his own way among the players. Despite the reluctance of Porter to listen to Majerle's advice, he became the shot doctor. When Alvin Gentry became the coach, Majerle was placed in charge of helping the wings. He was so well regarded that Majerle was interviewed for the Philadelphia 76ers head coaching position that was filled by Doug Collins.

In 2010, when Majerle met with Philadelphia 76ers President Ed Stefanshki, he impressed the 76ers brain trust. Gene Shue, who coached in the NBA, suggested that the 76ers would benefit from the Suns system. Although Majerle didn't get the job, he found his first head-coaching interview a positive one. There is no doubt that some day Majerle will be a head coach.

There are a number of things that Majerle does well as an assistant coach. The most important one is working with draft prospects and younger players. He knows something about taking a three point shot. He loves to work out draft prospects. His work ethic is legendary. "He loves the game and is very competitive and passionate," Steve Nash remarked.

On working for the Suns and Coach Alvin Gentry, Majerle said: "I want to be a head coach but I could work with Gentry for thirty years." Majerle is still the Sixth Man coming off the bench to help the Suns.

While coaching the 2012 Suns Summer League team in Las Vegas, Dan worked with newly drafted point guard Kendall Marshall. He told the young guard to be more aggressive. Majerle also mentored and recommended that P. J. Tucker be signed to a guaranteed roster contract. The Sun agreed, and the former Suns' draft choice was back in the NBA after five years of playing in Europe.

MEET DAN THE BUSINESSMAN

Dan Majerle may be one of the few players losing money working for the Suns. He has four high profile sports bars, he has countless commercials, he runs his own finances and somehow he finds time to coach.

During his NBA career, Majerle made almost 29 million dollars and by all accounts handled his money well. He has a keen business sense, and it shows in his sports bars, which are consistently nationally rated among the top ten because of his innovative and price friendly menu. When Majerle is on the road, he will find a burger in San Antonio or a sandwich in Chicago and call his restaurant to replicate it.

When Dan established his restaurant in downtown Phoenix near the arena, Barkley kidded him about having a place to hang out with his friends. When Majerle was featured in an issue of **Sports Illustrated** in a swimsuit, Barkley kidded him. I think Charles was jealous. He went to weight watchers and Barkley is still waiting for **Sports Illustrated** to call. "I look good in a bathing suit," Barkley commented.

Peter: "For once I have no comment."

THE UNIQUE PLAY OF DAN MAJERLE

The NBA is a league that keeps every type of imaginable statistic. For those who crave obscure statistics, Bill Simmons came up with the white guy NBA records. It is as follows:

THE WHITE GUY NBA RECORDS
POINTS IN A GAME: PETE MARAVICH, 68
BLOCKS: MARK EATON, 14
STEALS: JOHN STOCKTON, 9
3 POINT SHOTS MADE: DAN MAJERLE/REX CHAPMAN, 9

In the 1993 NBA finals, the Suns met the Chicago Bulls and while Charles Barkley was the face of the Suns, the Bulls were concerned with Majerle's three point shooting. Michael Jordan complained to the Chicago Bulls General Manager, Jerry Krause, that the Bulls were spending too much time looking at Majerle's potential. Not only was Dan unaware of Jordan's comments, he was perplexed by these remarks. In the 1993 finals, the Bulls and the Bulls-Suns six game series was a brilliant one. The Suns lost it in six games, and Majerle had three brilliant games.

In game three, Majerle scored 28 points and Jordan added 44, as the Suns beat the Bulls 129-121. This triple overtime game was one of the best in Suns history. In game five, Majerle came down with twelve rebounds and the Suns won 108 to 98. Majerle also had eleven points. In game six Majerle scored twenty-one points but the Bulls won 99 to 98 and with the victory came the NBA championship. During the series Jordan screamed: "Fuck You Dan." Maybe Charles Barkley was right, there was no sense pretending to be a role model.

The irony to the Bulls victory and Jordan's incandescent behavior is that Majerle did nothing to incite the Bulls superstar. Jordan thought he might have slighted him. Weird! But it was typical Jordan. He had strange ways to psyche himself up for a game.

The media types who covered Majerle's career believe that he was a better shot from twenty feet than he was from seventeen feet. When his teammate Steve Kerr shot the ball from thirty feet away from the basket he called it "the Dan Majerle three."

One of the strangest parts of Majerle's career took place in a game where the referees made Dan take off his lucky rubber band. It was during the playoffs with the Chicago Bulls. The complaining suspect was allegedly Michael Jordan. He would do anything for an advantage. He wanted to get into Majerle's head.

CHARLES BARKLEY HAS THE LAST WORD ON MAJERLE

In summarizing Majerle's career, it is necessary to let Charles Barkley have the last word. He announced that only three white guys could have their jersey worn in the ghetto, Larry Bird, Steve Nash and Dirk Nowitzki. When a reported asked if his old friend Dan Majerle would be a safe pick, Barkley responded: "I love Dan Majerle but you can't wear his jersey in the hood, it's only three white approved guys jersey you can walk around in…." Still Charles is Majerle's best friend.

Dan Majerle is a constant in the Valley of the Sun. He is a marvelous coach, a respected businessman, and he has a great family. He also makes his brother do most of the work in the restaurants. He is my kind of guy. With Charles Barkley on weight watchers the Barkley burger is in danger at Majerle's Sports Bar. It is now a mini-burger like Charles.

chapter

25

THE SUNS SPECIAL EVENTS OR WHY YOU NEED TO GET SEASON TICKETS: A SHAMELESS PLUG AND THE FUTURE

"THE PHOENIX SUNS ARE THE BEST ENTERTAINMENT BARGAIN IN TOWN, THEY ALSO PLAY PRETTY GOOD BASKETBALL," HARVEY SCHWARTZ

An invitation to special events, small parties, little luncheons and chitchat about the Phoenix Suns is what season ticket holder's experience. At the end of the 2012 season the U. S. Airways Center was open to fans for a special four-quarter game. It wasn't basketball, it was a thank you from the Suns organization. The event was labeled, "Inside The Huddle," and it allowed season ticket holders to go through the locker room, to eat pretzels, later hot dogs and salads, all for free. All the soft drinks and cookies you could eat were in various spots of the arena. Nothing was out of limits. The Suns locker room the training room, the coaches' offices and all parts of the arena allowed the fans an intimate look at the Suns. There is no organization in basketball with this level of intimacy.

Tanya Wheeless, the Suns' Senior Vice President for Communications and Public Affairs, summed up the organizations commitment:

"There was a desire to do something that would really be an exclusive, behind the scenes feel for our season-ticket holders." It worked. The fans loved it. As fans were divided into four groups and filled the arena, there were speaking areas where Robert Sarver, Steve Nash and Channing Frye manned one table. Aaron Nelson, the head trainer, was with Grant Hill at another table. Mike Elliott, a conditioning coach, explained the state of the art equipment that allows the Suns to extend the careers of players like Grant Hill or more recently Michael Redd. The players who were on hand shared his stories of the miracle of the training staff. It really isn't a miracle. It is simply hard work, hard science and a commitment to the player's conditions. Shaquille O'Neal, who no longer plays for the Suns, is seen around the arena and he calls for conditioning tips. He is unrelenting in his criticism that the team needs to revise its approach.

The man who runs the Suns' show, Lon Babby, appeared in a special room with Mark West talking about the Suns future. I cornered West and asked him all sorts of questions. He answered every one of my inane requests. The players were milling around and signing autographs. It was a chance for the fans to see everyone up close. West is one of the most articulate and open-minded people in the NBA. He tells the fans exactly what he thinks, and his experiences, as a player and executive, makes him an interesting source The Suns are always tweaking the fan experience. One year it is four places to visit and learn about the team. The next year it is small gatherings. There are constant information seminars, ticket upgrades and parties. I am going to have to talk to Robert Sarver about all the money that he is spending. Maybe I should talk to Mrs. Sarver.

THE EVENTS FOR FANS AND WHAT THEY MEAN

The Suns reach out to fans that have attended games. They do so with special events. While the hope is to sell season tickets, there is also no pressure. The notion of attending a VIP event, is an important one. I attended such a luncheon at the Monte Lucia in Scottsdale and there were pictures taken, a nice lunch and some interesting comments from a wide range of Suns' executives including owner-managing partner, Robert Sarver, and the Chief of Operations Lon Babby. The purpose of this meeting was to discuss free agency and let the fans know that the Suns were building a roster for future playoff runs.

The Suns also host events around the Valley and they are invariably for charitable causes. The Suns' "Operation Orange" campaign is designed to bring the mascot, the Gorilla, the Suns dancers, the Solar

Squad and the Verve Sol Patrol to shopping centers, restaurants, movie theaters and arenas to celebrate the Suns' contribution to the Valley of the Sun.

THE NEW ROSTER AND THE SUNS FUTURE

The new Suns roster emerged in a period from July 15 to August 15, 2012 in the frenetic period after the draft, but the transition began when Jason Richardson was traded to Orlando on December 2010. From that point on the Sun scrapped together more than 23 million dollars in salary cap money to sign some new players. Welcome Michael Beasley. He is the beneficiary of this management plan.

"We want to compete for championships every year, but you have to recognize there's a process," Lon Babby said. Stay tuned.

On October 1 the Suns opened training camp in La Jolla, California. The future was uncertain and no one knew what to expect. There is no doubt that Goran Dragic can run the pick and roll. He is not Steve Nash but Dragic is a brilliant floor leader and a good point guard. Michael Beasley can create his own shot and at 6-10 he is an excellent small forward. This will create a logjam with Channing Frye who can play power forward. Beasley is only twenty-three and has a strong up side. The same can be said of Wesley Johnson who as a 6-7 shooting guard reminds the Suns of Joe Johnson. The problem here is that Jared Dudley is a pretty good shooting guard who can also play small forward. For Coach Alvin Gentry these are good problems to have as it gives the Suns flexibility. Kendall Marshall is the sleeper on the roster, if he can come close to his ten assists a game that he average in college, he will be a bargain. There is also Sebastian Telfair as a back up point guard.

The Suns will be different and perhaps more exciting. Regardless of what happens a new phase begins in the Suns storied history. Coach Alvin Gentry is in the final year of his contract. He deserves an extension and there are a number of players who also need to be signed to long-term deals. Sebastian Telfair and Shannon Brown are on that list. The economics of the NBA at times prevents players from returning to their team.

For the Suns there remains a continuity and a fan friendly atmosphere that is important to the franchise. The sound of "Sarver You Suck" will sometimes come from a disgruntled fan. But that is the price of paying more than four hundred million dollars for an NBA franchise.

There will be fewer injuries and even fewer exhausted players in the 2012-2013 season. From January through March 2012 the Suns played forty-seven games in 90 days. Do the math, this is to many games, too much travel and too little time to plan game strategy. This will not happen in the 2012-2013 season and it will make for more coaching decisions. Coach Gentry is the best at game time match ups and the Suns should have a winning season. The playoffs? Who knows!

SUBSTANCE OVER STYLE

As the 2012-2013 season reached Christmas, Coach Gentry not only changed the Suns' starting lineup, but he began to advocate substance over style. What Gentry meant was that defense would win gems. Michael Beasley was left out of the starting lineup and Jerod Dudley came back in as the small forward. P. J. Tucker was inserted toward the end of most game for defensive purposes, and then Tucker did the unthinkable he started scoring in double figures. It is not easy to get players into a defensive mode as the NBA is an offensive game. Gentry doesn't care about bruised egos, play defense or get benched. This is certainly a new mode for the Suns.

On January 1, 2013, as this book went to press, things were not going well for the Suns. They had eleven wins and twenty-one losses and Coach Gentry hadn't been in Paradise Bakery since the season started. There was a sense of urgency as the Suns played well but they couldn't close out the close games. They had six and seven game losing stretches and two of the new players, Michael Beasley and Wesley Johnson, hadn't performed to their capabilities.

The main problem with the Suns was interior defense. The only strong inside defensive player, P. J. Tucker, comes off the bench. At times Marcin Gortat and Jermaine O'Neal had an inside presence but they lacked consistency. The Suns have dug themselves into a double-digit hole in twenty-four of the first thirty-two games. Coach Gentry has said time and time again that they can't come back from these deficits to win. He is right. There has to be some changes. What are they? Wait until next years book, they haven't happen but they will one way or another. Stay tuned.

Jermaine O'Neal summed up the early part of the 2012-2013 season: "We don't have an every night perimeter scorer. We have to be more focused." This sums up the early Suns' problems.

The Suns remain one of the best sports experiences in the Valley of the Sun. Don't miss Happy Hour at Legends on Monday as it is burger madness night. By the way the basketball is still pretty good. If that doesn't interest you, go for the hamburger.

Peter: "Or perhaps Howard you could get a life." Peter did become more articulate over the course of the book.

APPENDIX

I

THE PHOENIX SUNS DRAFT HISTORY

RoundSelection

1968	1	8	Gary Gregor
1968	2	21	Dick Cunningham
1968	3	36	Art Beatty
1968	4	50	Rich Jones
1968	5	64	Harry Holines
1968	6	77	Rodney Knowles
1968	7	92	Charles Parkes
1968	8	105	Brian Clare
1968	9	120	Merv Jackson
1968	10	133	Lee Davis
1968	11	147	Ron Boone
1968	12	160	Bill Davis
1969	1	2	Neal Walk
1969	2	23	Gene Williams
1969	3	30	Floyd Kerr
1969	3	33	Lamar Green
1969	3	39	Lloyd Kerr
1969	4	44	Dennis Stewart
1969	5	58	Rich Jones
1969	6	72	Dan Sadlier
1969	7	86	Bill Sweek
1969	8	100	Bob Edwards
1969	9	114	Steve Jennings
1969	10	128	Rick Abramson
1969	11	142	Fred Lind
1969	12	156	Bob Miller
1969	13	169	Andy White
1969	14	180	Marv Schmidt
1969	15	189	Bob Beamon
1970	1	10	Greg Howard
1970	2	27	Fred Taylor
1970	2	29	Joe Depre
1970	3	44	Greg McDivitt
1970	3	48	Vann Williford
1970	4	61	Bob Lienhard
1970	5	78	John Canine
1970	6	95	Joe Thomas
1970	7	112	Heyward Dotson
1970	8	129	Steve Patterson
1970	9	146	Carl Ashley
1970	10	163	G. Schreur
1970	11	178	Jim Walls
1970	12	190	Ric Cobb
1970	13	200	Fred Carpenter
1970	14	210	Chad Calabria
1970	15	219	Walt Williams
1971	1	14	John Roche
1971	3	48	Dennis Layton
1971	4	65	Walt Szczerbiak
1971	5	82	Ken Gardner
1971	5	84	Bob Kissane
1971	6	99	William Graham
1971	7	116	Ralph Brateris
1971	8	133	Vernell Eltzy
1971	9	149	Mike Johnson
1971	10	165	Tom Newell
1971	11	179	Paul Leitz
1971	12	192	Floyd Mason
1971	13	204	Ron Dorsey
1971	14	213	Ken Booker
1971	15	222	Curtis Carter
1972	1	4	Corky Calhoun
1972	3	33	Scott English
1972	3	34	Don Buse
1972	3	42	Claude Terry
1972	4	59	Matt Gantt
1972	5	75	Wardell Dyson

1968	1	8	Gary Gregor
1968	2	21	Dick Cunningham
1968	3	36	Art Beatty
1968	4	50	Rich Jones
1968	5	64	Harry Holines
1968	6	77	Rodney Knowles
1968	7	92	Charles Parkes
1968	8	105	Brian Clare
1968	9	120	Merv Jackson
1968	10	133	Lee Davis
1968	11	147	Ron Boone
1968	12	160	Bill Davis
1969	1	2	Neal Walk
1969	2	23	Gene Williams
1969	3	30	Floyd Kerr
1969	3	33	Lamar Green
1969	3	39	Lloyd Kerr
1969	4	44	Dennis Stewart
1969	5	58	Rich Jones
1969	6	72	Dan Sadlier
1969	7	86	Bill Sweek
1969	8	100	Bob Edwards
1969	9	114	Steve Jennings
1969	10	128	Rick Abramson
1969	11	142	Fred Lind
1969	12	156	Bob Miller
1969	13	169	Andy White
1969	14	180	Marv Schmidt
1969	15	189	Bob Beamon
1970	1	10	Greg Howard
1970	2	27	Fred Taylor
1970	2	29	Joe Depre
1970	3	44	Greg McDivitt
1970	3	48	Vann Williford
1970	4	61	Bob Lienhard
1970	5	78	John Canine
1970	6	95	Joe Thomas
1970	7	112	Heyward Dotson
1970	8	129	Steve Patterson
1970	9	146	Carl Ashley
1970	10	163	G. Schreur
1970	11	178	Jim Walls
1970	12	190	Ric Cobb
1970	13	200	Fred Carpenter
1970	14	210	Chad Calabria
1970	15	219	Walt Williams
1971	1	14	John Roche
1971	3	48	Dennis Layton
1971	4	65	Walt Szczerbiak
1971	5	82	Ken Gardner
1971	5	84	Bob Kissane
1971	6	99	William Graham
1971	7	116	Ralph Brateris
1971	8	133	Vernell Elizy
1971	9	149	Mike Johnson
1971	10	165	Tom Newell
1971	11	179	Paul Leitz
1971	12	192	Floyd Mason
1971	13	204	Ron Dorsey
1971	14	213	Ken Booker
1971	15	222	Curtis Carter
1972	1	4	Corky Calhoun
1972	3	33	Scott English
1972	3	34	Don Buse
1972	3	42	Claude Terry
1972	4	59	Matt Gantt
1972	5	75	Wardell Dyson

1972	6	92	Charles Edge
1972	7	109	Bernie Fryer
1972	8	125	Russell Golden
1972	9	140	Bill Kennedy
1972	10	153	Al Vilchek
1972	11	164	John Belcher
1972	12	172	Mark Soderberg
1972	13	179	Kelly Utley
1972	14	186	Ray Golson
1973	1	8	Mike Bantom
1973	2	38	Gary Melchionni
1973	3	42	Joe Reaves
1973	3	43	Steve Mitchell
1973	4	60	Ronnie Robinson
1973	5	77	Clinton Harris
1973	6	94	Gene Doyle
1973	7	111	Jerry Bisbano
1973	8	128	Jim Owens
1973	9	144	Sandy Smith
1973	10	158	Claude White
1973	11	170	Lynn Greer
1973	12	179	Lyman Williamson
1973	13	186	Kalevi Sarkalahti
1974	1	4	John Shumate
1974	2	31	Fred Saunders
1974	3	40	George Gervin
1974	3	49	Earl Williams
1974	4	58	Randy Allen
1974	5	76	Ralph Bobik
1974	6	94	Collis Temple
1974	7	94	Clyde Dickey
1974	8	130	Tom Holland
1974	9	148	Ted Evans
1974	10	165	Mark Wasley
1975	1	4	Alvan Adams
1975	1	16	Ricky Sobers
1975	2	35	Allen Murphy
1975	2	36	Jimmy D. Connor
1975	3	54	Bayard Forrest
1975	4	58	Sam McCants
1975	5	76	Joe Pace
1975	6	94	Biff Burrell
1975	7	112	Dave Edmunds
1975	8	130	Jack Schrader
1975	9	147	Owen Brown
1975	10	163	Mike Moon
1976	1	10	Ron Lee
1976	2	30	Al Fleming
1976	2	33	Butch Feher
1976	3	45	Ira Terrell
1976	4	62	Paul Miller
1976	5	79	Ralph Walker
1976	6	97	Carl Brown
1976	7	115	Brad Warble
1976	8	133	Tom DeBerry
1976	9	151	John Irving
1976	10	169	Gary Jackson
1977	1	5	Walter Davis
1977	3	66	Mike Bratz
1977	4	71	Greg Griffin
1977	5	93	Cecil Rellford
1977	6	115	Billy McKinney
1977	7	137	Alvin Scott
1977	8	159	Alvin Joseph
1978	1	19	Marty Byrnes
1978	3	63	Joel Kramer
1978	4	85	Bob Miller

Year	Round	Pick	Player
1978	4	88	Wayne Smith
1978	5	107	Andre Wakefield
1978	6	128	Charles Thompson
1978	7	149	Steve Malovic
1978	8	167	George Fowler
1978	9	184	Nate Stokes
1978	10		Lewis Cohen
1979	1	22	Kyle Macy
1979	2	24	Johnny High
1979	3	64	Al Green
1979	4	86	Malcomb Cesare
1979	5	107	Mark Eaton
1979	6	127	Dale Shackelford
1979	7	148	Ollie Matson
1979	8	177	Charley Jones
1979	9	196	Hosea Champine
1979	10	215	Korky Nelson
1980	2	42	Kimberly Belton
1980	3	59	John Campbell
1980	3	65	Doug True
1980	4	88	Leroy Stampley
1980	5	111	Mark Stevens
1980	6	134	Coby Leavitt
1980	7	157	Ron Williams
1980	8	179	Jim Connolly
1980	9	200	Keith French
1980	10	220	Randy Carroll
1981	1	20	Larry Nance
1981	3	62	Sam Clancy
1981	3	66	Craig Dykema
1981	5	112	Paul Heuerman
1981	6	135	Pete Harris
1981	7	158	David Williams
1981	8	180	Steve Risley
1981	9	200	Brian Johnson
1981	10	220	Felton Sealey
1982	1	15	David Thirdkill
1982	2	39	Kevin Magee
1982	3	61	Charles Pittman
1982	4	86	Rory White
1982	5	108	Marvin McCrary
1982	6	130	Jake Bethany
1982	7	155	Phil Ward
1982	8	177	Rick Elrod
1982	9	199	Ken Lyles
1982	10	221	Dale Wilkinson
1983	2	28	Rod Foster
1983	2	45	Paul Williams
1983	3	51	Dereck Whittenburg
1983	4	89	Sam Mosley
1983	5	113	Rick Lamb
1983	6	135	Edward Bona
1983	7	159	Fred Brown
1983	8	181	Mike Mulquin
1983	9	204	Joe Dykstra
1983	10	225	Bo Overton
1984	1	13	Jay Humphries
1984	2	6	Charles Jones
1984	3	59	Murray Jarman
1984	4	82	Jeff Collins
1984	5	105	Bill Flye
1984	6	128	Herman Veal
1984	7	151	Raymond Crenshaw
1984	8	174	Mark Fothergill
1984	9	196	Buddy Cox
1984	10	218	Ezra Hill, Jr.
1985	1	10	Ed Pinckney

1985	2	32	Nick Vanos
1985	3	56	Jerry Everett
1985	4	78	Granger Hall
1985	5	102	Shawn Campbell
1985	6	124	Charles Rayne
1985	7	148	Georgi Glouchkov
1986	1	6	William Bedford
1986	2	31	Joe Ward
1986	2	39	Rafael Addison
1986	2	46	Jeff Hornacek
1986	3	55	Kenny Gattison
1986	4	77	Grant Gondrezick
1986	5	101	Greg Spurling
1986	6	123	Jim McCaffrey
1986	7	147	Damon Goodwin
1987	1	2	Armon Gilliam
1987	2	46	Bruce Dalrymple
1987	3	53	Winston Crite
1987	4	76	Steve Beck
1987	5	99	Brent Counts
1987	6	122	Marcel Boyce
1987	7	145	Ron Singleton
1988	1	7	Tim Perry
1988	1	14	Dan Majerle
1988	2	28	Andrew Lang
1988	2	38	Dean Garrett
1988	2	50	Steve Kerr
1988	3	55	Rodney Johns
1989	1	24	Anthony Cook
1989	2	46	Ricky Blanton
1989	2	51	Mike Morrison
1989	2	51	Greg Grant
1990	1	21	Jayson Williams
1990	2	31	Negele Knight
1990	2	48	Cedric Ceballos
1990	2	50	Miloš Babić
1991	2	32	Chad Gallagher
1991	2	46	Richard Dumas
1991	2	50	Joey Wright
1992	1	22	Oliver Miller
1992	2	48	Brian Davis
1992	2	49	Ron Ellis
1993	1	27	Malcolm Mackey
1993	2	49	Mark Buford
1993	2	54	Byron Wilson
1994	1	23	Wesley Person
1994	2	29	Antonio Lang
1994	2	50	Charles Claxton
1994	2	52	Anthony Goldwire
1995	1	21	Michael Finley
1995	1	27	Mario Bennett
1995	2	56	Chris Carr
1996	1	15	Steve Nash
1996	2	9	Russ Millard
1996	2	43	Ben Davis
1997	2	42	Stephen Jackson
1999	1	9	Shawn Marion
2000	1	25	Iakovos "Jake" Tsakalidis
2001	2	51	Alton Ford
2002	1	9	Amaré Stoudemire
2002	1	22	Casey Jacobsen
2003	1	17	Žarko Čabarkapa
2004	1	7	Luol Deng
2005	1	21	Nate Robinson
2005	2	57	Marcin Gortat
2006	1	21	Rajon Rondoe

2006	1	27	Sergio Rodríguez
2007	1	24	Rudy Fernández
2007	1	29	Alando Tucker
2007	2	59	D.J. Strawberry
2008	1	15	Robin Lopez
2008	2	48	Malik Hairston
2009	1	14	Earl Clark
2009	2	48	Taylor Griffin
2009	2	57	Emir Preldžič
2010	2	46	Gani Lawal
2010	2	60	Dwyane Collins
2011	1	13	Markieff Morris
2012	1	13	Kendall Marshall

APPENDIX

II

2012 WESTERN CONFERENCE FINAL STANDINGS

Western	W	L	PCT	GB	CONF	DIV
San Antonio[1w]	50	16	0.758	0.0	35-13	12-4
Oklahoma City[2nw]	47	19	0.712	3.0	34-14	10-3
L.A. Lakers[3p]	41	25	0.621	9.0	32-16	9-5
Memphis[4x]	41	25	0.621	9.0	26-22	7-8
L.A. Clippers[5x]	40	26	0.606	10.0	29-19	7-7
Denver[6x]	38	28	0.576	12.0	22-26	6-7
Dallas[7x]	36	30	0.545	14.0	26-22	8-5
Utah[8x]	36	30	0.545	14.0	25-23	9-4
Houston°	34	32	0.515	16.0	23-25	6-8
Phoenix°	33	33	0.500	17.0	23-25	9-5
Portland°	28	38	0.424	22.0	20-28	4-10
Minnesota°	26	40	0.394	24.0	19-29	4-9
Golden State°	23	43	0.348	27.0	16-32	7-8
Sacramento°	22	44	0.333	28.0	16-32	3-10
New Orleans°	21	45	0.318	29.0	14-34	3-11

x-Clinched Playoff Berth

APPENDIX

III

SUNS TRIVIA: POINTS OF FUN AND FAME

1. PAT RILEY PLAYED FOR THE SUNS IN 1975-1976 AVERAGING 13.1 MINUTES A GAME WHILE AVERAGING 4.7 POINTS A GAME. HE WAS ACQUIRED FROM THE LOS ANGELES LAKERS. WHATEVER HAPPENED TO THIS OBSCURE FORMER UNIVERSITY OF KENTUCKY PLAYER.

2. DICK VAN ARSDALE AVERAGED OVER TWENTY POINTS A GAME IN HIS FIRST THREE SUNS SEASONS AND DURING THE NEXT FIVE SEASONS HE AVERAGED BETWEEN 16.1 AND 19.7 POINTS A GAME. THIS IS WHY H4 IS THE FIRST SUN.

3. AT CENTER, DENNIS AWTREY PLAYED TWO YEARS WITH THE SUNS FROM 1974 THROUGH 1976. HIS CLAIM TO FAME IS THAT HE WAS FROM STEVE NASH'S SCHOL SANTA CLARA.

4. STEVE NASH SPENT EIGHT YEARS SITTING ON THE FLOOR TO EASE HIS BAD BACK.

5. AMARE STOUDEMIRE WAS BROUGHT IN FOR A WORK-OUT. HE WENT ONE ON ONE WITH A WALK ON PLAYER JUST OUT OF JAIL. AMARE TERROIZED THE GUY ON THE COURT.

6. WHILE PLAYING IN A JUNIOR COLLEGE BASKETBALL TOURNAMENT IN MESA, ARIZONA, SHAWN MARION VISIT-ED THE SUNS ARENA. HE GOT TO GO ON THE COURT AND SHOOT A THREE POINTER. IT WENT IN AND MARION SAW THAT AS AN OMEN.

7. THE MOST OBSCURE RECENT DRAFT CHOICE IS Emir Preldžič.

8. A SUNFLOWER WAS THE FIRST SUNS' MASCOT.

9. THE TWO BEST TICKET TAKERS ON THE SUNS STAFF ARE CARLOS AND SAUL. FOR A FREE BOOK E MAIL ME WHAT GATE THEY TAKE TICKETS ON.

10. TOM CHAMBERS NEEDS A PAY RAISE IN THE BROAD-CAST BOOTH SO HE CAN PURCHASE SOME NICE SLACKS. THOSE JEANS ARE GETTING RATTY. THE SPORT COAT STILL LOOKS NICE.

11. PAUL SHIRLEY MADE THE SUNS ROSTER IN 2005. THEY CUT HIM BEFORE THE FIRST GAME. THEN THE SUNS RESIGNED SHIRLEY AND HE HUNG AROUND. WHY IS HE IM-PORTANT? HE IS THE LITERARY SUN. HE WROTE CAN I KEEP MY JERSEY: 11 TEAMS, 5 COUNTRIES AND MY FOUR YEARS AS A BASKETBALL VAGABOND (NEW YORK, 2007) SHIRLEY'S BLOG ON A SUNS FIVE DAY ROAD TRIP EARNED HIM RECOG-NITION AND SOME CRITICISM FOR HIS HONESTY.

12. SEBASTIAN TELFAIR WAS A MR NEW YORK BASKET-BALL AND HE HAD A SHOE ENDORSEMENT DEAL BEFORE HE ENTERED THE NBA.

13. DICK "MOON" MULLINS, THE SUNS FIRST INFORMA-TION DIRECTOR CAME OVER FROM ARIZONA STATE UNI-VERSITY, AND HE HAD A CONTEST FOR A TEAM NICKNAME. THERE WERE OVER 28,000 ENTRIES AND MRS. SELINDA KING WON THE CONTEST WITH THE NAME THE SUNS. SHE RE-CEIVED A THOUSAND DOLLARS AND TWO SEASON TICKETS.

14. THE PHOENIX SUNS FIRST LEASE FOR THE COLISE-UM WAS FOR $1,000 A YEAR FOR THREE YEARS.

15. WHEN THE PHOENIX SUNS WERE AWARDED A FRAN-CHISE, THE ONLY PERSON FROM THE VALLEY OF THE SUN IN-

VOLVED IN STARTING UP THE FRANCHISE WAS KARL ELLER. THE REMAINDER OF THE FOUNDERS PRIMARILY LIVED IN LOS ANGELES OR TUCSON.

16. BOB VACHE WAS THE SUNS FIRST RADIO VOICE. HE BROADCAST THE GAMES ON THIRTEEN RADIO STATIONS. HE WORKED AT KTAR RADIO AND TELEVISION, AND HE WAS REC-OMMENDED FOR THE SUNS JOB BNY ARIZONA STATE UNIV-ERISTY PUBLIC RELATIONS DIRECTOR DICK "MOON" MULL-INS.

17. IN THEIR FIRST SEASON THE SUNS AVERAGED 4,300 FANS A GAME.

18. WHEN ALVAN ADAMS TURNED INTO AN ALL STAR IT SURPRISED A LOT OF PEOPLE AS HE WAS UNDER THE RADAR. JERRY COLANGELO BEGAN CALLING HIM "THE FIND."

19. THE BEST-DRESSED SUNS COACH WHO WAS THE WORST COACH IN THE HISTORY OF THE SUNS. ANSWER: BUTCH VAN BREDA KOLFF. ONE NIGHT IN 1972 I WAS IN PHOE-NIX FOR A CONVENTION OF PROFESSORS. THAT WAS MY DAY JOB. IF YOU COULD CALL IT A DAY JOB. I WALKED INTO THE KON TIKI BAR AND SPENT THE NIGHT TALKING TO THE SUNS COACH. HE WAS FIRED A SHORT TIME LATER. I THINK THAT IS MY MOST IMPORTANT CONTRIBUTON TO THE TEAM.

20. THE PHOENIX SUNS ARE THE ONLY TEAM IN WHICH THE GENERAL MANAGER, JERRY COLANGELO, FIRED THE COACH JERRY COLANGELO.

21. THE SUNS MOST OBSCURE DRAFT PICK IS MILOS BAB-IC IN 1990. HE WAS A SEVEN-FOOT, 240 POUND SERBIAN CEN-TER. HE WAS DRAFTED AND IMMEDIATELY TRADED TO THE CLEVELAND CAVALIERS. HE PLAYED IN THE NBA FOR TWO SEASONS AVERAGING 1.8 POINS A GAME AND 1.0 REBOUNDS IN 4.1 MINUTES OF PLAYING TIME.

22. VERNE BOATNER OF THE ARIZONA REPUBLIC WROTE: "NO OTHER PLAYER CAPTURED THE IMAGINATION OF VALLEY FANS LIKE CONNIE HAWKINS." THIS QUOTE SUG-GESTS THAT WHEN THE HAWK ARRIVED IN THE VALLEY OF THE SUN THERE WAS A NEW POPUALRITY TO THE TEAM AND THEY BEGAN THEIR EARLIEST SELL OUTS.

23. HOT ROD HUNDLEY THE SUNS PLAY BY PLAY AND COLOR MAN WAS THE FIRST PICK IN THER 1958 NBA DRAFT BY

THE CINCINNATI ROYALS. HE PLAYED IN THE NBA THROUGH 1963 AND HE WAS AN ALL STAR. HE ALSO HAD MORE FUN THAN MOST OTHER NBA PLAYERS. HE WAS ALSO AN ALL AMERICAN AT WEST VIRGINIA AND HE SPEND HIS CAREER WITH THE MINNEAPOLIS/LOS ANGELES LAKERS. HE RE-TIRED AT TWENTY-EIGHT WITH BAD KNEES.

24. KARL ELLER, AN ORIGINAL SUN PARTNER DROPPED OUT TO PUSUE A PROFESSIONAL FOOTBALL TEAM AND TO WORK ON RUNNING A PROFESSIONAL HOCKEY TEAM. HE WAS THE ONLY PERSON FROM PHOENIX DIRECTLY INVOLVED WITH SECURING THE SUNS A FRANCHISE.

25. TONY CURTIS WAS AN INITIAL SUNS INVESTOR. THE ACTOR WAS A LONG TIME BASKETBALL FAN.

26. THE INITIAL REACTION TO THE SUNS FRANCHISE IN PHOENIX WAS LUKE WARM. THE ARIZONA REPUBLIC RE-PORTED THE STORY OF THE SUNS COME TO PHOENIX ON PAGE FOUR OF THE SUNDAY JANUARY 21ST ISSUE.

27. RUTH DRYJANSKI WAS THE SUNS FIRST SECRETARY AS COELANGELO BROUGHT HER FROM THE CHICAGO BULLS TO THE VALLEY OF THE SUN.

28. JOE PROSKI WAS THE FIRST TRAINER AND HE CAME FROM THE CHICAGO BULLS.

29. JOHN "RED" KERR WAS THE FIRST COACH AND HE WAS SIGNED TO A THREE-YEAR CONTRACT. HE WAS FIRED ONE AND A HALF YEARS INTO HIS CONTRACT. HE WAS AN OLD STYLE COACH IN A NEW STYLE LEAGUE.

30. CRAIG SPITZER WAS THE SUNS' FIRST SEVEN-FOOT PLAYER AND HE WAS TAKEN IN THE SUPPLEMENTAL DRAFT. IRONICALLY, HE NEVER SET FOOT IN THE VALLEY OF THE SUN.

31. THE SUNS' FIRST YEAR THEME SONG BLARING THROUGH THE ARENA WAS "WHERE HAVE ALL THE FLOW-ERS GONE?"

32. THE NEW YORK KNICKS DAVE DEBUSSCHERE SAID THAT THE SUNS ARENA WAS THE ONLY PLACE IN THE NBA WHERE A CORN COB THROWN AT HIM IN A GAME STRUCK HIM. HE DIDN'T FEEL BAD ABOUT IT, THE KNICKS WON THE GAME.

33. DICK VAN ARSDALE SCORED THE SUNS FIRST BASKET AND THIS IS A FITTING TRIBUTE TO THE ORIGINAL SUN.

34. WHEN THE SUNS CALLED HEADS AND LOST THE COIN FLIP TO DRAFT KAREEM ABDUL JABBAR, COLANGELO TOOK THE BLAME. HE HAD SUNS FANS VOTE ON WHETHER THE COIN FLIP SHOULD BE HEADS OR TAILS. THEY VOTED HEADS AND SUNS OWNER RICHARD BLOCH CALLED HEADS AND LOST KAREEM ABDUL JABBAR. HE WAS KNOWN AS LEW ALCINDOR AT THE TIME.

35. AFTER THE SUNS LOST THE KAREEM ABDUL JABBAR COIN FLIP THEY SELECTED NEAL WALK IN THE DRAFT. HE HAD AN ACCEPTABLE CAREER BUT HE WASN'T KAREEM.

36. SCOTT WILLIAMS, THE SUNS BROADCASTER, WON THREE TITLES WITH THE CHICAGO BULLS. HE WAS UNDRAFTED BUT IN 1990 HE SIGNED WITH THE CHICAGO BULLS. HE PLAYED WITH THE SUNS IN TWO SEPARATE SEASONS.

37. ANN MEYERS DRYSDALE, THE SUNS VINCE PRESIDENT AND NOW A BROADCASTER, WAS THE FIRST WOMAN TO TRY OUT FOR AN NBA TEAM. SHE PLAYED SIX GAMES WITH THE INDIANA PACERS. THEY CUT HER. THEN SHE WENT ON TO PUT WOMEN'S PROFESSIONAL BASKETBALL ON THE MAP.

38. THE PHOENIX SUNS BROADCASTER, STEVE ALBERT, WAS A BALL BOY FOR THE NEW YORK KNICKS. HE IS ALSO IN THE WORLD BOXING HALL OF FAME DUE TO 24 YEARS OF CALLING FIGHTS ON SHOWTIME.

39. MOST VISITING NBA TEAMS STAY IN THE RITZ CARLTON, 2401 E. CAMELBACK RD. PHOENIX.

40. STEVE NASH WAS BORN IN JOHANNESBURG, SOUTH AFRICA ON FEBRUARY 7, 1974 AND HE MOVED WITH HIS FAMILY TO REGINA IN THE PROVINCE OF SASKATCHEWAN WHEN HE WAS EIGHTEEN MONTHS OLD. HIS EARLY ATHLETE INTERESTS WERE IN SOCCER AND ICE HOCKEY. HE DIDN'T START PLAYING BASKETBAL UNTIL THE EIGHTH GRADE.

41. GRANT HILL WAS THE HENRY IBA AWARD WINNER IN 1992 AS THE BEST COLLEGE DEFENSIVE PLAYER.

42. GRANT HILL WAS THE CO-ROOKIE OF THE YEAR IN THE NBA IN 1995 SHARING THE AWARD WITH JASON KIDD.

43. CHANNING FRYE'S FAVORITE PORTLAND RESTAURANTS: 1.) JOHN'S LANDING. HIS FAVORITE DISH: CHAN-

NING'S FRIES 2.) THE NOBLE ROT IS A WINE BAR WITH GREAT FOOD. SEE FRYE'S BLOG FOR THIS EATERY. 3.) THE POK POK HAS THE BEST ASIAN FOOD IN PORTLAND.

44. IN 2012 STEVE NASH MADE TH ENBA ALL STAR TEAM FOR THE EIGHTH TIME AND THIS WAS THE SIXTH TIME THAT HE DID IT AS A SUN. THIS MATCHED SUNS RING OF HONOR PLAYER WALTER DAVIS.

45. IN 2012 STEVE NASH BROKE KEVIN JOHNSON'S SUNS CAREER ASSIST RECORD ON FEBRUARY 1, 2012 WHEN HE GOT HIS 6,518 ASSIST.

46. THE STRIKE SHORTENED 2011-2012 SEASON HAD 66 GAMES IN 115 DAYS.

47. P. J. TUCKER PLAYED IN A COUNTRY WHERE MOST OF THE TEAMS WERE LOCATED IN TWO CITIES. THAT COUNTRY IS GREECE.

48. RONNIE PRICE SIGNED WITH THE PORTLANF TRAIL-BLAZERS AFTER LEAVING THE SUNS.

49. WHEN THE FIRST SUNS OWNER, RICHARD BLOCH, MET NBA COMMISSIONER J. WALTER KENNEDY AT NEW YORK'S FAMED RESTAURANT TOOTS SHOR'S, BLOCH TOLD KENNEDY HE WAS APPLYING FOR AN NBA FRANCHISE IN PHOENIX AND HE HAD A $100,000 CHECK WHICH WAS THE APPLICATION FEE. KENNEDY ORDERED HIS LUNCH AND SAID TO BLOCH: "YOU MUST BE NUTS." THE COMMISSIONER DIDN'T THINK PHOENIX WAS A BIG ENOUGH MARKET.

50. THE FIRST SUNS GAME PLAYED IN ARIZONA WAS AN EXHIBITION GAME IN THE SMALL MINING TOWN OF MIAMI. ON SEPTEMBER 26, 1968 A CROWD OF 2000 WAS ON HAND IN A HIGH SCHOOL GYM TO WATCH THE SUNS WIN AN EXHIBI-TION GAME 104-99 OVER THE SEATTLE SUPER SONICS.

51. BY 2012 STEVE NASH MADE EIGHT APPEARANCES IN NBA ALL STAR GAMES AND SIX OF THESE WERE AS A SUN.

52. IN THE 2011-2012 SEASON THE SUNS WERE 21-10 WHEN JARED DUDLEY AND CHANNING FRYE SCORED IN DOUBLE FIGURES.

53. THE LARGEST MARGIN OF VICTORY FOR A SUNS TEAM IN 2012 WAS 25 POINTS AND THEY DID IT TWICE AGAINST THE PORTLAND TRAIL BLAZERS AND THE CLEVELAND CAVA-LIERS.

54. THE BIGGEST BLOWN LEAD FOR THE SUNS IN 2012 WAS SIXTEEN POINTS AGAINST THE OKLAHOMA CITY THUNDER ON MARCH 7.

55. THE SUNS USED NINE DIFFERENT STARTING LINE UPS IN THE 2012 SEASON.

56. THE SUNS HIGHEST SCORING GAME IN 2012 WAS 125 POINTS AGAINST THE LOS ANGELES LAKERS ON APRIL 7 AND THE PORTLAND TRAIL BLAZERS ON APRIL 16.

57. THE LOWEST SCORING SUNS GAME IN 2012 WAS 71 POINTS AGAINST THE PORTLAND TRAIL BLAZERS ON JANUARY 27/

58. THE LOWEST NUMBER OF FIRST QUARTER POINTS SCORED BY THE SUNS WAS 13 AGAINST THE SAN ANTONIO SPURS ON APRIL 14.

59. THE LOWEST NUMBER OF SECOND QUARTER POINTS SCORED BY THE SUNS WAS 9 AGAINST THE PORTLAND TRAIL BLAZERS ON JANAURY 27, 2012.

60. THE HIGHEST NUMBER OF FIRST HALF POINTS WAS 67 AGAINST THE MILWAUKEE BUCKS ON FEBRUARY 7, 2012.

PETER: "CAN BE CONCLUDE THIS, I AM GETTING BORED."

61. CEDRIC CEBALLOS SCORED MORE THAN 1400 POINTS WITH THE SUNS.

62. ERIC PIATKOWSKI WAS KNOWN AS THE POLISH RIFLE FOR HIS CLUTCH THREE POINT SHOOTING. MARCIN GORTAT IS THE PRESENT POLISH PLAYER WITH THE NICKNAME THE POLISH HAMMER.

63. PAUL WESTPHAL HAD 2429 ASSISTS, WHICH IS A TEAM RECORD FOR A SHOOTING GUARD.

64. GORAN DRAGIC'S FINEST MOMENT AS A SUN CAME IN 2010 WHEN HE SCORED 23 POINTS IN GAME 3 OF THE WESTERN CONFERENCE SEMI FINALS AGAINST THE SAN ANTONIO SPURS AND THE SUNS WON THE GAME AS A RESULT OF HIS PROLIFIC SCORING. THE IRONY WAS THAT HE HURT HIS FOOT STEPPING ON GLASS AT HOME AND HE WAS TRAGED MIDWAY THORUGH THE 2010-2011 SEASON TO THE HOUSTON ROCKETS. HE IS BACK AND THE SUNS DID MAKE A MISTAKE TRADING HIM. BUT ALL IS WELL NOW.

65. DICK SNYDER WAS THE SUNS FIELD GOAL PERCENT-
AGE LEADER IN 1968-1969. HE WAS FROM DAVIDSON COLLEGE
AND HE PLAYED TWO YEARS WITH THE SUNS.

66. STAN MCKENZIE WAS THE SUNS BEST EARLY FREE
THROW SHOOTER WITH A .763 AVERAGE PER GAME. HE AT-
TENDED NYU AND HE PLAYED DURING THE SUNS FIRST TWO
SEASONS.

67. PAT BURKE FROM AUBURN WAS THE SUNS' MOST POP-
ULAR PLAYER OFF THE BENCH FROM 2005 TO 2007. WHILE HE
DIDN'T PLAY MUCH THE CENTER HAD TREMENDOUS FAN
SUPPORT.

68. AFTER BURKE LEFT THE SUNS LOUIE AMUNDSOM
FROM UNLV BECAME THE NEXT FAN FAVORITE WITH THE
ROARING CHANT: "LOU LOU LOU" GREATING HIM. HE
PLAYED WITH THE SUNS FROM 2008 TO 2010 AND THEN HE
WENT ON THE PLAY WITH THE GOLDEN STATE WARRIORS
AND THE INDIANA PACERS.

69. WAYMAN TISDALE, WHO PLAYED FOR THE SUNS
FROM 1994 THROUGH 1997, RELEASED A NUMBER OF HIGHLY
REGARDED JAZZ ALBUMS. HE WAS FEATURED ON THE LIFE-
STYLES OF THE RICH AND FAMOUS. CHARLES BARKLEY COM-
PLAINED THAT HE WAS NEVER ON THE TV SHOW THE LIFE-
STYLES OF THE RICH AND FAMOUS.

69. CHARLES BARKLEY HAD THE LOWEST SHOOTING
PERCENTAGE OF ANY PLAYER WITH A 1000 OR MORE SHOTS
SINCE THE NBA ADOPTED THE THREE POINT SHOT IN 1979.

70. THE SUNS VIDEO COORDINATOR, ELIVS VALCARCEL,
IS FROM NEW JERSEY AND HE PREVIOUSLY WORKED FOR SE-
TON HALL UNIVERSITY AS A VIDEO COORDINATOR.

71. THE 2012-2013 SUNS ROSTER HAS AN AVERAGE AGE OF
26.4 AND THIS IS THE YOUNGEST ROSTER SINCE THE 2009-
2010 SEASON.

72. AS THE 2012-2013 SEASON BEGAN JARED DUDLEY WAS
THE LONGEST TENURED SUNS PLAYER.

73. ON NOVEMBER 9, 2012 THE SUNS CAME BACK FROM
A 26 POINT DEFICIT TO DEEAT THE CLEVELAND CAVALIERS.
THIS IS THE THIRD LARGEST COMEBACK IN FRANCHISE HIS-
TORY.

74. IN ITS 21ˢᵀ NBA SEASON THE U.S. AIRWAYS ARENA IS EXPANDED IN 2012-2013 WITH MORE THAN 7000 NEW SEATS AND 900 IN THE SUITE LEVEL.

75. EVERY PLAYER ON THE 2012-2013 SUNS ROSTER WAS ACQUIRED BY OR EXTENDED BY THE CURRENT BASKETBALL OPERATIONS DEPARTMENT OF LON BABBY, LANCE BLANKS AND MARK WEST.

76. IN 1992 THE SUNSMOVED INTO THEIR NEW ARENA IN DOWNTOWN PHOENIX, THE AMERICAN WEST ARENA, NOW THE U. S. AIRWAYS CENTER

77. IN THE 200-2001 SEASON TAHE PHOENIX SUNS INTRO-DUCED THREE NEW LOGOS MODERIZNING THE THEMES AND ADDING THE GRAY COLOR.

78. FOR THE FIRST ELEVEN SEASONS THE SUNS HAD NO MASCOT. THERE WAS AN ATTEMPT AT A SUNFLOWER COS-TUME. IN THE WINTER OF 1980 A SINGING TELEGRAM FROM EASTERN ONION WAS SENT TO THE ARENA IN A GORILLA COSTUME. THE SECURITY ASKED THE GORILLA TO STICK AROUND AND ENTERTAIN PEOPLE. HENCE, THE ORIGINS OF THE GORILLA AS THE SUNS MASCOT.

79. RON LEE AS NOT ONLY DRAFTED BY THE PHOENIX SUNS, BUT HE WAS SUCH A GOOD ATHELTE THAT HE WAS DRAFTED BY THE NFL AND THE NORTH AMERICAN SOCCER LEAGUE.

80. IN 987 THE SUNS TRIED TO HIRE RICK PITINO TO COACH THE TEAM.

0	Michael Beasley	F	6-10	235	01/09/1989
26	Shannon Brown	G	6-4	210	11/29/1985
1	Goran Dragic	G	6-3	190	05/06/1986
3	Jared Dudley	G-F	6-7	225	07/10/1985
8	Channing Frye	F-C	6-11	245	05/17/1983
10	Diante Garrett	G	6-4	190	11/03/1988
4	Marcin Gortat	C	6-11	240	02/17/1984
2	Wesley Johnson	F	6-7	215	07/11/1987
12	Kendall Marshall	G	6-4	195	08/19/1991
11	Markieff Morris	F	6-10	245	09/02/1989
20	Jermaine O'Neal	C	6-11	255	10/13/1978
14	Luis Scola	F	6-9	245	04/30/1980
31	Sebastian Telfair	G	6-0	170	06/09/1985
17	P.J Tucker	F	6-6	224	05/05/1985
40	Luke Zeller	F-C	6-11	245	04/07/1987

HEAD COACH
Alvin Gentry (College–Appalachian State)

ASSISTANT COACHES
Elston Turner (College–Mississippi)
Dan Majerle (College–Central Michigan)
Igor Kokoskov (College–Belgrade University)
Noel Gillespie (College–Wisconsin-Whitewater)

ATHLETIC TRAINER
Aaron Nelson (College–Iowa State)

APPENDIX

V

INDIVIDUAL AND TEAM STATISTICS

SUNS TEAM LEADERS 2011-2012
POINTS: MARCIN GORTAT: 15.4
REBOUNDS: MARCIN GORTAT: 10
ASSISTS: STEVE NASH: 10.7
STEALS: RONNIE PRICE: 0.9
BLOCKS: MARCIN GORTAT: 1.5

SUNS TEAM STATISTICS
POINTS SCORED PER GAME: 98.4 (8TH OVERALL IN NBA)
REBOUNDS PER GAME: 41.7 (19TH OVERALL IN NBA)
ASSISTS PER GAME: 22.5 (6TH OVERALL IN NBA)
POINTS ALLOWED: 98.6 (21ST OVERALL IN NBA)

APPENDIX

VI

PLAYER SALARIES 2012-2013

GORAN DRAGIC: $7.5 MILLION
MARCIN GORTAT: $7,258,960
CHANNING FRYE: $6 MILLION
MICHAEL BEASLEY: $5,750,000
WESLEY JOHNSON: $4,285,560
JARED DUDLEY: $4,250,000
LUIS SCOLA: $4,500,000
SHANNON BROWN: $3.5 MILLION
MARKIEFF MORRIS: $2,2051,040
KENDALL MARSHALL: $1,919,160
SEBASTIAN TELFAIR: $1,567,500
JERMAINE O'NEAL: $854,389
P. J. TUCKER: $762,195
DIANTE GARRETT: $473,604
LUKE ZELLER: $473,604

APPENDIX

VII

CHARLES BARKLEY TRIVIA

1. HE WAS NAMED AS ONE OF THE FIFTY GREATEST NBA PLAYERS OF ALL TIME.

2. HE WAS A MEMBER OF THE 1992 AND 1996 OLYMPIC BASKETBALL TEAMS.

3. HE WAS THE NBA MVP IN 1993 AND HE APPEARED IN ELEVEN ALL STAR GAMES.

4. CHARLES WAS AN ALL NBA SECOND TEAM MEMBER FOR FIVE YEARS AND HE EVEN MADE THE ALL NBA THIRD TEAM ONCE.

5. IN 2006 HE WAS INDUCTED INTO THE NAISMITH ME-MORIAL BASKETBALL HALL OF FAME

6. THE NATIONS SPORTSWRITERS NAMED BARKLEY TO THE ALL NBA INTERIVEW TEAM FOR HIS COOPERATION WITH THE PRESS DURING HIS LAST THIRTEEN SEASONS IN THE LEAGUE.

7. IN HIS JUNIOR YEAR IN HIGH SCHOOL AT 5-10 AND 220 POUNDS CHARLES WAS CUT FROM THE LEEDS HIGH SCHOOL BASKETBALL TEAM. THEN BARKLEY GREW TO 6-4 AND HE AVERAGED 19.1 POINTS A GAME IN HIS SENIOR YEAR AND 17.9 REOBUNDS AS HE LED HIS TEAM TO A 26-3 RECORD AND THE ALABAMA STATE SEMIFINALS.

8. WHEN HE ATTENDED AUBURN, BARKLEY MAJORED IN BUSINESS MANAGEMENT. HE HAS DONE WELL WITH HIS MONEY.

9. THE ROUND MOUND OF REBOUND WAS CHARLES' GRATUITIOUS NICKNAME. HE WORKED OUT HARD AND LOST THIS MONIKER.

10. IN HIS NBA CAREER CHARLES AVERAGED 22.1 POINTS A GAME AND 23 IN THE PLAYOFFS.

11. HE IS THE SECOND ALL TIME LEADER IN STEALS FOR A POWER FORWARD.

12. IN HIS CAREER CHARLES MADE 23,757 POINTS, 12,546 REBOUNDS AND 4,215 ASSISTS.

13. ON THE DREAM TEAM BARKLEY'S JERSEY WAS NUMBER 4 AND THIS WAS THE LAST NUMBER HE WORE WHILE FINISHING HIS CAREER WITH THE HOUSTON ROCKETS.

14. CHARLES BARKLEY PUNCHED DETROIT'S BILL LAIMBEER IN THE FACE AND HE RECEIVED A ONE GAME SUSPENSION. WHY IS THIS IMPORTANT? LAIMBEER OUTWEIGHED BARKLEY AND HE WAS TALLER. CHARLES WAS FEARLESS.

15. NICKNAME: SIR CHARLES

CHARLES BARKLEY: 60 OF HIS BEST QUOTES

1. "AUBURN SUFFERED A GREAT LOSS WHEN I LEFT."

2. "I'M STILL GOING TO DISNEYLAND." CHARLES SPEAKING AFTER LOSING TO THE CHICAGO BULLS IN THE NBA FINALS.

3. "THERE WILL NEVER BE ANOTHER PLAYER LIKE ME. I'M THE NINGTH WONDER OF THE WORLD." A QUOTE FROM A PHILADELPHIA NEWSPAPER, 1994

4. "I CAN BE BOUGHT. IF THEY PAID ME ENOUGH, I'D WORK FOR THE KLAN."

5. "YOU GOT TO BELIEVE IN YOURSELF. HELL, I BELIEVE I'M THE BEST-LOOKING GUY IN THE WORLD AND I MIGHT BE RIGHT."

6. "I DON'T HATE ANYONE, AT LEAST NOT FOR MORE THAN 48 MINUTES, BARRING OVERTIME."

7. "WE BETTER NOT BE DOING THE BULLS THIS YEAR. MAN, THEY SUCK! BUNCH OF HIGH SCHOOL KIDS WITH $70 MILLION CONTRACTS. DAMN! I HATE MY MOTHER FOR HAVING ME TOO SOON."

8. "YOU CAN TALK WITHOUT SAYING A THING. I DON'T EVER WANT TO BE THAT TYPE OF PERSON."

9. AFTER RETIRING FROM BASKETBALL "I'M JUST WHAT AMERICA NEEDS–ANOTHER UNEMPLOYED BLACK MAN.

10. ERNIE: "DID THEY RECOGNIZE YOU IN SOUTH DAKOTA?"

CHARLES: "YES, THEY DID. IT WAS EASY BECAUSE I WAS THE ONLY BLACK PERSON THERE. WHEN THEY SEE ME WALKING DOWN THE STREET THEY SAY 'THERE HE GOES AGAIN'. AND WHEN I COME BACK THE NEXT YEAR THEY SAY 'HE'S BACK YAWL!'"

11. RIGHT AFTER PEJA WON THE 3-POINT CONTEST: "KENNY SAID IT WAS GOING TO BE AN ALL-INTERNATIONAL NIGHT. I WANT TO KNOW WHICH INTERNATIONAL BROTHER IS GOING TO WIN THE SLAM DUNK CONTEST."

12. ON THE ENRON SCANDAL INVESTIGATION: "ALMOST ALL THOSE POLITICIANS TOOK MONEY FROM ENRON, AND THERE THEY ARE HOLDING HEARINGS. THAT'S LIKE O.J. SIMPSON GETTING IN THE RAE CARRUTH JURY POOL."

13. "I HAD TO EXPLAIN TO MY DAUGHTER WHY THAT SKANK MONICA LEWINSKI HAS AN HOUR SPECIAL ON HBO THIS WEEKEND."

14. ERNIE: "AUBURN IS A PRETTY GOOD SCHOOL. TO GRADUATE FROM THERE I SUPPOSE YOU REALLY NEED TO WORK HARD AND PUT FORTH MAXIMUM EFFORT."
CHARLES: "20 PTS AND 10 REBOUNDS WILL GET YOU THROUGH ALSO!"

15. "EVERY TIME I THINK ABOUT CHANGING A DIAPER, I RUN A LITTLE BIT HARDER AND A LITTLE BIT FASTER TO MAKE SURE I CAN AFFORD A NANNY UNTIL MY DAUGHTER'S OLD ENOUGH TO TAKE CARE OF THAT HERSELF."

16. EJ: "DID YOU GRADUATE FROM AUBURN?"
CHARLES: "NO, BUT I HAVE A COUPLE PEOPLE WORKING FOR ME WHO DID."

17. "DICK BAVETTA AND MOSES PARTED THE RED SEA TOGETHER."

18. ERNIE JOHNSON, ON REGGIE EVANS BEING CAUGHT GRABBING THE ROCKS OF CHRIS KAMAN: "(REGGIE EVANS) GOT CAUGHT WITH HIS HAND IN THE COOKIE JAR."CHARLES BARKLEY: "ERNIE, I DON'T KNOW WHERE YOU GET YOUR COOKIES AT BUT THE REST OF US DON'T GET OURS THERE."

19. ON HIS 17-YEAR OLD DAUGHTER NOT DATING YET: "THANK GOODNESS. I JUST HOPE SHE DOESN'T START BEFORE I GO IN THE HALL OF FAME. THAT WAY, I WON'T HAVE TO KILL ANYBODY BEFORE I GET INDUCTED."

20. KENNY: "THERE'S GUYS WHO GO OVER TO EUROPE AND PLAY OVERSEAS FROM AMERICA, AND THEY DOMINATE!"
CHARLES: "THOSE ARE CALLED 'BROTHERS'

21. AFTER WANG ZHIZHI HAS A SHOT BLOCKED, BARKLEY COMMENTED ON THE CHINESE PLAYER WHO WAS ON THE DALLAS MAVERICKS ROSSTER: "HE'S GOT TO BRING SOMETHING STRONGER THAN THAT. THAT'S LIKE BRINGING MILK TO A BAR, IT'S NOT STRONG ENOUGH"

22. BARKLEY ON TURNER SPORTS OFFICE HAVING A BETTING POOL ON HIS WEIGHT: "THAT IS STARTING TO HURT MY FEELINGS. I DON'T MIND SKINNY PEOPLE MAKING FUN OF ME, WE ALL DO THAT, BUT I DON'T WANT FAT PEOPLE MAKING FUN OF ME."

23. "WE ARE IN THE BUSINESS OF KICKING BUTT AND BUSINESS IS VERY, VERY GOOD."

24. WHEN THE DREAM TEAM WAS ABOUT TO PLAY THE ANGOLA NATIONAL TEAM, DURING PRE-GAME INTERVIEWS THE OTHER USA PLAYERS PROVIDED DIPLOMATIC, FACE SAVING COMMENTS ABOUT HOW THEY WOULD PLAY HARD AND FELT STRONGLY THEY WOULD WIN. WHEN CHUCK WAS ASKED ABOUT ANGOLA AND THE GAME, HE REPLIED: "THEY'RE IN A LOT OF TROUBLE."

25. CHARLES BARKLEY ON HIS THOUGHTS ABOUT RETIRING BEFORE THE SEASON: "I REMEMBER SITTING DOWN WITH THE ROCKETS AND SAYING, 'YEAH. I'M GOING TO RETIRE.' THEY SAID, 'WELL, WE'LL GIVE YOU $9 MILLION.' AND I SAID, 'YOU GOT A PEN ON YOU?'"

26. MAN, EVERYTHING GETS BLAMED ON THE CLINTONS, EVERY SINGLE THING IN THIS WORLD. I THINK BILL CLINTON SHOT JFK, TOO.

27. "I KNOW WHY HIS NAME IS DMX. BECAUSE HIS REAL NAME IS EARL. IMAGINE IF HIS NAME WAS EARL THE RAPPER."

28. "IF YOU GO OUT WITH A GIRL AND THEY SAY SHE HAS A GREAT PERSONALITY, SHE'S UGLY. IF THEY TELL YOU A GUY WORKS HARD, HE CAN'T PLAY A LICK. SAME THING."

29. AFTER KEVIN GARNETT THREW A BALL INTO THE CROWD OUT OF FRUSTRATION AND WAS EJECTED. THEY SHOWED FOOTAGE OF THE MAN THAT GOT HIT BY THE BALL BEING TAKEN AWAY IN A STRETCHER AND HIS DAUGHTER

WAS CRYING. CHARLES COMMENTED THAT PLAYERS TAKE PASSES TO THE FACE ALL THE TIME. HE TOPPED IT OFF BY SAYING: "YOU KNOW WHY THAT LITTLE GIRL'S CRYING? IT'S BECAUSE SHE'S THINKING 'MY DADDY'S A WUSSY'".

30. BARKLEY ON ERNIE JOHNSON AND KENNY SMITH EATING A BOX OF HOT KRISPY KREME DONUTS IN FRONT OF HIM: "BOTH OF Y'ALL ARE2 GOING TO HELL FOR THAT. Y'ALL ARE GOING TO HELL WITH A FIRST-CLASS TICKET. IS THAT HOW YOU TREAT YOUR PARTNER? KRISPY KREME MIGHT BE THE GREATEST INVENTION IN THE HISTORY OF CIVILIZATION WHEN THEY'RE HOT. Y'ALL ARE CRUEL MAN."

31. "IT'S KINDA GREAT TO SEE THE CELTICS DOIN WELL AGAIN CUZ THAT WAS SO MUCH FUN IN MY DAY TO GO TO THE BOSTON GARDEN AND THEY SPIT AT YOU AND THROW THINGS AT YOU AND TALK ABOUT YOUR MOM. IT SOUNDS LIKE DINNER AT KENNY SMITH'S HOUSE."

32. "I THINK THAT THE TEAM THAT WINS GAME FIVE WILL WIN THE SERIES. UNLESS WE LOSE GAME FIVE."

33. CHARLES BARKLEY AFTER SEEING A PICTURE OF SAM CASSELL ON THE SCREEN: "PHONE HOME." AND LATER HE REMARKS TO KENNY, "SAM CASSELL IS A GOOD GUY, BUT HE'S NOT GOING TO WIND UP ON THE COVER OF GQ ANYTIME SOON."

34. WHILE WATCHING SOMEONE IN AUSTRALIA PUT $1 MILLION WORTH OF RUBIES ON A TABLE: "DAMN, MUST NOT BE ANY BLACK FOLKS IN AUSTRALIA. YOU CAN'T JUST LEAVE $1 MILLION WORTH OF JEWELRY LYING AROUND THE 'HOOD."

35. ASKED IF HE HAD EVER BEEN IN THE GOVERNOR'S OFFICE IN MONTGOMERY, BARKLEY SAID NO. "THEY DON'T LET MANY BLACK PEOPLE IN THE GOVERNOR'S MANSION IN ALABAMA," HE SAID, "UNLESS THEY'RE CLEANING."

36. ON THE GOAL OF THE '92 OLYMPIC DREAM TEAM WHEN PLAYING PANAMA IN THE TOURNAMENT OF THE AMERICAS: "TO GET THE CANAL BACK."

37. TO KENNY: "HAKEEM COULDN'T KICK YOUR ASS CUZ YOU WERE TOO CLOSE, KISSIN HIS!"

38. BARKLEY ON HANNO MOTTOLA, WHO, AS EJ RE-MARKED "IS THE FIRST NBA PLAYER FROM FINLAND". CHARLES REPLIES: "OF COURSE HE IS THE FIRST NBA PLAY-ER FROM FINLAND, HE'S THE ONLY PERSON IN FINLAND."

39. ON SUPERSIZED OLIVER MILLER: "YOU CAN'T EVEN JUMP HIGH ENOUGH TO TOUCH THE RIM, UNLESS THEY PUT A BIG MAC ON IT."

40. "ALL I KNOW IS, AS LONG AS I LED THE SOUTHEAST-ERN CONFERENCE IN SCORING, MY GRADES WOULD BE FINE."

41. ON NORTH CAROLINA MISSING 22 OF ITS LAST 23 SHOTS IN LOSING TO GEORGETOWN IN THE NCAA TOURNA-MENT LAST WEEKEND: "STEVIE WONDER COULD MAKE ONE OF 23 SHOTS."

42. I'D NEVER BUY MY GIRL A WATCH ... SHE'S ALREADY GOT A CLOCK OVER THE STOVE.

43. "I ALWAYS LAUGH WHEN PEOPLE ASK ME ABOUT REBOUNDING TECHNIQUES. I'VE GOT A TECHNIQUE. IT'S CALLED JUST GO GET THE DAMN BALL."

44. ON THE PORTLAND TRAIL BLAZERS (BACK WHEN THEY WERE KNOWN AS THE JAIL BLAZERS) SERVING THANKS-GIVING MEALS: "IN BETWEEN ARRESTS THEY DO COMMUNI-TY SERVICE."

45. "YEAH ERNIE, IT'S CALLED DEFENSE, I MEAN I WOULDN'T KNOW ANYTHING ABOUT IT PERSONALLY BUT I'VE HEARD ABOUT IT THROUGH THE GRAPEVINE.

46. "WELL, WHEN I WENT OFF TO COLLEGE, THE GUYS I USED TO HANG WITH WERE PUMPING GAS AND VOTING DEMOCRAT. TODAY THEY'RE STILL PUMPING GAS AND VOTING DEMOCRAT. GUESS THE DEMOCRATS DIDN'T DO MUCH FOR THEM."

47. "WHEN I WAS RECRUITED AT AUBURN [UNIVERSITY], THEY TOOK ME TO A STRIP JOINT. WHEN I SAW THOSE TITTIES ON BUFFY, I KNEW THAT AUBURN MET MY ACADEMIC REQUIREMENTS."

48. "HEY STANLEY, YOU COULD BE A GREAT PLAYER IF YOU LEARNED JUST TWO WORDS: I'M FULL."—BARKLEY YELLING TO 300-PLUS-POUND HOUSTON ROCKETS TEAMMATE STANLEY ROBERTS

49. "I HEARD TONYA HARDING IS CALLING HERSELF THE CHARLES BARKLEY OF FIGURE SKATING. I WAS GOING TO SUE HER FOR DEFAMATION OF CHARACTER, BUT THEN I REALIZED I HAVE NO CHARACTER."

50. ON THE ALL-STAR GAME: "HELL, THERE AIN'T BUT 15 BLACK MILLIONAIRES IN THE WHOLE COUNTRY & HALF OF 'EM ARE RIGHT HERE IN THIS ROOM."

51. ON JERRY KRAUSE STILL BEING ABLE TO KEEP HIS JOB AS GM OF THE CHICAGO BULLS: "JERRY KRAUSE MUST HAVE PICTURES OF HIS BOSS'S WIFE HAVING SEX WITH A MONKEY."

52. AFTER THROWING A GUY THROUGH A 1ST FLOOR WINDOW IN A BAR CHARLES WAS IN FRONT OF THE JUDGE.
JUDGE: "YOUR SANCTIONS ARE COMMUNITY SERVICE AND A FINE, DO YOU HAVE ANY REGRETS?"

CHARLES: "YEAH I REGRET WE WEREN'T ON A HIGHER FLOOR"

53. AFTER AN OLYMPIC DREAM TEAM VICTORY OVER ANGOLA, IN WHICH THEY WON 116-48, CHARLES GOT INTO A PHYSICAL ALTERCATION WITH A MEMBER OF ANGOLA TOWARDS THE END OF THE GAME, AFTERWARDS HE SAYS THE PLAYER DESERVED IT.

54. "SOMEBODY HITS ME, I'M GOING TO HIT HIM BACK. EVEN IF IT DOES LOOK LIKE HE HASN'T EATEN IN A COUPLE WEEKS. I THOUGHT HE WAS GOING TO PULL A SPEAR ON ME."

55. "YOU KNOW IT'S GOING TO HELL WHEN THE BEST RAPPER OUT THERE IS WHITE AND THE BEST GOLFER IS BLACK."

56. "MY INITIAL RESPONSE WAS TO SUE HER FOR DEFAMATON OF CHARACTER, BUT THEN I REALIZED THAT I HAD NO CHARACTER."

57. "POOR PEOPLE CANNOT RELY ON THE GOVERNMENT TO COME TO HELP YOU IN TIMES OF NEED. YOU HAVE TO GET YOUR EDUCATION. THEN NOBODY CAN CONTROL YOUR DESTINY.

58. "MY FAMILY GOT ALL OVER ME BECAUSE THEY SAID BUSH IS ONLY FOR THE RICH PEOPLE. THEN I REMINDED THEM, 'HEY I'M RICH."

59. "I LOVE NEW YORK CITY, I'VE GOT A GUN."

60. "THESE ARE MY NEW SHOES. THEY'RE GOOD SHOES. THEY WON'T MAKE YOU RICH LIKE ME, THEY WON'T MAKE YOU REBOUND LIKE ME. THEY'LL ONLY MAKE YOU HAVE SHOES LIKE ME. THAT'S IT."

APPENDIX

VIII

AN ALL TIME LIST OF SUNS PLAYERS

A

Player			Pos.	From	To	School	Pts	Rebs	Asts
Alvan Adams	33	C/F	1975	1988	Oklahoma	13,9 10	6,937	4,012	
Rafael Addison		12	G/F	1986	1987	Syracuse	359	106	45
Danny Ainge		22	SG	1992	1995	BYU	2,12 4	454	650
Louis Amundson		17	PF	2008	2010	UNLV	692	616	59
Robert Archibald		21	F/C	2003	2003	Illinois	1	1	1
Dennis Awtrey	·	21	C	1974	1978	Santa Clara	1,87 3	1,655	846

B

Player	Ntn.	No.	Pos.	From	To	School	Pts	Rebs	Asts
James Bailey		2	F/C	1987	1988	Rutgers	288	210	42
Toby Bailey		12	G	1999	2000	UCLA	241	126	43
Marcus Banks		2	PG	2006	2008	UNLV	346	58	85
Mike Bantom		40	F/C	1973	1975	Saint Joseph's	1,811	1,095	325
Leandro Barbosa		10	G	2003	2010	Brazil	5,874	1,098	1,208
Charles Barkley		34	F	1992	1996	Auburn	6,556	3,232	1,219
Matt Barnes		22	F	2008	2009	UCLA	788	421	212
Andre Barrett		12	PG	2006	2006	Seton Hall	9	3	2
Earl Barron		30	C	2010	2010	Memphis	36	40	4
Kenny Battle		3	SF	1989	1991	Northern Illinois	338	177	53
William Bedford		50	C	1986	1987	Memphis	334	246	57
Charlie Bell		14	G	2001	2001	Michigan State	8	4	2
Raja Bell		19	SG	2005	2008	Florida International	3,406	842	600
Mario Bennett		8	F	1995	1996	Arizona State	85	49	6
Ed Biedenbach		12	G	1968	1969	UNC-Asheville	4	2	3
Corie Blount		43	PF	1999	2001	Cincinnati	161	198	18
Dexter Boney		10	G	1997	1997	UNLV	19	6	0
Dudley Bradley		7	F/G	1981	1982	North Carolina	325	87	80
Mike Bratz		23	PG	1977	1980	Stanford	1,697	423	525
Aaron Brooks		0	PG	2011	2011	Oregon	240	27	104
Chucky Brown		52	SF	1996	1996	North Carolina State	34	16	4
Dee Brown		11	PG	2008	2009	Illinois	5	1	3
Gerald Brown		4	G	1999	1999	Pepperdine	80	22	31
Mike Brown		45	C/F	1997	1997	George Washington	16	25	5
Randy Brown		0	G	2002	2003	New Mexico State	41	26	35
Shannon Brown		26	SG	2011	present	Michigan State			
Mark Bryant		2	F/C	1996	1998	Seton Hall	671	456	93
Jud Buechler		26	SF	2001	2001	Arizona	6	8	3
Pat Burke		11	C	2005	2007	Auburn	201	120	21
Steve Burtt		15	PG	1991	1992	Iona	187	34	59
Don Buse		10	PG	1977	1980	Evansville	1,952	699	1,067
Marty Byrnes		45	F	1978	1979	Syracuse	291	97	61

C

Player	Ntn.	No	Pos.	From	To	School	Pts	Rebs	Asts
Žarko Čabarkapa		11	PF	2003	2005	Serbia	212	102	40
Corky Calhoun		20	SF	1972	1974	Pennsylvania	1165	778	215
Chris Carr		43	SG	1995	1996	Southern Illinois	240	102	43
Joe Barry Carroll		2	C	1991	1991	Purdue	37	24	11
Vince Carter		25	SG	2010	2011	North Carolina	689	185	82
Sam Cassell		10	PG	1996	1996	Florida State	325	50	99
Cedric Ceballos		23 1	SF	1990 1997	1994 1998	Cal State Fullerton	3,91 6	1,480	337
Bill Chamberlain		24	SF	1973	1974	North Carolina	153	80	37
Jerry Chambers		44	SF	1969	1970	Utah	657	219	54
Tom Chambers		24	F/C	1988	1993	Utah	7,81 7	2,491	858
Rex Chapman		3	SG	1996	2000	Kentucky	2,78 7	538	556
Josh Childress		1	F/G	2010	2012	Stanford	272	155	42
Bob Christian		31	C	1973	1974	Grambling State	386	339	98
Earl Clark		55	F	2009	2010	Louisville	169	79	25
John Coker		40	C	1995	1996	Boise State	8	2	1
Jarron Collins		20	C	2009	2010	Stanford	34	62	6
Jeff Cook		45	C	1979 1987	1983 1988	Idaho State	1,63 9	1,244	457
Duane Cooper		10	PG	1993	1994	USC	48	9	28
Tyrone Corbin		23	F/G	1988	1989	DePaul	863	528	177
Mel Counts		31	C	1970	1972	Oregon State	1,27 4	760	232
Joe Courtney		40	PF	1993	1994	Mississippi State	103	27	9
Joe Crispin		11	PG	2002	2002	Penn State	69	10	24
Winston Crite		12	F	1987	1989	Texas A&M	87	65	15

D

Player	Ntn.	No	Pos.	From	To	School	Pts	Rebs	Asts
Ben Davis		43	PF	1996	1997	Arizona	33	36	2
Josh Davis		15	F	2006	2006	Wyoming	4	1	0
Mark Davis		43	F/G	1988	1989	Old Dominion	4	1	0
Walter Davis		6	G/F	1977	1988	North Carolina	15,666	2,472	3,340
Todd Day		11	G/F	1999	2000	Arkansas	396	129	65
Tony Delk		00	PG	2000	2002	Kentucky	1,440	385	241
Vinny Del Negro		8 15	G	2001	2001	North Carolina State	179	51	66
Boris Diaw		3	F	2005	2008	France	2,697	1,337	1,218
Zabian Dowdell		22	PG	2011	2011	Virginia Tech	121	20	51
Goran Dragić		2 1	PG	2008 2012	2011 **present**	Slovenia	1,234	360	501
Chris Dudley		14	C	2000	2001	Yale	72	183	18
Jared Dudley		3	SF	2008	**present**	Boston College	1,805	745	260
Richard Dumas		21 12	SF	1992 1994	1993 1995	Oklahoma State	839	252	67
Tony Dumas		27	SG	1996	1997	UMKC	14	2	3
T. R. Dunn		25	G	1989	1989	Alabama	33	60	25
Devin Durrant		17	SF	1985	1985	BYU	17	8	5
Craig Dykema		35	SF	1981	1982	Cal Long Beach	43	12	15

E

Player	Ntn.	No	Pos.	From	To	School	Pts	Rebs	Asts
James Edwards		53	C	1983	1988	Washington	3,933	1,490	530
Howard Eisley		12	PG	2004	2004	Boston College	240	63	117
Mario Elie		17	G/F	2000	2001	American International	299	155	131
Scott English		14	F	1972	1973	UTEP	93	44	15
Keith Erickson		14	F/G	1973	1977	UCLA	2,632	1,133	664

F

Player	Ntn.	No	Pos.	From	To	School	Pts	Rebs	Asts
Butch Feher		7	G	1976	1977	Vanderbilt	248	74	36
Michael Finley		4	G/F	1995	1996	Wisconsin	1,585	494	357
Alton Ford		4	PF	2001	2003	Houston	171	113	8
Sharrod Ford		23	PF	2005	2005	Clemson	4	3	0
Bayard Forrest		35	C	1977	1979	Grand Canyon	569	565	296
Rod Foster		10	PG	1983	1986	UCLA	1,562	258	479
Jim Fox		31	C	1968	1970	South Carolina	1,747	1,249	236
Channing Frye		8	F/C	2009	**present**	Arizona	1,880	940	209

G

Player	Ntn.	No	Pos.	From	To	School	Pts	Rebs	Asts
Rubén Garcés		21	PF	2000	2001	Providence	16	22	4
Pat Garrity		8	PF	1998	1999	Notre Dame	217	75	18
Kenny Gattison		44	PF	1986	1989	Old Dominion	405	271	36
Armen Gilliam		35	PF	1987	1989	UNLV	2,134	1,045	132
Gordan Giriček		2	G/F	2008	2008	Croatia	193	51	35
Georgi Glouchkov		16	PF	1985	1986	Bulgaria	239	163	32
Grant Gondrezick		3	SG	1986	1987	Pepperdine	349	110	81
Gail Goodrich		25	PG	1968	1970	UCLA	3,555	777	1,123
Marcin Gortat		4	C	2010	**present**	Poland	1,734	1,172	162
Brian Grant		55	F/C	2005	2006	Xavier	61	57	7
Greg Grant		10	PG	1989	1990	Trenton State	208	59	168
A. C. Green		45	F/C	1993	1996	Oregon State	2,885	2,114	353
Lamar Green		16	PF	1969	1974	Morehead State	1,806	2,186	247
Gary Gregor		44	PF	1968	1969	South Carolina	885	711	96
Greg Griffin		25	F	1977	1978	Idaho State	145	103	24
Taylor Griffin		32	F	2009	2010	Oklahoma	10	2	1
Tom Gugliotta		24	PF	1999	2004	North Carolina State	2,311	1,438	353

H

Player	Ntn.	No	Pos.	From	To	School	Pts	Rebs	Asts
Penny Hardaway		1	G	1999	2004	Memphis	2,924	1,071	986
Art Harris		23	G	1969	1972	Stanford	1,118	255	361
Donnell Harvey		4	F	2003	2004	Florida	141	92	13
Clem Haskins		11	PG	1970	1974	Western Kentucky	4,407	989	1,135
Connie Hawkins		42	F	1969	1973	Iowa	6,368	2,806	1,341
Nate Hawthorne		32	SG	1974	1976	Southern Illinois	776	301	85
Gar Heard		24	PF	1976	1980	Oklahoma	2,313	2,181	442
Skeeter Henry		4	SG	1994	1994	Oklahoma	4	2	4
Johnny High		12 22 11	SG	1979	1984	Nevada	1,396	617	525
Grant Hill		33	SF	2007	2012	Duke	3,872	1,541	782
Craig Hodges		25	SG	1988	1988	Long Beach State	271	37	52
Michael Holton		15	PG	1984	1985	UCLA	636	136	205
Jeff Hornacek		14	SG	1986	1992	Iowa State	6,420	1,753	2,523
Robert Horry		25	F	1996	1997	Alabama	220	119	54
Eddie House		50	PG	2005	2006	Arizona State	796	132	148
Greg Howard		44	F/C	1970	1971	New Mexico	173	119	26
Jay Humphries		24	G	1984	1988	Colorado	3,165	835	1,862
Steven Hunter		45	C	2004	2005	DePaul	348	227	13

J

Player	Ntn.	No.	Pos.	From	To	School	Pts	Rebs	Asts
Greg Jackson		24	PG	1975	1975	Guilford	174	67	93
Jim Jackson		21	SG	2005	2006	Ohio State	451	218	128
Casey Jacobsen		23	G/F	2002	2005	Stanford	1,046	351	208
Dennis Johnson		24	G	1980	1983	Pepperdine	4,140	1,108	1,048
Eddie Johnson		8	SF	1987	1990	Illinois	4,081	916	466
Frank Johnson		3	PG	1992	1994	Wake Forest	656	195	334
Gus Johnson		13	F	1972	1972	Idaho	163	136	31
Joe Johnson		2	G/F	2002	2005	Arkansas	3,847	1,189	968
Kevin Johnson		7	G	1988 2000	1998 2000	California	12,747	2,332	6,518
Linton Johnson		43	SF	2008	2008	Tulane	15	13	3
Neil Johnson		11	PF	1968	1970	Creighton	512	443	146
Charles Jones		34	PF	1984	1986	Louisville	854	587	180
Dwyane Jones		21	C/F	2010	2010	Saint Joseph's	0	2	0
James Jones		22	SF	2005	2007	Miami	1,184	429	102
Jumaine Jones		20	SF	2006	2007	Georgia	40	23	1

K

Player	Ntn.	No.	Pos.	From	To	School	Pts	Rebs	Asts
Rich Kelley		53	C/F	1980	1982	Stanford	1,339	1,056	625
Tim Kempton		8	F/C	1992	1994	Notre Dame	56	39	19
Steve Kerr		4	G	1988	1989	Arizona	54	17	24
Jason Kidd		32	PG	1996	2001	California	4,440	1,985	3,011
Joe Kleine		35	C	1993 1999	1997 1999	Arkansas	875	731	152
Brevin Knight		22	PG	2003	2003	Stanford	2	3	4
Negele Knight		32	PG	1990	1993	Dayton	899	181	448
Rod Knowles		23	F/C	1968	1969	Davidson	9	9	0
Joel Kramer		50	F	1978	1983	San Diego State	1,257	916	343

L

Player	Ntn.	No	Pos.	From	To	School	Pts	Rebs	Asts
Maciej Lampe		30	PF	2004	2005	Poland	140	76	10
Andrew Lang		28	C	1988	1992	Arkansas	1,350	1,267	100
Antonio Lang		21	SF	1994	1995	Duke	11	4	1
Dan Langhi		14	PF	2002	2003	Vanderbilt	183	87	21
Dave Lattin		43	F/C	1968	1969	UTEP	409	323	48
Gani Lawal		31	PF	2010	2011	Georgia Tech	0	0	0
Mo Layton		1	PG	1971	1973	USC	1,194	241	386
Ron Lee		30	PG	1976	1979	Oregon	2,260	666	700
Tim Legler		23	SG	1990	1990	La Salle	28	8	6
Randy Livingston		2	PG	1999	2000	LSU	393	132	173
Horacio Llamas		17	C	1997	1999	Grand Canyon	58	36	5
Ian Lockhart		51	PF	1990	1991	Tennessee	4	0	0
Luc Longley		13	C	1999	2000	New Mexico	791	544	122
Robin Lopez		15	C	2008	2012	Stanford	1,051	582	23
Maurice Lucas		20	PF	1982	1985	Marquette	3,306	2,081	567
Phil Lumpkin		10	PG	1975	1976	Miami (Ohio)	70	23	48

M

Player	Ntn.	No	Pos.	From	To	School	Pts	Rebs	Asts
Malcolm Mackey		27	F/C	1993	1994	Georgia Tech	32	24	1
Don MacLean		25	PF	1999	2000	UCLA	42	23	8
Kyle Macy		4	PG	1980	1985	Kentucky	4,180	923	1,555
Dan Majerle		9	G/F	1988 2001	1995 2002	Central Michigan	8,034	2,823	1,824
Danny Manning		15	F/C	1994	1999	Kansas	3,703	1,499	644
Stephon Marbury		3	PG	2001	2004	Georgia Tech	4,188	646	1,601
Shawn Marion		31	F	1999	2008	UNLV	12,134	6,616	1,332
Sean Marks		4	F/C	2006	2008	California	65	39	4
Bill Martin		26	SF	1987	1988	Georgetown	40	27	6
Walter McCarty		0	PF	2004	2005	Kentucky	98	61	11
Ted McClain		12	PG	1978	1979	Tennessee State	166	69	60
George McCloud		21	G/F	1997	1999	Florida State	884	380	163
John McCullough		8	PG	1981	1982	Oklahoma	21	4	3
Xavier McDaniel		35	SF	1990	1991	Wichita State	1,046	476	149
Antonio McDyess		34 14	PF	1997 2003	1998 2004	Alabama	1,363	751	122
Mike McGee		40	G/F	1989	1990	Michigan	102	36	16
Stan McKenzie		40	F/G	1968	1970	NYU	967	344	175
McCoy McLemore		34	F/C	1968	1969	Drake	367	168	50
Paul McPherson		23	SG	2000	2001	DePaul	112	48	16
Gary Melchionni		25	PG	1973	1975	Duke	1,074	329	298
Loren Meyer		40	C	1996	1998	Iowa State	188	96	12
Marko Milič		20	G/F	1997	1999	Slovenia	108	30	14
Oliver Miller		25 8	C	1992 1999	1994 2000	Arkansas	1,272	1,012	430
Otto Moore		34	C/F	1971	1972	Texas Pan–Am	614	540	88

						Am			
Ron Moore		53	C	1987	1988	West Virginia State	14	6	0
Chris Morris		34	SF	1998	1999	Auburn	184	121	23
Markieff Morris		11	PF	2011	**present**	Kansas			
Mike Morrison		32	G	1989	1990	Loyola Maryland	72	20	11
Jerrod Mustaf		0	F/C	1991	1994	Maryland	453	283	63

N

Player	Ntn.	No.	Pos.	From	To	School	Pts	Rebs	Asts
Larry Nance		22	F/C	1981	1988	Clemson	8,430	3,791	1,248
Steve Nash		13	PG	1996 2004	1998 2012	Santa Clara	9,940	2,107	6,333
Ed Nealy		45	PF	1988 1990	1989 1992	Kansas State	302	317	81
Mike Niles		40	F	1980	1981	Cal State Fullerton	115	58	15

O

Player	Ntn.	No.	Pos.	From	To	School	Pts	Rebs	Asts
Jimmy Oliver		11	G/F	1998	1999	Purdue	3	0	0
Jermaine O'Neal		20	C	2012	**Present**	Eau Claire (HS)			
Shaquille O'Neal		32	C	2008	2009	LSU	1,695	929	174
Bo Outlaw		45 46	PF	2001 2004	2003 2005	Houston	749	756	247
Jim Owens		45	F	1973	1975	Arizona State	177	52	64

P

Player	Ntn.	No.	Pos.	From	To	School	Pts	Rebs	Asts
Milt Palacio		10	PG	2001	2002	Colorado State	79	23	29
Smush Parker		1	PG	2004	2005	Fordham	15	3	4
Curtis Perry		18	F	1974	1978	Missouri State	2,746	2,269	495
Elliot Perry		2	PG	1993 2000	1996 2001	Memphis	1,734	368	946
Tim Perry		34	F/C	1988	1992	Temple	1,686	961	196
Wesley Person		11	SG	1994	1997	Auburn	2,939	814	366
Eric Piatkowski		52	G/F	2006	2008	Nebraska	66	21	14
Mickaël Piétrus		12	F/G	2010	2011	France	283	76	23
Ed Pinckney		54	F	1985	1987	Villanova	1,518	888	206
Charles Pittman		32	PF	1982	1986	Maryland	1,060	718	204
Ronnie Price		2	PG	2011	2012	Utah Valley			

R

Player	Ntn.	No	Pos.	From	To	School	Pts	Rebs	Asts
Kurt Rambis		31	F	1989	1993	Santa Clara	641	783	209
Joe Reaves		24	SF	1973	1974	Bethel	16	8	1
Michael Redd		22	SG	2012	2012	Ohio State			
Terrence Rencher		14	PG	1995	1996	Texas	3	2	0
Shawn Respert		2	SG	1998	1999	Michigan State	37	13	8
Jason Richardson		23	SG	2008	2011	Michigan State	2,672	776	289
Quentin Richardson		3	G/F	2004	2005	DePaul	1,176	479	158
Pat Riley		12	SG	1975	1976	Kentucky	278	47	57
Rick Robey		8	C/F	1983	1986	Kentucky	524	345	128
Cliff Robinson		30	F/C	1997	2001	Connecticut	4,775	1,330	759
Rumeal Robinson		20	PG	1996	1997	Michigan	36	7	8
Truck Robinson		21	PF	1978	1982	Tennessee State	4,789	2,505	566
Rodney Rogers		54	F	1999	2002	Wake Forest	2,757	1,047	422
Jalen Rose		8	G/F	2006	2007	Michigan	108	23	16
Trevor Ruffin		8	PG	1994	1995	Hawaii	233	23	48
Stefano Rusconi		51	C/F	1995	1996	Italy	8	6	3

S

Player	Ntn.	No	Pos.	From	To	School	Pts	Rebs	Asts
Mike Sanders		7 11	G/F	1983	1988	UCLA	2,40 5	798	379
Daniel Santiago	/	15 55	C	2000	2002	Saint Vincent	178	109	13
Fred Saunders		30	SF	1974	1976	Syracuse	480	290	93
Danny Schayes		24	C	1994	1995	Syracuse	303	208	89
Dale Schlueter		54	C	1976	1977	Colorado State	70	80	38
Alvin Scott		14	F/G	1977	1985	Oral Roberts	3,08 8	1,992	847
Charlie Scott		33	SG	1971	1975	North Carolina	5,16 3	860	1,103
Dennis Scott		4	SF	1997	1998	Georgia Tech	181	50	24
Paul Shirley		17	PF	2004	2005	Iowa State	12	2	3
John Shumate		34	F/C	1975	1976	Notre Dame	487	240	62
Paul Silas		29	F	1969	1972	Creighton	3,36 0	2,886	804
Garret Siler		20	C	2010	2012	Augusta State	45	28	3
Alvin Sims		19	G	1998	1999	Louisville	11	4	5
Courtney Sims		4	C	2008	2009	Michigan	0	0	0
Sean Singletary		14	PG	2008	2009	Virginia	34	16	12
Brian Skinner		54	F/C	2007	2008	Baylor	219	238	15
Tony Smith		14	SG	1995	1996	Marquette	189	56	86
Dick Snyder		10	F/G	1968	1970	Davidson	1,03 4	343	220
Ricky Sobers		4 40	G	1975	1977	UNLV	1,78 9	493	453
Alex Stivrins		11	F	1992	1993	Colorado	22	8	1
Amar'e Stoudemire		32 1	F/C	2002	2010	Cypress Creek (HS)	11,0 35	4,613	677
Paul Stovall		23	G	1972	1973	Arizona State	76	61	13
D. J. Strawberry		8	G	2007	2008	Maryland	73	28	30
Stromile Swift		4	PF	2008	2009	LSU	39	33	2
Aaron Swinson		4	SF	1994	1995	Auburn	24	8	3

T

Player	Ntn.	No.	Pos.	From	To	School	Pts	Rebs	Asts
Yuta Tabuse		1	PG	2004	2005	BYU-Hawaii	7	4	3
Fred Taylor		10	G/F	1970	1972	Texas Pan Am	314	103	58
Sebastian Telfair		31	PG	2011	**present**	Abraham Lincoln (HS)			
Ira Terrell		32	F/C	1976	1977	Southern Methodist	665	387	103
David Thirdkill		40	F/G	1982	1983	Bradley	194	72	36
Joe Thomas		40	F	1970	1971	Marquette	55	43	17
Kurt Thomas		40	F/C	2005	2007	TCU	763	794	81
Tim Thomas		2	SF	2005	2006	Villanova	287	127	18
Bernard Thompson		7	F/G	1985	1988	Fresno State	819	248	201
Brooks Thompson		4	G	1997	1998	Texas A&M	26	5	3
Dijon Thompson		1	G/F	2005	2006	UCLA	28	11	1
Wayman Tisdale		23	PF	1994	1997	Oklahoma	1,668	581	123
Sedric Toney		15	PG	1985	1986	Dayton	75	23	26
Cezary Trybański		15	C	2003	2004	Poland	0	1	0
Jake Tsakalidis	/	25	C	2000	2003	Georgia	908	737	55
Nikoloz Tskitishvili		15	F/C	2005	2006	Georgia	33	20	3
Alando Tucker		29	SF	2007	2010	Wisconsin	203	46	15
P.J. Tucker		17	SF	2012	**present**	Texas			
Hedo Türkoğlu		19	F	2010	2010	Turkey	237	100	58

V

Player	Ntn.	No.	Pos.	From	To	School	Pts	Rebs	Asts
Dick Van Arsdale		5	G/F	1968	1977	Indiana	12,060	2,452	2,396
Tom Van Arsdale		4	G/F	1976	1977	Indiana	444	184	67
Nick Vanos		30	C	1985	1987	Santa Clara	222	240	59
Jake Voskuhl		43	C	2001	2005	Connecticut	1,062	910	128
Jackson Vroman	/	4	F/C	2004	2005	Iowa State	16	13	7

W

Player	Ntn.	No	Pos.	From	To	School	Pts	Rebs	Asts
Neal Walk		41	C	1969	1974	Florida	6,010	3,637	966
John Wallace		22	SF	2001	2002	Syracuse	231	85	29
Bob Warlick		23	G/F	1968	1969	Pepperdine	507	151	131
Hakim Warrick		21	PF	2010	2012	Syracuse	669	296	69
Jeff Webb		10	G	1971	1972	Kansas State	67	17	16
Walt Wesley		31	C	1972	1973	Kansas	144	113	24
Mark West		41	C	1987 1999	1994 2000	Old Dominion	3,761	3,241	231
Paul Westphal		44	G	1975 1983	1980 1984	USC	9,564	1,002	2,429
John Wetzel		25	F/G	1970 1975	1972 1976	Virginia Tech	481	256	189
Jahidi White		55	F/C	2003	2004	Georgetown	261	261	7
Rory White		7	PF	1982	1984	South Alabama	486	167	44
Earl Williams		55	C/F	1974	1975	Winston-Salem	371	456	95
Hot Rod Williams		18	F/C	1995	1998	Tulane	1,251	1,246	211
Micheal Williams		21	PG	1989	1990	Baylor	5	1	4
Scott Williams		47	F/C	2002	2004	North Carolina	390	265	28
George Wilson		21	C	1968	1969	Cincinnati	475	505	76
David Wood		10	F	1995	1996	Nevada	4	5	2

Y

Player	Ntn.	No	Pos.	From	To	School	Pts	Rebs	Asts
Michael Young		43	F/G	1984	1985	Houston	4	2	0

APPENDIX

IX

COACHES AND THEIR RECORDS

WLGC %

1	Johnny Kerr	1968-1969	31	89	120	.258
2	Jerry Colangelo*	1970	44	24	20	.545
3	Cotton Fitzsimmons	1970–1972	164	97	67	.591
4	Butch van Breda Kolff	1972	7	3	4	.429
—	Jerry Colangelo*	1972–1973	75	35	40	.467
5	John MacLeod	1973–1987	1122	579	543	.516
6	Dick Van Arsdale*	1987	26	14	12	.538
7	John Wetzel*	1987–1988	82	28	54	.341
—	Cotton Fitzsimmons	1988–1992	328	217	111	.662
8	Paul Westphal	1992–1996	279	191	88	.685
—	Cotton Fitzsimmons	1996	49	27	22	.551
9	Danny Ainge*	1996–1999	226	136	90	.602
10	Scott Skiles	1999–2002	195	116	79	.595
11	Frank Johnson*	2002–2003	134	63	71	.470
12	Mike D'Antoni	2003–2008	389	253	136	.650
13	Terry Porter	2008–2009	51	28	23	.549
14	Alvin Gentry	2009–present	195	112	83	.574

APPENDIX

X

SUNS SEASON RESULTS

WL%

Season	Team	W	L	WL%	Finish	Division	W	L	%	Result
2011-2012	Phoenix	33	33	.500	3rd	Pacific Division	-	-	-	DNQ
2010-11	Phoenix	40	42	.488	2nd	Pacific Division	-	-	-	DNQ
2009-10	Phoenix	54	28	.659	2nd	Pacific Division	10	6	.625	Lost West Conf Finals
2008-09	Phoenix	46	36	.561	2nd	Pacific Division	-	-	-	DNQ
2007-08	Phoenix	55	27	.671	2nd	Pacific Division	1	4	.200	Lost West Conf 1st Rd
2006-07	Phoenix	61	21	.744	1st	Pacific Division	6	5	.545	Lost West Conf Semis
2005-06	Phoenix	54	28	.659	1st	Pacific Division	10	10	.500	Lost West Conf Finals
2004-05	Phoenix	62	20	.756	1st	Pacific Division	9	6	.600	Lost West Conf Finals
2003-04	Phoenix	29	53	.354	6th	Pacific Division	-	-	-	DNQ
2002-03	Phoenix	44	38	.537	4th	Pacific Division	2	4	.333	Lost West Conf 1st Rd
2001-02	Phoenix	36	46	.439	6th	Pacific Division	-	-	-	DNQ
2000-01	Phoenix	51	31	.622	3rd	Pacific Division	1	3	.250	Lost West Conf 1st Rd
1999-00	Phoenix	53	29	.646	3rd	Pacific Division	4	5	.444	Lost West Conf Semis
1998-99 *	Phoenix	27	23	.540	3rd	Pacific Division	0	3	.000	Lost West Conf 1st Rd
1997-98	Phoenix	56	26	.683	3rd	Pacific Division	1	3	.250	Lost West Conf 1st Rd
1996-97	Phoenix	40	42	.488	4th	Pacific Division	2	3	.400	Lost West Conf 1st Rd
1995-96	Phoenix	41	41	.500	4th	Pacific Division	1	3	.250	Lost West Conf 1st Rd
1994-95	Phoenix	59	23	.720	1st	Pacific Division	6	4	.600	Lost West Conf Semis
1993-94	Phoenix	56	26	.683	2nd	Pacific Division	6	4	.600	Lost West Conf Semis
1992-93	Phoenix	62	20	.756	1st	Pacific Division	13	11	.542	**Lost NBA Finals**
1991-92	Phoenix	53	29	.646	3rd	Pacific Division	4	4	.500	Lost West Conf Semis
1990-91	Phoenix	55	27	.671	3rd	Pacific Division	1	3	.250	Lost West Conf 1st Rd
1989-90	Phoenix	54	28	.659	3rd	Pacific Division	9	7	.563	Lost West Conf Finals
1988-89	Phoenix	55	27	.671	2nd	Pacific Division	7	5	.583	Lost West Conf Finals

Season	Team	W	L	Pct	Finish	Division	W	L	Pct	Result
1987-88	Phoenix	28	54	.341	4th	Pacific Division	-	-	-	DNQ
1986-87	Phoenix	36	46	.439	5th	Pacific Division	-	-	-	DNQ
1985-86	Phoenix	32	50	.390	3rd	Pacific Division	-	-	-	DNQ
1984-85	Phoenix	36	46	.439	3rd	Pacific Division	0	3	.000	Lost West Conf 1st Rd
1983-84	Phoenix	41	41	.500	4th	Pacific Division	9	8	.529	Lost West Conf Finals
1982-83	Phoenix	53	29	.646	2nd	Pacific Division	1	2	.333	Lost West Conf 1st Rd
1981-82	Phoenix	46	36	.561	3rd	Pacific Division	2	5	.286	Lost West Conf Semis
1980-81	Phoenix	57	25	.695	1st	Pacific Division	3	4	.429	Lost West Conf Semis
1979-80	Phoenix	55	27	.671	3rd	Pacific Division	3	5	.375	Lost West Conf Semis
1978-79	Phoenix	50	32	.610	2nd	Pacific Division	9	6	.600	Lost West Conf Finals
1977-78	Phoenix	49	33	.598	2nd	Pacific Division	0	2	.000	Lost West Conf 1st Rd
1976-77	Phoenix	34	48	.415	5th	Pacific Division	-	-	-	DNQ
1975-76	Phoenix	42	40	.512	3rd	Pacific Division	10	9	.526	**Lost NBA Finals**
1974-75	Phoenix	32	50	.390	4th	Pacific Division	-	-	-	DNQ
1973-74	Phoenix	30	52	.366	4th	Pacific Division	-	-	-	DNQ
1972-73	Phoenix	38	44	.463	3rd	Pacific Division	-	-	-	DNQ
1971-72	Phoenix	49	33	.598	3rd	Midwest Division	-	-	-	DNQ
1970-71	Phoenix	48	34	.585	3rd	Midwest Division	-	-	-	DNQ
1969-70	Phoenix	39	43	.476	3rd	Western Division	3	4	.429	Lost West Div Semis
1968-69	Phoenix	16	66	.195	7th	Western Division	-	-	-	DNQ

BIBLIOGRAPHICAL SOURCES

On the Phoenix Suns' early history see the brilliant book, Joe Gilmartin, **The Little Team That Could And Darn Near Did!** (Phoenix, 1976). This is an early history of the Suns' organization put out by the team. This book is filled with priceless anecdotes and it is beautifully written. For the NBA lockout see Seth Pollack, "NBA Free Agency: Phoenix Suns Stifled By Lockout But Have Options," **SB Nation**, June 27, 2011 http://arizona.sbnation.com/phoenix-suns/2011/6/27/2246607/ nba-free-agency-phoenix-suns-stifled-by-lockout-but-have-options Also see Paul Coro, "Phoenix Suns In Transition As Possible NBA Lockout Looms," **AZ Central.com**, April 7, 2011 http://www.azcentral.com/ sports/suns/articles/2011/04/07/20110407phoenix-suns-transition- nba-lockout.html On the lockout and strike, see Lacy J. Banks, "NBA's 66 Game Schedule Is Definitely Hectic," **Chicago Sun Times**, November 27, 2011; Sean Gregory, "The NBA Lockout And The Economy: An Overstated Impact," **Time**, November 7, 2011 and Howard Beck, "Two Exhibition Games For N. B. A. Teams," **The New York Times**, November 28, 2011

For Joe Proski, the first trainer's comments on training camp fun times, see, "Suns' Trainer A Wealth of Phoenix Anecdotes," **The Spokesman Review**, October 25, 1982 http://news.google.com/news papers?nid=1314&dat=19821025&id=tvlLAAAAIBAJ&sjid=2e4DAAA AIBAJ&pg=7016,4518831 Also on Proski's observations see, "One-On-One With Joe Proski," http://www.nba.com/suns/interactive/proski

transcript_010329.html For thirty two seasons Proski administered his training magic to 196 players. On John MacLeod see, Paul Coro, "John MacLeod Added Stability To Helm Of Phoenix Suns," **The Arizona Republic**, February 2,5 2012.

For a cranky and unfair assessment of Robert Sarver during the lockout see Seth Pollack, "Robert Sarver Rapidly Destroying 43 Years of Phoenix Suns Goodwill," **Arizona SBNation**, October 5, 2011 http://arizona.sbnation.com/phoenix-suns/2011/10/5/2470872/robert-sarver-phoenix-suns-nba-lockout An even nastier attack on Sarver which lacks research and credibility is in the following website http://politicomafioso.blogspot.com/2012/06/liberal-loser-robert-sarver drafts_28.html When he bought the team, Sarver had an open door policy with reporters. He as become a bit more careful over the years as a number of reporters have turned on him. No one is nastier toward Sarver than **Sports Illustrated** writer Jack McCallum. For a conversation with McCallum about his book and some excellent quotes and conclusions, see "Jack McCallum Talks Phoenix Suns," http://espn.go.com/blog/truehoop/post/_/id/2619/jack-mccallum-talks-phoenix-suns

The D'Antoni New York Knicks coaching debacle and how it impact perceptions of D'Antoni is analyzed in Jack McCallum, "Mike D'Antoni On Knicks Resignation: 'An Obstacle had To Be Removed,'" **Sports Illustrated**, May 21, 2012 http://sportsillustrated.cnn.com/2012/writers/jack_mccallum/05/21/dantoni.knicks/index.html

The Nash-D'Antoni relationship is examined in Derek Page, "Did Steve Nash Make Mike D'Antoni?" **Hoops World http://www.hoopsworld.com/did-steve-nash-make-mike-dantoni/**

For the 2012 draft see Dan Bickley "Suns Are Hoping Luck Falls Their Way," **The Arizona Republic**, May 30, 2012, p. C 1, 7 and for Lance Blanks front office role and plans for the team, see, Paul Coro, "Phoenix Suns New GM Lance Blanks Wants To Take 'Great' To Greater," **Arizona Republic**, August 25, 2010. Bickley and Coro are excellent beat writers, and Bickley is a great columnist. At times, they both want to run the team. Fortunately, Robert Sarver, Lon Babby, Lance Blanks and Mark West are still in charge. For the Phoenix Suns GM and his explanation of the needed in-depth changes on the roster and within the organization see, Dan Devine, "Phoenix Suns GM Lance Blanks Likes Luis Scola Because He Is Gross," **Bleacher report**, August 15, 2012 http://bleacherreport.com/tb/d8dLY?utm_source=newsletter&utm_medium=newsletter&utm_campaign=phoenix-suns and also see the article by Dan Devine, "Phoenix Suns GM Lance Blanks Takes A Hard View Of Human Existence," **Yahoo! Sports**, June 28, 2012 http://bleacherreport.com/tb/d8dLY?utm_source=newsletter&utm_medium=newsletter&utm_campaign=phoenix-suns For a conversation with Blanks see, "Chat With Cavaliers Assistant General Manager Lance Blanks," **Sports Nation**, **http://espn.go.com/sportsnation/chat//id/9357**

For Blanks extensive and insightful comments on the 2012-2103 roster see, Paul Coro, "Phoenix Suns Focus On Young Roster," **AzCentral.Com**, August 27, 2012 http://www.azcentral.com/sports/heatindex/articles/20120827phoenix-suns-focus-young-roster.html Also see the excellent and highly analytical article by Dan Bickley, "Phoenix Suns' Future In Lance Blanks; Hands," **The Arizona Republic**, June 27, 2012 http://www.azcentral.com/sports/suns/articles/2012/06/27/20120627phoenix-suns-future-lance-banks-hands.html Also see the analytical and in-depth article on Blank by Paul Coro, "Presiding Theme Is Commitment," **The Arizona Republic**, August 14, 2012 http://www.azcentral.com/arizonarepublic/sports/articles/2012/08/14/20120814phoenix-suns-presiding-theme-commitment.html

For Gregg Popovich's impact upon Lance Blanks development see, J. A. Adande, "Gregg Popovich's Portable Program," **ESPN NBA**, May 5, 2012 http://espn.go.com/nba/playoffs/2012/story//page/Adande-120504/nba-playoffs-gregg-popovich-spurs-effect

Rich Wolfe with Al McCoy, **The Real McCoy** (Phoenix, n. d.) is a great read about the Suns long time announcer. See Chris Ballard, **The Art of A Beautiful Game: The Thinking Fans Tour of the NBA** (New York, 2009), pp. 93-108 for material on Steve Nash. See David Wolf, **The Connie Hawkins Story** (New York, 1972) and Rodger Citron, "Foul!: An Appreciation, Revisiting The Classic Basketball Book On Its 40th Anniversary, **Far Post**, August 2, 2012 http://www.slamonline.com/online/nba/2012/08/foul-the-connie-hawkins-story-an-appreciation/

For Nash leaving the Suns see, Paola Boivin, "No, Not L. A., **The Arizona Republic**, July 5, 2012, pp. 1A, 8A and Paul Coro, "Over And Out: Nash Era With Suns Comes To A Close With Deal To Lakers," **The Arizona Republic**, July 5, 2012, pp. C1, C3. Also see, Mike Bresnahan, "The Two Time MVP Wanted To Come To LA," **The Los Angeles Times**, July 5, 22012, CI, C7, Bill Plaschke, and "This Is A Great Move And Now For The Next One" **The Los Angeles Times**, July 5, 2012, p. C1, C7. Both articles congratulate the Lakers and treat the Suns like they are country bumpkins. Both articles suggest that Nash's signing cleared the way for a Dwight Howard trade. Time will tell. **The Arizona Republic** accorded the Nash signing a front page story and also the front of the sports page. Phoenix fans were clearly surprised and most of them were upset. The outcry against owner Robert Sarver was contrary to the facts. At least the good business facts, if not the emotional ones Sarver did everything he could to grant Nash's wish to join the Los Angeles Lakers. Most people didn't buy this explanation.

.For Nash's agent view of the Phoenix Suns and how the trade took place and the logistics behind it, see, Paul Coro, "Steve Nash's Agent Describes How Phoenix Suns Trade With Los Angeles Lakers Went Down," **The Arizona Republic**, July 6, 2012 http://www.azcentral.com/arizonarepublic/sports/articles/2012/07/05/20120705steve-nash-phoenix-suns-los-angeles-lakers-trade-turn-of-events.html For Nash's reaction to signing with the Lakers see Greg Beacham, "Steve Nash Elaborates On Reasons He Chose Lakers," **SF Gate**, July 5, 2012 http://www.sfgate.com/sports/article/Steve-Nash-elaborates-on-reasons-he-chose-Lakers-3686855.php Also see, Mark Whacker, "In Steve Nash, L. A. Lakers Will Make Many Components Better," **Orange County Register**, July 7, 2012 http://www.newsobserver.com/2012/07/07/2185829/in-nash-the-lakers-will-make-many.html On Nash's training see "Nash And Celebrini-Keys To The Success of the Phoenix Suns," **Sportmedbc** **http://sportmedbc.com/news/nash-and-celebrini---keys-success-phoenix-suns** and Stefan Swiat, "Steve Nash's MVP Workout," http://www.nba.com/suns/news/mvpworkout_071107.html

On the legacy of Steve Nash see, Paul Coro, "Steve Nash Leaves Legacy of Revamping Phoenix Suns Franchise," **The Arizona Republic**, July 7, 2012 http://www.azcentral.com/arizonarepublic/sports/articles/2012/07/07/20120707steve-nash-leaves-legacy-revamping-phoenix-suns-franchise.html For Don Nelson's remarks on Nash and what he meant to this legendary coach, see Tom Tolbert, "Don Nelson Proud of Resume, Happy To Be In Hall, **San Francisco Chronicle**, April 1, 2012 http://www.sfgate.com/sports/article/Don-Nelson-proud-of-resume-happy-to-be-in-Hall-3450538.php

On access to the Suns organization, see the excellent article by Paul Coro, "Phoenix Suns Capitalize On Suns Intimacy," **The Arizona Republic**, May 31, 2012. On the Suns' draft picks including successes, failures and maybe selections, see Paul Coro, "A Look Back At The Phoenix Suns' Draft History," **The Arizona Republic**, June 17, 2012 http://

www.azcentral.com/sports/heatindex/articles/20120617look-back-phoenix-suns-nba-draft-history.html

For in depth view of the 2012 draft selection and the process of selection, see Paul Coro, "Phoenix Suns Draft PG Kendall Marshall With 13th Pick In NBA Draft," **The Arizona Republic**, June 29, 2012. For Marshall's struggles early in the 2012-2013 season see Bob Young, "Marshall Having Tough Time Adjusting to Bench," **The Arizona Republic**, November 22, 2012, p. C1, C

On Lance Blanks philosophy, see, Dan Devine, "Phoenix Suns GM Lance Blanks Takes A Hard View Of Human Existence," **Yahoo! sports**, June 28, 2012 http://sports.yahoo.com/blogs/nba-ball-dont-lie/phoenix-suns-gm-lance-blanks-takes-hard-view-171621943—nba.html Kristofer Habbas, "Lunch With Lance: Blanks Lays Out Phoenix suns Plans For Draft..Sort Of," **SB Nation**, June 4, 2012. Chris Broussard, "Suns Hire Lance Blanks As GM," **ESPN The Magazine**, August 6, 2010 http://sports.espn.go.com/nba/news/story?id=5441283

See Elliott Kalb, **Who's Better, Who's Best In Basketball** (New York, 2004) pp. 195-203 for a summary of Charles Barkley's talent. Also see Charles Barkley and Roy Johnson, Jr., **Outrageous** (New York, 1991) for Barkley's view of his life and Charles Barkley and Michael Wilbon, **I May Be Wrong But I Doubt It: Some Things I've Learned So Far** (New York, 2002)

See Paul Coro, "Phoenix Suns: Free Agency Pursuits Open with Michael Beasley, Eric Gordon," **The Arizona Republic**, July 1, 2102.

On Alvin Gentry see Paul Coro, "Home-Grown Humility, Dedication," **The Arizona Republic**, October 25, 2009. On Gentry's career see, for example, **Chicago Sun Times**, April 29, 1998, p. 124; **Detroit Free Press**, April 29, 1998, p. D1, May 8, 1998, p. C1; **Detroit News**, February 3, 1998, p. E5, April 19, 1998, p. D1, April 29, 1998, pp. D1, D3, May 7, 1999, p. F1, September 15, 1999, p. D1. See Mark Bonavita, et. al., editors, **The Sporting News Official NBA Register: 1998-199 Edition** (The Sporting News, 1999) for information on Gentry. For a recent view of Gentry see, T. J. Simers, "Phoenix Coach Alvin Gentry Is A Normal Guy, And That's Not Average," **The Los Angeles Times**, January 10, 2012. For Gentry ripping the Suns in 2012 for lax play, see, Sean Deveney, "Phoenix Suns Coach Alvin Gentry Rips Team To Media After Loss," **The Sporting News**, February 23, 2012. On Gentry's deserving contract extension see the brilliant analysis by Dan Bickley, "Gentry Caught Between Clashing Agenda Inside Planet Orange," **The Arizona Republic**,

November 14, 2012 http://mail.aol.com/37185-111/aol-6/en-us/Suite.aspx

On Terry Porter see, Paul Coro, "Terry Porter Hoping For Redemption After Suns Stay," **The Arizona Republic**, March 3, 2102. For Porter's transgressions see, for example, Paul Coro, "Gentry In, Porter Out For Suns, **The Arizona Republic**, February 16, 2009 http://www.azcentral.com/sports/suns/articles/2009/02/15/20090215spt-sunsporter.html The Terry Porter era was the worst few months in recent Suns history. Porter is a person of high character. He is simply a lousy coach. The Milwaukee Buck as their head coach fired him after finishing two seasons and the reasons were the same ones. He is an uncompromising disciplinarian. The Suns should have investigated his coaching practices in more detail. But he was Steve Kerr's buddy.

See Paul Coro, "Sun Is Setting On Colangelo Era," **The Arizona Republic**. July 1, 2012, p. C 6. Also see Dan Bickley, "Suns Need To Move On, Rebuild As High Flying Nash Era Winds Down," **The Arizona Republic**, July 1, 2012, p .C1, C6. This article is a precursor to the end of the Steve Nash-Grant Hill dynasty. On Nash and Hill, see, for example, Nick Fasulo, "Steve Nash Trade: Grant Hill Could Follow To Los Angeles," **SB Nation**, July 4, 2012 http://www.sbnation.com/nba/2012/7/4/3137986/steve-nash-trade-grant-hill-could-follow-to-los-angeles; Melissa Rohlin, "The Clippers' Acquisition of Grant Hill Sparks Various Reactions," **The Los Angeles Times**, July 20, 2012 http://articles.latimes.com/2012/jul/20/sports/la-sp-sn-grant-hills-decision-to-come-to-the-clippers-has-sparked-varied-reactions-20120720

For the Tim Donaghy scandal see, Sean Patrick Griffin, **Gaming The Game: The Story Behind The NBA Betting Scandal and The Gambler Who Made It Happen** (New York, 2011). Also see Tim Donaghy, **Personal Foul: A First Person Account Of the Scandal That Rocked the NBA** (Sarasota 2009). What is weird about this book is that the publishing company, Four Daughters, is obviously Donaghy's. The analysis gets even stranger when Donaghy indicts most other officials for honesty. He claims that they have tendencies that the players and coaches can figure out. So Donaghy says that they are helping the gamblers by being themselves. Am I missing something in his explanation? There is only one mention of a Phoenix Suns player. When Donaghy victimizes former Suns' great Charles Barkley in his book for having a difficult personality, there is very little evidence to back this claim. This is typical of Donaghy who doesn't blame himself for his predicament. The cheap shots that

Donaghy takes at Barkley suggest his level of integrity. The Suns' fans are still waiting for the real story. The little weasel will never tell it. Don't worry the real story is still to be told, but stay tuned.

On Donaghy's post jail life and the question of gambling, see Kurt Mensching, "Former NBA Referee Tim Donaghy Still A Gamblin' Man," **SB Nation**, November 4, 2012 http://www.sbnation.com/nba/2012/11/4/3597608/tim-donaghy-nba-ref-gambling

See Pat Jordan, "After The Buzzer," **The New York Times Magazine**, January 7, 2011 for a view of Donaghy's life and what was left of his future as he was released from prison http://www.nytimes.com/2011/01/09/magazine/09FOB-Encounter-t.html?_r=0 Also see Jeff Garcia, "Ex-NBA Referee Donaghy Talks 2007 Spurs-Suns Series," **Project Spurs**, June 27, 2011 http://www.projectspurs.com/2011-articles/june/ex-referee-donaghey-talks-2007-spurs-suns-series.html

On Cheryl Wolfe-Ruiz in Phoenix and her connection to referee Tim Donaghy and his activities in the Valley of the Sun and elsewhere, see, for example, Jana Winter and Dan Managan, "Dirty Ref's Sideline Gal Eyed By Feds," **The New York Post**, August 27, 2007 http://www.nypost.com/p/news/national/item_kW509WacNrGg3MYaWIqXSJ

On the Suns' training staff see the in depth article Michael Schwartz, "The Secret Behind The Phoenix Suns' Elite Training Staff," **Valley of The Suns**, April 5, 2012 http://valleyofthesuns.com/2012/04/05/secret-behind-phoenix-suns-elite-training-staff/ Also see, Henry Abbott, "The Secrets of The Suns Training Staff," **ESPN NBA** http://espn.go.com/blog/truehoop/post/_/id/40143/the-secrets-of-the-suns-training-staff An excellent overview of Nelson's achievements, the methods used by the Phoenix Suns and it impact is Seth Pollack, "Phoenix Suns Trainer Aaron Nelson Named Athletic Trainer of the Year," **SB Nation**, September 18, 2009 http://www.brightsideofthesun.com/2009/9/18/1036946/phoenix-suns-trainer-aaron-nelson

On Mark West see, Thomas R. Garrett and Clay Shampoe, **Old Dominion University Men's Basketball** (Charleston, 2007), chapter 5 and Paul Coro, "Phoenix Suns: Mark West To Represent Team At NBA Draft Lottery," **The Arizona Republic**, May 11, 2011. Also see Paul Coro, "Phoenix Suns' Presiding Them Is Commitment," **The Arizona Republic**, August 14, 2012 http://www.azcentral.com/sports/suns/articles/2012/08/14/20120814phoenix-suns-presiding-theme-commitment.html for West's importance in player development.

378

For free agency, see, for example, "Suns Withdraw Qualifying Offer to Aaron Brooks," **Yahoo! Sports**, July 7, 2012 http://sports.yahoo.com/news/suns-withdraw-qualifying-offer-aaron-234733870—nba.html for the glut of point guards. On the Eric Gordon contract and why didn't work, see Chris Broussard, "Eric Gordon, Suns Agree on Contract," **ESPN NBA**, July 4, 2012 http://espn.go.com/nba/story/_/id/8128612/2012-nba-free-agency-eric-gordon-phoenix-suns-agree-max-salary-deal Also see Stefan Swiat, "Five Things You Don't Know About Jermaine O'Neal," **Blog.Suns.Com**, August 20, 2012 http://blog.suns.com/2012/08/6431/ for a thoughtful analysis of what O'Neal brings to the table.

On the NBA and moneyball using academic computer models with a statistical emphasis, see Adam Smith, "Can USC Researchers Change the NBA Through Science?" **USC News** http://news.usc.edu/#!/article/35821/moneyball-for-basketball-using-science-to-change-the-nba/ For Jeremy Lin as a moneyball player see, "A 'Moneyball' Statistician Predicted Jeremy Lin's Success," http://q-ontech.blogspot.com/2012/02/statistician-predicted-jeremy-lin.html This prediction took place in may 2010 when Professor Qaissaunee predicted Lin's emergence as an effective NBA point guard.

Also see Michael Lewis, **Moneyball** (New York, 2003). The concept of moneyball has become a part of most professional sports franchises and in a few colleges. There is still skepticism as to whether it translates into basketball. On the use of the amnesty rule on Josh Childress and how it impacted the Suns, see, Craig Grialou, "Josh Childress: I'm Not Upset At All," **Arizona Sports**, July 16, 2012 http://arizonasports.com/41/1559581/Josh-Childress-Im-not-upset-at-all

For Cotton Fitzsimmons problems with Pete Maravich see, Mark Kriegel, **Pistol: The Life of Pete Maravich** (New York, 2008), pp. 220-230.

There are some strange Phoenix Suns books not worth the price, see, for example, Aaron Frisch, **Phoenix Suns** (Phoenix, 2007) for thirty-two pages on the team. Also see, Steve Silverman, **The Story of the Phoenix Suns (NBA A History of Hoops)** (Creative Education, 2010) for a forty-eight page kids book.

A serious basketball book that helped this tome is David Halberstam, **The Breaks of The Game** (New York, 2009), which examines the Portland Trail Blazers 1979 season before big money changed the game.

On Dan Majerle as a coach and businessman, see, Paul Coro, "Phoenix Suns Legend Dan Majerle Loves Coaching," **The Arizona Re-**

public, February 3, 2011 http://www.azcentral.com/sports/suns/articles/2011/02/03/20110203phoenix-suns-dan-majerle-coaching.html

On the Barkley-Majerle friendship and the years behind it as well as their mutual respect, see "To Majerle, Barkley Is A Special Friend," September 8, 2006 http://www.azcentral.com/sports/columns/articles/0908boivin0908.html Also see Greg Esposito, "Dan Majerle Is Still A Valley Favorite," **Arizona Sports.com**, March 28, 2011 http://arizonasports.com/?nid=41&sid=1397649 On Majerle's first three year contract and its provisions and guarantees with the Suns see Mike Huguenin, **OrlandoSentinelhttp://arizonasports.com/?nid=41&sid=139764**

See Shaquille O'Neal with Jackie MacMullan, **Shaq Uncut: My Story** (New York, 2011) for his comments on the Suns. Shaq added a great deal to the Suns' box office and he was a team player. He followed what the coach wanted to a letter.

On Elston Turner's hiring see Paul Coro, "Phoenix Suns Hire Elston Turner As New Defensive Assistant Coach," **The Arizona Republic**, July 11, 2011. After a dozen games in the 2102-20123 season Turner's defense was analyzed see Paul Coro, "Defensive Woes Mount When Suns' Lose Focus, **The Arizona Republic**, November 27,2912, p.C 3.

On Channing Frye see Mark Hester, "Channing Frye Will Keep Honeymoon Short," **The Portland Oregonian**, August 17, 2009. When he signed with the Suns, Frye was elated, see Stefan Swiat, "Frye Returns Home To Play For Suns," **NBA.com**, July 14, 3009 http://www.nba.com/suns/news/frye_signs_090714.html Also see Paul Coro, "Channing Frye Selected For 3-Point Shootout," **The Arizona Republic**, January 31, 2010 http://www.azcentral.com/sports/suns/articles/2010/01/31/20100131spt-suns-channing-frye-three-point-contest.html For Frye's medical condition, see Paul Coro, "Channing Frye Says He'll Likely To Miss The Upcoming Season With An Enlarged Hart,"" **AZcentral.com**, September 20, 2012 http://www.azcentral.com/sports/suns/articles/20120920phoenix-suns-channing-frye-enlarged-heart.html

For Goran Dragic's strange NBA path and his future, see Jacob Padilla, "The Curious Career of Goran Dragic: How Good Will He Be For The Phoenix Suns?" http://www.brightsideofthesun.com/2012/8/21/3256122/the-curious-career-of-goran-dragic-how-good-will-he-be-for-the-suns Also see Loren Jorgensen, "Utah Jazz: Little Known Dragic Enjoys Career Night For Suns," **Deseret News**, January 26, 2010 http://www.deseretnews.com/article/705361116/Utah-Jazz-Little-known-Dragic-enjoys-career-night-for-Suns.html For Dragic during the NBA lockout, see Ben Golliver, "Goran Dragic Signs With Caja Laboral In Spain," **CBS Sports**, November 19, 2011 http://www.cbssports.com/mcc/blogs/entry/22748484/33388324

For the up and down NBA career of Sebastian Telfair see, Craig Meyer, "The Curious Case of Sebastian Telfair: From NYC Phenomenon to NBA Bust," **Bleacher Report**, August 5, 2009 http://bleacherreport.com/articles/230844-the-curious-case-of-sebastian-telfair-from-nyc-phenom-to-nba-bust Also see, Ian O'Connor, **The Jump: Sebastian Telfair And The High-Stakes Business of High School Ball** (New York, 2005). As the 2012-2013 season began Telfair was injured but looked to play an important back up role at point guard, see Sarah McLellan, "Suns' Guard Telfair Dealing With 'Knickknack' Injuries," **The Arizona Republic**, October 17, 2012, p. C3. For Telfair's Adidas shoe deal and the pressures on him during his days at Abraham Lincoln High School, see Darren Rovell, "Telfair Signs Multiyear Deal With Adidas," **Sports Business**, May 6, 2004 http://sports.espn.go.com/espn/sportsbusiness/news/story?id=1794856 On Telfair's new found defensive skills see Paul Coro, "Telfair, Tucker Carrying Heavy Load Defensively," **The Arizona Republic**, December 18, 2012, p. C2.

On the Suns 2012 playoff hopes and injuries that derailed that drive see, Alex Laugan, "Injuries Hurting Suns' Playoff Push," **Bright Side of the Road**, April 22, 2012 http://www.brightsideofthesun.com/2012/4/22/2966558/injuries-hurting-phoenix-suns-playoff-push

See Rod Hundley with Tom McEachin, **Hot Rod Hundley: You Gotta Love It Baby** (Champaign, 2008) for his experiences as a Suns broadcaster. Also, see Mike Furfari, "Hot Rod Hundley Still Going Strong," **West Virginian Times, June 10, 2008. http://www.apbr.org/forum/viewtopic.php?t=1649** and the in-depth personal look into his life by Kathleen Gage, "Hot Rod Hundley: The Man With A Lot To Smile About," http://www.albaspectrum.com/Articles1/Sport/500/00466.html

On Steve Albert's hiring and his intriguing background see, Paul Coro, "Phoenix Suns Hire Play-By-Play Announcer Steve Albert," **The Arizona Republic**, July 27, 2012 http://www.azcentral.com/sports/suns/articles/20120727phoenix-suns-hire-play-by-play-announcer-steve-albert.html On Gary Bender's retirement, his extensive media skills and his place in the pantheon of Suns media personalities, see Bob Young, "Suns Broadcaster Gary Bender Announces Retirement," **The Arizo-**

na **Republic**, march 28, 2011 http://www.azcentral.com/sports/suns/ articles/2011/03/28/20110328suns-broadcaster-bender-announces-retirement.html

See Leonard Koppett, **24 Seconds to Shoot: An Informal History of the National Basketball Association** (New York, 1968) for the league history as the Suns entered the NBA.

For Grant Hill =see, **The New York Times**, September 30, 1994 for his rookie contract. Jalen Rose's egregious comments are highlighted and analyzed in a brilliant and thoughtful article by Jason Reid, "Jalen Rose's Comments On Race in ESPN Documentary Are Misguided," **The Washington Post, March 12, 2011** http://www.washingtonpost.com/sports/jalen-roses-comments-on-race-in-espn-documentary-are-misguided/2011/03/12/ABFHbLS_story.html

On Hill's tenure with the Suns, see, for example, Chad Ford, "Hill To Sign With Phoenix After Agreeing to Two Year Deal," **ESPN NBA**, July 6, 2007 http://sports.espn.go.com/nba/news/story?id=2926650

For coverage of Grant Hill's career see, **Boston Globe**, December 1, 1994, p. 79; **Esquire**, February 1995, p. 60; **GQ**, April 1995, p. 170; **Los Angeles Times**, January 5, 1995, p. C1; **People**, January 23, 1995, p. 74; **Sports Illustrated**, February 1, 1993, p. 58 and January 22, 1996, p. 59; **Time**, February 13, 1995, p. 78; **USA Today**, December 6, 1994, p. C1; **Washington Post**, February 12, 1995, p. D1.

See Jalen Rose, "Jalen Rose On Duke Vs. Michigan, The Feb Five's Legacy-And Grant Hill," **The Wall Street Journal**, March 20, 2011 for a defense of his comments. For Grant Hill's response to Rose, See **The New York Times**, March 16, 2011. See Brad Cohen, "Michael Wilbon: Grant Hill And Jalen Rose Ain't All That Different," **Sports Grid**, March 11, 2011 http://www.sportsgrid.com/ncaa-basketball/michael-wilbon-grant-hill-and-jalen-rose-aint-all-that-different/ for a strange argument that the two are alike. Grant Hill is also a documentary producer and he graciously refrained from criticizing the ESPN 30 Minute film on the Fab Five. He took the high road. Rose took the low road.

The Suns future is discussed in Paul Coro, "Rebuilding Was Two Years In Making," **The Arizona Republic**, September 9, 2012, pp. C 1, C 9. On the acquisition of Wesley Johnson and what it means, see, Roberto Payne, "Report: Phoenix Suns To Get Wesley Johnson IN Three-Way Trade," **Bleacher Report**, July 24, 2012 http://bleacherreport.com/articles/1271357-breaking-news-phoenix-suns-to-get-wesley-johnson-in-three-way-trade Also see Paul Coro, "New Leaders Will

Be Key To Success For Phoenix Suns," **The Arizona Republic**, September 11, 2012 http://www.azcentral.com/arizonarepublic/sports/articles/2012/09/10/20120910new-leaders-will-key-success-phoenix-suns.html Also see, the excellent article by Paul Coro, "Phoenix Suns Look To Rise Again After Disappointing Season," **The Arizona Republic**, April 16, 2011 http://www.azcentral.com/sports/suns/articles/2011/04/16/20110416phoenix-suns-2011-2012-season-improvements.html

On the end of the 2011-2012 season and what the next year portends, see, Stefan Swiat, "Suns Close The Book On 2011-2012 Season," **NBA.Com**, April 25, 2012 http://www.nba.com/suns/news/seasonfinale_120425.html

The Suns first exhibition game in Miami, Arizona is briefly mentioned in **The Milwaukee Journal**, September 27, 1968.

On Tom Chambers career, see, Bruce Newman, "They're Tall, But That Ain't All, **Sports Illustrated**, March 2, 1981. Also see the incisive piece by Norm Clark, "Colorado's All Time Top Prep Star? Tom Chambers By A Spurt," **The Seattle Times**, February 25, 1990 http://community.seattletimes.nwsource.com/archive/?date=19900225&slug=1057825;

"Tom Chambers On 1993," http://www.nba.com/suns/chambers_93.html and Glenn Nelson, "Move Has Chambers Jazzed—Utah Now Ex-Sonics Place in Sun," **The Seattle Times**, November 8, 1993 and for his work with Tom Leander on TV see, Paul Coro, "Suns Give And Go: Broadcaster Tom Leander," **The Arizona Republic**, March 3, 2012.

For Lon Babby's use of cap space see Paul Coro," Phoenix suns Exec Lon Babby Cautious Over Utilizing Cap Space," **The Arizona Republic**, May 2, 2012. Also on Babby see, Bob Young, "Phoenix Suns Introduce Lon Babby As Executive," **The Arizona Republic**, July 20, 2010 and Josh Greene, "Babby Named Suns President OF Basketball Operations," **NBA.com**, July 20, 2010 http://www.nba.com/suns/news/babby_newsroom_100720.html Also see Paul Coro, "Phoenix Suns' Rebuilding Plan Coming Full Circle Under Lon Babby," **The Arizona Republic**, September 8, 2012 http://www.azcentral.com/sports/suns/articles/20120907phoenix-suns-rebuilding-plan-coming-full-circle-under-lon-babby.html

On the 2012-2013 season and the hopes for the playoffs see, Sarah McLellan, "Retooled Team Hits Court," **The Arizona Republic**, October 10, 2012, p. C5 and Dan Bickley, "Is It Boom Time Or Bust?" **The Arizona Republic**, October 10, 2012, p. C1, C5. The Bickley article deals with Lon Babby's role in revitalizing the Suns roster.

For Hakim Warrick and Robin Lopez in New Orleans, see Jimmy Smith, "New Orleans Trade For Robin Lopez, Hakim Warrick Now Official," **The New Orleans Times Picayune**, July 27, 2012 and John Reid, "New Orleans Hornets' Roger Mason Jr. and Hakim Warrick Drawing Respect As Veteran Leaders," **The New Orleans Times Picayune**, October 4, 2012.

On Marcin Gortat's expiring contract see, Paul Coro, "Gortat: No Extension Until Present Deal Up," **The Arizona Republic**, November 26, 2012, p. C4. As the 2012-2013 NBA season began, Gortat had some struggles, for his comments, see, Sarah McLellan, "Gortat Looking To Regain Hunger," **The Arizona Republic**, December 21, 2012, p. C5. For Gortat's interview with a Polish newspaper, see Kelly Dwyer, "Marcin Gortat Interview With A Polish Publication Reveals His Uneasiness With The Suns' Offense," **Yahoo Sports**, November 19, 2012, http://sports.yahoo.com/blogs/nba-ball-dont-lie/marcin-gortat-interview-polish-publication-reveals-uneasiness-suns-201829760—nba.html

For P. J. Tucker see, for example, the comments on Coach Alvin Gentry on Tucker, Randi Hill, "Some Good, Some Bad Found in Suns' Overall," **Bleacher Report**, November 26, 2012 http://bleacherreport.com/tb/d9214?utm_source=newsletter&utm_medium=newsletter&utm_campaign=phoenix-suns, Scott Hosaard Cooper, "P.J. Tucker Rises In Phoenix," **Sekou Smith's Hang Time Blog**, November 25, 2012 http://hangtime.blogs.nba.com/2012/11/25/p-j-tucker-rises-up-in-phoenix/

For a look at Ron Lee in Sweden and with the Suns, see, Joel Horn, "Where In The World Is Ron Lee?" http://www.nba.com/suns/history/00608069.html?nav=ArticleList On substance versus style for the Suns see the excellent article by Dan Bickley, "Substance Over Style," **The Arizona Republic**, November 19, 2012, p. C1, C4.

For Bob Vache's obituary see the **Prescott Evening Courier**, January 18, 1970, p. 11. Also see the **Phoenix Suns Yearbook: 2013** for key information n the players and management.

ABOUT THE AUTHOR AND ACKNOWLEDGEMENTS

Howard A. DeWitt is Professor Emeritus of History at Ohlone College, Fremont, California. He received his B. A. from Western Washington State University, the M. A. from the University of Oregon and a PhD from the University of Arizona. He also studied at the University of Paris, Sorbonne and the City University in Rome. Professor DeWitt is the author of twenty-two books and has published over 200 articles and more than 200 reviews in a wide variety of popular and scholarly magazines.

DeWitt has also been a member of a number of organizations to promote the study of history. The most prestigious is the Organization of American Historians.

For more forty-five years he has taught full and part time at a number of U. S. colleges' is best known for teaching two college level courses in the History of Rock n Roll music. He continued to teach the History of Rock and Roll music on the Internet until 2011. Among people he brought to class were Bo Diddley, Mike Bloomfield, Jimmy McCracklin, Paul Butterfield, George Palmerton and Pee Wee Thomas. In a distinguished academic career, he has also taught at the University of California, Davis, the University of Arizona, Cochise College and Chabot College. In addition to these teaching assignments, Professor DeWitt is a regular speaker at the Popular Culture Association annual convention and at the National Social Science Association meetings. He has delivered a number of addresses to the Organization of American Historians.

He wrote the first book on Chuck Berry, which was published by Pierian Press under the title **Chuck Berry: Rock N Roll Music** in 1985. DeWitt's earlier brief biography, **Van Morrison: The Mystic's Music**, published in 1983, received universally excellent reviews. On the English side of the music business DeWitt's, **The Beatles: Untold Tales**, originally published in 1985, was picked up by the Kendall Hunt Publishing Company in the 1990s and is used regularly in a wide variety of college courses on the history of rock music. Kendall Hunt also published **Stranger in Town: The Musical Life of Del Shannon** with co-author Dennis M. DeWitt in 2001. In 1993's **Paul McCartney: From Liverpool To Let It Be** concentrated on the Beatle years. He also co-authored **Jailhouse Rock: The Bootleg Records of Elvis Presley** with Lee Cotten in 1983.

Professor DeWitt's many awards in the field of history include founding the Cochise County Historical Society and his scholarship has been recognized by a number of state and local government organizations. DeWitt's book, **Sun Elvis: Presley In The 1950s**, published by Popular Culture Ink. was a finalist for the Deems-ASCAP Award for the best academic rock and roll book.

Professor DeWitt is a renaissance scholar who publishes in a wide variety of outlets that are both academic and popular. He is one of the few college professors who bridge the gap between scholarly and popular publications. His articles and reviews have appeared in **Blue Suede News, DISCoveries, Rock 'N' Blues News**, the **Journal of Popular Culture**, the **Journal of American History, California History**, the **Southern California Quarterly**, the **Pacific Historian, Amerasia**, the **Western Pennsylvania Historical Magazine**, the **Annals of Iowa**, the **Journal of the West, Arizona and the West**, the **North Beach Review, Ohio History**, the **Oregon Historical Quarterly**, the **Community College Social Science Quarterly, Montana: The Magazine of the West, Record Profile Magazine, Audio Trader**, the **Seattle Post-Intelligencer** and **Juke Box Digest**.

For forty plus years DeWitt has combined popular and academic writing. He has been nominated for numerous writing awards. His reviews are combined with articles to form a body of scholarship and popular writing that is frequently footnoted in major work. As a political scientist, Professor DeWitt authored three books that questioned American foreign policy and its direction. In the Philippines, DeWitt is recognized as one of the foremost biographers of their political leader Jose Rizal. His three books on Filipino farm workers remain the standard in the field.

During his high school and college years, DeWitt promoted dances in and around Seattle, Washington. Such groups as Little Bill and the Bluenotes, Ron Holden and the Playboys, the Frantics, the Wailers and George Palmerton and the Night People among others played at such Seattle venues as the Eagle's Auditorium and Dick Parker's Ballroom.

My thanks to my wonderful and supportive brother and sister in law, Ken and Barb Marich, for their sane and intelligent choice of wine and food. My brothers Dennis and Duane DeWitt listened to me, and one of them, known as Nostradamus Junior, provided opinions on real estate, music and life. Fortunately, for the reader, none of these views are in this book. Nor are Dennis' comments about me getting a real estate wedgie. Dennis sad: "Howard, the Highlighters weren't with Bobby Darin. That is not a picture of Ron Holden. I am not talking to you again. You never threw dances at Parker's." Poor guy. Delusion is not a country in Eastern Europe. Maybe it is. Duane DeWitt is normal, thank God for him.

Marc and Gaby Magg Bristol are good friends and they publish my ranting on rock and roll music in **Blue Suede News**. Thank you Marc and Gaby for not only being critical editors but good friends. They have edited my rock, blues, country and rockabilly articles for almost thirty years. Thanks for being such good friends. Neil Skok and Fred Hopkins are friends who listened to this project.

My friends in Scottsdale Claude and Cindy Amerson, Peter Serena, Arnie and Merle Weiner, Betty Vyskocil, Ron and Carolyn Brock, Sandy Polo and Pat Maudsley listened to me but they have nothing to do with this book. Jackie and Joe, Rebecca and Jerry, and Ed and Jean in the East Valley are good friends who offered a sympathetic ear.

Howard has two grown children. They both live in Los Angeles. His wife of forty plus years, Carolyn, is an educator, an artist and she continues to raise Howard. She is presently retired and vacationing around the world. The DeWitt's divide their time between Scottsdale, Arizona and the Silver Lake area of Los Angeles. That is when they are not in Paris looking for art, books and music. Howard is working on a book on Paris. That is a year away and a study of Rodriguez is next.

Professor DeWitt has a private detective series with the first novel, **Stone Murder**, now out and selling well. His book on the president **Obama Detractor's: In The Right Wing Nut House** is a marvelous look at the radical rifght. It was also the reason that his friends in Scottsdale and Saddlebrooke no longer talk to him. **Stone Murder** features a San Francisco P.I. Trevor Blake III, and much of the story line will evolve around crimes that DeWitt witnessed while working four years and two days as an agent with the Bureau of Alcohol, Tobacco and Firearms. He was a street agent for the BATF and his tales of those years are in manuscript waiting for publication. He was also a key figure in the BATF Union.

He is currently working on a series of rock and roll mystery novels featuring Trevor Blake III, a private eye in San Francisco. The first novel **Stone Dead** can be ordered through Amazon. He also writes fiction under another name.

Any corrections or additions to this or the subsequent volumes that will follow this study can be sent to Horizon Books, P. O. Box 4342, Scottsdale, Arizona 85258. DeWitt can be reached via e-mail at <u>Howard217@aol.com</u>

17663971R00238

Made in the USA
Charleston, SC
22 February 2013